Lecture Notes in Social Networks

More information about this series at http://www.springer.com/series/8768

Tomayess Issa · Pedro Isaias
Piet Kommers
Editors

Social Networking and Education

Global Perspectives

Springer

Editors
Tomayess Issa
Curtin University
Perth, WA
Australia

Pedro Isaias
Universidade Aberta
Lisbon
Portugal

Piet Kommers
Department of Media, Communication and Organisation
University of Twente
Enschede
The Netherlands

ISSN 2190-5428   ISSN 2190-5436 (electronic)
Lecture Notes in Social Networks
ISBN 978-3-319-17715-1   ISBN 978-3-319-17716-8 (eBook)
DOI 10.1007/978-3-319-17716-8

Library of Congress Control Number: 2015948163

Springer Cham Heidelberg New York Dordrecht London

Printed on acid-free paper

Springer International Publishing AG Switzerland is part of Springer Science+Business Media (www.springer.com)

Foreword

If we explore the timeline of man's scientific discoveries, we may observe a spiral acceleration and evolution, escalating from century to century as we are approaching the present moment. Our tools extended our legs, arms, senses and minds so to visit, work, think and understand ourselves and the world around us. Each scientific revolution was reflected in our everyday lives, impacting our environment to serve our purposes; and in turn, our environment impacted us. One recent discovery is the Internet; it is the invisible net connecting us together, breaking time and space boundaries and allowing us to be omnipresent and multifaceted in myriads of real and imaginary worlds. Consequently, the related human abilities to adapt and learn in a constantly changing outer and virtual world are also accelerating. On such cognitive development and learning, Piaget said in a conference at Cornell University in 1964, that the principal goal of education is to create individuals who are capable of doing new things, not simply of repeating what other generations have done—humans who are creative, inventive and discoverers. Also, the second goal of education is to form minds which can be critical, can verify, and not accept everything they are offered.

It seems that the first educational target Piaget suggested is fully accomplished in the past, present and future technical accomplishments. However, according to Nicholas Carr in his book 'The Shallows' published in 2010, the second goal is still to be reached. As the human thought has been shaped through the centuries by 'tools of the mind', every information technology carries an intellectual ethic—a set of assumptions about the nature of our knowledge and intelligence. Instead of focusing our attention, and promoting deep and creative thought, contemplation and reflection, the Internet encourages the rapid, distracted sampling of small bits of information. As such, its ethic is the ethic of the industrialist, an ethic of speed and efficiency, of optimized production and consumption. Now the Internet is remaking us in its own image; we are becoming 'the shallows'.

It seems that more than the investigating mind, new tools and enthusiasm for discovery exists on the online world. This gap possibly finds its fulfilment within the educational field and the ways our cognitive development and learning are connected with the world and the society around us. The key then exists in the manner we interact with our environment; the world and the society. According to Vygotsky in 1979, there are two dimensions in building our consciousness: the social dimension which is primary in time and in fact, and the individual dimension which is derivative and secondary. Therefore, the mental functioning of the individual is not simply derived from social interaction; rather, the specific structures and processes revealed by individuals can be traced to their interactions with others. The tools facilitate our interactions and exist as our society and community artefacts, impacting us back in our interactions.

Building upon the evolution of the human and the tools, this book suggests the new Social Networking (SN) revolution and provides the missing mediators for the second Piaget's goal to be fully accomplished as well as solutions to Carr's argument. It can be utilised by individuals, communities, organisations, companies and governments, to name a few. The provision of specific methodologies can expand communication in two ways, by enhancing our collaboration and co-creativity opportunities and abilities targeting in our active engagement with our colleagues, or as in education, with our teachers and co-students. The authors offer tools and techniques anchored in diverse special interests and affinities so that learning occurs by immersing ourselves in SN as authentic educational collaborative environments. They function as complementary to the traditional on-site classrooms by extending the wall and timetable boundaries. The book's methods and frameworks for cross-cultural communication and collaboration fulfil both Piaget's purposes and without risks. They aid at supporting both educators and students to engage in on-site and online educational activities, acquire a complete set of knowledge skills and abilities, protect their privacy and be critical, verify and refuse to accept everything they are offered.

This book on Social Networking in education promotes active engagement for co-creation, exchange of best practices and joint development. Such opportunities accessible for collective exchange and development lead to organic educational evolution, progressing human cognitive and social development, knowledge building, skills and competencies, as well as physical development, based upon human characteristics inherent in our DNA. The book on Social Networking in education from a global viewpoint ultimately supports individuals, groups and communities to co-construct the sense of belonging and co-develop the shared dreams for the new twenty-first century civilisation.

London
January 2015

Dr. Niki Lambropoulos
Global Operations Division, London, UK
University of Patras, Greece

Acknowledgments

We acknowledge the support of all people who contributed directly or indirectly to this book.

Tomayess Issa owes special gratitude first to the almighty and to her parents: V. Rev. Fr. Boutros Touma Issa; Bathqyomo Marine Khoury-Issa. Her sister Dr. Theodora, her brother Dr. Touma, his wife Siba, and their daughter Talitha; her Sister Tamara, her husband Tony, and their children Tabitha, Antoinette, Jacob, and finally to her bother Theodore, his wife Mary, and their children Cephas and Mary; for their continuous support and encouragement, since without their help, this work would never have been completed. Tomayess would like to acknowledge the support of the School of Information Systems—Curtin University; Australia for their inspiration and encouragement.

Pedro Isaias would like to acknowledge Universidade Aberta and Curtin University for their support to this author specifically. Also, a special acknowledgment to the other authors of this book for their cooperation and work. Finally, he would like to acknowledge the support of his family. Without their assistance, this work would not be possible at all.

Piet Kommers: We want to express our acknowledgement to all institutional leaders, professors and students who enabled the publication of this book. Without their loyal contribution to our surveys we could not have reached this level of clarity.

Perth, WA, Australia — Tomayess Issa
Lisbon, Portugal — Pedro Isaias
Enschede, The Netherlands — Piet Kommers

Contents

Part I
Social Networking

Social Networking

Tomayess Issa, Pedro Isaias and Piet Kommers

Abstract Technology has become an essential element of many sectors ranging from business to education as a means by which people connect, communicate and collaborate with one another; moreover, this type of connection is easy and accessible both locally and globally. Currently, web technologies have streamlined and strengthened links worldwide, allowing people to interact to distribute information and practices. There is no doubt that the second generation of the internet called Web 2.0 has been used by various sectors since businesses have become highly dependent on this technology which enables collaboration between reader and writer. Social networking (SN) is an example of one of the best aspects of the Web 2 revolution. Currently, educational institutions are in the process of introducing social networking as a teaching and learning tool by adopting a specific platform (i.e. wiki; blog; discussion board etc.) especially regarding assessments, as a means of improving students' personal skills (i.e. motivation; leadership; negotiation, communication, problem solving, time management, and reflection) and professional skills (i.e. reading. writing, research, information, critical thinking, decision making technology, digital oral presentation, visual representations and teamwork) to enhance students' learning in the academic environment and to prepare them for the workplace in the future. This chapter will examine and discuss the history of the Internet, the history of social networking and its various web types, and social networking applications which are relevant to and useful in the education sector.

T. Issa (✉)
School of Information Systems, Curtin University, Perth
Western Australia
e-mail: Tomayess.Issa@cbs.curtin.edu.au

P. Isaias
Universidade Aberta, Palácio Ceia, Rua da Escola Politécnica, n. 141–147,
1269-001 Lisbon, Portugal
e-mail: pisaias@uab.pt

P. Kommers
University of Twente, Enschede, Netherlands
e-mail: p.a.m.kommers@utwente.nl

T. Issa et al. (eds.), *Social Networking and Education*,
Lecture Notes in Social Networks, DOI 10.1007/978-3-319-17716-8_1

Keywords Internet history · Social networking history · Web types · SN applications

1 Introduction

Technology has been steadily evolving in order to meet the need for information sharing. Education systems locally and globally have for many years been monitoring students' and businesses' needs in order to update and enhance the curriculum so as to improve students' skills and meet business needs by using the latest technology in their teaching and learning practices. Nowadays, social networking has been improved by Web 2.0, since it has become a significant factor in altering students' attitudes toward teaching and learning in the higher education sector. SN can create and develop communication and collaboration between peers and cultivate a niche community with similar interests and knowledge in education as well as in business.

The adoption of Social Networking has been very useful in the education sector as a means of improving knowledge acquisition and encouraging social interaction between students' and students, and students and lecturers. Currently, web technologies are being used by enterprises to help the organisation and the customers to interact, communicate and collaborate since the interface design has been developed with intellectual features to increase the interaction among the users; however, this tool has opportunities as well as some risks; therefore the use of this technology in the higher education sector will increase the interaction among students and lecturers; however, specific guidelines should be established so that opportunities to students can be maximised and risks or potential risks can be decreased or eliminated.

In this chapter, the authors will closely examine the evolution of the Internet, since the Internet has been used to generate many sophisticated online tools such as social networking, among others. Furthermore, this chapter will identify social networking and education applications which are associated with education, especially in the higher education sector.

2 The History of the Internet

Communication technology aims to enhance collaboration, communication, cooperation and connection among communities, education and business. This communication technology was termed 'the Internet' which is an effective network of networks that can rapidly connect people [17].

The Internet concept was developed and introduced by J. Licklider of MIT in 1962 to connect people locally and globally to share communication and knowledge via the exchange of packets [4, 7, 38]. This idea started to develop further and further to connect networks around the world in order to exchange ideas and viewpoints between researchers. In 1990, the Internet took off to cover tens of thousands of isolated networks, enabling them to be integrated into a global entity. This step encouraged people to share their knowledge, information and data. This tool rapidly gained popularity especially among businesses and students. Further technological development saw this tool evolve from read only to read and write which became known as ‘web technologies’ which have made a substantial contribution to the overall well-being of humanity.

Fatimah et al. [11] confirm that technologies, particularly the communication technologies, play a major role in the education sector and are the history of the Internet, used in the higher education mainly to increase participation and interaction among students and lecturers and to enhance students’ professional and personal skills.

3 Web Types

World Wide Web (WWW) is derived from the term Web, and the web plays an essential role in obtaining the necessary information for the users with the help of the technology. Social networking applications are based on variations of web technology, namely: Web 1.0; Web 2.0; Web 3.0; Web 4.0 and Web 5.0.

According to Patel [36, p. 410], “Web 1.0 referred as a web of information or percipience, Web 2.0 as web of verbalization, Web 3.0 as web of affiliation and Web 4.0 as a web of integration and Web 5.0 as web of decentralized smart communicator”.

Several studies [1, 12, 15, 19, 23, 33, 36, 37, 46] define Web 1.0 as the first generation of the web, which is mainly focused on static information and read-only web; this generation allows users to connect webs in order to share information and knowledge. This web was created by Tim Burners-Lee in 1989. The Web 1.0 technologies include HTML, HTTP, URI Newer Protocols, XML, XHTML, ASP, PHP, JSP, CGI, JavaScript, VBScript and Flash.

Web 2.0 is the second generation of WWW and consists of concepts and technology. This web allows users to read and write by means of collaboration, user-generated content and social networking. The user of Web 2.0 has more interaction with less control. Web 2.0 allows users to support collaboration and cooperation between users nationally and locally via specific applications such as MySpace, Facebook, Twitter, Orkut, Flicker and others.

Web 3.0 is the third generation of WWW, refer to connecting intelligence (known as semantic web) to identify a web-based data and to make the search more effective and efficient. This technology was coined by John Markoff of the New York Times in 2006 [42]. This web aims to use semantic web, microformats, natural language search, data-mining, machine learning, recommendation agents, and artificial intelligence technologies, which emphasize machine-facilitated understanding of information in order to provide a more productive and intuitive user experience [42].

Web 4.0 technology is based on wireless communication (mobile devices or computers) connecting users world-wide to the physical or virtual world in real time. Web 4.0 is considered as an Ultra-Intelligent Electronic Agent, symbiotic web and ubiquitous web [23, 36]. This web technology will be read write concurrency web, and will allow a mass participation in online networks. For example, if you visit amazon.com more than once, it will recognize you and provide relevant and personalized advice. One of the most critical developments of Web 4.0 is the migration of online functionality into the physical world. To use one of the simplest examples, imagine being able to Google your home to locate your car keys or the remote control [36, p. 416].

Finally, Web 5.0 technology is the sensory and emotive web, designed to allow computers to interact with human begins to measure and compute their effects and emotions by dealing with the technology. This technology allows researchers to track users' behaviours and emotions by neuro technology through headphones, which have been created by the Emotive Systems Company. Using the headphones, users can interact with content that responds to their emotions or changes the facial expression of their avatars in real time. If interactions can then be personalised to create experiences that excite users, then Web 5.0 will undoubtedly be more user-friendly than its predecessors [2, p. 277].

4 Social Networking Applications

The web technologies serve as a platform for users and business to interact and communicate with other parties globally and locally. The Web 2.0 applications permit social interaction and accessibility of information regardless of distance and time; this service is flexible, efficient, effective and easy to use so as to meet users' and businesses' needs and requirements. Under this section, we will discuss some of the social network applications namely: Wikis, Blogs, Mashups, Tags, and Podcasts.

4.1 Wiki

Wiki is an elemental tool for generating contents by using the content management system. Wiki allows users to upload articles, information, data, images, videos and others items. The beauty of this tool is that the user is able to edit, modify and delete contents based on his/her needs. Currently, this tool is critical in the teaching and learning process, and it is part of the learning management systems since it fosters students' professional and personal skills via assessments. This technology has the potential to enhance online collaboration, communication, cooperation and connection between users, including students in the higher education sector [20, p. 4].

4.2 *Blogs*

The blog is considered to be the most important revolution of Web 2.0 technology; this type of application is web-based since users world-wide can interact and comment on others' ideas. Also, this tool allows users to add images, videos, links and various types of files. The blog idea is very simple and easy since the marketing idea is cheap and inexpensive, and users can interact by shifting from one blog to other blogs and posts since participation and subscription are free; furthermore, users can receive an email when new information and data are added and generated in these blogs [16, 48].

4.3 *Mashups*

Mashups have become a crucial tool for business and education since they gather information and data from numerous sources, and later, users can compare and contrast the acquired information based on their needs. This information is presented in a special platform with all the resources found in order to expedite decision-making processes in businesses and education. Further researchers [3, 44] indicate that this tool is easy to use and useful for creating and generating a mashup application rather than generating the whole content from scratch, thereby saving time and providing accurate information.

4.4 *Tags*

The Tag is a non-hierarchical keyword or word assigned to an article, image and information. This tool helps to describe these items and allows users to locate them by browsing or searching. Currently, the majority of websites, blogs, wikis and other tools use the tagging approach [39, 41, 45].

4.5 *Podcasts*

A podcast is a digital channel, which consists of audio, digital radio, PDF which can be directly downloaded. Podcasts are available in several formats from MP3 and MP4, and these files can be played in any music players and from any device. Issa et al. [21, p. 16] confirm that it was observed that by embedding Audio Feedback technology into teaching and learning practices, especially in higher education, students were becoming more interested in their studies and in sharing their knowledge and skills with their colleagues, thereby making classes fully interactive.

5 Social Networking and Education

Over the previous decades, the World Wide Web has become the historical information medium for various users locally and globally to exchange information, knowledge and data. According to Kemp [26] (see Fig. 1), the Asia Pacific region has the largest share of social networking usage in the world, followed by North America, Western Europe, Eastern Europe, South America, Central America Middle East and finally Africa. This development and the variety of user languages on the web will develop and create several opportunities and risks via this tool for both the business and education sectors.

SN is a virtual, online application whereby users can generate accounts and public profiles in order to interact and connect with and meet real friends based on their mutual interests [18]. The social networking concept is intended to facilitate the exchange of ideas, communication collaboration and connection among users from various sectors including businesses and education. Social networking allows users to post, publish and write articles or comments in sites such as Facebook and Google [6]. Furthermore, SN has web aplications which enable information-sharing, interoperability, user-centred design and collaboration in the WWW [2, p. 276].

Social networking is also available in the learning management system through wiki, blogs, and discussion boards. These tools will assist students to interact with their peers and lecturers. The lecturers will use these tools to assign specific assessments to foster and enhance students' professional and personal skills [20].

The social networking usage for educational purposes has changed teaching and learning approaches in higher education. Students become more responsible for their own learning by being provided with the appropriate tools of social networking such as wiki. These tools allow more interaction, participation, debate and

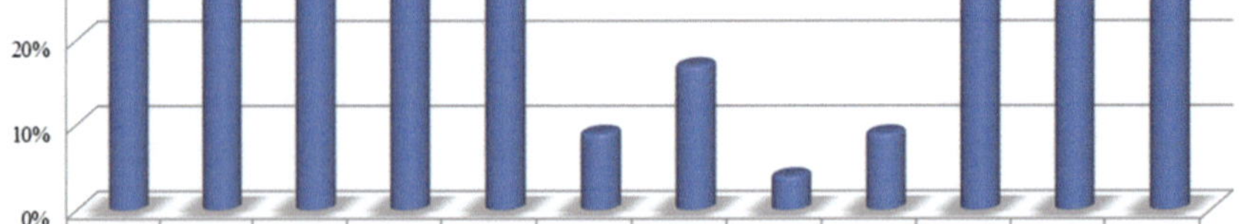

	North America	Central America	South America	West Europe	East Europe	Africa	Middle East	Central Asia	South Asia	East Asia	South East Asia	Oceania
Percentage	58%	37%	48%	47%	45%	9%	17%	4%	9%	43%	32%	45%

Fig. 1 Social networking usage worldwide (2015) prepared by the authors (*Data Source* Kemp 2015)

discussion among students and lecturers in various assessments and activities in the class [20, p. 13]. Furthermore, Taraghi et al. [44] confirm that using technology for teaching and learning will allow students to manage and organize their learning based on their individual needs. This will decrease the management overhead and resource negotiations while enhancing students' personal and professional skills.

On the other hand, to ensure a smooth transition from traditional teaching practices to e-learning teaching, lecturers will play a key role in the effective delivery of teaching, since the lecturer will facility the teaching and learning, not the technology [40]. Wilson [47] suggests that three characteristics of the lecturer will control the degree of learning: attitude towards technology, teaching style and the control of technology.

Several studies [14, 22, 30, 34, 35, 49] confirm that working and learning with social networking facility in the higher education sector will bring new opportunities for students namely: exposure to cutting edge knowledge; the opportunity for collaboration and inter-crossing relationships; enhanced communication skills; acquisition of new acquaintances, and an awareness of an environment-friendly means of communication. However, this tool can create risks related to cognitive development, social development; physical development and security (see Figs. 2 and 3).

Based on several [5, 8–10, 13, 24, 25, 27–29, 31, 32, 43] studies, this book's editors developed a survey to examine and assess social networking opportunities and risks in the education sector, especially in the higher education sector of various regions: Asia-Pacific, Europe, Mediterranean, America, Middle East and Caribbean. A total of 3477 participants from 15 countries in six regions responded to the questionnaire. These participants are from Australia, Malaysia, India, South Korea, Pakistan, Netherlands, Portugal, Greece, Italy, Turkey, USA, Mexico, Jordan, Saudi Arabia, and Puerto Rico (see Table 1).

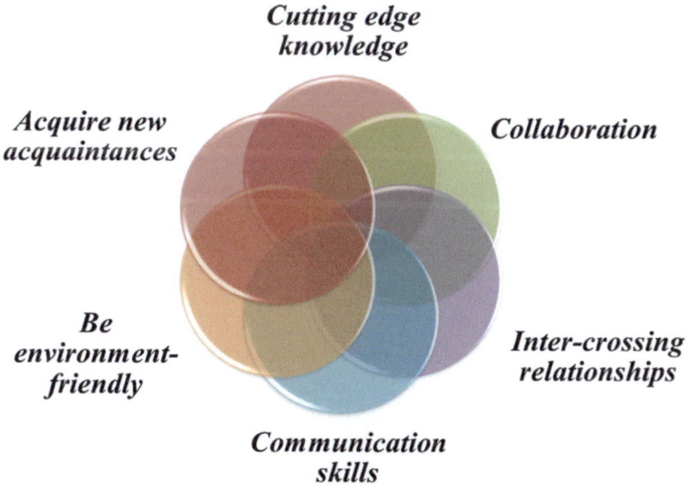

Fig. 2 Social networking opportunities in the higher eduation—prepared by the authors

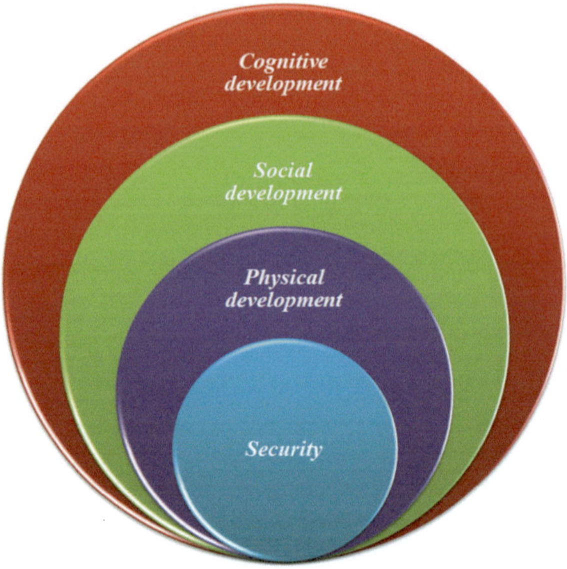

Fig. 3 Social networking risks in the higher education—prepared by the authors

Table 1 Participating country details—(prepared by the authors)

Data grouping			
Region	Country	Participants	
Asia Pacific	Australia	153	
	Malaysia	74	
	India	85	
	South Korea	231	
	Pakistan	153	
Total Asia Pacific			*696*
Europe	Netherlands	135	
	Portugal	130	
	Greece	245	
	Italy	324	
Total Europe			*834*
Mediterranean	Turkey	457	
Total Mediterranean			*457*
America	USA	564	
	Mexico	150	
Total America			*714*
Middle East	Jordan	495	
	Saudi Arabia	101	
Total Middle East			*596*
Caribbean	Puerto Rico	134	
Total Caribbean			*134*
Total all			*3431*

The book is organized into a total of nineteen chapters; with an introductory chapter; seventeen chapters from the above countries, since we have three chapters from Turkey. The final chapter aims to present the global statistic from the all the countries and later present a model proposal.

6 Conclusion

This chapter discussed and examined web technology history, social networking web types and education, in addition to applications and the opportunities and risks associated with the use of social networking, especially in the higher education sector. To minimize the risks and maximise the opportunities to students in higher education, the editors developed an online survey distributed to countries in the following regions: Asia-Pacific, Europe, Mediterranean, America, Middle East and Caribbean to examine students' attitudes to the use of social networking as a teaching and learning tool.

References

1. Acerbis R, Bongio A, Brambilla M, Butti S, Ceri S, Fraternali P (2008) Web applications design and development with WebML and WebRatio 5.0. In: Objects, components, models and patterns. Springer, Berlin, pp 392–411
2. Benito-Osorio D, Peris-Ortiz M, Armengot C, Colino A (2013) Web 5.0: the future of emotional competences in higher education. Glob Bus Perspect 1(3):274–287. doi:10.1007/s40196-013-0016-5
3. Blatt AJ (2015) Collaborative mapping. In: Health, science, and place. Springer, New York, pp 63–75
4. Campbell-Kelly M, Garcia-Swartz DD (2013) The history of the internet: the missing narratives. J Inf Technol 28(1):18–33
5. Chen R (2013) Member use of social networking sites—an empirical examination. Decis Support Syst 54(3):1219–1227. doi:10.1016/j.dss.2012.10.028
6. Christoffersen MB, Boukaouit D, Weeke Hervit BH, Winther Brødreskift D, Makilä RM, Pingel Vogel KE, Wolter Strate S (2012) Social media ethics
7. Cohen-Almagor R (2011) Internet history. Int J Technoethics 2(2):45–64
8. Conole G, Culver J (2010) The design of Cloudworks: applying social networking practice to foster the exchange of learning and teaching ideas and designs. Comput Educ 54(3):679–692. doi:10.1016/j.compedu.2009.09.013
9. Din N, Yahya S, Suzan R, Kassim R (2012) Online social networking for quality of life. Procedia Soc Behav Sci 35:713–718. doi:10.1016/j.sbspro.2012.02.141
10. eMarketer (2013) Social networking reaches nearly one in four around the world. http://www.emarketer.com/Article/Social-Networking-Reaches-Nearly-One-Four-Around-World/1009976. Accessed 24 July 2013
11. Fatimah H, Gazi MA, Saedah S (2010) Information and communication technology for participatory based decision-making-E-management for administrative efficiency in higher education. Int J Phys Sci 5(4):383–392

12. Fifarek A (2007) Web 2.0? I am not finished with 1.0 yet! back to basics at the 2007 American library association conference. Libr Hi Tech News 24(8):43–43. doi:10.1108/07419050710836045
13. Fitzpatrick A (2010) Facebook and social networking—inappropriate use by employees. http://www.gadens.com.au/Publications-View.aspx?documentid=1704#article2. Accessed 2 Feb 2015
14. Fox J, Moreland JJ (2015) The dark side of social networking sites: an exploration of the relational and psychological stressors associated with Facebook use and affordances. Comput Hum Behav 45:168–176. doi:10.1016/j.chb.2014.11.083
15. Franklin T, Van Harmelen M (2007) Web 2.0 for learning and teaching in higher education. The observatory of borderless higher education, London
16. Godwin-Jones B (2003) Blogs and Wikis: environments for on-line collaboration. Lang Learn Technol 7:12–16
17. Gordon D, Wirz M, Roggen D, Tröster G, Beigl M (2014) Group affiliation detection using model divergence for wearable devices. Paper presented at the proceedings of the 2014 ACM international symposium on wearable computers, Seattle, Washington
18. Griffiths MD, Kuss DJ, Demetrovics Z (2014) Chapter 6—Social networking addiction: an overview of preliminary findings. In: Feder KPRC (ed) Behavioral addictions. Academic Press, San Diego, pp 119–141. doi:10.1016/B978-0-12-407724-9.00006-9
19. Hsu Y-C, Ching Y-H, Grabowski B (2014) Web 2.0 applications and practices for learning through collaboration. In: Spector M, Merrill MD, Elen J, Bishhop MJ (eds) Handbook of research on eduational communications and technology. Springer, New York, pp 747–758
20. Issa T (2014) Learning, communication and interaction via Wiki: an Australian perspective. In: Kaur H, Tao X (eds) ICTs and the millennium development goals. Springer, New York, pp 1–17
21. Issa T, Isaias P, Issa T (2014) Does MP3 audio feedback enhance student's learning skills? Int J Learn 19:15–28
22. Issa T, Kommers P (2013) Social networking for web-based communities. Int J Web Based Communities 9(1):5–24
23. Kambil A (2008) What is your Web 5.0 strategy? J Bus Strategy 29(6):56–58. doi:10.1108/02756660810917255
24. Keenan A (2009) Sociability and social interaction on social networking websites. Libr Rev 58 (6):438–450
25. Kelin K (2008) Are social networking sites useful for business? http://www.businessweek.com/print/smallbiz/content/aug2008/sb2008086_346094.htm. Accessed 22 Nov 2011
26. Kemp S (2015) Digital, social and mobile worldwide in 2015. http://wearesocial.net/tag/sdmw/. Accessed 22 Jan 2015
27. Kontos E, Emmons K, Puleo E, Viswanath K (2010) Communication inequalities and public health implications of adult social networking site use in the United States. J Health Commun 15(S3):216–235
28. Lakhani A (2013) Social networking sites and the legal profession: Balancing benefits with navigating minefields. Comput Law Secur Rev 29(2):164–174. doi:10.1016/j.clsr.2013.01.008
29. Langheinrich M, Karjoth G (2010) Social networking and the risk to companies and institutions. Inf Secur Tech Rep 15(2):51–56. doi:10.1016/j.istr.2010.09.001
30. Mathew B (2014) Using a social networking tool for blended learning in staff training: sharing experience from practice. J Neonatal Nurs 20(3):90–94. doi:10.1016/j.jnn.2014.03.005
31. McCarroll N, Curran K (2013) Social networking in education. IGI Global. doi:10.4018/jide.2013010101
32. Medaglia R, Rose J, Nyvang T, Saebo O (2009) Characteristics of social networking services. In: MCIS 2009, Athens 2009
33. O'reilly T (2007) What is Web 2.0: design patterns and business models for the next generation of software. Commun Strat (1):17
34. Oh HJ, Ozkaya E, LaRose R (2014) How does online social networking enhance life satisfaction? The relationships among online supportive interaction, affect, perceived social

support, sense of community, and life satisfaction. Comput Hum Behav 30:69–78. doi:10.1016/j.chb.2013.07.053
35. Pan Y, Xu Y, Wang X, Zhang C, Ling H, Lin J (2015) Integrating social networking support for dyadic knowledge exchange: a study in a virtual community of practice. Inf Manag 52 (1):61–70. doi:10.1016/j.im.2014.10.001
36. Patel K (2013) Incremental journey for world wide web: introduced with Web 1.0 to recent Web 5.0–a survey paper. Int J Adv Res Comput Sci Softw Eng 3(10):410–417
37. Redzuan F, Lokman AM, Othman ZA (2014) Kansei semantic space for emotion in online learning. In: 2014 3rd international conference on user science and engineering (i-USEr). IEEE, pp 168–173
38. Russell AL (2012) Histories of networking vs. the history of the internet. In: SIGCIS Workshop
39. Sinclair J, Cardew-Hall M (2008) The folksonomy tag cloud: when is it useful? J Inf Sci 34 (1):15–29
40. Singh G, O'Donoghue J, Worton H (2005) A study into the effects of e-Learning on higher education. J Univ Teach Learn Pract 2(1):3
41. Smith W, Kidder D (2010) You've been tagged! (Then again, maybe not): employers and Facebook. Bus Horiz 53(5):491–499
42. Spivack N (2015) (N.Y) Web 3.0: The third generation web is coming. http://lifeboat.com/ex/web.3.0. Accessed 1 Feb 2015
43. Steinfield C, DiMicco J, Ellison N, Lampe C (2009) Bowling online: social networking and social capital within the organization paper presented at the C & T '09. University Park, Pennsylvania
44. Taraghi B, Ebner M, Schaffert S (2009) Personal learning environments for higher education: a mashup based widget concept. In: Wild F, Kalz M, Palmér M, Müler D (ed) Mash-up personal learning environments: proceedings of the workshop in conjunction with the 4th European conference on technology-enhanced learning (ECTEL'09). Citeseer, pp 15–22
45. Tseng G, Schleier-Smith J (2009) User created tags for online social networking. Google Patents
46. Turban E, King D, Lee JK, Liang T-P, Turban DC (2015) E-commerce: mechanisms, platforms, and tools. In: Electronic commerce. Springer, Berlin, pp 51–99
47. Wilson J (2001) Lessons of a virtual timetable: education. Economist 17(4):27–41
48. Zein R (2014) Explorative study on the ways of using Blogs and Wikis as teaching and learning tools in mathematics. Paper presented at the society for information technology & teacher education international conference 2014, Jacksonville, Florida, United States
49. Zhu DH, Chang YP, Luo JJ, Li X (2014) Understanding the adoption of location-based recommendation agents among active users of social networking sites. Inf Process Manage 50 (5):675–682. doi:10.1016/j.ipm.2014.04.010

Part II
Social Networking in Asia-Pacific

Social Networking in Australia: Opportunities and Risks

Tomayess Issa

Abstract Social Networking (SN) and its associated applications have their opportunities and risks; however, if the implementation of this tool is appropriately planned and is adopted in higher education, students will obtain the necessary benefits to enhance their personal and professional skills. In this chapter, the author employed an online survey with 153 respondents from Australia to examine students' attitudes and behaviors towards Social Networking usage. The survey results produced four new opportunities and three risks associated with students' use of Social Networking in Australia. Further research will be carried out in future to examine more varied groups of students to reinforce the research findings.

Keywords Social networking · Opportunities · Risks · Australia

1 Introduction

Social Networking (SN) is a tool that simplifies universal interaction among people and individuals world-wide. SN is a virtual and mass communication media whereby individuals connected to this tool can view information and knowledge from other individuals as well as their contributions. The aims of this interaction are: to develop communication, cooperation, collaboration and connection in order to exchange information and ideas; and to give users the opportunity to interact with and learn about each other's cultures, particularly in view of the fact that usage is widespread among individuals living in various countries. This situation will lead to a two-way communication between individuals, who in many cases may not have met personally. Thus, it is reasonable to state that SN increases an individual's circle of associates on a worldwide scale.

T. Issa (✉)
School of Information Systems, Curtin University, GPO BOX U1987
Perth, WA 6845, Australia
e-mail: Tomayess.Issa@cbs.curtin.edu.au

T. Issa et al. (eds.), *Social Networking and Education*,
Lecture Notes in Social Networks, DOI 10.1007/978-3-319-17716-8_2

In today's world where information is measured as an indispensable foundation of wealth, SN (such as Wiki, Blogs, Forums, Discussion Board, Blackboard, Moodle etc.) plays the role of mass media whereby even the public can communicate their views to the whole world that is waiting to listen.

The simplicity and affordability of Internet access to the general masses has increased the use of SN locally and globally. The amount of knowledge and information made available to large proportions of the population has risen exponentially with the general public taking advantage of the convenience of the Internet, and the obtainability of devices such as mobile phones and tablet computers in the market at affordable prices.

SN has plenty of applications in every sector, including the business and education sectors, as this tool can be used as a source of knowledge management. Currently, the education sector has begun to integrate it in their curriculum to improve students' personal skills (such as motivation, leadership, negotiation, communication, problem solving, time management, and reflection) and professional skills (such as reading, writing, research, information gathering, critical thinking, decision making, digital oral presentation, drawing (i.e. concept maps) and teamwork) to enhance students' learning in their current studies and prepare them for the workplace in the future. The use of SN in higher education is intended to encourage critical thinking, debate and discussion among students and between students and lecturer, and to ascertain whether students have acquire a thorough understanding of the topics. SN can assist students to reduce printing costs and travel costs, and it creates more independent learners who can delve more deeply into the topics presented by their teachers. Furthermore, SN use has revolutionized the educational system and transformed the classroom into an interactive podium where students question what is taught and strive to contribute information to the discussion by adding their comments, documents, concept maps or power point slides.

In general, SN in higher education can improve students' personal and professional skills such as writing, speaking, listening, discussion, and debating via the Internet. Furthermore, it encourages students to respect and acknowledge the views of their colleagues and lecturers. This tool can encourage weak students to better understand the topics discussed in class through the weekly activities, with the lecturer and colleagues helping to answer their queries and dispel their doubts.

Notwithstanding the opportunities of using SN in higher education, this tool can bring some risks from four perspectives: (1) Cognitive Development, (2) Social Development, (3) Physical Development and (4) Security. This chapter aims to examine and inspect SN usage among students in Australian high education. This chapter is organized as follows: (1) Introduction; (2) Social Network; (3) Research Method and Questions; Survey Design; (4) Participants; (5) Results, Discussion and Significance.

2 Social Networking

Social Networking is a web-based interface intended to establish and facilitate interaction, communication, collaboration and connection between individuals and groups by utilizing numerous tools such as emails, blogs, wiki, tweets, instant messaging, to enable the sharing of digital information [20, 36, 56]. The SN interface is easy to use, and learn, and each user is able create an account in order to share information and interact with family and peers to obtain knowledge and new ideas; moreover, it gives them the freedom to choose with whom s/he will correspond and share information. Currently, Social Networking applications are becoming a common tool among people world-wide, such as Myspace, Facebook, YouTube, LinkedIn, Twitter, Wikis, Blogs and Podcasts, to interact, explore, share, communicate, and provide view and arguments and ideas based on the topics. Furthermore, this tool is changing how sectors, including business and education, interact with customers, employees, and students and teachers now and in future.

The SN tool can have a significant influence on the education and learning sectors, since it offers a pioneering means of involving students in the learning process. Currently, universities recognize that SN tool will assist students to communicate and engage with their peers and lecturers to enhance their learning and their personal and professional skills [7, 16, 37, 52]. Therefore, the majority of universities, especially in developed countries, have introduced SN in the syllabus to enhance students' knowledge and learning and to foster students' independent learning in their tertiary studies, their future workplace, and life in general [31, 32]. Figures 1 and 2 identify the SN opportunities based on the current literature [9, 32, 33, 35, 37, 38, 46, 47, 55, 57]. These opportunities are: cutting edge knowledge, collaboration, inter-crossing relationships, communication skills; environment-friendly and provides opportunities to acquire new acquaintances. Figure 2 depicts the SN opportunities in further detail.

On the other hand, using SN in higher education can create several risks in terms of: (1) Cognitive Development, (2) Social Development, (3) Physical Development and (4) Security. Figures 3 and 4 explain the risks of SN based on the current literature [2, 4–6, 20, 21, 37, 39, 41, 42]. Figure 4 explains the risks in detail.

Generally speaking, using SN in higher education provides students with an outstanding opportunity to since it improve their learning process and their skills. However, this tool should be implemented by using specific models for SN in order to minimize risks and increase the opportunities available to both students and lecturers.

3 Research Method and Questions; Survey Design

This study aims to address and examine the two questions, namely: "what are the opportunities and risks associated with social networking usage by students in Australia? "What is the relationship between the Social Networking use and the

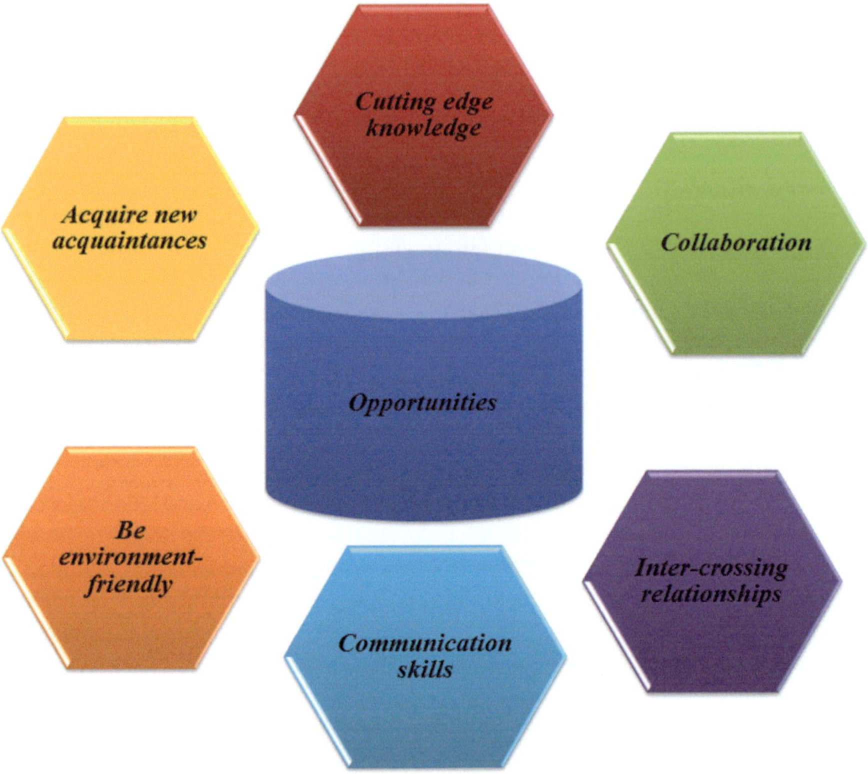

Fig. 1 SN opportunities—Prepared by the author

notion of sustainability awareness among the students in Australia?" and "What is the relationship between Social Networking and the development of a professional attitude among students in Australia?" To examine these questions, the researcher devised an online survey to assess the opportunities and risks of Social Networking. The online survey was generated and developed based on a review of the current literature. Online surveys are designed to provide interaction between participant and survey via online or face-to-face modes. The beauty of using this tool is that data downloaded from it are ready for immediate analysis using SPSS or other statistical programs; while the findings can be presented in numerous formats such as tables, figures, calculations of mean and standard deviation based on the researcher's requirements [8, 14, 15, 18, 19, 23, 50]. Via the online survey, participants can provide rich and historical information which the researcher can utilize for the research objectives and aims. An online survey is a "pre-formulated written set of questions to which respondents record their answers, usually within rather closely defined alternatives." In addition, "online surveys are an efficient data collection mechanism when the researcher knows exactly what is required and how to measure the variables of interest" [49, 236].

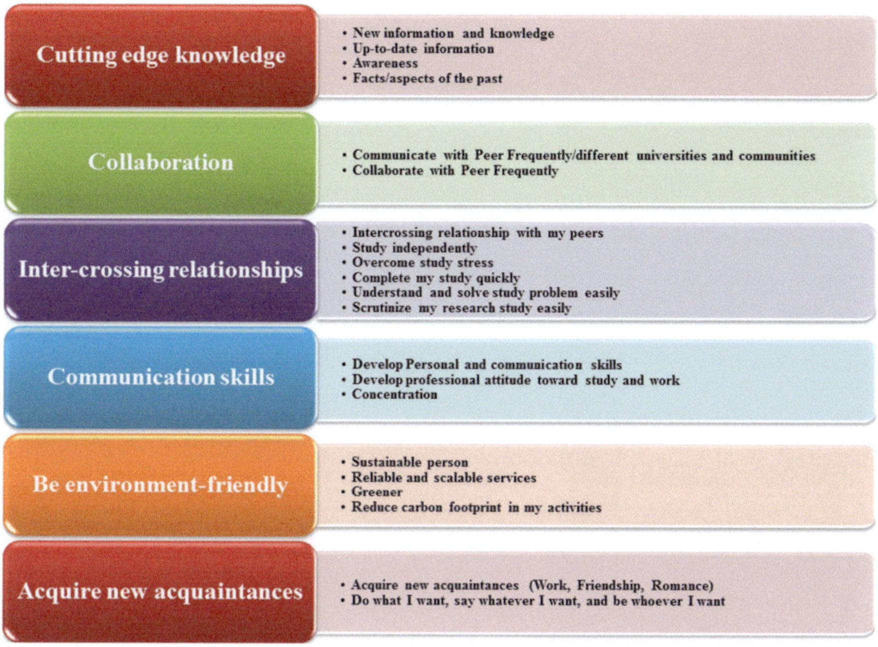

Fig. 2 SN opportunities in details– Prepared by the author

Fig. 3 SN risks—Prepared by the author

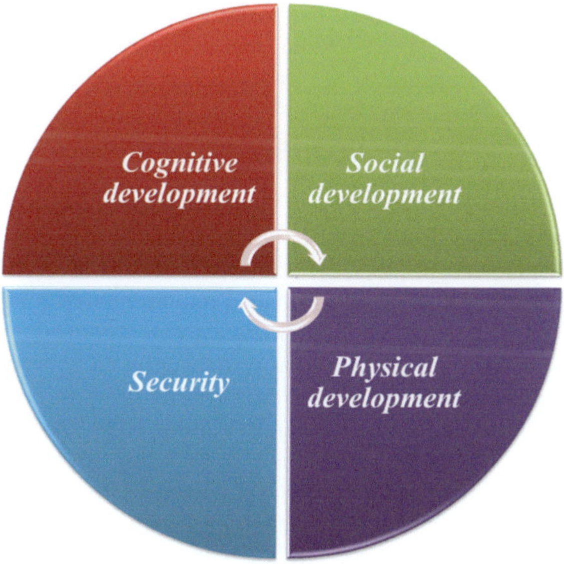

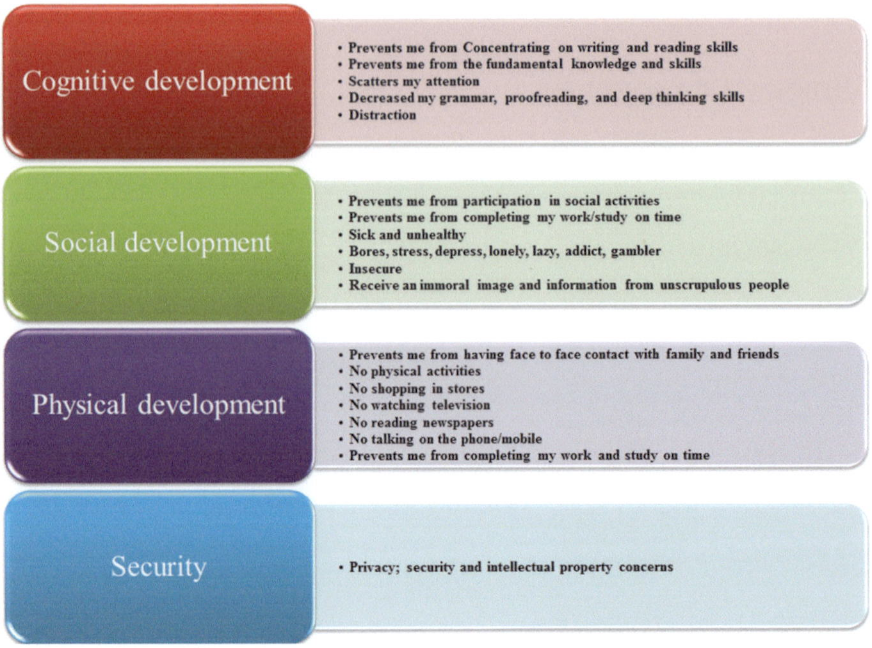

Fig. 4 SN risks in details– Prepared by the author

The online survey has many strengths as it is less expensive, provides greater anonymity, it is easy to manage and accessible, less error-prone, and reduces paper usage compared to the paper and pencil survey, thereby confirming that online surveys are more sustainable compared with the traditional survey methods [27, 43–45]. However, the online survey has several weaknesses in relation to technical failure including computer viruses and hacking which can decrease the response rate according to Fan and Yan [18]. The online survey design offers self-motivated interaction between the respondent and the survey than can be achieved via email or paper surveys [13, 14].

The online survey is divided into three parts namely: background, opportunities and risks components. The researcher set seven questions for the background to obtain the participants' background as well as some information related to social networking usage. As for the opportunities; the researchers developed twenty-five [29] statements pertaining to cutting edge knowledge, coloration, inter-crossing relationships, communication skills, being environment-friendly and acquiring new acquaintance. The thirty (30) statements for the risks focus mainly on cognitive development, social development, physical development and security. Also, a comment section for the last parts is provided where participants can offer additional opinions. A five-point Likert scale is used in each part of the online survey to "examine how strongly subjects agree or disagree with statements" [49, 197]. The five-point Likert scale ranges: Strongly disagree, Disagree, Neutral, Agree, and

Strongly Agree. The online survey contained clear instructions at the top of the page and a progress bar along the bottom to offer feedback to users about their proximity to the finishing point. Furthermore, three questions per page presented to minimize scrolling and the concluding page thanked participants for their participation. The survey was created online using Qualtrics software. Qualtrics website (www.qualtrics.com) distributed the online survey to 153 participants in Australia. Qualtrics is an online survey tool with an outstanding reputation since it is used to develop and summarize the survey results to allow the researchers to accomplish data collection and analysis [34, 40]. The response validity was 100 % for this study.

4 Participants

The participants for this study were 153 from across Australia. 41 % are male, while 59 % are female. The participants' ages ranged from 18 to 52 years, and the highest response rate for 42–52 was 30, 29 % for 22–32, 27 % for 32–42, and finally 14 % for the 18–22 age group (see Table 1).

The participants' fields of study comprised Information Technology (10 %), Management (11 %), Health Sciences (12 %), and Accounting (7 %) while the rest (24 %) from Business Law, Economics and Finance, Information Systems, Computer Science, Marketing, Humanities, Science and Engineering and Art and Design. As for the others (35 %) studied various related fields such as Construction, Education, Building, Manufacturing, Payroll, Real Estate, and Human Resources (see Table 2).

Table 3 shows that the majority of participants (37 %) are Higher/Secondary/Pre-University, and 24 % have a Bachelor's degree.

Furthermore, the online survey examined the participants' daily use of social networking. From the survey results (see Table 4), it was noted that the majority (53 %) of the participants spend on social networking (not including email) less

Table 1 Gender—Prepared by the author

Gender		
	Response	%
Male	63	41
Female	90	59
Total	153	100
Age		
18–22	21	14
22–32	44	29
32–42	42	27
42–52	46	30
Total	153	100

Table 2 Field of study—Prepared by the author

Field of study		
	Response	%
Accounting	10	7
Business law	5	3
Economics and finance	5	3
Information systems	1	1
Information technology	16	10
Computer science	3	2
Management	17	11
Marketing	2	1
Health sciences	19	12
Humanities	9	6
Science and engineering	5	3
Art and design	7	5
Others—Please specify	54	35
Total	153	100

Table 3 Highest education level—Prepared by the author

Highest education level		
	Response	%
Primary Education	8	5
Higher Secondary/Pre-University	57	37
Professional Certificate	13	8
Diploma	18	12
Advanced/Higher/Graduate Diploma	6	4
Bachelor's Degree	36	24
Post Graduate Diploma	4	3
Master's Degree	11	7
Total	153	100

Table 4 Number of hours spent on social networking daily, not including email? (Per day)

How many hours do you spend on the social networking daily, not including email? (Per day)		
	Response	%
Less than an hour	81	53 %
Up to five hours	52	34 %
Five to ten hours	11	7 %
Ten to twenty hours	7	5 %
Over twenty hours	2	1 %
Total	153	100 %

Table 5 Number of hours spent on the Internet for email (per day?)

How many hours do you spend on the internet for email? (Per day)		
	Response	%
Less than an hour	82	54
Up to five hours	53	35
Five to ten hours	14	9
Ten to Twenty hours	1	1
Over twenty hours	3	2
Total	153	100

than an hour daily; on the other hand, 34 % of the participants spend 34 % daily on the social networking.

Moreover, from the survey results we noted that participants spend the same time on the Internet as they do on social networking; this means that users are spending the same amount of time using these tools to interact, communicate, and chat (Table 5).

Table 6 shows that 91 % of the participants are using the Internet for Email, 67 % for banking online; 63 % for shopping online; 51 % for buying goods or services, 42 % for study, work, and researching hobbies, 36 % for making or researching travel information or reservations; 35 % for playing or chatting, 9 % for investment and 5 % for using Skype, Facebook or listening to music.

Table 6 Internet usage—Prepared by the author

Do you **prefer** using the internet for: (you can choose more than one option)?		
	Response	%
Email	139	91
Play Games	54	35
Study	65	42
Work	65	42
Shop Online	96	63
Chat	54	35
Researching hobbies	64	42
Banking online	102	67
Buying goods or services	78	51
Buying stocks or investing online	14	9
Making or researching travel information or reservations	55	36
Others—Please specify	7	5
Total	153	100

5 Results, Discussion and New Significance

A total of 153 participants from Australia responded to the questionnaire. There was no missing data, resulting in all 153 cases being valid responses for Australia for the following Factor Analysis, where the analysis was conducted separately for responses from Opportunities Group and Risks Group. The Opportunities group consisted of 25 questions and Risks group consisted of 30 questions. Based on the Mean and STD Deviation results, it was confirmed that the majority of the respondents agreed on the opportunities of SN usage, while there was a mixture reaction to the SN risks (see Tables 7 and 8).

The researcher examined the online survey results for the opportunities and risks sections. The researcher employed principal axis factoring for factor extraction, and to allow the variable to correlate, oblique rotation (rather than orthogonal rotation) was applied using the promax method [11, 12, 58]. To measure the sampling

Table 7 Descriptive statistics—Opportunities

Descriptive Statistics		
	Mean	Std. Deviation
Q 9_1 Learn new information and knowledge	3.59	1.017
Q9_2 Gain up-to-date information	3.74	0.849
Q9_3 Be more aware of global issues/local issues	3.68	0.878
Q9_4 To remember facts/aspects of the past	3.58	0.886
Q9_5 Communicate with my peers frequently	3.79	0.886
Q 9_6 Collaborate with my peers frequently	3.63	0.834
Q9_7 Communicate with my peers from different universities	3.35	0.990
Q9_8 Communicate with my different communities	3.58	0.871
Q9_9 Develop intercrossing relationships with my peers	3.42	0.964
Q9_10 Study independently	3 22	1.051
Q9_11 Overcome study stress	3.12	1.057
Q9_12 Complete my study more quickly	3.12	1.088
Q9_13 Understand and solve study problems easily	3.32	1.049
Q9_14 Scrutinize my research study more easily	3.27	1.027
Q9_15 Develop my personal and communication skills	3.39	0.967
Q9_16 Concentrate more on my reading and writing skills	3.16	0.976
Q9_17 To prepare my professional attitude toward study and work	3.14	1.013
Q9_18 Be more sustainable person	3.19	0.944
Q9_19 Provide reliable and scalable services	3.20	0.948
Q9_20 Become more "Greener" in my acuities	3.05	1.062
Q9_21 Reduce carbon footprint in my activities	2.98	1.103
Q9_22 Acquire new acquaintances—work related	3.44	0.965
Q9_23 Acquire new acquaintances—friendship relationship	3.54	0.966
Q9_24 Acquire new acquaintances—romance relationship	3.12	1.106
Q9_25 Do whatever I want, say whatever I want, and be whoever I want	3.42	0.998

Table 8 Descriptive statistics—Risks

Descriptive Statistics		
	Mean	Std. deviation
Q11_1 Prevents me from concentrating more on writing and reading skills	3.09	1.035
Q11_2 Presents me from remembering the fundamental knowledge and skills	2.90	.978
Q11_3 Scatters my attention	3.29	1.038
Q11_4 Decreases my grammar and proof reading skills	3.08	1.076
Q11_5 Decreases my deep thinking	3.05	1.031
Q11_6 Distracts me easily	3.31	1.065
Q11_7 Prevents me from participating in social activities	2.84	1.033
Q11_8 Presents me from completing my work it study on time	2.91	1.047
Q11_9 Makes me sick and unhealthy	2.57	1.024
Q11_10 Bores me	2.80	.974
Q11_11 Stresses me	2.58	.971
Q11_12 Depresses me	2.58	.984
Q11_13 Makes me feel lonely	2.63	1.063
Q11_14- Make me lazy	2.97	1.066
Q11_15 Makes me addict	2.85	1.012
Q11_16 Makes me more gambler	2.35	.996
Q11_17 Makes me insecure to release my personal details from the theft of personal information	3.03	1.063
Q11_18 Makes me receive an immoral images and information from unscrupulous people and it is difficult to act against them at present	2.84	1.029
Q11_19 Prevents me from having face to face contact with my family	2.74	1.081
Q11_20 Prevents me from having face to face contact with my friends	2.81	1.075
Q11_21 Prevents me from participating in phvsical activities	2.90	1.101
Q11_22 Prevents me from shopping in stores	2.68	1.055
Q11_23 Prevents me from watching television	2.75	1.072
Q11_24 Prevents me from reading the newspapers	2.75	1.065
Q11_25 Prevents me from talking on the phone/mobile	2.63	1.025
Q11_26 Prevents me from completing my work on time	2.74	.998
Q11_27 Prevents me from completing my study on time	2.80	1.026
Q11_28 Increase privacy concerns	3.31	1.003
Q11_29 Increase securitv concerns	3.29	1.069
Q11_30 Increase intellectual property concerns	3.08	1.026

adequacy for the Opportunities and Risks, researcher carried out specific testing using Cronbach's Alpha, Kaiser-Meyer-Olkin and Bartlett's test.

For the Opportunities section, the Cronbach's Alpha for all 25 variables was 0.961 indicates an excellent internal consistency of the items in the scale [10, 53]. Moreover, the Kaiser-Meyer-Olkin measure of sampling adequacy was 0.920; this measure indicates that a good sample size is obtained from the analysis [24]. Finally, The Bartlett's test of sphericity is highly significant, $\chi^2 = 3420.299$, df = 300, p < 0.000, indicating that the items of the scale are sufficiently correlated to factors to be found [3, 48].

For the Risks section, The Cronbach's Alpha for all 30 variables was 0.970, indicating an excellent internal consistency of the items in the scale [22]. A Kaiser-Meyer-Olkin measure of sampling adequacy of 0.924 indicates a good sample size is obtained from the analysis [24]. Finally, the Bartlett's test of sphericity is highly significant, $\chi^2 = 4498.143$, df = 435, p < 0.000, indicating that the items of the scale are sufficiently correlated to factors to be found [17, 54] Lastly, the communalities for the Opportunities and Risks statements were over 0.5 (see Tables 9 and 10) only the last statement "Do whatever I want, say whatever I want, and be whoever I want" in the opportunities section is less than 0.5, indicates to the

Table 9 Communalities –Opportunities

Communalities		
	Initial	Extraction
Q9_1 Learn new information and knowledge	0.741	0.753
Q9_2 Gain up-to-date information	0.769	0.820
Q9_3 Be more aware of global issues/local issues	0.628	0.619
Q9_4 To remember facts/aspects of the past	0.622	0.539
Q9_5 Communicate with my peers frequently	0.732	0.520
Q9_6 Collaborate with my peers frequently	0.713	0.620
Q9_7 Communicate with my peers from different universities	0.654	0.651
Q9_8 Communicate with my different communities	0.779	0.743
Q9_9 Develop intercrossing relationships with my peers	0.721	0.642
Q9_10 Study independently	0.737	0.714
Q9_11 Overcome study stress	0.719	0.648
Q9_12 Complete my study more quickly	0.852	0.923
Q9_13 Understand and solve study problems easily	0.800	0.725
Q9_14 Scrutinize my research study more easily	0.827	0.728
Q9 15 Develop my personal and communication skills	0.692	0.524
Q9_16 Concentrate more on my reading and writing skills	0.760	0.636
Q9_17 To prepare my professional attitude toward study and work	0.814	0.754
Q9_18 Be more sustainable person	0.824	0.792
Q9_19 Provide reliable and scalable services	0.788	0.696
Q9_20 Become more "Greener" in my activities	0.821	0.732
Q9_21 Reduce carbon footprint in my activities	0.858	0.755
Q9_22 Acquire new acquaintances—work related	0.726	0.629
Q9_23 Acquire new acquaintances—friendship relationship	0.725	0.629
Q9_24 Acquire new acquaintances—romance relationship	0.555	0.528
Q9_25 Do whatever I want, say whatever I want, and be whoever I want	0.416	0.285

Extraction method: maximum likelihood

Table 10 Communalities—Risks

Communalities		
	Initial	Extraction
Q11_1 Prevents me from, concentrating more on writing and reading skills	0.760	0.676
Q11_2 Prevents me from remembering the fundamental knowledge and skills	0.830	0.669
Q11_3 Scatters my attention	0.775	0.743
Q11_4 Decreases my grammar and proofreading skills	0.717	0.547
Q11_5 Decreases my deep thinking	0.778	0.665
Q11_6 Distracts me easily	0.664	0.576
Q11_7 Presents me from participating in social activities	0.772	0.582
Q11_8 Prevents me from completing my work/study on time	0.779	0.706
Q11_9 Makes me sick and unhealthy	0.769	0.645
Q11_10 Bores me	0.606	0.435
Q11_11 Stresses me	0.830	0.708
Q11_12 Depresses me	0.823	0.881
Q11_13 Makes me fed lonely	0.797	0.719
Q11_14 Makes me lazy	0.557	0.349
Q11_15 Makes me addict	0.691	0.500
Q11_16 Makes me more rambler	0.732	0.557
Q11_17 Makes me insecure to release my personal details from the theft of personal information	0.575	0.393
Q11_18 Makes me receive an immoral images and information from unscrupulous people and it is difficult to act against them at present	0.736	0.633
Q11_19 Prevents me from having face to face contact with my family	0.828	0.651
Q11_20 Prevents me from having face to face contact with my friends	0.861	0.699
Q11_21 Prevents me from participating in physical activities	0.857	0.708
Q11_22 Prevents me from shopping in stores	0.731	0.634
Q11_23 Prevents me from watching television	0.779	0.695
Q11_24 Prevents me from reading the newspapers	0.808	0.787
Q11_25 Prevents me from talking on the phone mobile	0.745	0.645
Q11_26 Prevents me from completing my work on time	0.892	0.776
Q11_27 Prevents me from completing my study on time	0.883	0.773
Q11_28 Increase privacy concerns	0.870	0.881
Q11_29 Increase security concerns	0.856	0.899
Q11_30 Increase intellectual property concerns	0.786	0.704

Extraction method: maximum likelihood

researcher that participants are taking into account the type of information that they need to post via social networking, especially for studies and work.

Furthermore, the researchers used principle components analysis to estimate the factor loading matrix for the factor analysis model as well the standard correlation

Table 11 Total variance explained—Opportunities

Total variance explained							
	Initial eigenvalues			Extraction sums of squared loadings			Rotation sums of squared loadings[a]
Factor	Total	%of Variance	Cumulative %	Total	%of Variance	Cumulative %	Total
1	11.796	53.616	53.616	11.357	51.623	51.623	8.990
2	2.228	10.127	63.743	1.970	8.954	60.576	8.606
3	1.444	6.562	70.305	1.052	4.784	65.360	8.663
4	1.003	4.558	74.863	0.878	3.989	69.349	6.984

Table 12 Total variance explained—Risks

Total variance explained							
	Initial Eigenvalues			Extraction sums of squared loadings			Rotation sums of squared loadings[a]
Factor	Total	% of Variance	Cumulative %	Total	% of Variance	Cumulative %	Total
1	12.738	55.384	55.384	12.069	52.472	52.472	11.495
2	2.011	8.745	64.128	1.841	8.005	60.477	9.274
3	1.466	6.504	70.633	1.408	6.120	66.597	7.035

matrix. The Eigen values for the opportunities were assessed to determine the number of factors accounting for the correlations amongst the variables.

As demonstrated in Table (11), this model of four factors accounts for a total of 69.349 % of the variation. The Eigen values and the amount of variances explained by each of these factors are presented below (after rotation).

As for the Risks section, as demonstrated in Table (12), this model of two factors accounts for a total of 66.597 % of the variation. The Eigen values and the amount of variances explained by each of these factors are presented below (after rotation).

Furthermore, to measure the regression coefficients (i.e. slopes), the researchers carried out the factor loadings. The factor loadings for the Opportunities and Risks are high enough and the one with the cleanest fact structured to be considered as important [11], and to exclude several items under each factors where the factor loading below 0.5 based on the rule of thumb of Stevens [51] for a sample size above 100.

Four factors are revealed by the Pattern Matrix for the Opportunities Group:

1. Factor 1: Be a "green" and "economical" user, use to improve professionalism and literacy skill; operational benefits
2. Factor 2: Teamwork-building instrument, channel for professional and personal networking

3. Factor 3: As tool for study or work independently
4. Factor 4: As alternative channel to gain knowledge or information (Table 13)

Three factors have been revealed by the Pattern Matrix for Risks Group:

1. Factor 1: Impediment to traditional information source, changes to regular daily activity, anxiety trigger, inhibitor of sociability, leads to sedentary lifestyle

Table 13 Pattern matrix—Opportunities

Pattern Matrix[a]				
	Factor			
	1	2	3	4
Q9_18 Be more sustainable person	0.903			0.188
Q9_21 Reduce carbon footprint in my activities	0.823		0.120	–0.127
Q9_20 Become more "Greener" in my activities	0.750		0.184	
Q9_ 17 To prepare my professional attitude toward study and work	0.660		0.163	0.115
Q9_19 Provide reliable and scalable services	0.614		0.137	0.119
Q9_ 16 Concentrate more on my reading and writing skills	0.578		0.157	
Q9_7 Communicate with my peers from different universities	–0.236	0.795	0.302	
Q9_8 Communicate with my different communities	–0.141	0.756		0.217
Q9_23 Acquire new acquaintances—friendship relationship	0.223	0.746	–0.289	
Q9_24 Acquire new acquaintances—romance relationship	0.258	0.740		–0.384
Q9_9 Develop intercrossing relationships with my peers	0.177	0.661		
Q9_22 Acquire new acquaintances—weak related	0.300	0.648	–0.109	
Q9 6 Collaborate with my peers frequently		0.628		0.273
Q9_5 Communicate with my peers frequently	–0.219	0.559		0.321
Q9_ 12 Complete my study more quickly		–0.153	10.001	
Q9_13 Understand and solve study problems easily	0.134		0.685	
Q9_10 Study independently	0.162		0.675	0.124
Q9_11 Overcome study stress			0.652	
Q9_14 Scrutinize my research study more easily	0.171	0.183	0.650	
Q9_2 Gain up-to-date information		0.141		0.820
Q9_1 Learn new information and knowledge	0.173			0.817
Q9_3 Be more aware of global issues/local issues				0.731

Extraction method: maximum likelihood. rotation method promax with kaiser normalization
[a]Rotation converged in 10 iterations

2. Factor 2: Inhibitor of developing literacy and fundamental skills, reduction of further thinking capability and inability to focus on one matter for any length of time
3. Factor 3: Cynicism regarding data security (Table 14)

A score was calculated for each factor by averaging across each individual item. The mean and standard deviation of each factor average for the Opportunities group are presented below (see Table 15):

The mean and standard deviation of each factor average for the Risks group is presented in Table 16:

The Australian results indicated that social networking can offer several opportunities to Australian students since this tool will improve their personal and

Table 14 Pattern matrix—Risks

Pattern Matrix[a]			
	Factor		
	1	2	3
Q11_24 Prevents me from reading the newspapers	0.867	–0.111	0.114
Q11_22 Prevents me from shopping in stores	0.856	–0.199	0.120
Q11_23 Prevents me from watching television	0.836		
Q11_16 Makes me mere gambler	0.836		–0.208
Q11_25 Prevents me from talking on the phone/mobile	0.788		
Q11_12 Depresses me	0.776	0.163	–0.242
Q11_9 Makes me side and unhealthy	0.769		
Q11_13 Makes me feel lonely	0.733		
Q11_20 Prevents me from having face to face contact with mv friends	0.726		0.108
Q11_11 Stresses me	0.721	0.189	
Q11_21 Prevents me from participating in physical activities	0.691		0.226
Q11_19 Prevent me from having face to face contact with mv family	0.673		0.169
Q11_27 Prevents me from completing my study on time	0.657	0.253	
Q11_7 Prevents me from participating in social	0.584	0.267	
Q11_1 Prevents me from concentrating more on		0.827	
Q11_3 Scatters my attention		0.811	0.160
Q11_5 Decreases my deep thinking		0.790	
Q11_6 Distracts me easily		0.751	
Q11_2 Prevents me from remembering the	0.197	0.727	
Q11_4 Decreases my grammar and proofreading skills		0.686	
Q11_29 Increase security concerns			0.962
Q11_28 Increase privacy concerns			0.955
Q11_30 Increase intellectual property concerns		0.189	0.668

Extraction method maximum likelihood. rotation method: Promax with Kaiser Normalization
[a]Rotation convened in 6 iterations

Table 15 Factors—Opportunities

Factors	Mean	Std. Deviation
Factor 1: Be a "Green" and "economical" user, use to improve profesionalism and literacy skill	3.1209	1.0080
Factor 2: Teamwork building instrument, channel for professional and personal networking	3.484	0.948
Factor 3: As tool for study or work independently	3.209	1.05
Factor 4: As alternative channel to gain knowledge or information	3.669	0.915

Table 16 Factors—Risks

Factors	Mean	Std. Deviation
Factor 1: Impediment to traditional information source, changes to regular daily activity, anxiety trigger, inhibitor of sociability, leads to sedentary lifestyle	2.69	1.04
Factor 2: Inhibitor of developing literacy and fundamental skills, reduction of further thinking capability and inability to focus on one matter for any length of time	3.12	1.04
Factor 3: Cynicism regarding data security	3.23	1.03

professional skills, especially reading and writing. Using this tool will encourage students to develop teamwork skills by facilitating collaboration, communication, debate, activities and oral presentation. These skills will assist students in their studies as well as the workforce in the future. These skills are required by organizations locally and globally; therefore, higher education institutions have begun to integrate and adopt these tools in their assessments and class activities to promote students' professional and personal skills.

Several studies [1, 26, 28] confirm that using technology in higher education will enhance students' skills, since technology has become a necessity for tertiary studies and the workforce. These outcomes answered the study research question—question 3—that there is a relationship between social networking and the development of a professional attitude among students in Australia.

Furthermore, the study produced two interesting findings: that social networking will produce more economical and 'green aware' students. This result shows an increased awareness among the students in Australia about the relationship between the use of social networking and the notion of sustainability. This result proved to be most interesting and an exceptional achievement since, by means of this tool, students changed their mind-sets and became good stewards of sustainable development for their current studies and in future. Academics and higher education sectors should take a leading role in transforming society's and students' critical thinking about using technology tools and raising their awareness of the relationship between technology and sustainability among students to benefit our community, society and the earth [25, 30]. This result confirmed the research question—question 2—that this tool enables students to become aware, understand and acknowledge the relationship between social networking use and sustainability since the majority of students indicated that using this tool is more sustainable, simple, and with less paper usage; it is less time consuming and more green.

Finally, the survey indicated several opportunities and skills that could be acquired through social networking use by students in Australia (see Fig. 5 and 6); Green aware, Promoting skills (Teamwork; Professional; Personal) Work Independently and New Channels for the acquisition of knowledge or information. From these results, we recognised that the use of Social Networking can bring several opportunities to students in higher education. The aforementioned skills are an example of ways in which SN usage can assist students in their studies and this

Fig. 5 New SN opportunities for Australia—Prepared by the author

Fig. 6 New SN risks for Australia—Prepared by the author

may encourage higher education institutions to implement this tool in their curriculum, especially in universities.

On the other hand, using this tool without monitoring and observing can lead to enormous risks namely: impeding traditional information source/media; anxiety and worry; no social life; changes to regular daily activity; lack of foundation skills including literacy and thinking capability; inability to focus on one matter for any length of time and security, especially regarding data storage. These are serious risks for students, and higher education institutions should implement SN tools by using a specific model to minimize or eliminate these risks.

As previously indicated, SN tools can provide excellent opportunities for students to increase their knowledge and experience locally and globally and this will assist them not only in their studies but in the workforce in future. Therefore, higher education institutions should and must take these risks into consideration when implementing SN in the higher education curriculum. This can be achieved by using SN models for higher education and lecturers should track and monitor students' progress via the SN. By using these techniques, these risks should be minimized. The study outcomes answered the research question by ascertaining the opportunities and risks to students who engage in social networking.

Finally, this study added new significant contributions to the current literature especially regarding Australia as new opportunities and risks emerged associated with SN usage amongst students in higher education. This study will assist students, academics, and researchers to understand and recognize how technology has begun to change students' attitudes and behaviour towards their studies and for the workforce in future.

This study was limited to 153 students from Australia. Its purpose was to examine students' attitudes to SN usage. Through the results of this study there emerged several new opportunities and risks associated with SN usage, especially in higher education. Further research with larger and more diverse groups of students is required in the future to strengthen the research findings.

6 Conclusion

The purpose of this study is to examine students' attitudes and behaviours toward Social Networking use in Australia. Social Networking technology in higher education will allow teachers and students to communicate, collaborate, connect and cooperate with each another more effortlessly. This tool is easy to use, easy to learn, inexpensive, and a simple means to promote business, health, school, and university activities and information-sharing. SN has become an essential tool in universities to foster students' professional and personal skills since, currently, lecturers have started to integrate Social Networking (such as Wiki, Blog, Discussion Board… etc.) in assessments and class activities to create productive communication between students and teachers. Current literature indicates that the use of Social Networking in any sector, including the education sector, has numerous opportunities but also and risks. These may differ from country to country and depend on the country's culture, security, privacy policies and ethical issues. This study conducted an online survey with 153 respondents, and based on the online survey, four opportunities and three risks emerged from the Australian perspective. Further research will be carried out in future to examine more varied groups of students in order to reinforce the research findings.

References

1. Benson V, Morgan S, Filippaios F (2014) Social career management: social media and employability skills gap. Comput Hum Behav 30:519–525. doi:10.1016/j.chb.2013.06.015
2. Bright LF, Kleiser SB, Grau SL (2015) Too much Facebook? An exploratory examination of social media fatigue. Comput Hum Behav 44:148–155. doi:10.1016/j.chb.2014.11.048
3. Burns R, Burns R (2008) Business research methods and statistics using SPSS. SAGE, New York

4. Carr N (2008) Is Google making us stupid? The Atlantic Monthly
5. Carr N (2010) The Shallows: how the internet is changing the way we think, read and remember. Atlantic Books USA
6. Carr N (2011) The Shallows: what the internet is doing to our brains. W. W. Norton USA
7. Chen R (2013) Member use of social networking sites—an empirical examination. Decis Support Syst 54(3):1219–1227. doi:10.1016/j.dss.2012.10.028
8. Cho Y, Park J, Han SK, S (2011) Development of a web-based survey system for evaluating affective satisfaction. International Journal of Industrial Ergonomics 41:247–254
9. Choi J, Lee JK (2015) Investigating the effects of news sharing and political interest on social media network heterogeneity. Comput Hum Behav 44:258–266. doi:10.1016/j.chb.2014.11.029
10. Connelly LM (2011) Cronbach's Alpha. Medsurg Nursing 20(1):44–45
11. Costello A, Osborne J (2005) Best Practices in exploratory factor analysis: four recommendations for getting the most from your analysis. Pract Assess Res Eval 10(7):1–9
12. de Winter JCF, Dodou D, Wieringa PA (2009) Exploratory factor analysis with small sample sizes. Multivar Behav Res 44(2):147–181. doi:10.1080/00273170902794206
13. Dillman D (2007) Mail and internet surveys "The Tailored Design Method", 2nd edn. Wiley, USA
14. Dillman D, Glenn P, Tortora R, Swift K, Kohrell J, Berck J, Messer B (2009) Response rate and measurement differences in mixed-mode surveys using mail, telephone, interactive voice reponse (IVR) and the Internet. Soc Sci Res 38:1–18
15. Dillman D, Reipus U, Matzat U (2010) Advice in Surveying the general public over the Internet. Int J Internet Sci 5(1):1–4
16. Din N, Yahya S, Suzan R, Kassim R (2012) Online Social networking for quality of life. Procedia—Soc Behav Sci 35:713–718. doi:10.1016/j.sbspro.2012.02.141
17. Dziuban CD, Shirkey EC (1974) When is a correlation matrix appropriate for factor analysis? Some decision rules. Psychol Bull 81(6):358
18. Fan W, Yan Z (2010) Factors affecting response rates of the web survey: a systematic review. Comput Hum Behav 26(2):132–139
19. Fink A (2010) Survey research methods. Educ Res Methodol: Quant Methods Res:152–160
20. Fox J, Moreland JJ (2015) The dark side of social networking sites: An exploration of the relational and psychological stressors associated with Facebook use and affordances. Comput Hum Behav 45:168–176. doi:10.1016/j.chb.2014.11.083
21. Frison E, Eggermont S (2015) The impact of daily stress on adolescents' depressed mood: The role of social support seeking through Facebook. Comput Hum Behav 44:315–325. doi:10.1016/j.chb.2014.11.070
22. Gliem J, Gliem R (2003) Calculating, interpreting, and reporting Cronbach's alpha reliability coefficient for likert-type scales. Paper presented at the 2003 Midwest research to practice conference in adult, continuing and community education
23. Gordon J, McNew R (2008) Developing the Online Survey. Nurs Clin N Am 43(4):605–619
24. Hill BD (2012) The sequential Kaiser-Meyer-Olkin procedure as an alternative for determining the number of factors in common-factor analysis: a Monte Carlo simulation proquest. Umi Dissertation Publishing USA
25. Isaias P, Issa T (2013) E-learning and sustainability in higher education: an international case study. Int J Learn High Educ 20(4):77–90
26. Isaias P, Issa T (2014) Promoting communication skills for information systems students in Australian and Portuguese higher education: action research study. Educ Inf Technol 19 (4):841–861
27. Issa T (2013) Online survey: best practice. In: information systems research and exploring social artifacts: approaches and methodologies. IGI Global, pp 1–19. doi:10.4018/978-1-4666-2491-7.ch001
28. Issa T, Isaias P, Issa T (2014) Does MP3 audio feedback enhance student's learning skills? Int J Learn 19:15–28

29. Issa T, Issa T, Chang V (2011) Would teaching sustainable development business strategies shift students' mindsets: an Australian perspective. Int J Environ Cult Econ Social Sustain 7 (5):258–272
30. Issa T, Issa T, Chang V (2014) Sustainability and Green IT education practice for incorporating into the Australian Higher Education curriculum. Int J Sustain Educ 9(2):21–30
31. Issa T, Issa T, Kommers P (2014) Feedback and learning support that fosters students' independent learning: an Australian case study. Int J Learn 19:29–39
32. Issa T, Kommers P (2013) Social networking for web-based communities. Int J Web Based Commun 9(1):5–24
33. Kemp S (2015) Digital, social and mobile worldwide in 2015. http://wearesocial.net/tag/sdmw/. Accessed 22 Jan 2015
34. Kocher M (2015) Recipes and research: a survey of cookbook collection users. J Agric Food Inf 16(1):53–59
35. Lalonde M, Castro JC (2015) Amplifying youth cultural practices by engaging and developing professional identity through social media. Youth practices in digital arts and new media: learning in formal and informal settings, p 40
36. Mathew B (2014) Using a social networking tool for blended learning in staff training: Sharing experience from practice. J Neonatal Nurs 20(3):90–94. doi:10.1016/j.jnn.2014.03.005
37. McCarroll N, Curran K (2013) Social networking in education. IGI Global. doi:10.4018/jide.2013010101
38. Mulligan N (2013) The WorldWide state of social networks http://wearesocial.net/blog/2013/06/worldwide-state-social-networks/. Accessed 24 July 2013 2013
39. Pan Y, Xu Y, Wang X, Zhang C, Ling H, Lin J (2015) Integrating social networking support for dyadic knowledge exchange: a study in a virtual community of practice. Inf Manag 52 (1):61–70. doi:10.1016/j.im.2014.10.001
40. Peer E, Paolacci G, Chandler J, Mueller P (2012) Selectively recruiting participants from Amazon Mechanical Turk using qualtrics. SSRN 2100631
41. Jvd Peijl, Klein J, Grass C, Freudenthal A (2012) Design for risk control: The role of usability engineering in the management of use-related risks. J Biomed Inform 45(4):785–812. doi:10.1016/j.jbi.2012.03.006
42. Picazo-Vela S, Gutierrez-Martinez I, Luna-Reyes LF (2012) Understanding risks, benefits, and strategic alternatives of social media applications in the public sector. Gov Inf Q 29(4):504–511
43. Porter S (2004) Pros and cons of paper and electronic surveys new directions for institutional resaerch, vol 2004. Wiley Periodicals, Inc
44. Prahalad CK, Rangaswami MR (2009) Why sustainability is now the key driver of innovation Harvard Bus Rev 56–64
45. Prasad A, Saha S, Misra P, Hooli B, Murakami M (2010) Back to green. J Green Eng 89–110
46. Rennie F, Morrison T (2013) e-Learning and social networking handbook resources for higher education. Routledge
47. Roman LA (2014) Using social media to enhance career development opportunities for health promotion professionals. Health Promotion Pract 15(4):471–475. doi:10.1177/1524839914535213
48. Schaefer HS, Larson CL, Davidson RJ, Coan JA (2014) Brain, body, and cognition: Neural, physiological and self-report correlates of phobic and normative fear. Biol Psychol 98:59–69
49. Sekaran U (2003) Research methods for business "A Skill Building Approach", 4th edn. Wiley, New York
50. Smyth J, Dillman D, Christian L, O'Neill A (2010) Using the internet to survey small towns and communities: Limitations and Possibilities in the early 21st Century. Am Behav Sci 53:1423–1448
51. Stevens J (1992) Applied multivariate statistics for the social sciences. Erlbaum, Hillsdale, NJ
52. Swensrud K (2011) Best practices for enterprise social networking. http://thenextweb.com/socialmedia/2011/04/18/best-practices-for-enterprise-social-networking/ Accessed 16 Nov 2011

53. Tavakol M, Dennick R (2011) Making sense of Cronbach's alpha. Int J Med Educ 2:53
54. Tobias S, Carlson JE (1969) Brief report: Bartlett's test of sphericity and chance findings in factor analysis. Multivar Behav Res 4(3):375–377
55. UNCP (2013) The Brief history of social media. http://www.uncp.edu/home/acurtis/NewMedia/SocialMedia/SocialMediaHistory.html. Accessed 24 July 2013
56. Velasquez A, Graham C, McCollum K (2009) Online social networking used to enhance face to face and online pre-servicve teacher education courses. In: Society for information technology and teacher education international conference USA, 2009 pp 560–566
57. Wang Y-C (2014) Using wikis to facilitate interaction and collaboration among EFL learners: a social constructivist approach to language teaching. System 42:383–390. doi:10.1016/j.system.2014.01.007
58. WIlliams B, Onsman A, Brown T (2010) Exploratory factor analysis: A five-step guide for novices. J Emer Primary Health Care (JEPHC) 8(3):1–13

Students' Perception Towards the Potential and Barriers of Social Network Sites in Higher Education

Marva Mirabolghasemi, Noorminshah A. Iahad and Nor Zairah Ab. Rahim

Abstract Social Network Sites (SNS) offer several benefits for all groups of people, particularly students. Based on previous studies, it is considered that studies on the usage of SNS among students in Malaysia are still limited. Therefore, the main purpose of this study is to investigate the Positive Effects (Advantages) and Negative Effects (Disadvantages) of SNS in order to help students to take full advantages of such tools. Moreover, this study seeks to help students in avoiding its negative effects. This study conducted an online survey through Facebook and E-mail consisting of 55 questions among students from a public university in the southern region of peninsular Malaysia. The total number of respondents is one hundred and nine students. Factor analysis in this study identified three categories of SNS positive effects such as information seeking, social presence, and academic and social activities fulfilment; also four categories of SNS negative effects such as negative feelings, reduction of cognitive development, social isolation, and security concerns. The outcomes of this study expect to be a starting point intended for instructors to be aware of the positive and negative effects of SNS before engaging students in using SNS for teaching and learning activities.

Keywords Cognitive development · Information seeking · Negative effects · Positive effects · Security concerns · Social network sites · Social presence · Social isolation

---

M. Mirabolghasemi · N.A. Iahad (✉) · N.Z.Ab.Rahim
Universiti Teknologi Malaysia (UTM), 81310 Skudai, Malaysia
e-mail: minshah@utm.my

M. Mirabolghasemi
e-mail: mmarva3@live.utm.my

N.Z.Ab.Rahim
e-mail: nzairah@utm.my

T. Issa et al. (eds.), *Social Networking and Education*,
Lecture Notes in Social Networks, DOI 10.1007/978-3-319-17716-8_3

1 Introduction

Social Network Sites (SNS) is a free online communication technology that allows online users' to connect with each other [5, 21]. Moreover, it is defined as "a Web-based system that aims to create and support specific types of relationships between people" [6]. Lenhart and Madden [15] also define social networks as any online location where the user can create his/her profile and establish a personal network with other users. According to Mahajan [16], the concept of social networking is the formation of a community over the internet, to facilitate sharing their thoughts, and to interact with each other in accordance with a common goal.

Facebook is ranked as the most popular SNSs visited by Internet users in Malaysia. With 12.2 million Facebook users, Malaysia is currently ranked 17th in the world in terms of Facebook accounts per person. The largest age group is currently 18–24, followed by 25–34 year old [4]. This shows young people are the largest group of Facebook users in Malaysia. In Malaysia, the Youth Development Act 2007 defined Youth as those who are aged between 15 and 40 years old. Most of this age group are college or university students. Under the Ninth Malaysia Plan (2006–2010), the government has allocated RM2.2 billion for activities related to the expansion of these young people.

SNS provide users with facilities such as: promoting themselves in an online environment and continuing to communicate with other users [7], sharing the content they created [13] and discovering new friendships [23]. The use of SNS for educational purposes is discussed extensively [22]. Masrom and Usat [17], reviewed the current published research studies, focusing on the use of SNS by students in Malaysia and found that there are still limited studies related to SNS usage among students. In addition, the positive and negative effects of SNS among university students in Malaysia are still less explored. Therefore, the main research question of this research is the following:

- *What are the positive and negative effects of SNS for university students in Malaysia?*

2 Social Network Sites Applications

Social networked learning refers to learning using new learning media commonly referred to social software tools [18]. Social software tools that support social networked learning include weblogs, social bookmarking, RSS feeds, social networking sites (e.g. Facebook, Twitter, MySpace), podcasts, e-portfolios, del.icio.us, YouTube, Skype, online office and tagging [2, 3].

Social software tools connect learners in the virtual space enabling them to interact and collaborate as they execute learning activities. By participating in social networked learning, learners are actively engaged in the learning process and experience flexible environments for communication, global information sharing, personalized learning and independent learning with respect to place and time. Social networked learning enables borderless learning, and its focus is toward learner-centred and process driven learning environments as opposed to content-driven learning [19]. In the literature, there are various definitions of social networks and networking. Online social networking is a set of activities used by the group of people through social technologies [11]. According to Mahajan [16], the concept of social networking is the formation of a community over the internet, to facilitate sharing their thoughts and interacting with each other in accordance with a common goal. Although, SNS are popular and regularly accessed by students, these sites have not yet been considered as a tool for teaching and learning processes [20].

2.1 The Advantages of Social Network Sites for the Students

The intention of using SNS may vary in different areas. SNS provide users with facilities such as: promoting themselves in an online environment and continuing to communicate with other users [7], sharing the content they created [13] and discovering new friendships [23]. SNS can be used to improve cooperation and solidarity in higher education [1]. Similarly, Grant [9], points out that usage of SNS in educational environments provides more effective communication between students and teachers, so instructors know their students much better. Moreover, Ferdig [8], indicated that social networking applications are closely related to many pedagogical points in the constructivist approach and claimed that these applications support pedagogical approaches like active learning, social learning and communities of practice and learning. In a study conducted by Helou and Rahim [12], the majority of respondents clearly indicated that SNS can be used for group discussions, discuss assignments as well as to improve interaction between lecturers and classmates in Malaysian university context. Additionally, Hamat et al. [10], also found that students mainly used SNS for informal learning, consisting of communicating with peers and arranging meeting in a Malaysia University.

2.2 The Disadvantages of Social Networks for the Students

Social networks capture the concentration of people and may lead to their social isolation, which has a negative effect on people's well-being. Scholars used a variety of scales that included measures of loneliness, depression, and overall life satisfaction [14]. Another negative outcome of SNS use is flaws in privacy safety. SNS offer users a degree of freedom to control their privacy settings. Masrom and Usat [17] stated that SNS drawbacks include addiction, cyber bullying, identity theft, and cybercrime. The impacts of SNS addiction are physical changes, insomnia, inferiority, loss of concentration and loss of productivity [17].

Consequently, Helou and Rahim [12], found that addiction to SNS has affected the academic life of students in a public university of Malaysia.

3 Methodology

The participants of this study were a group of total 109 students from a public university in the southern region of peninsular Malaysia in the 2012–2013 academic year. The instrumentation of this study was a set of questionnaire distributed on a Facebook page of the university. In addition, the online version of the questionnaire was also sent through email. The questionnaire consisted of a total of 55 questions divided into three sections: Background of Information, Positive Effects of SNS (Advantages), and Negative Effects of SNS (Disadvantages).

Questions addressing the Positive Effects of SNS were mainly concerned with the positive ways for students to organize and maintain work, study, and their social life. On the other hand, students were asked about the Negative Effects of SNS from four perspectives namely cognitive development, social development, physical development, and security concerns. Questionnaire items for both the Positive and Negative Effects were 5-point Likert scale, from 1 (indicating strongly disagree) to 5 (indicating strongly agree).The data gathered from the questionnaire was analyzed using SPSS version 18.

4 Results

4.1 The Advantages of Social Network Sites

KMO and Bartlett's Test is a measure of sampling adequacy that is recommended to check the case to variable ratio for the analysis being conducted. The KMO value is always between 0 and 1. Values greater than 0.6 are acceptable, while closer to 1 is the best. Table 1 illustrates the results of KMO and Bartlett's test on the advantages of SNS.

The KMO value related to the advantages of SNS is 0.699 which is acceptable. The Bartlett's test is significant at a 0.05 level. Table 2 illustrates the component Matrix for the advantages of SNS.

Table 1 KMO and Bartlett's test

Kaiser-Meyer-Olkin measure of sampling adequacy		0.699
Bartlett's test of sphercity	Approx. Chi-Square	1192.447
	df	300
	Sig.	0.000

Table 2 The component matrix for the advantages of social network sites

Question	Comp. 1	Comp. 2	Comp. 3
Learn new information and knowledge	0.489		
Gain up-to-date information	0.543		
Be more aware of global issues/local issues	0.486		
To remember facts/aspects of the past	0.424		
Communicate with my peers frequently		0.630	
Collaborate with my peers frequently		0.602	
Communicate with my peers from different universities		0.713	
Communicate with my different communities		0.509	
Develop intercrossing relationships with my peers (i.e. Artistic talents, sport and common interests)			0.466
Study independently			0.657
Overcome study stress			0.698
Complete my study more quickly			0.597
Understand and solve study problems easily			0.677
Scrutinize my research study more easily			0.673
Develop my personal and communication skills			0.679
Concentrate more on my reading and writing skills			0.567
To prepare my professional attitude toward study and work			0.670
Be more sustainable person			0.637
Provide reliable and scalable services			0.704
Become more "Greener" in my activities			0.625
Reduce carbon footprint in my activities			0.699
Acquire new acquaintances—work related			0.731
Acquire new acquaintances—friendship relationship			0.698
Acquire new acquaintances—romance relationship			0.613
Do whatever I want, say whatever I want, and be who ever I want			0.335

Generally, the results of Component Matrix through factor analysis yielded three categories of advantages of SNS, students considered that SNS has positive effects in terms of enabling them to seek information, to communicate and collaborate, enabling them to fulfil their academic and social activities. Therefore, this research identified two additional categories of positive effects of SNS compared to previous research in Malaysian university that highlighted only social presence.

Table 3 KMO and Bartlett's test

Kaiser-Mayer-Olkin measure of sampling adequacy		0.821
Bartlett's test of sphercity	Approx. Chi-Square	1989.899
	df	453
	Sig.	0.000

4.2 The Disadvantages of Social Network Sites

This section presents the findings of analysis on SNS disadvantages. Table 3 illustrates the results of KMO and Bartlett's test on SNS disadvantages.

The KMO value for the disadvantages of SNS is 0.821 which is acceptable. The Bartlett's test is significant at a 0.05 level. Table 4 illustrates the component Matrix for the disadvantages of SNS.

Compared to previous research in Malaysian universities highlighted the privacy concerns [10, 12], as shown in Table 4, the disadvantages of SNS are divided into four categories which are negative feeling, social isolation, reduced critical thinking, and privacy concerns.

5 Discussion

Social networks are applications that support interest in a common space around sharing resources, collaboration, communications and interactions. In this digital and social environment with high connectivity anywhere and anytime it can be concluded that there is a need to investigate the advantages and disadvantages of SNS in order to help students to take full advantages of such tools. There are very limited studies on the students' perception of positive effects and negative effects of SNS in Malaysia [17]. Therefore, this research determines the positive and negative effects of SNS for university students in Malaysia.

Previous research in the Malaysian university context found that the advantage of SNS are mainly for social presence [10, 12]. The results of this research demonstrate that social presence, information seeking, and fulfilment of academic and social activities are the positive effects of SNS. On the other hand, students perceived that SNS caused negative effects through negative feeling and social isolation in addition to reduction of critical thinking and privacy concerns.

Government regulatory agencies such as the Malaysian Communication and Multimedia Commission (MCMC) and Ministry of Education (MOE) which are responsible for monitoring internet activities could benefit from the findings of the study to outline or improve any existing guidelines of SNS usage for students [10, 12]. In addition, based on the findings of the study, universities and other institutions of higher learning could take advantage of SNS in higher education.

Table 4 The component matrix for the disadvantages of social networks

Question	Comp. 1	Comp. 2	Comp. 3	Comp. 4
Scatters my attention	0.635			
Decreases my grammar and proofreading skills	0.529			
Distracts me easily	0.634			
Prevents me from participating in social activities	0.641			
Prevents me from completing my work/study on time	0.703			
Makes me sick and unhealthy	0.694			
Bores me	0.614			
Stresses me	0.714			
Depresses me	0.753			
Makes me feel lonely	0.770			
Makes me lazy	0.752			
Makes me addict	0.606			
Makes me more gambler	0.716			
Makes me insecure to release my personal details from the theft of personal inform ation	0.736			
Makes me receive an immoral images and information from unscrupulous people and it is difficult to act against them at present	0.689			
Prevents me from participating in physical activities	0.826			
Prevents me from completing my work on time	0.805			
Prevents me from completing my study on time	0.765			
Prevents me from having face to face contact with my family		0.368		
Prevents me from having face to face contact with my friends		0.455		
Prevents me from shopping in stores		0.617		
Prevents me from watching television		0.795		
Prevents me from reading the newspapers		0.709		
Prevents me from talking on the phone/mobile		0.771		
Prevents me from concentrating more on writing and reading skills			0.352	
Prevents me from remembering the fundamental knowledge and skills			0.504	
Decreases my deep thinking			0.306	
Increase privacy concerns				0.661
Increase security concerns				0.732
Increase intellectual property concerns				0.763

6 Conclusions and the Future Works

This research intended to conduct a survey on students' perceptions of the advantages and disadvantages of SNS at a public university in Malaysia. Online questionnaires were distributed through Facebook and by e-mails. The results of this research show three categories of SNS positive effects such as information seeking, social presence, and academic and social activities fulfilment plus four categories of SNS negative effects such as negative feelings, reduction of cognitive development, social isolation, and security concerns. The outcomes of this study are expected to be used for exploring the advantages and disadvantages of SNS in Malaysian university before engaging students in using SNS for teaching and learning activities. The small group of participants was one of the limitations of this research. In future studies the survey instrument can be tested further with larger sample involving students from more than one university.

References

1. Ajjan H, Hartshorne R (2008) Investigating faculty decisions to adopt Web 2.0 technologies: theory and empirical tests. Internet High Educ 11(2):71–80
2. Alexander B (2008) Social networking in higher education. The Tower and the Cloud 197–201
3. Awodele O, Idowu S, Anjorin O, Adedire A, Akpore V (2009) University enhancement system using a social networking approach: extending e-learning. Issues in Informing Science & Information Technology 6
4. Ayu A, Abrizah A (2011) Do you Facebook? Usage and applications of Facebook page among academic libraries in Malaysia. Int Inf Libr Rev 43(4):239–249
5. Boyd DM, Ellison NB (2007) Social network sites: definition, history, and scholarship. J Comput Mediat Commun 13(1):23. doi:11
6. Coenen T (2006) Structural aspects of online social networking systems and their influence on knowledge sharing. In: Proceedings web based communities San Sebastian, Spain
7. Ellison NB, Steinfield C, Lampe C (2007) The benefits of Facebook "friends:" Social capital and college students' use of online social network sites. J Comput Mediat Commun 12 (4):1143–1168
8. Ferdig RE (2007) Editorial: examining social software in teacher education. J Technol Teach Educ 15(1):5–10
9. Grant N (2008) On the usage of social networking software technologies in distance learning education. In: Society for information technology & teacher education international conference, 2008, vol 1. pp 3755–3759
10. Hamat A, Embi MA, Hassan HA (2012) The use of social networking sites among Malaysian university students. Int Educ Stud 5(3):56
11. Hamid S, Chang S, Kurnia S (2009) Identifying the use of online social networking in higher education. In: ASCILITE 2009 conference, 2009. pp 6–9
12. Helou AM, Rahim NZA (2013) The influence of social networking sites on students'academic performance in Malaysia. Int J Electron Commer 4(2)
13. Kim W, Jeong O-R, Lee S-W (2010) On social Web sites. Inf Syst 35(2):215–236

14. Kraut R, Patterson M, Lundmark V, Kiesler S, Mukophadhyay T, Scherlis W (1998) Internet paradox: a social technology that reduces social involvement and psychological well-being? American psychologist 53(9):1017
15. Lenhart A, Madden M (2007) Teens, privacy & online social networks: how teens manage their online identities and personal information in the age of MySpace. Pew Internet & American Life Project
16. Mahajan P (2009) Use of social networking in a linguistically and culturally rich India. Int Inf Libr Rev 41(3):129–136
17. Masrom M, Usat S (2013) Understanding students'behavior on the use of online social networking
18. Nichols M, Anderson B (2005) Strategic e-learning implementation. Educ Technol Soc 8 (4):1–8
19. Siritongthaworn S, Krairit D, Dimmitt NJ, Paul H (2006) The study of e-learning technology implementation: A preliminary investigation of universities in Thailand. Educ Inf Technol 11 (2):137–160
20. Stanciu A, Mihai F, Aleca O (2012) Social networking as an alternative environment for education. Accounting & Management Information Systems/Contabilitate si Informatica de Gestiune 11(1)
21. Subrahmanyam K, Reich SM, Waechter N, Espinoza G (2008) Online and offline social networks: use of social networking sites by emerging adults. J Appl Dev Psychol 29(6):420–433. doi:10.1016/j.appdev.2008.07.003
22. Tiryakioglu F, Erzurum F (2011) Use of social networks as an education tool. Contemporary Educational Technology 2(2)
23. Wang SS, Moon S-I, Kwon KH, Evans CA, Stefanone MA (2010) Face off: implications of visual cues on initiating friendship on Facebook. Comput Hum Behav 26(2):226–234

Effect of Social Networking on Higher Education in India

Samant Saurabh and Ashok Singh Sairam

Abstract Several studies have been carried out to research the impact of social networking on society. In this work, we aim to study both the positive and negative aspects in which social-networking is affecting our lives. In this paper, we formulate a research questionnaire comprising several questions to evaluate the mindset of the respondents towards the use and impact of social networks. The questions basically try to gain information about age, gender, educational qualification of the respondents and then assess their social networking usage patterns and behaviors. The survey was exclusively carried in India and respondents were mostly from educational institutes. The survey revealed several interesting results. It shows that there are more male social-media users than female ones. Most of the social networking users are young people in the age group of 18–42 years of age. Among different departments in universities Computer Science and Engineering people are the chief users of Internet and social networking. 60 % of people spend less than an hour for email usage whereas around 90 % of them spend up to 5 h on social networking. 60 % of them use Internet heavily for online shopping, banking, travelling, research study and work. Around 60 % of them believe that social network helps them positively in personality development, freedom of expression, developing hobbies and increasing domain knowledge. However, around 50 % of them also agree about negative aspects of social networking like addiction, no social participation, insecurity and poor health. We also used factor analysis to categorize related set of questions and gain insight into these categories.

Keywords Social networks · Internet · Factor analysis · Effect of social networking · Indian society · Survey

---

S. Saurabh (✉) · A.S. Sairam
Department of Computer Science, Indian Institute of Technology, Patna, Bihar, India
e-mail: ssaurabh@iitp.ac.in

A.S. Sairam
e-mail: ashok@iitp.ac.in

T. Issa et al. (eds.), *Social Networking and Education*,
Lecture Notes in Social Networks, DOI 10.1007/978-3-319-17716-8_4

1 Introduction

Social networking has become a global network that connects millions of people around the world. Since the emergence of the social networking, its use and implications on individuals and the society as a whole has become a topic of hot discussion. At one extreme, there are people, who only see the brighter side and benefits of social networking. They consider it as a remarkable instrument that provides connectivity, commerce, freedom of expression and an overabundance of other social benefits. On the other extreme, there are people who seriously criticize and lament the disadvantages and negative effects of it. They consider it to be an extremely potent and grave threat to the existing social institutions, moral values, culture and human relationships [7].

Internet and social networking are undeniably one of the most astounding and path-breaking inventions. There are a large number of positive ways in which they affect our lives but at the same time there are quite a few negative side-effects too. A large community uses them for their betterment. They use it to promote their social and economic status and in improving their knowledge and health. But, unfortunately there is significant number of users, mostly in teenagers and youth, who use social networking for unconstructive and downbeat purposes which wastes their time, makes them addicted to Internet and social network besides causing health problems [2].

Keeping all these points in mind, we planned to conduct a survey of people's notion about various aspects of social-media usage. As we know, a survey research is often used to assess thoughts, opinions, and feelings of mass towards any matter or issue. For this, we formulated a set of diversified and highly inferential questionnaire to record the responses of Indian people (mostly students, teachers and staff members working in Indian Universities) towards the impact of social networking on the Indian Society. The survey consisted of questions regarding age, gender, educational qualification, and course specialization of individuals. It also comprised a set of questions on both positive and negative effects of social networking use where the responses were recorded in the form of agreement, neutrality and disagreement. The survey was carried out by sending the questionnaire's link to several people (mostly students) and their responses were recorded. A study was then conducted to understand the responses and to mine useful information and knowledge from the survey data using SPSS and other database tools. We carried out factor analysis on questions related to positive and negative effect of social networking on society. Using factor analysis we categorized the questions into lesser number of independent groups so that our study could become more precise and clear.

2 Social Networking Background

In today's world, social networking has highly revolutionised our life in both the best and worst possible ways. Numerous studies have been carried out to study the impact of social networking sites on individuals and society in different dimensions of life. In this section, we try to do a literature survey of some of the important research works.

A large number of people think that digital content and online tools like social networking have helped students by providing them with online video lectures, study-materials and presentations from the best professors in the world. In fact it has also made professors the new YouTube stars [9]. Social networking has provided people with freedom of expression and a platform for communicating their views to a larger and diverse platform [12]. Most people agree that these digital tools have made the process of writing, blogging, teaching and content creation much easier than before. Internet has made online shopping, banking and planning of trips much more easy and smooth than before. People are using social networking and Internet for study, work and for pursuing their hobbies much more than before [11]. People are using emails for all their personal and official works. They are meeting and interacting with their friends and families in far off land by using social networks like Facebook, chatting and conferencing [10]. It has been found that social networks and blogs continue to dominate Americans' time online, now accounting for nearly a quarter of total time spent on the Internet. According to the statistics, social networks have become a fundamental part of the global online experience.

However, besides these wonderful advantages, social networking too has dark side attached to it. Quite a vast number of people have started to use social networking in such a way that social networking addiction has become a sizzling topic of debate [1]. There is a yet another conflict that's centred on the potential educational value of computers, on the grey area of 'edutainment', and on the use of so-called 'educational' applications [4]. On one hand there is a notion that social networking is making people confident learners and expert in grasping and learning new information; on the other hand, there also lies notion pertaining to concern and worry about students losing their retention power and creativity due to easy access to everything. Free Internet access to small children has also made them vulnerable to pornography and its negative effects [14]. Somewhere around 4–5 % of teenage boys are very frequently indulge themselves in pornography per week [13]. Yet another study revealed that spending a lot of time on social networking and Internet is one of the prime reasons for a lot of health hazards like eye problem, back-pain, obesity, loneliness and insecurity among its users [1]. Besides a lot of malicious activities and attacks like identity theft, spamming, frauds and phishing attacks are happing daily which makes social networking and Internet not so safe for layman [3].

As can be seen from this section, much has already been done on finding the effect of social networking on people. One of the major contributions of our work is that we try to find the effect of social networking on people of India. We have conducted a survey on finding the impact of social networking on Indian people and tried to find out how people are getting influenced by it. Furthermore, we conduct our survey mostly on people from universities across our country and expect to see how the learned people react to this new revolution.

3 Research Method

In our research work, our main focus was to find the effect of social networking on people in the Indian society. We developed an online survey to get answer of this question from people studying and working in technical universities in India.

Research Question: In our paper, we study the following research questions.

- We wanted to find how social-networking was affecting individuals in developing country like India and what future lies for it in this country.
- What are the positive and negative impacts of social-networking in the Indian higher-education in particular?

We created an online survey. The survey tried to gain information about the respondents. It asked questions like age, sex, qualification, department of study and occupation of the respondents. Then it asked some behavioural questions pertaining to number of hours spent on Internet (on email and social networks) and usage of Internet for various activities like online shopping, banking, study, research etc. Finally, we tried to analyse what the respondent feels about the positive and negative impact of social networking on our lives. The link to the survey was sent to various universities in India and high percentage of the respondents was students.

Before preparing the questionnaire, written objectives for the research were clearly decided. It was reviewed by our peer group. Literature related to the objective was reviewed and questions were designed such that we could get clear answers regarding our survey questions. The feasibility of administering questionnaire to the Indian population was determined carefully. Then a clear time-line was developed for taking the survey. A descriptive title was prepared for the questionnaire along with a suitable introduction. Questions were grouped according to content and suitable subtitle was given for each one of them.

The survey was open for around 3 months. Then we collected survey responses in a database. After this step we analyzed the recorded responses and tried to extract useful information from these data. We populated the responses in mySql database and used database queries to get the answers to several interesting and important questions.

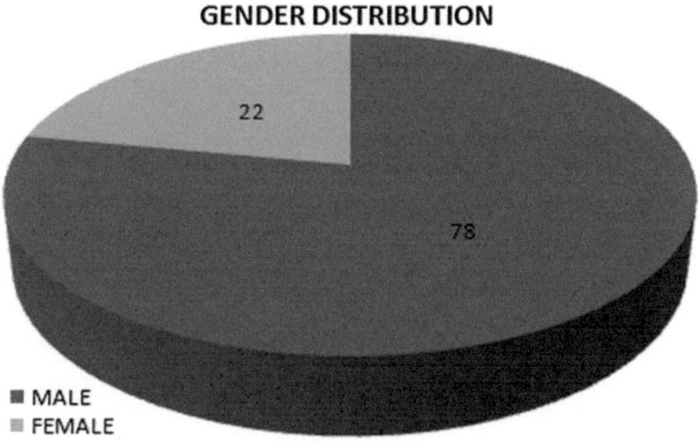

Fig. 1 Pie chart showing the gender distribution of users

4 Findings of the Survey

In this section, we discuss the major findings of our survey.

4.1 Gender Distribution of Surveyed People

Figure 1 shows the gender distribution of the surveyed people. Our data shows that 78 % of the people who took this survey were male while 22 % of them were female. This survey was conducted mostly in the engineering colleges of India and shows that percentage of female is very less compared to males in these technical institutes. We need to encourage Indian girls to study and pursue higher degree engineering courses like boys.

4.2 Age Distribution of Surveyed People

Figure 2 shows the age distribution of the surveyed people. 66 % of them are in the age group of 18–22 years of age. 22 % of them are between 22 and 32 years of age. 11 % are between the ages of 32–42 years. Only 2 % of them are above 42 years of age. This result suggests that most of the people surveyed were undergraduate students who were between 18 and 22 years of age. People in the age group of 22–32 years are Masters or PhD students or even some young professors. Participants in age group of 32 and above would mostly be teaching faculty and staff members.

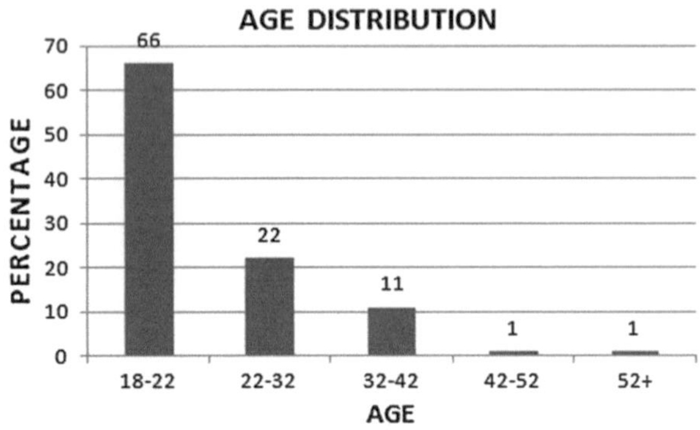

Fig. 2 Age distribution of the surveyed people

4.3 *Popular Fields of Study of Respondents*

Figure 3 shows the main fields of study of the participants of the survey. 49 % of the people are from Computer Science Department. 33 % are from Science and Engineering background. 10 % of the participants are from Management background. 2 % are from Humanities and rest of the 6 % is from other departments. This shows that most of the participants are from Engineering-background. Internet use is highly popular among students/people associated with computer science as their field of study.

4.4 *Educational Level and Internet Use*

Figure 4 shows the highest educational level of the participants of survey for both males and females. We also provide the overall result. It could be inferred that 50 % of the participants have Bachelor's degree as their highest education level. Around 23 % have master's degree as their highest educational level. Around 22 % have higher secondary as their highest degree. It's clear that Internet use is a favorite time

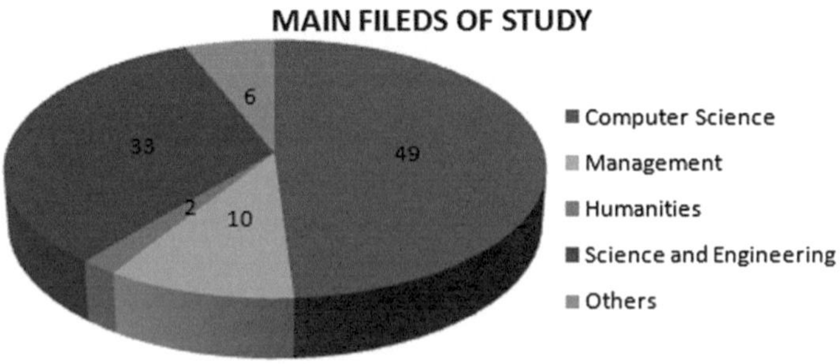

Fig. 3 Pie chart showing the main fields of study of participants of survey

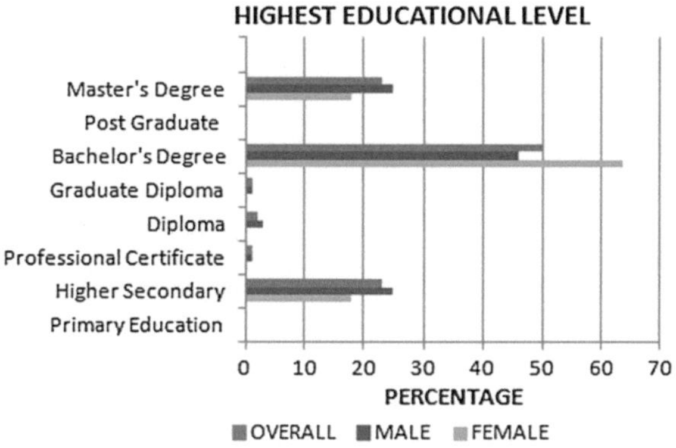

Fig. 4 Highest educational level of participants

pass or need of students of bachelor degree followed by teenagers of higher secondary level. The Internet use has truly revolutionized the world of teenagers and college goers in both positive and negative ways.

4.5 Social Networking Versus Emails in Terms of Time Spent on Internet Per Day

Through Fig. 5 we especially looked at the time spent by users on social networks and on emails. Overall, 72 % of the users spent less than an hour on emails. Around 85 % of females use less than an hour on email. While only 68 % of male use email for less than an hour, around 21 % of them spent up to 5 h on emails. Around 10 % of male spend around 5–10 h on reading and writing email per day. Very few female spend more than an hour on email.

Figure 6 tells us that overall, 62 % of the users spend less than an hour on social networks. Around 37 % spend up to 5 h on social networks as compared to 21 %

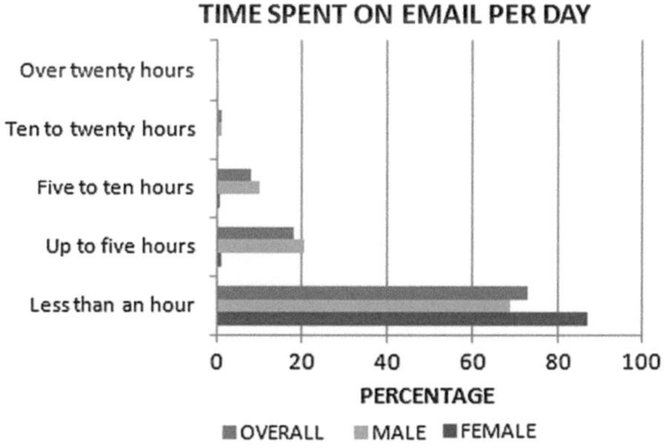

Fig. 5 Time spent on email per day

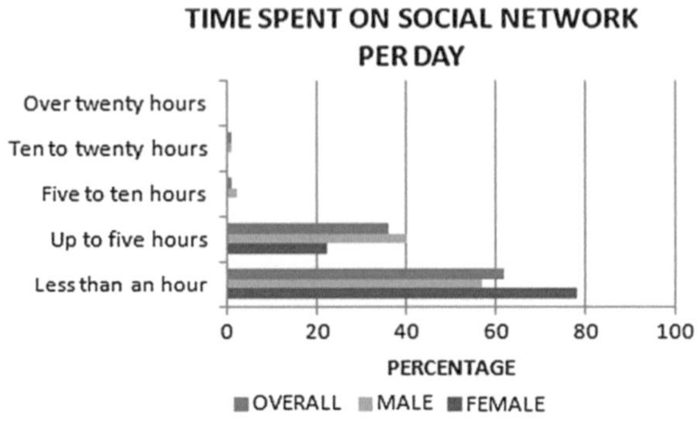

Fig. 6 Time spent on social network per day

spending same time on emails. We find that participants spend more time on social network than on emails. This seems natural as social network provides lot more activities than simple email. Again, most of the females spend lesser time on social network than males. Around 12 % of males spend between 10 and 15 h on social network per day.

4.6 Time Spent on Email and Social Network Per Day

4.6.1 As a Function of Age

In our case we had sufficient data for users of only two age groups, those between 18 and 22 years and those who are between 22 and 32 years of age. From Fig. 7 we find that 62 % of users in age group of 22–32 use social network for less than an hour whereas 35 % of them use it for up to 5 h. Here again we can observe that they spend less number of hours on email per day. Only 47 % of users in age group of

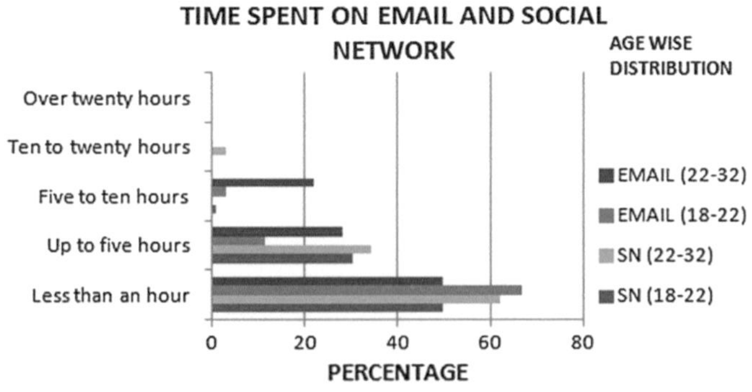

Fig. 7 Age wise distribution of time spent on email and social network per day

18–22 years use social network for less than an hour whereas 28 % spend up to five hours on social network.

4.6.2 As a Function of Area of Study

Next we study time spent on social network and email by people from different departments. Management students spend more time on social networks than engineering and Computer Science students. High percentage of them spends up to 5 h on social networks. However more computer and engineering students use email for longer hours as can be seen from Fig. 8.

4.7 Most Popular Uses of Social Networking and Internet

4.7.1 Diversified Common Uses of Social Networking and Internet

In **Fig.** 9, we study the distribution of usage of Internet for various activities. In our survey-questionnaire regarding uses of Internet, multiple options were provided and users could tick more than one option. More than 90 % of participants use Internet for checking emails and for doing their study. 65 % use Internet for online shopping and chatting with friends. Around 50 % of people use Internet for online banking and planning their trips. 20 % of them use it for playing games. The number of female respondents is less. We find that far lesser number of females uses Internet than males for various online activities. Only around 20–25 % of them use it for shopping, travelling, studies, banking and other activities.

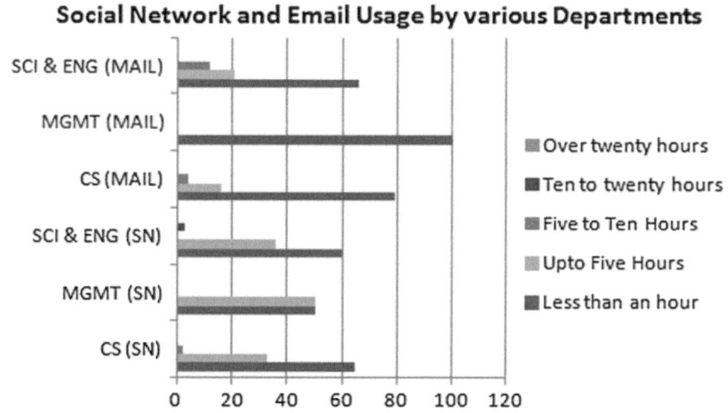

Fig. 8 Department wise distribution of time spent on email and social network/day

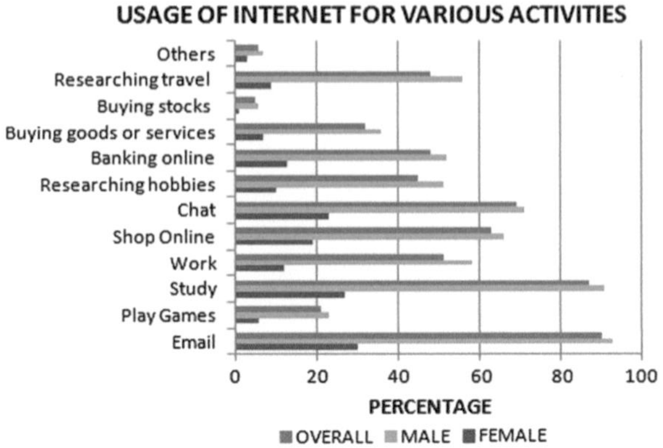

Fig. 9 Usage of Internet for various activities

4.7.2 Internet and Social Networking Use Based on Age

In Fig. 10, we study the use of Internet for various activities based on the people's age. We find that people in age group of 32–42 years are highest users of email. Around 85 % of them use Internet for email. Only 75 % of people in age group of 18–22 years use Internet for email. People in age group of 18–22 are the most vigorous online buyers. People in age group of 32–42 years of age are the most avid users of Internet for work. A very strange revelation is that people in age groups of 18–22 and 32–42 play more game than people in age group of 22–32 years. May be this group is more busy in establishing themselves.

4.8 Study Oriented Use of Social Networking and Internet

In Fig. 11, we study the time spent on study per day by people of various departments. We find that students of computer science use Internet maximum for

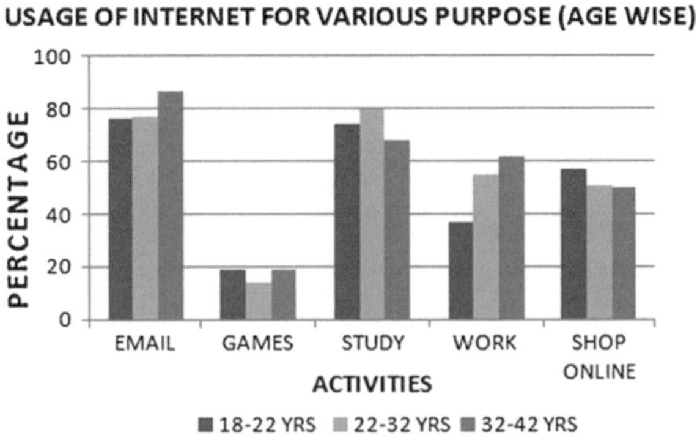

Fig. 10 Age wise distribution of usage of Internet for various activities

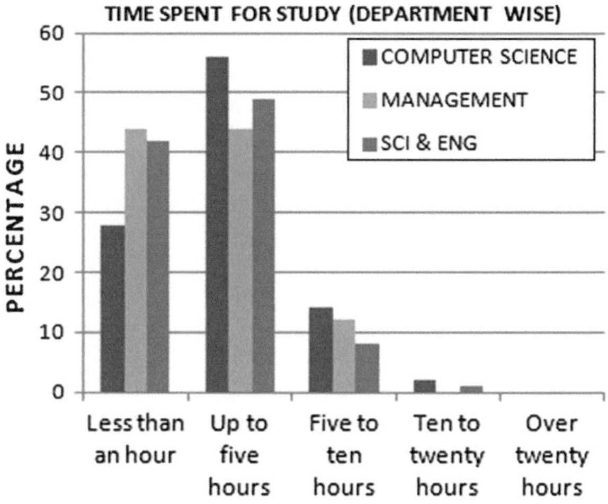

Fig. 11 Department wise distribution of time spent on study per day

their studies. However, people from all departments spend lot of time studying their course from Internet.

5 Effects of the Social Networking

To study the effect of social networking on Indian society, we conducted a survey which had two set of questions. First set assessed the positive impact of social networking on Indian people and the second set of questions tried to gauge the negative effect of social networking on our population. To categorize correlated set of questions into group, we use factor analysis. Factors or group of questions are formed that are relatively independent of each other. Factor analysis allows us to gain insight into categories.

A total of 85 participants from India responded to the questionnaire. There was no missing data. All the above cases were found to be valid for factor analysis. Factor analysis was conduct separately for questions from Group Questions 9 (Q9) which related with Positive impact and Group Q11 (Q11) which related with Negative impact. There were 25 questions in group Q9 whereas group Q11 had 30 questions.

Even though, the number of valid cases was less than 100, attempt to run Factor Analysis for India sample was conducted. In this section we describe the method used for our factor analysis and the reason behind using them.

Extraction and Rotation Method

Extraction method: We employed *Principal Axis Factoring* for factor extraction.

Rotation: To allow correlation among the variables, *oblique rotation* (rather than orthogonal rotation) was applied using the *Promax* method [6, 8].

Following is the report for the Preliminary Analysis

For Q9 Group:

- The Cronbach's Alpha for all 25 variables from Q9 group was 0.904 which indicated that there was excellent internal consistency of the items in the scale [11].
- A Kaiser-Meyer-Olkin measure of *sampling adequacy* of .804 indicated a good sample size for the conducted survey.
- The Bartlett's test of sphericity is highly significant, $\chi^2 = 1242.529$ $df = 300$, $p < 0.000$. It indicated that the items of the scale are sufficiently correlated to factors to be found.

For Q11 Group:

- The Cronbach's Alpha for all 30 variables from Q11 group was 0.941 which indicated an excellent internal consistency of the items in the scale [5].
- A Kaiser-Meyer-Olkin measure of sampling adequacy of 0.799 indicates a good sample size is obtained from the analysis
- The Bartlett's test of sphericity is highly significant, $\chi^2 = 1964.280$, $df = 435$, $p < 0.000$, indicated that the items of the scale are sufficiently correlated to factors to be found.

For Q9 group there are five factors were extracted on the final run with Kaiser Normalisation (Eigenvalues greater than one).

As demonstrated in the following table, this model of five factors explains a total of 62.407 % of the variation. The Eigen values and the amount of variances explained by each of these factors are presented below (after rotation). (Table 1)

For Q11 group there are six factors able to be extracted on the final run with Kaiser Normalisation (Eigenvalues greater than one).

As demonstrated in the following table, this model of six factors explains a total of 68.701 % of the variation. The Eigen values and the amount of variances explained by each of these factors are presented below (after rotation). (Table 2)

For Q9 and Q11 groups:

Table 1 Total variance explained (Q9 group)

Total variance explained							
Factor	Initial eigenvalues			Extraction sums of squared loadings			Rotation sums of squared loadings[a]
	Total	% of variance	Cumulative %	Total	% of variance	Cumulative %	Total
1	5.975	31.448	31.448	3.191	16.797	16.797	4.980
2	3.301	17.372	48.820	2.046	10.766	27.563	2.955
3	1.775	9.342	58.162	3.482	18.325	45.888	3.651
4	1.209	6.362	64.524	2.247	11.824	57.712	2.277
5	1.126	5.929	70.453	0.892	4.695	62.407	2.958

Table 2 Total variance explained (Q11 group)

Total variance explained							
Factor	Initial eigenvalues			Extraction sums of squared loadings			Rotation sums of squared loadings[a]
	Total	% of variance	Cumulative %	Total	% of variance	Cumulative %	Total
1	8.903	38.710	38.710	8.608	37.428	37.428	6.219
2	2.436	10.591	49.300	2.119	9.211	46.639	5.382
3	2.018	8.774	58.075	1.699	7.389	54.027	4.226
4	1.795	7.803	65.878	1.493	6.493	60.521	5.466
5	1.348	5.863	71.740	1.086	4.722	65.243	3.561
6	1.061	4.612	76.353	0.795	3.458	68.701	6.061

Extraction method: principal axis factoring
[a]When factors are correlated, sums of squared loadings cannot be added to obtain a total variance

It was found that factor loading of most of the items were quite high. The ones with the cleanest structured were considered as important. With sample size (N = 85) is < 100, work in [5] suggested the sufficient factor loading based on sample size between 85 and 99 is 0.60.

Following is the Q9 Group (Positive Impact) Pattern Matrix:(Table 3)

Five factors revealed from the Pattern Matrix for Q9 Group are given as follows:

1. As study or work tool
2. Teamwork building instrument
3. As alternative channel to gain knowledge or information
4. Channel for personal networking
5. Be a “Green” User

Following is the Q11 Group (Negative Impact) Pattern Matrix:(Table 4).

The six factors revealed from the Pattern Matrix for Q11 Group are as follows:

1. Trigger anxiety, losing interest and health concern
2. Inhibitor to focus on one matter for longer time and reduce thinking capability
3. Impede to traditional information source and inhibitor to be more social
4. Inhibitor to accomplish higher priority as scheduled
5. Cynicism on data security
6. Inhibitor on in-person or personal contact leads to sedentary lifestyle

Descriptive statistics on factors

A score was calculated for each factor by averaging across each individual item. The mean and standard deviation of each factor average for Group Q9 is presented below:

From Table 5, we can observe that people in India firmly believe that social networking is an excellent alternative to gain knowledge and get huge amount of information. They consider social networking to be highly important in increasing

Table 3 Pattern matrix for Q9 group

Pattern matrix[a]					
	Factor				
	1	2	3	4	5
Q9_13 Understand and solve study problems easily	0.985	.128			
Q9_12 Complete my study more quickly	0.820		−0.105	-0.156	
Q9_14 Scrutinize my research study more easily	0.783	0.106			
Q9_16 Concentrate more on my reading and writing skills	0.638			0.187	
Q9_17 To prepare my professional attitude toward study and work	0.616				0.156
Q9_10 Study independently	0.601		0.137		
Q9_11 Overcome study stress	0.408				
Q9_6 Collaborate with my peers frequently		0.990	−0.111	−0.105	
Q9_5 Communicate with my peers frequently		0.818			
Q9_7 Communicate with my peers from different universities	−0.145	0.624	0.103	0.237	
Q9_8 Communicate with my different communities		0.554			−0.105
Q9_2 Gain up-to-date information			0.803		
Q9_3 Be more aware of global issues/local issues	−0.121		0.773		0.176
Q9_1 Learn new information and knowledge	0.282		0.745		
Q9_23 Acquire new acquaintances—friendship relationship				1.003	−0.161
Q9_22 Acquire new acquaintances—work related		0.120		0.635	0.104
Q9_24 Acquire new acquaintances—romance relationship		−0.106	−0.203	0.499	0.242
Q9_21 Reduce carbon footprint in my activities					0.977
Q9_20 Become more "Greener" in my activities	0.211				0.647

Extraction method: maximum likelihood
Rotation method: promax with Kaiser normalization
[a]Rotation converged in 6 iterations

their personal network. People in India are using Linked In, Facebook and Google + to connect with each other, to make user-groups and to seek jobs. They also believe that social networking provides them with an excellent platform for

Table 4 Pattern matrix for Q11 group

Pattern matrix[a]						
	Factor					
	1	2	3	4	5	6
Q11_10 Bores me	0.928				0.148	−0.269
Q11_11 Stresses me	0.889		0.111			
Q11_9 Makes me sick and unhealthy	0.804					
Q11_12 Depresses me	0.730					0.315
Q11_13 Makes me feel lonely	0.727		−0.146			0.153
Q11_3 Scatters my attention		0.975				−0.126
Q11_6 Distracts me easily	-0.180	0.759				
Q11_5 Decreases my deep thinking	0.206	0.600		−0.131		0.113
Q11_1 Prevents me from concentrating more on writing and reading skills	0.101	0.598	0.168			
Q11_2 Prevents me from remembering the fundamental knowledge and skills	0.104	0.582				
Q11_23 Prevents me from watching television			0.900			
Q11_24 Prevents me from reading the newspapers			0.791			
Q11_25 Prevents me from talking on the phone/mobile			0.724			−0.140
Q11_22 Prevents me from shopping in stores			0.694		0.100	0.129
Q11_26 Prevents me from completing my work on time				0.983		
Q11_27 Prevents me from completing my study on time				0.880		
Q11_8 Prevents me from completing my work/study on time		0.321	−0.181	0.549		
Q11_28 Increase privacy concerns					0.844	0.126
Q11_29 Increase security concerns	0.208				0.779	−0.139
				0.239	0.708	

(continued)

Table 4 (continued)

Pattern matrix[a]						
	Factor					
	1	2	3	4	5	6
Q11_30 Increase intellectual property concerns						
Q11_19 Prevents me from having face to face contact with my family			0.116		−0.108	0.850
Q11_20 Prevents me from having face to face contact with my friends					0.110	0.847
Q11_21 Prevents me from participating in physical activities		−0.149		0.144		0.737

Extraction method: principal axis factoring
Rotation Method: promax with Kaiser normalization
[a]Rotation converged in 6 iterations

Table 5 Mean and standard deviation for factors for Q9 group

Factors	Mean	Std. deviation
Factor 1: As study or work tool	3.19	1.13
Factor 2: Teamwork building instrument	3.80	0.78
Factor 3: As alternative channel to gain knowledge or information	4.06	0.79
Factor 4: Channel for personal networking	3.84	0.78
Factor 5: Be a "Green" user	3.21	0.94

team building work. In the 2014 elections, social networking was used intensively for the very first time and the party using it effectively could gain a land-slide victory. People also believe that social networking and Internet has reduced the amount of paper work required in offices and email and social networking have also reduced the need to travel for small matters. Social networking provides us with hangouts and video chatting by which travelling need is reduced considerably. They also feel that social networking has evolved as a study and work tool too.

The mean and standard deviation of each factor average for Group Q11 (Negative Impact) is presented below:

From the factor analysis of negative impact given in Table 6, we find that people are really concerned about the negative effects of social networking. Social networking is acting as inhibitor for in-person contact and is leading to sedentary life-style. As solution to lot of problems is readily available on Internet and social networking, people have lost their imagination and thinking capability. People are also becoming less social. People are becoming cynical about data protection. As

Table 6 Mean and standard deviation for factors for Q11 group

Factors	Mean	Std. deviation
Factor 1: Trigger anxiety, losing interest and health concern	2.715	1.060
Factor 2: Inhibitor to focus on one matter for longer time and reduce further thinking capability	3.275	1.102
Factor 3: Impede to traditional information source and inhibitor to be more socialable	2.891	1.099
Factor 4: Inhibitor to accomplish higher priority as scheduled	3.076	1.155
Factor 5: Cynicism on data security	3.46	0.84
Factor 6: Inhibitor on in-person or personal contact, leads to sedentary lifestyle	2.94	1.14

they have a lot of data online, security of data has become a major concern [14]. People are becoming more stressed and anxious due to high usage of social networking. It has also lead to Indian children becoming obese due to lack of physical activity.

Hence, it turns out that even though social networking has contributed a lot to the development of Indian society and people's life style, like any other thing in the world, it too has its dark side. We need to make efficient use of social networking so that it can serve us instead of harming us.

6 Conclusion, Limitations and Future Work

Social Networking and Internet, no doubt have evolved to become the de facto cyberspace facilitating communication, business, and entertainment on a global scale. Our study found out that social networking sites have become highly dominant among the Internet uses. Our survey showed that overall 56 % people consider social networking to have positive effects while overall 42 % agree that it has some negative effects too. We find that social networking and Internet have become major forces in India. Lot of people is using it for studies, work, education, entertainment, communication, banking and online shopping. From the survey results, it is very clear that social networking and Internet use is going to increase exponentially in the near future. However, as with everything in this world, they too have disadvantages. Many people feel that they will make us addicted to social networking. It will reduce our memory retention and imaginative powers. It is increasing online security problems and making people feel lonely in spite of being with hundreds of friends online. Besides all this, it is obvious from the survey that social networking and Internet have made huge impact on Indian people and its use is going to increase manifold in the near future. One of the limitations of our work has been that people surveyed do not represent India very accurately. People studying and working in technical universities do not represent our country accurately. These people are much more advanced and prosperous and we suspect that Internet and social networking usage would be far less if we take out this survey among the common people. As future work, we would like to take this survey on various other groups of people like those in Indian Government jobs, people having their own business and doctors.

References

1. Adiele I, Wole O (2104) Prevalence and determinants of Internet addiction among adolescents. Comput Hum Behav, Elsevier 31:100–110
2. Benevenuto F, Tiago R Meeyoung C, Almeida V (2009) Characterizing user behavior in online social networks. In: Proceedings of the 9th ACM SIGCOMM conference on Internet measurement conference. ACM
3. Gao H, Hu J, Huang T, Wang J, Chen Y (2011) Security issues in online social networks. Internet Comput IEEE 15(4):56–63
4. Gialamas V, Nikolopoulou K, Koutromanos G (2013) Student teachers' perceptions about the impact of internet usage on their learning and jobs. Comput Educ 62:1–7
5. Gliem JA, Gliem RR (2003) Calculating, interpreting, and reporting Cronbach's alpha reliability coefficient for Likert-type scales. In: Paper presented at the midwest research-to-practice conference in adult, continuing, and community education
6. Hair JF, Ringle CM, Sarstedt M (2011) PLS-SEM: indeed a silver bullet. J Market Theory Pract 19(2):139–152
7. Mendel T, Andrew P, Wagner B, Hawtin D, Torres N (2012) Global survey on internet privacy and freedom of expression
8. Osborne JW, Costello AB (2004) Sample size and subject to item ratio in principal components analysis. Pract Assess Res Eval 9 (11):8
9. Saurabh S, Sairam AS (2013) Professors-the new YouTube stars: education through Web 2.0 and social network. Int J Web Based Commun, Indersci 212–232
10. Shen J, Brdiczka O, Ruan, Y (2013) A comparison study of user behavior on Facebook and Gmail. Comput Hum Behav Elsevier 29(6):2650–2655
11. Wang L, Luo J, Luo J, Gao W Kong J (2013) The effect of Internet use on adolescents' lifestyles: a national survey. Comput Hum Behav Elsevier 28(6):2007–2013
12. Welch C (2011) Global internet freedom policy: evolution, action, and reaction. IEEE Internet Comput 15(6)
13. Wolak J, Mitchell K, Finkelhor D (2007) Unwanted and wanted exposure to online pornography in a national sample of youth Internet users. Pediatr Am Acad Pediatr 119 (2):247–257
14. Zwi K, Shanti R, Burgner D, Faniran S, Voss L, Blick, B, Osborn M, Borg C, Mitchell S (2007) Towards better health for refugee children and young people in Australia and New Zealand: The Royal Australasian College of Physicians perspective. J Paediatr Child Health, Wiley Online Libr 43(7):522–526

Age and Gender Differences in Social Networking: Effects on South Korean Students in Higher Education

Sooyoung Kim and Sun Joo Yoo

Abstract Social networking sites (SNS) are popular communication technologies in the world. Many Koreans have been using SNS to network and communicate with their acquaintances. The growing popularity of SNS usage affects teaching and learning in higher education. However, there are unknown territories of positive and negative effects of using SNS in higher education. The purpose of this study is to investigate both positive and negative impacts of using SNS and to examine the effects of gender and age differences in those impacts. Participants (n = 236) at five Korean universities were surveyed on their SNS usage. Factor analyses identified three positive effects of social networking: (1) information acquisition and communication, (2) efficiency in work, and (3) relationship building. The negative factors of using SNS were identified as (1) security, (2) completion of study/work, (3) emotion, (4) cognitive development, (5) social development, and (6) physical development. Independent *t*-tests and Mann-Whitney *U*-tests revealed there are age and gender differences in both positive and negative effects of SNS usage.

Keywords Social networking sites · Positive effects · Negative effects · Age · Gender · Higher education · South Korea

1 Introduction

According to the New Media Consortium Horizon Report (2014), more than 1.2 billion people use social media such as Facebook on a daily basis. The number of Social networking sites (SNS) users has dramatically increased worldwide in recent years. The number of Facebook users reached over 750 million, more than 100 million joined LinkedIn, Twitter had over 177 million tweets per day, and YouTube reached three billion views per day in 2012 [3]. Many Koreans also have been using

S. Kim · S.J. Yoo (✉)
Samsung SDS, West Campus, 125 Songpa-Gu, Samsung SDS Tower, Seoul, South Korea
e-mail: sunjoo.yoo@samsung.com

T. Issa et al. (eds.), *Social Networking and Education*,
Lecture Notes in Social Networks, DOI 10.1007/978-3-319-17716-8_5

social media. Seven million people are using SNS and the most frequent users are in their twenties and thirties [17]. According to Korea Information Society Development Institute (2013), 61 % of the young generation has used SNS in South Korea. In 2013, more than 90 % of young SNS users have used social networking sites such as Facebook, Twitter, *Kakaostory,* and *Cyworld* (Kakaostory and Cyworld are the Korean equivalent of Facebook). The number of SNS users is continuously increasing.

SNS users utilize social networking sites for social engagement, communication, and relationship building [18]. Using SNS helps students to maintain their network and to make new friends when they have to adjust to new environments, which are the cases for freshmen in universities [14]. Several universities have reported that SNS is being used as a learning tool for team activities [10, 30]. However, too much time spent on using SNS leads students to addiction, depression, and loneliness, which are serious consequences of using SNS [25, 27].

Using SNS brings negative influences as well as positive influences. Despite the popularity of social media, SNS users utilize them more for personal use. A relatively small number of students and faculty use social media for academic purposes [3, 18, 26]. Little is known about the specific effects of social media on South Korean students in higher education. Therefore, this research attempts to answer the following questions:

(1) What are the positive and negative effects of using social-network for South Korean students?
(2) How do the effects of social networking on South Korean students in higher education differ by age and gender?

2 Effects of Social Networking

Social media are technologies that facilitate social interaction and support collaboration, community building, participation, and sharing [2, 13]. Social networking sites include media sharing tools, file sharing tools, and networking platforms. Blogs, wikis, YouTube, Dropbox, Facebook, Twitter, LinkedIn, and Second Life are good examples of such sites [9].

Social media has both positive and negative impacts on its users. Social media strengthens the users' ability to socially adjust by helping them to grow their social networks [6, 14, 16, 21, 29]. In 2007, Ellison and others [6] found that Facebook use was associated with bonding users and maintaining social capital, which leads its users to get information and emotional satisfaction. According to Madge and others in 2009 [21], Facebook helped students to form a kind of social glue and adjust to their college life.

On the contrary, according to Kalpidou et al. (2011) [14], college students who spend a lot of time on Facebook are likely to have low self-esteem. Interestingly, using Facebook helped undergraduates with low self-esteem to increase their social capital. They found that undergraduates with a lot of Facebook friends showed strong social adjustment skills and attachment to their affiliations. According to Karpinski and others in 2013 [15], SNS decreased both efficiency and productivity of college students. They found SNS usage among college students (n = 857) had significantly negative effect on their academic grades. In 2011, Kuss and Griffiths [16] also found the positive and negative effects of using SNS. They found that the use of SNS is positively associated with user's social enhancement, particularly with the maintenance of their established networks. The use of SNS had negative effect by causing social face-to-face interaction, academic achievement, and relationship to decrease in real life. In 2013, Yang and Brown [29] conducted a self-report survey from 193 students (mostly European-Americans) attending a major Mid-Western university in the United States. They reported that using Facebook was associated with users' social adjustment. In 2008, Tufekci [28] also found that social media usage was not related to student's social engagement, even though the number of friends contacted through social media has increased weekly.

In summary, SNS are popular communication technologies in the world. Many Koreans have been using SNS as a way to network and communicate with their acquaintances. The growing popularity of SNS usage affects teaching and learning in higher education. However, there are unknown territories of positive and negative effects of using SNS in higher education. The purpose of this study is to investigate both positive and negative impacts of using SNS and to examine the effects of gender and age differences in those impacts.

3 Method

3.1 Participants and Data Collection

Participants were recruited from six classes of five different universities in South Korea. Two weeks before the data collection, in-class announcements were made and a research team visited the classes to distribute and collect the survey questionnaires. Data were collected for 4 weeks from December 2012 to January 2013. Participants voluntarily participated in the survey.

3.2 Instruments

The research team in South Korea used the same instruments as the other teams in other four countries. The instruments were composed of 25 items for surveying positive effects and 30 items for negative effects that SNS may have on students.

Demographic information such as age, gender, major, education level, and hours of SNS use were also taken into account. Effects of social networking were measured with a 5-point Likert Scale. See Table 1 for items included in this study.

Table 1 Factor loadings

Category	Subcategory	Item*	Factor loadings
Positive effects	Information acquisition and communication	P6_Collaborate with my peer frequently	0.780
		P7_Communicate with my peer from different universities	0.749
		P5_Communicate with my peer frequently	0.725
		P1_Learn new information and knowledge	0.668
		P3_Be more aware of global issues/local issues	0.653
		P2_Gain up-to-date information	0.613
		P8_Communicate with my different communities	0.606
	Efficiency in study	P13_Understand and solve study problems easily	−0.884
		P12_Complete my study more quickly	−0.871
		P14_Scrutinize my research study more easily	−0.827
		P10_Study independently	−0.797
	Relationship building	P24_Acquire new acquaintances—romance relationship	−0.857
		P23_Acquire new acquaintances—friendship relationship	−0.843
		P22_Acquire new acquaintances—work related	−0.729
Negative effects	Security	N29_ Increases security concerns	0.905
		N28_ Increases privacy concerns	0.858
		N17_ Makes me insecure to release my personal details from the theft of personal information	0.761
		N30_ Increase intellectual property concerns	0.751
		N18_ Makes me receive an immoral images and information from unscrupulous people and it is difficult to act against them at present	0.671
	Completion of study/work	N27_Prevents me from completing my study on time	0.918
		N26_Prevents me from completing my work on time	0.916

(continued)

Table 1 (continued)

Category	Subcategory	Item*	Factor loadings
		N8_Prevents me from completing my work/study on time	0.858
	Emotion	N12_Depresses me	0.888
		N13_Makes me lonely	0.866
		N11_Stresses me	0.856
		N10_Bores me	0.587
	Cognitive development	N3_Scatters my attention	0.790
		N2_Prevents me from remembering the fundamental knowledge and skills	0.741
		N1_Prevents me from concentrating more on writing and reading skills	0.708
		N4_Decreases my grammar and proofreading skills	0.707
		N6_Distracts me easily	0.669
		N5_Decreases my deep thinking	0.639
	Social development	N7_Prevents me from participating in social activities	−0.737
		N19_Prevents me from having face to face contact with my family	−0.676
		N20_Prevents me from having face to face contact with my friends	−0.676
		N16_Makes me more gambler	−0.654
	Physical development	N23_Prevents me from watching television	0.804
		N24_Prevents me from reading the newspapers	0.751
		N22_Prevents me from shopping in stores	0.625

Note Item numbers are from the original instruments

3.3 *Data Analysis*

The survey was distributed to 242 students. Six incomplete data sets were discarded. A total of 236 data sets were analyzed. Factor analysis and reliability analyses were conducted to examine the factors of positive and negative effects of social networking. Descriptive analyses and correlation analyses were conducted to examine social networking's positive and negative effects on students in higher education in South Korea. Independent *t*-tests were performed to examine the age the differences regarding the positive and negative effects of social networking. Mann-Whitney *U*-tests were conducted to compare gender differences on positive and negative effects of social networking.

4 Results

4.1 Demographics of Participants

Of the 236 completed surveys, 60 of them were completed by males (25.4 %) and 176 (74.6 %) by female students. The age of most participants ranged from 18 to 32 years: 116 (49.2 %) were 18–21 years old and 111(47 %) were 22–32 years old. 179 (75.8 %) participants were studying Humanities, 20(8.5 %) Health Sciences, 19 (8.1 %) Science and Engineering, and 15(6.4 %) Art and Design, respectively. Most of the highest education level was higher secondary/pre-university (78.8 %) and the rest was bachelor's degree (21.2 %).

4.2 Factor Analysis and Reliabilities

Exploratory Factor Analysis (EFA) was conducted to identify the factors of positive and negative effects of social networking to South Korean students in higher education. Upon carrying out Principle Factor Analysis (PFA) with *oblimin* rotation, of the three factors of the positive effects (information acquisition and communication, efficiency in study, relationship building) and six factors (security, completion of study/work, emotion, cognitive development, social development, and physical development) of the negative effects, the results identified the convergent validity in the study with acceptable factor loadings (≧ 0.50) [5]. See Table 1 for the factor loading results.

After EFA, 14 items for the positive effects and 25 items for the negative effects of social networking remained from the original instrument. The reliability analyses further indicated a good overall instrument reliability for positive effects (Cronbach's Alpha = 0.839) and negative effects (Cronbach's Alpha = 0.892). The analyses also showed acceptable (Cronbach's Alpha ≧ 60) subcategory reliabilities ranging from 0.672 to 0.911 (See Table 2).

Table 2 Scale and category reliability

Category	Subcategory	Item #	Cronbach's alpha
Positive effects	Information acquisition and communication	1, 2, 3, 5, 6, 7, 8	0.824
	Efficiency in study	10, 12, 13, 14	0.868
	Relationship building	22, 23, 24	0.757
Negative effects	Security	17, 18, 28, 29, 30	0.859
	Completion of study/work	8, 26, 27	0.911
	Emotion	10, 11,12, 13	0.833
	Cognitive development	1, 2, 3, 4, 5, 6	0.892
	Social development	7, 16, 19, 20	0.720
	Physical development	22, 23, 24	0.672

4.3 Effects of SNS on Students in Higher Education in Korea

Descriptive analyses and correlation analyses were conducted to describe the positive and negative effects of social networking and examine relationships among variables in interest. The results (Table 3) revealed that SNS have positive effects on the South Korean students in higher education in terms of information acquisition and communication (M = 3.98) and relationship building (M = 3.22) (See Table 3). However, the findings showed that social networking did not influence students much for efficiency in their study (M = 2.83). Age is significantly negatively associated with daily use of SNS ($r = -0.156$, $p < 0.05$) and with information acquisition and communication ($r = -0.230$, $p < 0.001$). Gender is significantly positively correlated with the use of SNS ($r = -0.236$, $p < 0.001$), information acquisition and communication ($r = -0.209$, $p < 0.01$), and with efficiency in study ($r = -0.255$, $p < 0.001$). Daily use of SNS is significantly associated with information acquisition and communication ($r = -0.335$, $p < 0.001$) and with completion of study/work ($r = -0.129$, $p < 0.05$).

Table 3 also showed that SNS have negative effects in terms of security (M = 3.34), completion of study/work (M = 3.32), and physical development (M = 3.20). The results also showed that the use of SNSs did not have great impacts on students' emotion, cognitive and social development (M = 2.26, 2.88, 2.27). Moreover, the findings showed that social networking did not influence much students on efficiency in their study (M = 2.83). Age is significantly negatively associated with completion of study/work ($r = -0.270$, $p < 0.001$). Gender is significantly positively correlated with security (r = −0.202, p < 0.01), and with completion of study/work ($r = -0.259$, $p < 0.001$). Daily use of SNS is significantly associated with completion of study/work ($r = -0.129$, $p < 0.05$).

4.4 Age Differences in Social Networking Effects

Independent t-tests were conducted to compare age differences in daily use of SNS and in positive and negative effects of social networking. There were no differences found in SNS use by age ($t = 1.823$, $p = 0.070$). The findings showed age differences in social networking effects. Younger group aged 18–21 is more likely to communicate and collaborate with their peers than an older group over the age of 21. In terms of negative effects of social networking, the younger group had a harder time completing study/work on time than the older group. The results revealed that both groups were not much influenced by social interaction with people. Compared to the older group, the younger group is less likely to have difficulty in having face-to-face contact with people. See Table 4 for detailed information.

Table 3 Correlations between variables

	N	*M*	*SD*	1	2	3	4	5	6	7	8	9	10	11	12
1. Age	236	1.74	0.67	1											
2. Gender	236	1.75	0.44	-0.276^{***}	1										
3. Use of SNS	236	1.74	0.67	-0.156^{*}	0.236^{***}	1									
4. PE1	236	3.98	0.62	-0.230^{***}	0.209^{**}	0.335^{***}	1								
5. PE2	235	2.83	0.94	0.030	0.255^{***}	0.104	0.327^{***}	1							
6. PE3	235	3.22	0.82	−0.030	−0.125	0.125	0.324^{***}	0.218^{**}	1						
7. NE1	229	3.34	0.87	−0.054	0.202^{**}	0.072	0.022	-0.162^{*}	−0.034	1					
8. NE2	231	3.32	1.08	-0.270^{***}	0.259^{***}	0.129^{*}	0.130^{*}	-0.211^{**}	-0.145^{*}	0.329^{***}	1				
9. NE3	230	2.26	0.78	−0.010	0.127	0.003	-0.152^{*}	−0.042	-0.221^{**}	0.277^{***}	0.317^{***}	1			
10. NE4	230	2.88	0.78	−0.037	0.114	0.004	−0.056	−0.074	−0.059	0.309^{***}	0.416^{***}	0.394^{***}	1		
11. NE5	230	2.27	0.76	0.140^{*}	0.102	−0.034	−0.091	0.060	−0.091	0.318^{***}	0.266^{***}	0.370^{***}	0.357^{***}	1	
12. NE6	230	3.20	0.92	0.015	0.163^{*}	0.128	0.118	0.085	−0.040	0.202^{**}	0.276^{***}	0.004	0.051	0.325^{***}	1

Note: PE Positive effects, *NE* Negative effects, *PE1* Information acquisition and communication, *PE2* Efficiency in study, *PE3* Relationship building, *NE1* Security, *NE2* Completion of study/work, *NE3* Emotion, *NE4* Cognitive development, *NE5* Social development, *NE6* Physical development

$^{*}p < 0.05$, $^{**}p < 0.01$, $^{***}p < 0.001$

Table 4 Age and effects of social networking by categories

			N	*M*	*SD*	*t*	*df*	*p*
Positive effects	Information acquisition and communication	18–21	116	4.08	0.56	2.105	225	0.036*
		21+	111	3.91	0.63			
	Efficiency in study	18–21	116	2.79	0.90	−0.509	224	0.611
		21+	110	2.86	0.98			
	Relationship building	18–21	116	3.22	0.83	−0.275	224	0.784
		21+	110	3.25	0.82			
Negative effects	Security	18–21	112	3.39	0.89	0.921	219	0.358
		21+	109	3.28	0.87			
	Completion of study/work	18–21	112	3.61	1.08	3.865	220	0.000***
		21+	110	3.06	1.02			
	Emotion	18–21	111	2.26	0.80	−0.043	219	0.966
		21+	110	2.26	0.79			
	Cognitive development	18–21	112	2.92	0.78	1.848	220	0.397
		21+	110	2.83	0.79			
	Social development	18–21	112	2.14	0.75	−2.332	220	0.021*
		21+	110	2.38	0.77			
	Physical development	18–21	112	3.11	0.96	−1.591	219	0.113
		21+	109	3.31	0.90			

$^*p < 0.05$, $^{**}p < 0.01$, $^{***}p < 0.001$

4.5 *Gender Differences in the Effects of Social Networking*

Mann-Whitney *U*-tests were conducted to compare gender differences in the daily use of SNS and in positive and negative effects of social networking. Gender differences were found in daily use of SNS. Females use SNS more on a daily basis than males (Table 5). The findings showed that the use of social networking has more impacts on female students regarding study/work. Females are more likely

Table 5 Daily use of SNS by gender

					Significance of difference between male and female			
		N	Mean ranks	Sum of ranks	Mann-Whitney *U*	Wilcoxon *W*	*Z*	Sig. (2-tailed)
Daily use of SNS (hours)	M	60	93.85	5631.00	3801	5631	−3.631	0.000***
	F	176	126.9	22335.0				

$^*p < 0.05$, $^{**}p < 0.01$, $^{***}p < 0.001$

Table 6 Gender and positive effects of social networking by categories

Subcategory					Significance of difference between male and female			
		N	Mean ranks	Sum of ranks	Mann-Whitney *U*	Wilcoxon *W*	*Z*	Sig. (2-tailed)
Information acquisition and communication	M	60	93.88	5633	3803	5633	−3.246	0.001**
	F	176	126.89	22333				
Efficiency in study	M	60	88.72	5323.5	3493	5323	−3.879	0.000***
	F	175	128.04	22407.5				
Relationship building	M	59	132.49	7817	4337	19913	−1.906	0.057
	F	176	113.14	19913				

*$p < 0.05$, **$p < 0.01$, ***$p < 0.001$

than males to study/work, acquire information, and communicate and collaborate with peers using social networks. See Table 6 for detailed information.

Moreover, the use of social networking had more negative impact on female students in terms of security, completion of study/work, emotion, and physical development. Female users of SNS are more concerned about security, have more difficulty in completing their study/work on time, are more influenced emotionally—such as being more depressed, stressed out, or feeling lonely—and are more negatively influenced in physical development. See Table 7.

Table 7 Gender and negative effects of social networking by categories

Subcategory					Significance of difference between male and female			
		N	Mean ranks	Sum of ranks	Mann-Whitney *U*	Wilcoxon *W*	*Z*	Sig. (2-tailed)
Security	M	59	93.43	5512.5	3742.5	5512.5	−2.911	0.004**
	F	170	122.49	20822.5				
Completion of study/work	M	59	85.11	5021.5	3251.5	5021.5	−4.148	0.000***
	F	172	126.60	21774.5				
Emotion	M	59	100.76	5945.0	4175	5945	−1.992	0.046*
	F	171	120.58	20620.0				
Cognitive development	M	58	101.28	6196.5	4163	5874.5	−1.888	0.059
	F	172	120.30	20599.5				
Social development	M	59	104.92	6190.5	4420.5	6190.5	−1.423	0.155
	F	171	119.15	20374.5				
Physical development	M	58	96.58	5601.5	3890.5	5601.5	−2.520	0.012*
	F	172	121.88	20963.5				

*$p < 0.05$, **$p < 0.01$, ***$p < 0.001$

5 Discussion

The findings revealed age differences in positive and negative effects of students using SNS. Younger students use SNS more to acquire information and communicate and collaborate with their peers, and the use of SNS makes it harder for them to complete their study/work on time compared to older students. Both groups were not much influenced by SNS use regarding social development, but the younger group is relatively less likely than the older group to be influenced by SNS. In 2011, Lewis and Nichols [19] found significant differences in age regarding student's beliefs on social media. The results showed that participants between the ages of 21–24 rated social media more positively than the participants between the ages of 18–20 did. This finding suggests that education is having an impact on student's attitude about using social media. Older college students may have been more exposed and accustomed to using social media than younger students. They might have spent more time using SNS to get information, which may hinder them from finishing their study on time.

This study also found that students are differently influenced by SNS depending on their gender. Females are more influenced by SNS in that they are more likely than males to acquire information, and communicate and collaborate with peers through SNS. Previous research [1] found that female adolescents who reported to have high positive collective self-esteem were more likely to report greater SNS use to communicate with their peers. Past studies [12, 23] reported that males generally showed more competence and more favorable attitude in using technology. However, recent studies [8, 11] indicated that there are no gender differences in social media usage. This means females have fairly similar opportunities to get information from SNS compared to their counterparts. In particular, the results of this study indicated that female students are more aware of the benefits of using social media in information acquisition and communication and efficiency in their studies compared to their counterparts. In 2011, Lewis and Nichols [19] also found that female college students rated social media more positively. Their upgraded competence in using SNS, positive attitude toward SNS, information acquisition skills, and communication and collaboration with their peers through the use of SNS all together may have enabled females to be more likely to study efficiently.

On the other hand, SNS have more negative impacts on females in that they are concerned more about security; they have more difficulty in completing their study/work on time; they are more depressed, stressed out, feel lonely; and their physical development is hindered by SNS. Consistent with previous studies [7, 20], our findings showed that female users were more concerned about security when using SNS. For instance, in 2009, Fogel and Nehmad [7] have found that female participants in their study expressed more concerns about privacy. In 2008, Lewis and others [20] has also found that women are more protective of their personal information and more likely to have private profiles. A study [22] has found that female users of Facebook update their profile photos more frequently than men and, therefore, they might need to be more concerned about privacy issues compared to male users.

The findings of this research also indicated that female students spend more time on SNS on a daily basis, which may keep them from completing their study/work on time. According to Chen and Lee, in 2013 [4], a survey of college students showed that frequent Facebook interaction is associated with greater distress ($N = 513$). The findings of this current study that females spend more time on SNS than males may explain why females are more distressed than males. This is consistent with previous research [23] that reported that using Facebook might make people feel anxious, inadequate, or miserable. Those who have high levels of anxiety resulting from frequent use of SNS may be less likely to visit stores, read newspapers in print, or watch television, but they would rather search up-to-date news through SNS. That is why female users of SNS are less likely than males to visit stores, read newspapers, or watch television.

6 Conclusion

The aim of this chapter was to investigate college students' perceptions of positive and negative effects of social media and to examine gender and age differences in both effects. The findings of the first research question suggest three positive effects of social networking which are: (1) information acquisition and communication, (2) efficiency in study and (3) relationship building. The study also suggests six negative effects of social media which are: (1) security, (2) completion of study/work, (3) emotion, (4) cognitive development, (5) social development, and (6) physical development.

According to the results of the second research question, age and gender had an impact on the positive and negative effects of using social media. In terms of age, the younger group acquires information and communicates and collaborates with their peers using SNS, more so than the older group. SNS also impacts students differently by gender in terms of information acquisition and communication, efficiency in study, security, completion of study/work, emotion, and physical development.

Another interesting finding was that gender differences in using social media are decreasing. Females are accustomed to using SNS efficiently, which gives them equal opportunities as their main counterparts to gain information, and communicate and collaborate with other students. Social media have the potential to engage students in forms of communication and collaboration with their friends on SNS. However, using social media does not guarantee students' learning. One of the advantages of SNS is that the good leading questions the facilitators post on SNS could lead students' cognitive development instead of their gossiping among members.

7 Limitations and Future Studies

There are a few limitations of this study: first, differences in types of SNS such as Facebook, Twitter, wikis, and blogs have not been considered. In the future research, it may be interesting to see how different types of SNS have different effects. Another limitation is that the qualities of interaction within SNS and individual differences (such as motivation for using SNS) have not been controlled. Therefore, future studies need to include those factors to investigate the impacts of individual differences on the effects of using SNS. The participants of this study are higher education students. For future research, employees at workplace might have different perception of using social media. It would be interesting to investigate their perspectives on using social media.

SNS are popular tools among people to globally share information and communicate with one another. Cultural differences might be one factor that should be considered to see how SNS have been utilized in different settings. Cross-cultural elements such as those from Hofstede's cultural dimension's theory could be included in the future studies.

References

1. Barker V (2009) Older adolescents' motivations for social network site use: the influence of gender, group identity, and collective self-esteem. CyberPsychol Behav 12(2):209–213
2. Bryer T, Zavattaro S (2011) Social media and public administration: theoretical dimensions and introduction to symposium. Adm Theor Prax 33(3):325–340
3. Chen B, Bryer T (2012) Investigating instructional strategies for using social media in formal and informal learning. Int Rev Res Open Distance Learn 13(1):87–100
4. Chen W, Lee KH (2013) Sharing, liking, commenting, and distressed? The pathway between Facebook interaction and psychological distress. Cyberpsychol Behav Soc Netw 16(10):728–734
5. Costello AB, Osborne JW (2005) Best practices in exploratory factor analysis: four recommendations for getting the most from your analysis. Pract Assess Res Eval 10(7):1–9
6. Ellison NB, Steinfield C, Lampe C (2007) The benefits of Facebook "friends: social capital and college students' use of online social network sites. J Comput Mediated Commun 12 (4):1143–1168
7. Fogel J, Nehmad E (2009) Internet social network communities: risk taking, trust, and privacy concerns. Comput Hum Behav 25(1):153–160
8. Gerlich RN, Browning L, Westermann L (2010) The social media affinity scale: implication for education. Contemp Issues Educ Res 3(11):35–41
9. Guy R (2012) The use of social media for academic practice: a review of literature. Ky J High Educ Policy Pract 1(2):1–21
10. Han S-Y, Choi M-H, Park M-K, Lee H-J (2013) The effects of SNS use on the social network: moderating effect of the gender. Inf Manag J 30(3):133–156
11. Huang WHD, Hood DW, Yoo SJ (2013) Gender divide and acceptance of collaborative web 2.0 applications for learning in higher education. Internet High Educ 16:57–65
12. Jackson LA, Ervin KS, Gardner PD, Schmitt N (2001) Gender and the internet: women communicating and men searching. Sex Roles 44(5–6):363–379

13. Junco R, Heibergert G, Loken E (2011) The effect of Twitter on college student engagement and grades. J Comput Assist Learn 27(2):119–132
14. Kalpidou M, Costin D, Morris J (2011) The relationship between Facebook and the well-being of undergraduate college students. Cyberpsychol Behav Soc Netw 14(4):183–189
15. Karpinski AC, Kirschner PA, Ozer I, Mellott JA, Ochwo P (2013) An exploration of social networking site use, multitasking, and academic performance among United States and European university students. Comput Hum Behav 29(3):1182–1192
16. Kuss DJ, Griffiths MD (2011) Excessive online social networking: can adolescents become addicted to Facebook? Educ Health 29(4):68–71
17. Lee JY (2012) A case study of learning communication through the use of SNS (social network service) in colleges. Soc Sci Res J 25(1):93–123
18. Lenhart A, Purcell K, Smith A, Zickuhr K (2010) Social media & mobile internet use among teens and young adults. Pew Internet & American Life Project. http://pewinternet.org/Reports/2010/Social-Media-and-Young-Adults.aspx
19. Lewis BK, Nichols C (2011) Attitudes and perceptions about social media among college students and professionals involved and not involved in strategic communications. In: Noor Al-Deen HS, Hendricks JH (eds) Social media: usage and impact. Lexington Books, Lanham, pp. 129–144
20. Lewis K, Kaufman J, Christakis N (2008) The taste for privacy: an analysis of college student privacy settings in an online social network. J Comput Mediated Commun 14(1):79–100. doi:10.1111/j.1083-6101.2008.01432.x
21. Madge C, Meek J, Wellens J, Hooley T (2009) Facebook, social integration and informal learning at university: It is more for socialising and talking to friends about work than for actually doing work. Learn Media Technol 34(2):141–155
22. McAndrew FT, Jeong HS (2012) Who does what on Facebook? Age, sex, and relationship status as predictors of Facebook use. Comput Hum Behav 28(6):2359–2365
23. Miller LM, Schweingruber H, Bradenburg CL (2001) Middle school students' technology practices and preferences: re-examining gender differences. J Educ Multimedia Hypermedia 10(2):125–140
24. Paddock C (2012) Facebook use feeds anxiety and inadequacy says small study. Medical news today. http://www.medicalnewstoday.com/articles/247616.php
25. Sheldon KM, Abad N, Hirsch CA (2011) A two-process view of Facebook use and relatedness need-satisfaction: disconnection drives use, and connection rewards it. J Pers Soc Psychol 100:766–775
26. Tiryakioglu F, Erzurum A (2011) Use of social networks as an educational tool. Contemp Educ Technol 2(2):135–150
27. Tokunaga RS, Rains SA (2010) An evaluation of two characterizations of the relationships between problematic internet use, time spent using the internet, and psychosocial problems. Hum Commun Res 36(4):512–545
28. Tufekci Z (2008) Grooming, gossip, Facebook and MySpace: What can we learn about these sites from those who won't assimilate? Inf Commun Soc 11(4):544–564
29. Yang CC, Brown BB (2013) Motives for using Facebook, patterns of Facebook activities, and late adolescents' social adjustment to college. J Youth Adolesc 42(3):403–416
30. Yu BM, Park HJ, Cha SB (2013) A study on the learning effect of the structural relationships model with the use of social networking services (SNS) in university classes. Educ Sci Res 44 (3):133–159

The Advantages and Risks of Using Social Networking in Higher Education in Pakistan

Sumaiya Pervaiz

Abstract To understand and affiliate themselves with the feelings of their own kind seems to be an inherent feature of mankind. Social networking sites are the product of this drive in the context of the modern world whose outlook has been completely changed by the advent of technology. It is a medium to virtually connect a multitude of people around the world through the internet. “Man is by nature a social animal”. This claim by Aristotle has stood the test of time. For this reason, humans want to interact with one another through communication channels. The internet has completely changed the face of world communication. Web 2.0 technology allows the people worldwide to communicate with each another more easily, frequently, timelessly and inexpensively to promote business, commerce, health care, school and universities etc. In such demanding contexts, social networking (via social networking sites) is used in different sectors such as government, health and commerce. In addition, higher education is seriously considering its implementations for e-teaching, e-learning and e-marketing. Universities and other education institutions have realized that Web 2.0 tools such as Facebook and Twitter have great potential to create constructive communication between students and teachers; therefore, they are considering them as well as other Web 2.0 features (blog, wiki, blackboard etc.) for pedagogical purposes. On the one hand, different researchers are discovering numerous positive factors (advantages) of social networking; on the other hand, they are also confronting negative factors (risks) of social networking. These risks and advantages are different in different countries because of varying security and privacy policies and cultural and moral issues. Before implementing these tools and technologies in higher education, it is important to do research demographically to know exactly what risks and advantages are related to different regions. Accordingly, this research focuses on Pakistan’s higher education sector. Therefore, for the data collection, only university students were targeted from different universities in Pakistan. An online survey was conducted and more than 150 participants’ valid responses were used for data analysis. The findings are based on four positive factors (advantages) and

---

S. Pervaiz (✉)
Curtin University, Perth, Western Australia
e-mail: SumaiyaPervaiz@hotmail.com

T. Issa et al. (eds.), *Social Networking and Education*,
Lecture Notes in Social Networks, DOI 10.1007/978-3-319-17716-8_6

five negative factors (risks) associated with the use of social networking in higher education in Pakistan. Some recommendations are given to mitigate those risks and maximize the benefits of opportunities for facilitating students, teacher and institution. In conclusion, this research has pinpointed directly and precisely the advantages and risks (positive and negative factors) of using social networking in the higher education sector in Pakistan.

Keywords Social networking · Sustainability · Web2.0 · Higher education in pakistan · Positive and negative factors of social networking · Pakistani students' attitudes to sustainability and social networking

1 Introduction

This chapter introduces the reader to the types of web2.0 applications the relationship between web 2.0 and social networking. It also throws light on the use of social networking in different sectors. Further it examines the capacity of social networking sites (Web 2.0) to act as a supportive tool in the sector of higher education. After that it presents the Positive/negative impacts of Social networking in the higher education context. It discusses the research methodology and research questions. Finally it arrives at the result, discussion of findings, research limitation and conclusion.

1.1 Types of Web 2.0 Applications

Aghaei et al. [1] mention different types of Web 2.0 including wikis, blogs, social networking, really simple syndication (RSS), mashups, podcasting, folksonomy, etc. The most popular Web 2.0 websites are Facebook, Myspace, Wikipedia, Flickr, YouTube, and Twitter.

1.1.1 Blogs

Jorn Barger first proposed the term 'weblog' in 1999. Blog is a type of website and includes different web pages that are called 'posts' which are published chronologically with the most recent at the top, in the style of a journal. Most blogs are textual, and therefore, visitors can add their comments, but there are other types such as Vlogs or videoblogs, podcasts, photoblogs or photo log which enable the users to use blog for other material such as graphics and video [1].

1.1.2 Wikis

Wiki is a set of web pages designed to allow anyone to have access in order to modify existing content or contribute their own content by using simplified markup language, which is used to create contributive websites. The most well-known wiki is Wikipedia. Wikis can be used in education sectors to enhance the systems of knowledge driven by students [13].

1.1.3 Mashups

Mashup is a website (web pages) that gathers services and information from multiple sources on the web. It can be assembled into seven categories: messaging, mapping, shopping, mobile, movies, search, and sports. Mapping mashups make up more than 40 percent of all mashups. It is quicker and easier to build mashups than to program applications from scratch in conventional ways; this ability is among the most valued features of Web 2.0. Mashups are commonly made by using application programming interfaces (API) For example, Google Maps API has been integrated into many other applications such as earth measurement and housing maps [1].

1.1.4 Social Network

A social network uses nodes to build a social structure generally around organizations or individuals which are linked by one or more particular kinds of interdependency. My Space and Facebook are the two biggest social networks. Twitter is a joint micro-blog service and social network which enables its users to read and send messages known as ‘tweets’. Tweets are text- Tweets are text-based messages which are shown on the profile page of the user and sent to other users who have subscribed to them (followers). Twitter is presently the fastest increasing social network [13].

1.1.5 Podcasts

A podcast is a digital media file (audio and video) that is freely available for download from the internet with the help of software that can treat RSS feeds. Users can play such digital media files on a personal computer or a mobile device at any time. Currently, the YouTube podcast is the most popular site to post. There are three types of podcasts: Video podcasts also known as VodCasts, Double Twist and Enhanced podcasts. Various reasons have accelerated the popularity of podcasts, one of them being that they can be played on various devices such as iPods, MP3, mobile phones, PDAs, laptop computers, or other portable devices [13].

1.1.6 Virtual Worlds

A virtual world is a computer-simulated environment that allows its users to communicate with each other without geographical restraints. In this environment, each user is acted by an avatar. This avatar which may be a common representation allotted to him or her, to some extent may look like the user (e.g. gender, color, hair, etc.) The avatar may be completely personalized in those virtual worlds, allowing greater complexity and customization according to the user's preferences. Within these limitless simulations available 24/7, users can explore the virtual world, solve cooperative challenges, and socialize.

At present, the largest virtual world with more than 1.5 million accounts registered is a Linden Lab's Second life (SL) [13].

1.1.7 Web Syndication

Web Syndication is a concept related to presenting data from different web pages on a single page. The format RSS (Really Simple Syndication) is used to publish digital content which is frequently updated, i.e. podcasts, Weblogs and news feeds. RSS software presents its information as an XML file called 'RSS channel' or RSS feed [7].

1.1.8 Twitter

Twitter is a kind of Web 2.0 application which amalgamates instant messaging, blogging, and short messaging service (SMS). The intention behind the designing of Twitter was emergency communication as distinct from high performance communication [14].

1.1.9 Social Search Engine

Social search engines are conceived as a part of Web 2.0 since they utilize the collective filtering of online communities to raise, using tagging, particularly interesting or relevant content. These descriptive tags add to the information implanted in web pages, in theory cultivating the results for specific keywords in time. A user will normally see recommended tags for a specific search term, signifying tags that have been added previously. Numerous distinct versions of social engines have been initiated including Sproose, Google Coop, Eurekster, Anoox, Yahoo's MyWeb2.0 and Rollyo [16].

1.2 The Relationship Between Web 2.0 and Social Networking

In order to thoroughly understand social networking, it is essential to understand the relationship between it and Web 2.0. To show the relationship between them, Darwish and Lakhtaria [5] mention that the Web 2.0's advent is evident in a broad range of social software including social networking websites, Wikipedia, instant messaging, blog etc. [5]. Web 2.0 enhances the Weberian idea of communication [8] and in the situation of social networking platforms, employs relatively novel forms of information and communication such as in the case of wikis, tagging and blogging. Expressions such as "Social Software" and "Web 2.0" that indicate that the Web has become strongly communicative are used repeatedly when defining such platforms [8].

Social networking websites such as My Space, Facebook and Twitter are becoming increasingly popular. They attract 100 million visitors each month. Because of this increased usage, companies have observed a strong engagement between consumer and creativity resulting from these technologies. Many organizations therefore, willing to control Web 2.0 internally, are experimenting with the tools or installing them on a test basis [3].

Moreover, Web 2.0 is a common word used to define social technologies that impact on the way in which people interact. At the same time, Web 2.0 technologies are being introduced to enterprise, profoundly changing the way in which customers, employees and applications collaborate and communicate [3].

1.3 Social Networking in Different Sectors

1.3.1 Industrial Sectors

Social media provide an excellent opportunity to demonstrate initiative and leadership raise brand awareness and build strong relationships with one's current and prospective customers, and partners. Social channels are a natural fit with content marketing because one can promote and distribute content such as white papers, videos, webinars, articles, case studies, eBooks and more through one's social channels.

For example, GlobalSpec offers suppliers the ability to include their social media links within their company profile pages, helping to build awareness and relevance for their social media efforts. Suppliers can also add video content to their GlobalSpec company profiles [17, 9, 10, 27].

1.3.2 Health Sector

The health sector can directly communicate with individuals who are relevant to the medical issue, instead of taking on a general approach. More people can gain access to useful information for better treatment online.

A lot of people rely on social media to obtain quick information about medical procedures, medicines and medical professionals. Creating a venue and initiating conversations focused on healthcare will greatly benefit the majority of social media users and increase awareness of treatments and procedures [18].

Social networking in the health sector can easily target and directly communicate with individuals regarding their medical issues, instead of giving just general information or guidelines. Greater people online can access useful information for better treatment. Therefore, numerous people are relying on social networking sites to obtain immediate responses and information about medicines, medical professionals and procedures. Establishing a venue and starting dialogues concerned with healthcare will significantly benefit mainstream social media users and enhance awareness on procedures and treatment [18].

1.3.3 Social Networking in Higher Education Sectors

It is believed that Web 2.0 platforms are increasingly playing an important role in transforming learning and teaching. Specific services and technologies contributing in higher education include wikis, syndication of content through RSS, media sharing, tag based folksonomies, social bookmarking, and social networking sites. Already, there are increasing numbers of users from higher education sectors who are applying Web 2.0 technologies in their teaching and learning activities. Therefore, it is essential to realize that Web 2.0 has something innovative to offer higher education—the creation of a clear picture of the characteristics that might create new ICT education in the 21st century: Pedagogy 2.0 [5].

Gülbahar [10] asserts that this latest web will significantly change the education environment in the 21st century, shaping how students access learning, how teachers approach teaching, and ever more, how educators are cooperating and learning from each other.

The internet has truly transformed the way in which knowledge is transferred. In the most developed economies of the world, ICTs have increased exponentially and affected virtually all areas of tertiary education such as online social networking spaces and e-mail deliver paths for academic cooperation and joint research. Electronic journals have become well-known and in some fields quite essential. Traditional publishers of journals and books have progressively turned to the Internet to circulate their publications. The movement of open educational resources has acquired substantial drive, giving free access to curricula, courses, and pedagogical approaches not locally accessible [4].

The notion of conveying educational activities by means of Web 2.0 tools is known as Learning 2.0. It is fundamentally an innovative online learning space used to provide learning and teaching. Learning 2.0 provides the latest participatory medium that is perfect for boosting several types of learning, specifically social learning. Parallel to the popularity of OSN, there are plenty of reports in universities on its repurposing and appropriation for educational purposes. Nevertheless, the applications are generally not university-wide as all of them are small-scale implementations and limited to a certain level of studies only (i.e. postgraduate students, first year students, discipline-oriented or subject-focused). Thus, searching educational aspects for the implementation of successful OSN for Learning 2.0 via Web2.0 is a productive research ground [11]. The usage of social technologies for educational purposes has altered the direction and demands of higher education. Teachers are being encouraged these days to employ social technologies in their pedagogy for the purpose of encouraging social learning and to prepare students as alumnae who will make contributions to a society that now depends greatly on social technologies. From the evidence delivered by the two professors in this research, we found that OSN activities were used to complement existing learning and teaching practices. The grouping of one or more social technologies to facilitate one or more OSN activities also indicates the confidence of the lecturers as well as the applicability of social technologies to provide learning and teaching [12].

1.4 Positive/Negative Impacts of Social Networking in the Higher Education Context

The discussion in this section uses the research modes mentioned above to analyse and summarize the findings related to the positive effects of social networking on college students in order to find out whether it is employed as a daily exercise affecting their daily lives or as a tool that they have been motivated or advised to use by their teachers. Since this examination does not intend to make a comparison of the merits and drawbacks of separate technologies, the common term "social networking" will be used for all sorts of collaborative Web 2.0 technologies mentioned here, regardless of their variance in different dimensions such as size, design, and form. Thus, notwithstanding the fact that the studies discussed are distinct in their scope and use of sample platforms, the dominant theme is that these technologies provide capacities for generating content sharing, socializing processes and shared collaboration both in academic practice and in daily routine [11] (Figs. 1 and 2).

1.5 Research Methodology

There are two methods of research: Qualitative and Quantitative. Quantitative research aims at defining phenomena by gathering mathematical data which is then

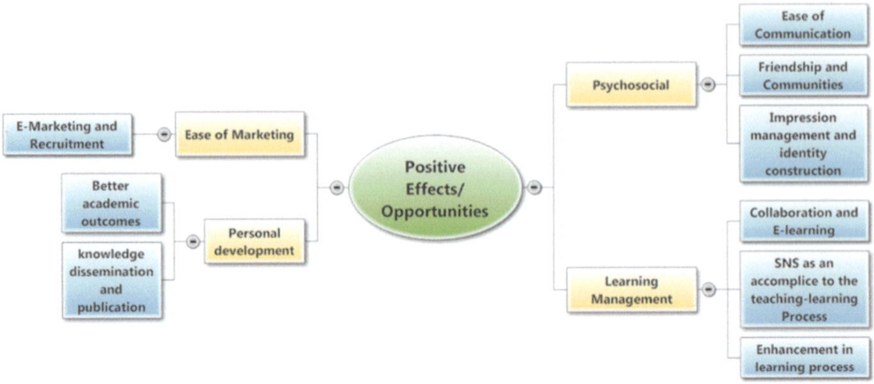

Fig. 1 Positive effects (advantages) of social networking on students and universities

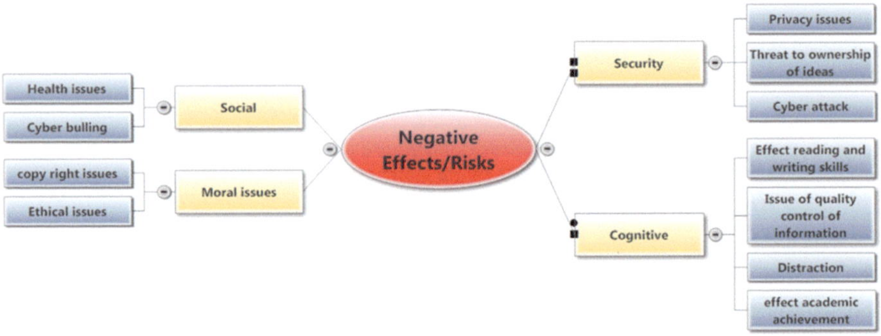

Fig. 2 Negative effects (risks) of Social Networking in higher education

analysed by employing mathematically-based methods (specifically, statistics). Quantitative research includes surveys and questionnaires [19].

The latter method will be used to determine the attitudes of Pakistani students regarding the use of SNs in higher education of Pakistan. It will help to explore the advantages and risks factors of SNs in higher education of Pakistan.

In qualitative research, there are three basic epistemological positions to select from namely: interpretive, positivist, or critical. Quantitative research, however, makes use of the positivist approach alone; the interpretive and critical positions have no meanings here [15].

A quantitative research method is proposed for this research.

This approach has been replaced or to some extent complemented by an interest in using qualitative modes to acquire wider information stretching the boundaries of readily-measured variables [9].

Despite the fact that research approaches vary in research papers, this report swill adopt the positivist methodology by producing computable numerical data to measure the risks and advantages of social networking in the higher education sector in Pakistan. The data will be subjected to analysis and comparisons after it has been collected via an online survey.

1.6 Survey Research

The objective of compiling survey questions is to develop a questionnaire which every potential respondent will interpret in the same way, be able to respond to precisely, and be inclined to answer [6].

An online survey will serve as the means of collecting the primary data. The effectiveness of surveys is determined by their ability to gather practical data about views, approaches and events at a specific time. The quantitative analytical technique is then used to make inferences about the data and its interrelationships.

1.7 Research Questions

In the case of Pakistan, it is more vital since these technologies are going to be implemented for the first time and no assistance could be taken from cases of adequate practices existing previously as in the case of mainstream geographical regions. Also, the youth is generally considered naïve; they are young blood and are most likely to happily welcome any technology in the name of advancement and modernism without assessing it fully and considering those aspects which could prove harmful. Therefore, it is all the more important in education sectors to explore and think about addressing issues before working out their implementation for the consideration here is youth which is relatively sensitive to technological issues. This all leads to the primary research question: What are the risks and advantages of using Social Networking Sites in Pakistan's higher education sector?

The primary question also raises further questions which are discussed and considered as secondary questions in the research.

1.7.1 Secondary Research Question

It is inadequate to consider the advantages and risks of social networking only in the context of the educational sector. Despite the importance of social networking in the education sector, the issue should be dealt with on a global level. Nowadays, sustainability has attracted worldwide attention and is a current issue that must be addressed. Sustainability is the term globally used for environmental preservation initiative. As a human being, it is our duty to protect our planet's resources for future generations. It is essential to adopt sustainability in every aspect of our lives as well as to spread awareness about it so that the majority can contribute to this

Table 1 Research questions and objectives

Research question	Research objectives
Primary question:	Objective 1
What are the risks and advantages of social networking use in Pakistani higher education?	To identify the advantages and risks associated with social networking use in Pakistani higher education.
Secondary Question:	Objectives 2
What are Pakistani students' attitudes towards sustainability and the use of social networking in higher education?	To determine Pakistani students' attitudes to sustainability and social networking use in higher education.

mission. Hence, we arrive at the secondary question: What are the attitudes of tertiary students in Pakistan to sustainability?

Both research questions and research objectives are given in Table 1.

1.8 *Results/Findings*

A total of 153 valid survey responses were used for analysis. 72 % were from male respondents and 28 % were from females. In the reliability test, the alpha of advantages (positive effects) of social networking is 0.938 and risks (negative effect) are 0.950. Four positive factors (advantages) were found from the factor analysis.

The four {4} positive factors emerging from the Pattern Matrix are given in Table 2:

1.8.1 Primary Question Findings

Positive Effects (Fig. 3)

The five {5} Negative factors revealed from the Pattern Matrix for Group Q12 are given in Table 3:

Negative Effects/Risks (Fig. 4)

Table 2 Positive factors

Factors	Name of Factors
Factor 1	Assist study and developing network and professional skills, and gaining awareness of environment issues
Factor 2	Connect me with my peers and information from the past
Factor 3	Maintain current relationships and establish new networks
Factor 4	Information and learning channel

Fig. 3 Positive factors/advantages of social networking effects prepared by the author

Table 3 Negative factors

Factors	Name of Factors
Factor 1	Inhibits socializing, regular activities and in-person contact
Factor 2	Triggers anxiety and loss of interest
Factor 3	Cynicism about data security
Factor 4	Inhibits development of my cognitive skills
Factor 5	Decrease in motivation to undertake intelligent exercises and easy loss of focus

1.8.2 Secondary Question Findings

The secondary question of research is: what is Pakistani student/higher education's attitudes towards sustainability in terms of the relationship between sustainability and social networking? Survey findings revealed a mean of four different factors, which are "be more aware of global issues/local issues", "be more sustainable person", "become Greener in my activities" and "reduce carbon footprint in my activities" as: 0.6, 0.6, 0.5 and 0.6 respectively. The average mean 0.5 of these factors indicate that there is a connection between social networking and sustainability concerns, and the participants agreed on the concerns for the potentials of social networking for "green" awareness and decrease of carbon footprint.

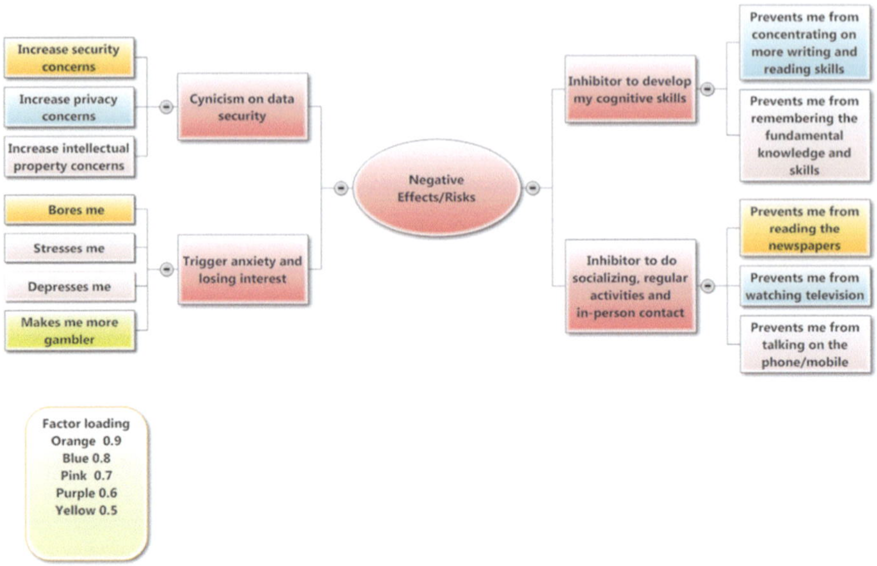

Fig. 4 Negative factors/risks of social networking effects prepared by the author

1.9 Discussion of Positive and Negative Findings

Hence a comparison of the conceptual model above with factors in the conceptual model based on the Literature Review (Fig. 1) proposes that despite some positive aspects (advantages) of social networking recognized in the previous model actually applicable to the Pakistan sample surveyed, many others did not emerge as substantial variables and factors. Therefore, Fig. 1 recognizes the new alignment of factors developing from the evaluation of data attempted in this dissertation related to the positive aspects (advantages) of social networking computed in the survey. The two variables with the highest factor loading were "Gain up-to-date information" (0.942) and "Complete my study more quickly" (0.911). Further, these findings are in line with the studies related to world-wide practices of social networking; for instance, Alkindi and Alhashmi [2] assert that 100 % of respondents utilized social networking for the collection of information with 85 % mentioning benefits to their studies. In the Pakistani context, it may be hypothesized that the reason for the high factor loading in "Gain up to date information" and "Complete my study more quickly" could be because people realize that social networking sites are reliable sources of information and used these sites to obtain current information which subsequently assisted them to complete their study activities more quickly.

As for the low loadings for the factors such as "Scrutinize my research study more easily", "Study independently", to "remember facts/aspects of the pasts" and "Develop Intercrossing relationship with my peers", this is because of the lower awareness of Pakistani students regarding the positive aspects of social networking sites. It is observed from the survey that Pakistani students mostly use these sites for fun and entertainment and are not fully informed about the maximum potential of these sites such as how the positive use of these sites can enhance their research work, study, history and relationship with their peers.

The capacity of social networking to be integrated into a university environment was highlighted by the fact that the respondents showed an inclination to use it as an educational tool, signalling its potential for positive and pedagogical usage.

Like the discussion section on the positives, this section is based on the negative aspects of social networking. The analysis of the negative effects of social networking revealed by the survey indicates that the highest area of concern is related to making users bored and concerned about security issues in social networking. Other factors with relatively higher loadings were related to privacy issues, i.e. "prevents me from concentrating on more writing and reading skills" and "decreases my deep thinking". While the low loadings concerning gambling and distraction show that they are not major negatives for the respondents of the survey.

To summarize, along with advantages, negative findings imply that concerns about potential risks emerging from social networking also exist. The use of social networking has some risks involved according to the Pakistani perspective which can prove to be an impediment to the success of Web 2.0 in higher education. Higher education has to consider them, be proactive, and take serious steps to mitigate these risks before implementing social networking in higher education.

1.10 Limitation

Every project has some limitations, and this research project is no exception. Its limitations are related to the scope, time, quality of the survey etc.… Each of these limitations is discussed below in detail:

1.10.1 Sample Size of Research

This research is based on the responses from 153 university students due to the limit of time and resources. Evidently, considering the research topic, there is a need for a larger sample size to extend the number of responses.

1.10.2 Time

As the time span for the completion of this research project was decided during the semester, the time constraints affected the quality of data and research.

1.10.3 Consideration of Web 2.0 Instruments/Scope

This research deals with a limited number of selected tools from the wide multitude of Web 2.0 technologies, which emerges as a limitation in the scope of the research.

Aspects omitted include Learner Management Systems such as discussion boards, Blackboards, instant messaging services, podcast technology, online sharing repositories such as Google Docs, Dropbox, as well as Skype and other latest technological features. Given these limitations and parameters, the research was deliberately focused on the use of low cost, open-source, collaborative tools in the higher education that were actually designed for leisure or social usages such as, wiki, blogs, Twitter, Facebook, mashups, social bookmarking, media sharing services, and virtual world applications.

1.10.4 Consideration of References

To support and strengthen the arguments in a research, it is important to include references from various other authors and researchers. Due to time constraints, a limited number of researcher comments are included in this paper. To enhance the quality of work, it is essential to study and include more researchers because the greater the spectrum of the study, the more promising and solid will be the results.

1.10.5 Poor Responses From Participants

A total of 186 participants responded to the questionnaire, with 33 found to be missing data resulting overall in 153 valid cases for the factor analysis. Even from these 153 participants, not all of the participant's responses were of high quality. Some inappropriate responses affected the quality of factor analysis which strongly emphasized the need to approach serious participants – sensitive to the importance of giving a sincere opinion and taking a serious approach demanded by an empirical study and who would honestly give their comments to enhance the quality of factor analysis/research.

1.11 Conclusion

In conclusion, it describes why the focus of the paper centres on Pakistan and those factors those emphasize the need for this focus such as the need to learn about the advantages of social networking in the area, and its risks and benefits. Moreover, it gives an overview of the research significance, research objective, and methodologies and sums up research findings, limitation.

It addresses the issue of social networking in different sectors and draws attention to the use of social networking specifically in the higher education sector of Pakistan.

In addition, it outlines the primary and secondary research questions that were used to explore the respondent data collected through online surveys. All the participants were Pakistani university students. In order to address the research questions, the quantitative research method was applied.

The results and findings of the entire research have summaries the chief aspects of this study. It also mentions the limitations of the research, the constraints in scale, times and scope of the web 2.0 applications selected for the study.

References

1. Aghaei S, Nematbakhsh MA, Farsani HK (2012) Evolution of the World Wide Web: from Web 1.0 to Web 4.0. Int J Web Seman Technol 3(1):1–10
2. Alkindi SSA, Alhashmi SM (2012) Use of social networking sites among shinas college of technology students in Oman. J Inf Knowl Manage 11(01):1250002-1250001–1250002-1250009
3. Almeida F (2012) Web 2.0 techonologies and social networking security fears in enterprises. Int J Adv Comput Sci Appl 3(2):152–156
4. Altbach PG, Reisberg L, Rumbley LE (2009) Trends in global higher education: tracking an academic revolution, pp 1–246
5. Darwish A, Lakhtaria KI (2011) The Impact of the New Web 2.0 technologies in communication, development, and revolutions of societies. J Adv Inf Technol 2(4):204–216
6. Dillmn D (2000) Mail and internet surveys: the tailored design method. Wiley. http://web.mit.edu/subjectevaluation/docs/TLL_ItemWritingTips-2.pdf. Accessed 11 sept 2014
7. Dorn J (2010) Social software (and Web 2.0)
8. Fuchs C, Hofkirchner W, Schafranek M, Raffl C, Sandoval M, Bichler aR (2010) Theoretical foundations of the web: cognition, communication, and co-operation. Towards an understanding of web 1.0, 2.0, 3.0 2 (1):41–59
9. Gephart R (1999) Paradigms and research methids, vol 4
10. Gülbahar Y (2013) Social networks from higher education students' perspective. Anadolu J Educ Sci Int 3(2):22–32
11. Hamid S, Chang S, Kurnia S (2009) Identifying the use of online social networking in higher education 419–422
12. Hamid S, Waycott J, Chang S, Kurnia S (2011) Appropriating online social networking (OSN) activities for higher education: two Malaysian cases
13. Harris AL, Rea A Web 2.0 and virtual world technologies: a growing impact on IS education. J Inf Syst Educ 20(2):137–144
14. Mills A, Chen R, Lee J, Rao HR (2009) Web 2.0 emergency applications: how useful can twitter be for emergency response? Twitter for Emergency Management and Mitigation
15. Quantitative, Positivist Research Methods in Information Systems. (2013). http://dstraub.cis.gsu.edu/quant/2philo.asp. Accessed 12/10/2014 2014
16. Rouse M (2011) Social search engine. http://whatis.techtarget.com/definition/social-search-engine. Accessed 11 Nov 2014
17. Social Media use in the Industrial Sector. IHS GlobalSpec Research Report
18. Vanessa D (2013) Social media analytics and the health Sector. https://www.hashtags.org/how-to/search/social-media-analytics-and-the-health-sector/. Accessed 26 Sept 2014 014
19. Wills K What is quantitiative research. http://www.marketingdonut.co.uk/marketing/market-research/what-is-quantitative-research. Accessed 10 Aug 2014 2014

Part III
Social Networking in Europe

Social Networking in Higher Education: Students in The Netherlands

Piet Kommers

Abstract Social networking (SN) has the reputation to promote societal coherence and promote the spread of experience and competence awareness. The crucial question in the chapter is whether social networking is estimated to be proliferate to formal education and higher professional training as well? In order to make a fair evaluation of SN's net added value for higher education it is inevitable to anchor the key dimensions of learning. In case, for instance, a certain study includes the skills to manage networks of experts, it will be clear that SN is easily legitimated. But also SN seems to be a necessary skill if the continuous life-long learning in a certain domain relies on "communities of practice" as defined by Wenger. This chapter describes the dominant opinions of higher education students on positive and negative aspects of SN on the essence of studying a certain curriculum.

Keywords Higher education · Social networking · Social media · Collaborative learning · Learning climate · Learning paradigm

1 Introduction

The goal of this chapter is to start from the common opinion that Social Networking (SN) is beneficial for the social components in studying like taking notice of peer students' ideas, motivations and cooperation in learning tasks, but also on the wide-spread experience that SN work as distractor for the pure academic concentration and hence dissipates a considerable amount of attention and thus causes cognitive overload; [1]. Despite that the report "Social Networking: The UK as a Leader in Europe" (Office of National Statistics [2]) mentions a high percentage (57 %) of citizens to use social media, The Netherlands is listed with an even higher

P. Kommers (✉)
Department of Media, Communication & Organisation, University of Twente, Enschede, The Netherlands
e-mail: kommers@edte.utwente.nl

T. Issa et al. (eds.), *Social Networking and Education*,
Lecture Notes in Social Networks, DOI 10.1007/978-3-319-17716-8_7

percentage of internet users: 65 %. Its data have been derived from the Office for National Statistics and Eurostat who study the number of people across Europe who are using social networks. The Netherlands tops the group at 65 %. It triggered the question whether or not this tendency can be found back in the penetration and the awareness on social media in the student population? More intricate is the intuition that SN contributes to a more autonomous study attitude and even facilitates the self-regulation of students as SN internalizes other students' peer coaching when panic and stress tend to overwhelm. In latter hypothesis of SN that help students to integrate regulative measures, it looks evident that its beneficial effects should be found in the curricular phases of so-called "higher-order learning" where problem solving and creative tasks are at stake. In summary, the common sense expectation is that SN helps the divergent phases of learning, however threatens the stage of focusing and memorization. We may expect that it will be hard to discern the pros and cons of SN as students also develop a certain capacity to cope with distraction and develop certain mechanisms for multi-tasking during their career. In any case it should be noted that social media and social networking have not been designed to support learning and studying; that's why we now face 'lateral thinking' in terms of creativity: How can students benefit from the exotic tools without hampering the prime learning process of concentration and memorization. This chapter dedicates to opinions by students themselves: How do students estimate the final contribution of social media and—networking at this very moment? In more operational terms we can formulate the question as follows: Do social media and—networking have intrinsic values for studying in HE (Higher Education) , or: Do they belong to the many distractive elements that threaten learning at a larger scale like entertainment, sensation and digression? [3]. Critical notion is the fact that HE students are on the verge of adolescent and adult; In other words their agenda is loaded with concerns on career, existential doubts and the need for emotional self-regulation. In other words: if social media and networking do not foster the pure curricular learning, it might be a positive indirect effect that manifests as beneficial for the studying at large. The bottom line for evaluating the potential benefit of social media in studying is if social media.

1. Draw on intrinsic—versus extrinsic incentives for academic learning; in how far is social media coaching students to sacrifice centrifugal—in favor of centripetal attention?
2. Add to the studying process because of social awareness is endemic to intellectual development itself?

The first and second alternative are not mutually exclusive; it might well be the case that convergence and knowing about who knows and knows-not go together quite well. Since the paradigm of collaborative learning and the notion of distributed cognition [4] we know that intellectual growth rests upon social cognition anyway [5]; knowledge is a product of social interaction anyway. Even more recent theories on the essence of postmodern learning theory is based on the fact that any human function relies upon social connectionism [6]. The question for this book is if students themselves are aware of these complementary elements or not?

2 Research Question

The current common sense opinion in Dutch Middle and Higher Education that social media are antagonistic to the learning attitude and dissipate considerable attention and delay in the study process. This study targets the pattern in international differences and in particular how the students in The Netherlands exist in this landscape of multi-cultural trends and commonalities as well.

3 The Research Method

The research method has been the survey that included 126 from the 148 entrant responding students from Higher Education in The Netherlands.

4 Patterns in Social Media Preferences Among Students in The Netherlands

In order to characterize students' preferences for using the Internet, also they were asked to estimate their preference for social media and their estimation of its benefit/disadvantage for the process of studying and professional learning attitude. For this sake 148 students entered the web site. 126 Actually participated and gave their opinions via a web-based survey formulary. 85 % of them actually completed the questionnaire. 22 Respondents (14.9 %) stopped their reaction rather quickly after having entered the web-based survey. 25 Items addressed students' estimation on how social media would affect their study behaviour. Its reliability was computed with Cronbach's Alpha and reached the level of 0.87.

5 Survey Coherence

The thirty survey questions have been analysed in terms of item/total correlation, both initial and also the total correlation after having extracted this item.

Table 1 shows that the next items embody ambiguity (in blue). They are: Distracts me easily, depresses me, makes me feel lonely, prevents me to have f2f and physic contact with my friends, and prevents me to complete my work in time, increase privacy, security and IPR concerns. Though these questions can be regarded as being meaningful, they obviously introduced a variety of interpretations by the respondents, and should be reformulated or clarified in future research.

Table 1 Item-total correlation, before and after extraction

	Initial	Extraction
Q11_1 Prevents me from concentrating more on writing and reading skills	,503	,419
Q11_2 Prevents me from remembering the fundamental knowledge and skills	,586	,653
Q11_3 Scatters my attention	,452	,316
Q11_4 Decreases my grammar and proofreading skills	,437	,338
Q11_5 Decreases my deep thinking	,603	,585
Q11_6 Distracts me easily	,500	,937
Q11_7 Prevents me from participating in social activities	,491	,366
Q11_8 Prevents me from completing my work/study on time	,646	,655
Q11_9 Makes me sick and unhealthy	,574	,540
Q11_10 Bores me	,488	,477
Q11_11 Stresses me	,724	,762
Q11_12 Depresses me	,836	,984
Q11_13 Makes me feel lonely	,759	,700
Q11_14 Makes me lazy	,455	,324
Q11_15 Makes me addict	,508	,404
Q11_16 Makes me more gambler	,456	,290
Q11_17 Makes me insecure to release my personal details from theft of personal information	,464	,362
Q11_18 Makes me receive an immoral images from unscrupulous people	,376	,314
Q11_19 Prevents me from having face to face contact with my family	,509	,489
Q11_20 Prevents me from having face to face contact with my friends	,605	,689
Q11_21 Prevents me from participating in physical activities	,669	,701
Q11_22 Prevents me from shopping in stores	,466	,381
Q11_23 Prevents me from watching television	,389	,425
Q11_24 Prevents me from reading the newspapers	,448	,587
Q11_25 Prevents me from talking on the phone/mobile	,454	,386
Q11_26 Prevents me from completing my work on time	,857	,957
Q11_27 Prevents me from completing my study on time	,824	,814
Q11_28 Increase privacy concerns	,782	,813
Q11_29 Increase security concerns	,790	,911
Q11_30 Increase intellectual property concerns	,660	,615

6 Main Factors in the Perceived Benefits of Social Networking

Built upon the questionnaire the search was after underlying sentiments in the Dutch students' perceived benefits of social networking (Table 2).

The discerned factors have been analysed for mutual correlation and can be seen in the Table 3 below. Typical contours are the contrasts between Factor 3 and all others. Factor 3 proves to stand for students' critical attitude towards ones' own study success, study more independently and more focussed towards problem solving. Obviously questions in this genre tend to be regarded quite differently from all other questions.

Six of the eight detected factors analysed further and were mapped back unto the 24 posed questions:

- Factor 1 explained 99, 61 and 48 % respectively of the students' perceived benefits: Acquire new friendship relations, romance and to a lesser extent,

Table 2 Underlying factors in the students' perceived benefits of social media

	Factor					
	1	2	3	4	5	6
Q9_23 Acquire new acquaintances —friendship relationship	0.991	−0.155	0.156	0.279	0.202	–
Q9_24 Acquire new acquaintances —romance relationship	0.609	–	0.132	0.181	0.201	–
Q9_22 Acquire new acquaintances —work related	0.477	−0.178	0.116	0.296	0.284	0.254
Q9_21 Reduce carbon footprint in my activities	0.187	−0.995	0.129	0.143	0.314	0.135
Q9_20 Become more "Greener" in my activities	0.176	−0.688	0.143	0.205	0.514	0.126
Q9_13 Understand and solve study problems easily	0.183	–	0.883	–	0.334	0.303
Q9_12 Complete my study more quickly	0.126	–	0.719	0.103	0.363	0.253
Q9_14 Scrutinize my research study more easily	0.351	−0.284	0.665	0.233	0.498	0.149
Q9_10 Study independently	0.144	–	0.580	–	0.302	0.350
Q9_8 Communicate with my different communities	0.308	−0.112	–	0.739	0.170	–
Q9_5 Communicate with my peers frequently	0.265	−0.125	–	0.731	0.131	0.234
Q9_6 Collaborate with my peers frequently	0.254	−0.165	0.172	0.610	0.145	0.116
Q9_7 Communicate with my peers from different universities	0.148	−0.149	–	0.573	–	−0.237
Q9_9 Develop intercrossing relationships with my peers	0.330	–	0.183	0.459	0.355	0.394
Q9_17 To prepare my professional attitude toward study and work	0.244	−0.251	0.524	–	0.796	0.209
Q9_19 Provide reliable and scalable services	0.246	−0.430	0.270	0.331	0.674	0.280
Q9_18 Be more sustainable person	0.322	−0.344	0.282	0.237	0.657	0.166
Q9_16 Concentrate more on my reading and writing skills	0.192	−0.203	0.388	–	0.593	0.265
Q9_3 Be more aware of global issues/local issues	–	–	0.327	–	0.181	0.694
Q9_2 Gain up-to-date information	–	−0.156	0.205	–	0.216	0.605
Q9_1 Learn new information and knowledge	0.141	−0.114	0.405	–	0.373	0.590

Extraction Method: Maximum Likelihood
Rotation Method: Oblimin with Kaiser Normalization

Table 3 Factor correlation matrix

Factor correlation matrix								
Factor	1	2	3	4	5	6	7	8
1	1.000							
2	0.159	1.000						
3	−0.078	−0.252	1.000					
4	0.206	0.309	−0.074	1.000				
5	0.254	0.283	−0.053	0.291	1.000			
6	0.267	0.384	−0.198	0.331	0.377	1.000		
7	0.148	0.416	−0.086	0.173	0.362	0.313	1.000	
8	0.316	0.281	−0.026	0.301	0.277	0.239	0.171	1.000

Extraction method: maximum likelihood
Rotation method: Oblimin with Kaiser normalization

finding new work related relationships. The smaller loadings were found in 'scrutinizing my research study mores easily', 'communicate with my different research communities', 'developing inter-crossing (traversal) relationships with my peers' and 'to be a mores sustainable person'. In summary: The dominant factor that underpins the Dutch students' perceived social networking benefits are social bonding, both for affinitive relations and study awareness.

- Factor 2 seems to be the antagonist of Factor 1; its contributing question responses show a typical negative pattern all over the set of the 18 of 24 questions. It can be summarized as that students admit that the expressed blessings of social media are at the same time counter productive for the sake of study processes.
- Factor 3 can be classified as orthogonal to the loadings of Factor 1. Typical loadings are on the benefit of social networking that help to understand and solve problems in the period of studying, complete and again scrutinize one's own study success, and, remarkably, to study more independently. This finding suggests that a certain part of the population sample recognizes that besides the incentive of social capital, the social network stimulates the studying process in itself, apart from the social stimuli that are brought along.
- Factor 4 lists the benefits of communicating with external communities and peers from other universities as well. It suggests that its underlying motive is the perceived benefit of having a wider intellectual horizon. Quite understandable the same students who support this view also admit that the prices of this wider intellectual circle is that the study period will last longer.
- Factor 5 has a wide spread on survey questions; however its mere accent is on the role of social networking on preparing for the coming professional context. Consciousness and being a sustainable person are recognized and point to the same wider time-scale dimension in the factor.
- Factor 6 expresses the mere ideological values of global issues like ethics and actuality. It typically correlates negatively with recognizing the virtue of communicating with a wider circle of students from other universities.

Summarizing the factor analysis, we can say that the polled Dutch students reflect a differentiated view on the positive/negative side effects of social networking. The crucial interpretation of the discriminant of the factors 1 and 2 is that a considerable proportion of the Dutch students show to be aware that the trade-off between speed and depth of studying is non trivial; social media are seen as socially- and intellectually-enriching, and at the same time entail to a more extended study period. Finally: the elicitation and ethical-/consciousness aspects during the study period are seen as congruent with the practising of social networking; another facet of opening one's mind for extra-curricular investments.

7 Underlying Factors in Social Media

So far we examined and assessed the risks and opportunities of social networking in the students' awareness in the Netherlands. In order to find the motivations that underlie these opinions we performed a study into the students' views on how their confidence on using social media depends on adjacent factors like attitude towards collaborative work, social skills and the degree of extroversion. Social media efficacy was postulated as superordinate factor; [7]. For this purpose the underlying model has been tested in the study by Voorn and Kommers [8] (Fig. 1).

The first order associations are that Groups Skills (both the conceived and the perceived self-skills) is strongly correlated with one's degree of Extroversion and collaborative learning. It is a considerably stronger tie than those stemming from Social Media Efficacy and the Non Collaborative Learning. The conclusion of this study was that introvert students consider social skills as less important and also consider that they are helped by social media in learning as they feel themselves as less skilled in social contacting. It means that social media might be a bridge for introvert students in order to become more alert in relationships anyhow.

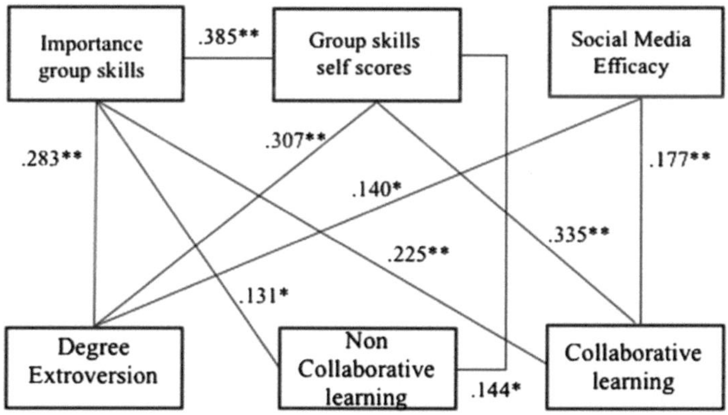

Fig. 1 Hypothesized model on students' preference for collaborative learning and social media

8 Discussion

The potential meaning of this characteristic as derived from the cohort of Dutch students can only be pinpointed when compared to the typical results from other countries. However it is the impression from interviews with both academic teachers and students, that in respect to the adoption of social media in education, The Netherlands shows a rather opportunistic and not very scrupulous attitude in this, even if its merits will only be seen years after Higher Education has been finalized. The essential discussion here is if this pro-active attitude towards new communicative media embodies a positive, neutral or even negative feature in the Dutch student population? This question is hard to answer as we would need to combine our data with students' final societal and economic success. So far we have no data that can justify or refute. We can just expect based upon educated guess, that the propagation of social media is so wide and deep that it will become a determinant of media literacy and self-efficacy anyway. In other words: yes it is likely that the coming years will show the self-propelling legitimation of social media, and will reify its existence autonomously, especially among students as by tradition they are in the best position to remove barriers and even excavate forgotten conventions like the social networking metaphor.

9 Significance of This Chapter

The main message of this chapter is that though the Dutch students of Higher Education adhere a great relevance to the use of social media, an ambiguity could be found in the student reports. It is that students have twofold intuitions. The first is that social media allow them to reach a more meaningful level of learning; more tuned to relevant dimensions like sustainability and ethical aspects. Also they feel that through the network communication they reach a higher level of reflection and critical thinking. The second one however is their awareness that participating in this deeper level of learning is not exactly rewarding in terms of speed and level of grades. So in fact students need to invest in other dimensions than the study program anticipated so far.

10 Limitations and Future Research

This study has been instigated to make a diagnostic survey of the higher education student perceptions and attitudes towards social media in and around the study process. Since the data from the other involved countries were not unveiled unfortunately, the characterization of the Dutch students could not be mirrored against the more global data that were available from the other countries. This is a pity and has caused trouble in the analysis above. Future research should build upon the new situation nowadays where students actually need social media to get involved in their future career communities of practice. The question can then be addressed to what extent this contextual orientation helps students to acquire and assimilate a professional attitude and capacity to solve contextual problems in the field.

11 Conclusion

The combination of the factor- and the path analysis shows that the Dutch students make a sensitive difference between the actual support of social media for the mainstream curricular goals and learning achievements at one side, and the potential of social media to enlarge one's horizon. Also the Dutch students' perception is that the added value of social media manifests through social media efficacy, social extraversion and collaborative learning. It comes down to the conclusion that students see the social- and collaborative skills as decisive, even if they are not included in formal grading procedures. It means that the students' social media awareness exceeds the actual curricular needs and that they have the intuition that social media skills are important for their careers nevertheless.

References

1. Sweller J, Chandler P, Tierney P, Cooper M (1990) Cognitive load factor in the structuring of technical material. J Exp Psychol Gen 119:176–192
2. Social networking: the UK as a leader in Europe: part of internet access—households and individuals, social networking: the UK as a leader in Europe release. Released: 13 June 2013
3. Kommers P (2011) Social media for learning by means of ICT, UNESCO Institute for Information Technologies in Education. UNESCO, Moscow, pp 1–10
4. Salomon G, Perkins DN (1998) Individual and social aspects of learning. In: Pearson PD, Iran-Nejad A (Special issue eds) Review of research in education, vol 23, pp 1–24
5. Vygotsky L (1986) Thought and language, (newly revised and edited by Alex Kozulin). The MIT press, Cambridge. ISBN:0-262-22029-6
6. Siemens G (2005) Connectivism: a learning theory for the digital age. Int J Instr Technol Distance Learn 2(1):3–10
7. Mazman SG, Usluel YK (2010) Modelling educational usage of Facebook. Comput Educ 55 (2010):444–453
8. Voorn RJJ, Kommers PAM (2013) Social media and higher education: introversion and collaborative learning from the student's perspective. Int J Soc Media Interac Learn Environ 1 (1):59–73. ISSN:2050-3954
9. Cabero-Almenara J, Marín-Díaz V (2014) Educational possibilities of social networks and group work. University students' perceptions. Comunicar 21(42):165–172. doi:10.3916/C42-2014-16
10. Mazzoni E, Iannone M (2014) From high school to university: impact of social networking sites on social capital in the transitions of emerging adults. Br J Educ Technol 45(2):303–315. doi:10.1111/bjet.12026

Higher Education Students' Perceptions of Positive and Negative Effects of Social Networking in Portugal

Paula Miranda, Pedro Isaias and Sara Pífano

Abstract The aim of this study was to examine students' perceptions of social networking in Portugal. One hundred and thirty (N = 130) students were surveyed online. Factorial analyses have been performed with results showing that social networking were had positive impacts in terms of being a tool for study or work independently and support personal or professional network, a Teamwork building instrument; contributing to being a "Green" user, and gaining updated information and knowledge. On the negative side, social networks impede to traditional information source, are an inhibitor to be more sociable and in-person contact and leads to sedentary lifestyle, trigger anxiety and losing interest, are an inhibitor on developing literacy skills, reducing further thinking capability and unable to focus on one matter for longer time, raise increasing privacy, security and intellectual property concerns, and lastly, are an inhibitor to accomplish higher priority as scheduled.

Keywords Social networking · Social media · Portuguese college students · Higher education · Web 2.0 · Positive impacts · Negative impacts

P. Miranda
Escola Superior de Tecnologia de Setúbal, IPS, Campus do IPS,
2910-761 Setúbal, Estefanilha, Portugal
e-mail: paula.miranda@estsetubal.ips.pt

P. Isaias (✉)
Universidade Aberta, Palácio Ceia Rua da Escola Politécnica,
n. 141-147, 1269-001 Lisbon, Portugal
e-mail: pisaias@uab.pt

S. Pífano
ISRLab – Information Society Research Laboratory,
Rua São Sebastião da Pedreira 100, 3, 1050-209 Lisbon, Portugal
e-mail: sarap@isrlab.org

T. Issa et al. (eds.), *Social Networking and Education*,
Lecture Notes in Social Networks, DOI 10.1007/978-3-319-17716-8_8

1 Introduction

Online social networks have been growing in number and nature. They have become highly popular and specialized. Also, their social character has evolved to embrace economy, education, health and many other areas of society.

Isaías et al. [11] define social networks as "platforms that allow internet users the possibility of having individual pages displaying their personal profiles, their network of contacts and other information that they may choose to share. Besides a venue, these websites also provide users with a multiplicity of means to interact with their contacts." [11]. Social Networks allow users the possibility to access and create online content, the swift dissemination of information, and the opportunity to address global issues (climate, terrorism) [8]. Social networks can also be valuable in terms of the participation of users in public domains [11].

Education is one of the sectors that has been exploring the benefits of social networks [5, 16]. Namely, scholars are using social networks for communication [20], participation, collaboration, information [18], to increase student satisfaction and to enhance the interaction between students [19]. On the other hand social networks' use in education have been associated to negative academic performance, namely due to the distraction they may constitute and the amount of time spent on these sites [19]. Privacy and security concerns [1] are also known pitfalls of social networks, along with copyright and intellectual property issues [6].

Portuguese users have intensified and varied their use of social networks. They have become more active inside social networks and they have also been using a wider array of social networks [2]. However, research in Portugal regarding the use of social networks in educational contexts is insufficient. The studies that are available seem to predict a growing involvement of social networks in higher education, but to move forward in this matter it is necessary to invest in more empirical research.

2 Social Networks in Portugal

Portugal has experienced an increase in the levels of internet use. In 2013, around 55 % of people in Portugal characterized themselves as internet users, while circa 38 % said they did not use the internet and about 6 % said that they had stopped using it in 2013 [2]. Eurostat [4] figures show that in the EU-28 in 2014, 80 % of the people used the internet in the last 12 months. In Portugal though, that rate is 67 %, showing a significant difference between the levels of internet use in Portugal the EU-28´s average.

Although the majority of Portuguese users (72.9 %), reported using the internet on a daily basis, solely 38.5 % of the users said that they resort to mobile devices to access the Internet [2]. The difference between gender in terms of use is insignificant, with 51 % of the users being male and 49 % being female. In terms of age, the internet utilisation rate decreases as the age of the user increases. Another aspect where there is a clear variation is the level of education of the users. The rate of internet use increases proportionally to the level of education [2].

With regard to the use of the internet for participating on online social networks, Portugal has a slightly higher numbers than the EU-28's average. In 2014, 47 % of Portuguese internet users stated that they used the internet for participating on social networks, while the EU-28's average was 76 % [3]. In 2014, Facebook was Portugal's preferred social network [7], maintaining its position from previous years. The figure below portraits the distribution of personal profiles of Portuguese users throughout different social networks and confirms Facebook´s unmistakable dominance (Fig. 1).

Facebook was the social network where 98 % of Portuguese users reported having a personal profile, which represents a overwhelming difference from the number two social network Google+ (13.7 %) [2]. Facebook is also the social network that the academia, in general, uses the most [20].

In contrast, a study conducted by Grupo Marktest [7] revealed that, in 2014, 27 % of internet users in Portugal had left a social network in the last year and 20 % of them expected to spend last time on social networks in the next 12 months.

The reasons that were given by people to justify social network abandonment included lack of interest, migration of their friends (or their own) to another social network, lack of time and the fact that the social network had become outdated [7]. Also, in general, social network participation often results in social anxiety, partly because users believe that they cannot meet the different expectations that their contacts have [14].

2.1 Social Networks and Higher Education

"The immediacy and extent of online social networks allied with their diversity in terms of interactive features have earned them the loyalty of millions of internet users." [10], namely students.

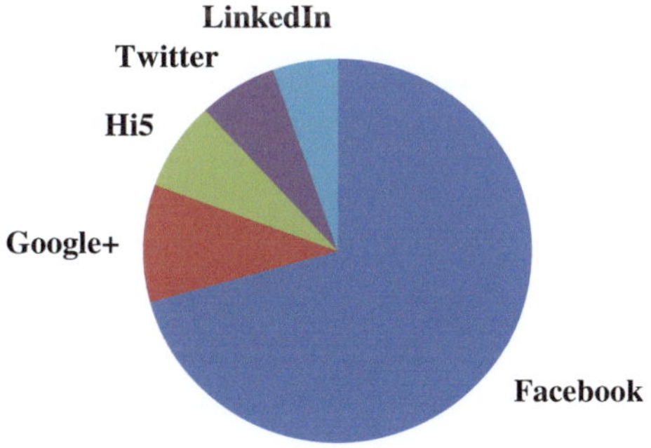

Fig. 1 Personal profiles per social networks in 2013 (adapted from [2])

Students are active social network users. They use these sites to reach their family and friends, to exchange information and ideas and to promote events and causes [13]. Eurostat [3] statistics shows that the participation of users in social network sites is directly proportionate to their educational level. Figures 2 and 3 show the percentage of individuals aged 16–74 with high formal education and low formal education, respectively.

Figures 2 and 3 show the predominance of EU-28 and Portuguese individuals with high formal education in terms of social network participation. Figure 4 further illustrates the discrepancy between education levels and social network participation in Portugal.

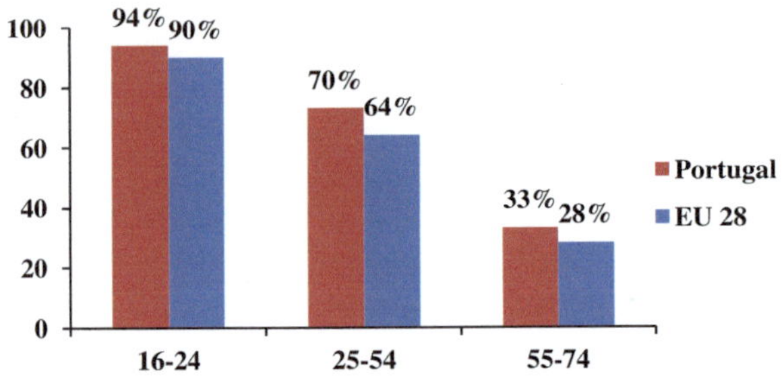

Fig. 2 Social network participation of individuals with high formal education per group [3]

Fig. 3 Social network participation of individuals with low formal education per group [3]

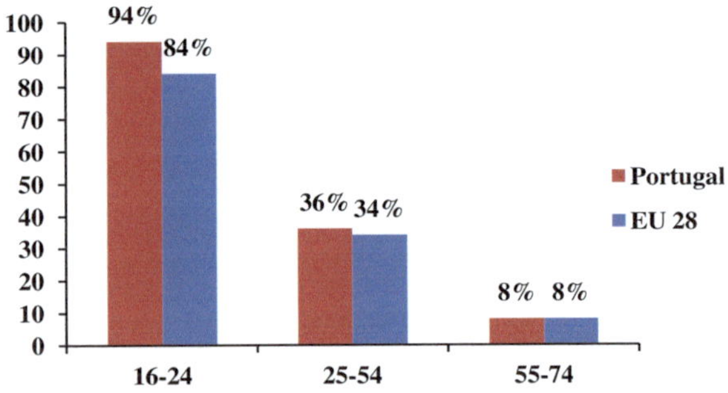

Fig. 4 Portuguese users' participation in social networks per age group and education level [3]

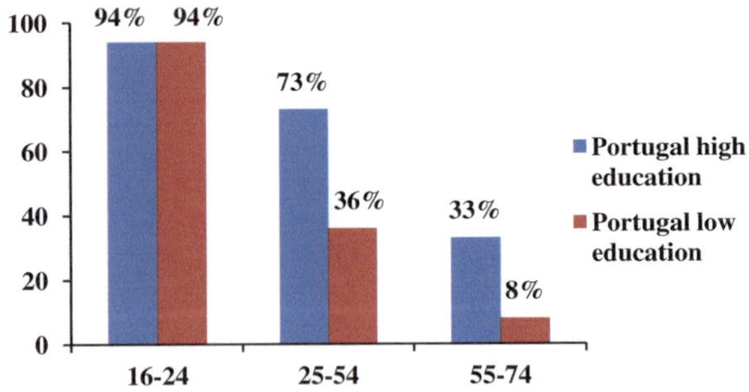

The only age group where participation is not affected by the level of education is the 16–24, where both low and high formal education levels register 94 % of social network users.

Inside educational settings, social networks are demonstrating their potential as platforms for connection and online communities' creation. They can benefit students by endowing them with a combination of pedagogy and entertainment [12]. On the other hand, social networks also represent a series of challenges that cannot be overlooked, namely in terms of cyberbullying and unwanted content [9].

In Portugal, research about the impact of Social Networks inside educational environments remains scarce, but the literature that already exists, forecasts a more widely spread use of social networks in higher education. Minhoto, Meirinhos [15] conducted a study on the use of Facebook by a 12th grade class (pre-university) of Biology. The students were asked to engage with a Facebook page that was created for the class with various features, such as, the wall, discussion forums, videos and photos. Although the students did engage with the page, the analysis of the forum entries revealed a low degree of student-to-student communication and collaboration, which can be explained by a persisting educational culture of individual learning and competition. On a more positive note, due to the students' familiarity with Facebook, no training period was necessary before introducing the social network [15]. Another study [17] using Facebook in a 1st year undergraduate course had more encouraging results. Patrício, Gonçalves [17] started to use Facebook with the students after the unsuccessful deployment of a b-learning platform, that contrary to its initial purpose of platform of interaction and engagement, became a mere repository of course material. A Facebook page was created to potentiate interaction and a more active participation and it began to be used as a platform for several educational resources, namely presentations, links, activities and a Facebook group to promote communication and address students' queries. Before the deployment of the Facebook page, 77 % of the students claimed to have a Facebook account and 88 % of the students agreed with the use of Facebook within the course. At the end of the experience, an expressive majority of the students claimed that using Facebook allowed the development of technological skills, a deeper knowledge of their colleagues, the improvement of group cohesion, an increase in their participation and engagement with the course content, more learning autonomy and self-management and the promotion of critical thinking. Additionally, 73 % of the students stated that the use of Facebook should be extended to other courses and modules [17].

This study addresses the following research question:

> What are the positive and negative effects of using social-network for Portuguese higher education students?

3 Methods

3.1 Participants

A total of 130 participants from Portugal have responded to an on-line questionnaire, with none missing data found, resulted with 130 valid cases of responses for Portugal, ages ranging from 18 to 52+ years. The participants were students that originated from Portuguese universities (ISEG—University of Lisbon and Universidade Aberta (Portuguese Open University)), from several different undergraduate and graduate course units.

A total of 130 students participated in this study. The students were recruited from several units.

3.2 Data Collection Instrument

The research team in Portugal used the same instrument as the other teams in other countries. The instrument was composed of 25 items for surveying positive effects of Social Networking and 30 items for negative effects of Social Networking. Items followed a 5-point Likert-type scale ranging from 1 = *strongly disagree* to 5 = *strongly agree*.

Demographic information such as age, gender, major, education level has been collected. The survey also assessed the amount of time participants spend in social networking, amount of time spent on email, and other types of activities performed online.

4 Results

4.1 Descriptive Statistics

Of the 130 answered surveys, 87 of them were answered by males (54 %) and 73 (46 %) by female students. The age of most participants ranged from 18 to 32 years: 63 (39 %) were 22–32 years old, the age group with more students, 40 (25 %) were 18–21 years old, and 36 (23 %) were 32–42 years old. As for the fields of study, 99 (63 %) participants were studying Management, 12(8 %) Science and Engineering, and 9 (6 %) Economics and Finance, as well as Computer Science. Most of the highest education level was higher secondary/pre-university 99 (63 %) and the second one being bachelor's degree 25 (16 %).

The majority of the participants 100 (65 %) reported to spend less than one hour per day in social networking, while 50 (32 %) of the participants reported to spend up to five hours social networking per day. Similarly, regarding E-Mail usage,

93 (60 %) reported spending less than one hour per day with E-mail, whilst 46 (30 %) reported spending up to five hours with E-mail per day.

Descriptive statistics have been calculated for questions from Group Questions 9 (Q9) which related with Positive impact and Group Q11 (Q11) which related with Negative impact. Q9 group consists of 25 questions and Q11 group consists of 30 questions (Table 1).

As for the questions relating to Negative Impact, the questions that had higher averages were the following (see Table 2): Q11.6 Distracts me easily (M = 3.52; SD = 1.101); Q11.3 Scatters my attention (M = 3.44; SD = 1.004); Q11.29 Increase security concerns (M = 3.33; SD = 1.157); Q11.28 Increase privacy concerns (M = 3.31; SD = 1.167); Q11.1 Prevents me from concentrating more on writing and reading skills (M = 3.23; SD = 1.023); Q11.30 Increase intellectual property concerns (M = 3.08; SD = 1.035).

Table 1 Mean and standard deviation of the 25 items in Q9 group—positive impact of SN

Descriptive statistics		
	Mean	Std. deviation
Q9_1 Learn new information and knowledge	3.85	0.867
Q9_2 Gain up-to-date information	4.06	0.842
Q9_3 Be more aware of global issues/local issues	3.85	0.846
Q9_4 To remember facts/aspects of the past	3.70	0.868
Q9_5 Communicate with my peers frequently	4.15	0.772
Q9_6 Collaborate with my peers frequently	3.99	0.849
Q9_7 Communicate with my peers from different universities	3.75	0.959
Q9_8 Communicate with my different communities	3.80	0.884
Q9_9 Develop intercrossing relationships with my peers	3.57	0.825
Q9_10 Study independently	3.25	1.208
Q9_11 Overcome study stress	3.26	1.053
Q9_12 Complete my study more quickly	3.12	1.155
Q9_13 Understand and solve study problems easily	3.34	1.111
Q9_14 Scrutinize my research study more easily	3.58	1.127
Q9_15 Develop my personal and communication skills	3.45	1.100
Q9_16 Concentrate more on my reading and writing skills	2.96	1.060
Q9_17 To prepare my professional attitude toward study and work	3.14	1.084
Q9_18 Be more sustainable person	3.17	1.043
Q9 19 Provide reliable and scalable services	3.15	0.858
Q9 20 Become more "Greener" in my activities	3.24	0.913
Q9_21 Reduce carbon footprint in my activities	3.22	0.948
Q9_22 Acquire new acquaintances—work related	3.64	0.956
Q9_23 Acquire new acquaintances—friendship relationship	3.65	0.861
Q9_24 Acquire new acquaintances—romance relationship	3.10	0.947
Q9_25 Do whatever I want, say whatever I want, and be whoever I want	3.11	1.247

Table 2 Mean and standard deviation of the 30 items in Q11 group—negative impact of SN

Descriptive statistics	Mean	Std. Deviation
Q11_1 Prevents me from concentrating more on writing and reading skills	3.23	1.023
Q11_2 Prevents me from remembering the fundamental knowledge and skills	2.65	0.895
Q11_3 Scatters my attention	3.44	1.004
Q11_4 Decreases my grammar and proofreading skills	2.89	1.058
Q11_5 Decreases my deep thinking	2.85	1.057
Q11_6 Distracts me easily	3.52	1.101
Q11_7 Prevents me from participating in social activities	2.53	1.101
Q11_8 Prevents me from completing my work/study on time	2.82	1.033
Q11_9 Makes me sick and unhealthy	2.09	1.045
Q11_10 Bores me	2.48	1.108
Q11_11 Stresses me	2.26	1.104
Q11_12 Depresses me	2.18	1.023
Q11_13 Makes me feel lonely	2.20	1.067
Q11_14 Makes me lazy	2.63	1.195
Q11_15 Makes me addict	2.70	1.268
Q11_16 Makes me more gambler	2.35	1.174
Q11_17 Makes me insecure to release my personal details from the theft of personal information	2.89	1.222
Q11_18 Makes me receive an immoral images and information from unscrupulous people and it is difficult to act against them at present	2.75	1.135
Q11_19 Prevents me from having face to face contact with my family	2.20	1.177
Q11_20 Prevents me from having face to face contact with my friends	2.25	1.188
Q11_21 Prevents me from participating in physical activities	2.15	1.171
Q11_22 Prevents me from shopping in stores	1.98	0.968
Q11_23 Prevents me from watching television	2.13	1.116
Q11_24 Prevents me from reading the newspapers	2.21	1.139
Q11_25 Prevents me from talking on the phone/mobile	2.03	1.056
Q11_26 Prevents me from completing my work on time	2.34	1.124
Q11_27 Prevents me from completing my study on time	2.45	1.175
Q11_28 Increase privacy concerns	3.31	1.167
Q11_29 Increase security concerns	3.33	1.157
Q11_30 Increase intellectual property concerns	3.08	1.035

4.2 *Factor Analysis*

An exploratory factor analysis was conducted on the survey items using maximum likelihood extraction method with Oblimin with Kaiser normalization rotation method for Positive items (Q9 group of questions) and Principal Axis Factoring extraction method with Promax with Kaiser Normalization rotation method for Negative items (Q11 group of questions).

For Q9 group, the following were calculated:

- The Cronbach's Alpha for all 25 variables from Q9 group was 0.936 indicates an excellent internal consistency of the items in the scale (Gliem and Gliem, 2003).
- A Kaiser-Meyer-Olkin (Blackmore, #1390) measure of sampling adequacy of 0.896 indicates a good sample size is obtained from the analysis.
- The Bartlett's test of sphericity is highly significant, $\chi^2 = 2282.454$ $df = 300$, $p < 0$, indicating that the items of the scale are sufficiently correlated to factors to be found.

For Q11 Group, the following were calculated:

- The Cronbach's Alpha for all 30 variables from Q11 group was 0.956 indicates an excellent internal consistency of the items in the scale (Gliem and Gliem, 2003).
- A Kaiser-Meyer-Olkin (Blackmore, #1390) measure of sampling adequacy of 0.872 indicates a good sample size is obtained from the analysis.
- The Bartlett's test of sphericity is highly significant, $\chi^2 = 3668.396$, $df = 435$, $p < 0$, indicating that the items of the scale are sufficiently correlated to factors to be found

Further to the reliability analyses presented in the previous paragraphs for Q9 and Q11 groups (0.936 and 0.956 respectively), a detailed reliability analyses also showed acceptable (Cronbach's Alpha≧60) subcategory reliabilities ranging from 0.649 to 0.925 (See Table 3).

Positive items (N = 25) and negative items (N = 30) were examined separately. Items with factor loadings of 0.5 were retained. From the original 25 positive items for Group Q9, there are four factors extracted on the final run with Kaiser Normalisation (Eigenvalues greater than one).

As demonstrated in the following table, this model of four factors explains a total of 58.178 % of the variation. The Eigenvalues and the amount of variances explained by each of these factors are presented on Table 4 (after rotation).

Table 5 presents the Pattern Matrix for Q9—Positive Impact of SN.

The four factors revealed from the Pattern Matrix for Group Q9 are:

- **Factor 1**: This factor has been designated as "As tool for study or work independently and support personal or professional network". This includes the following significant variables (by order of their contribution to the factor): Q9.13—Understand and solve study problems easily; Q9.14—Scrutinize my research study more easily; Q9.12—Complete my study more quickly; Q9.17—To prepare my professional attitude toward study and work; Q9.10—Study independently; Q9.22—Acquire new acquaintances—work related; Q9.11—Overcome study stress; Q9.18—Be more sustainable person;

Table 3 Category and subcategory reliability (Cronbach's alpha)

Category	Subcategory	Item #	Cronbach's subcategory alpha	Cronbach's category alpha
Positive effects	Information acquisition & communication	1, 2, 3, 5, 6, 7, 8	0.874	0.936
	Efficiency in study	10, 12, 13, 14	0.884	
	Relationship building	22, 23, 24	0.649	
Negative effects	Security	17, 18, 28, 29, 30	0.854	0.956
	Completion of study/Work	8, 26, 27	0.898	
	Emotion	10, 11,12, 13	0.925	
	Cognitive development	1, 2, 3, 4, 5, 6	0.846	
	Social development	7, 16, 19, 20	0.869	
	Physical development	22, 23, 24	0.896	

Table 4 Eigenvalues and amount of variances explained by each of the factors—Q9 positive impact of SN

Total variance explained							
	Initial eigenvalues			Extraction sums of squared loadings			Rotation sums of squared loadings[a]
Factor	Total	% of variance	cumulative %	Total	% of variance	Cumulative %	Total
1	9.948	41.448	41.448	9.241	38.506	38.506	8.148
2	3.100	12.915	54.363	2.834	11.808	50.314	5.120
3	1.524	6.349	60.711	1.073	4.471	54.786	4.458
4	1.174	4.891	65.602	0.814	3.393	58.178	6.139

Extraction method: maximum likelihood

[a]When factors are correlated, sums of squared loadings cannot be added to obtain a total variance

- **Factor 2**: This factor has been designated as "Teamwork building instrument". This includes the following significant variables (by order of their contribution to the factor): Q9.6—Collaborate with my peers frequently; Q9.7—Communicate with my peers from different universities; Q9.8—Communicate with my different communities; Q9.5—Communicate with my peers frequently;
- **Factor 3**: This factor has been designated as "Towards being a "Green" user". This includes the following significant variables (by order of their contribution to the factor): Q9.20—Become more "Greener" in my activities; Q9.21—Reduce carbon footprint in my activities (both with negative loadings);

Table 5 Pattern matrix for Q9—positive impact of SN

Pattern matrix[a]				
	Factor			
	1	2	3	4
Q9_13 Understand and solve study problems easily	0.981			
Q9_14 Scrutinize my research study more easily	0.906			
Q9_12 Complete my study more quickly	0.875	−0.124		
Q9_17 To prepare my professional attitude toward study and work	0.781			
Q9_10 Study independently	0.693		−0.143	
Q9_22 Acquire new acquaintances—work related	0.654	0.162		−0.141
Q9_11 Overcome study stress	0.612			
Q9_18 Be more sustainable person	0.586	0.101	−0.216	
Q9_6 Collaborate with my peers frequently		0.840		
Q9_7 Communicate with my peers from different universities		0.830		
Q9_8 Communicate with my different communities	0.106	0.745		0.121
Q9_5 Communicate with my peers frequently	−125	0.740		−0.230
Q9_4 To remember facts/aspects of the past	0.136	0.413		−0.182
Q9_9 Develop intercrossing relationships with my peers	0.112	0.395	−0.137	−0.186
Q9_20 Become more "Greener" in my activities	0.104		−0.829	−160
Q9_21 Reduce carbon footprint in my activities	0.127	0.115	−0.806	
Q9_19 Provide reliable and scalable services	0.278	0.120	−0.283	−0.131
Q9_3 Be more aware of global issues/local issues			−0.104	−0.823
Q9_2 Gain up-to-date information		0.113		−0.791
Q9_1 Learn new information and knowledge	0.188			−749
Q9_15 Develop my personal and communication skills	0.350			−363
Q9_24 Acquire new acquaintances—romance relationship		0.125		−0.297
Q9_25 Do whatever I want, say whatever I want, and be whoever I want		0.127	0.175	−0.237
Q9_23 Acquire new acquaintances—friendship relationship	118	0.194	−0.133	−232

Extraction method: maximum likelihood
Rotation method: Obliminwith Kaiser normalization
[a]Rotation converged in 7 iterations

- **Factor 4**: This factor has been designated as "Updated information and knowledge". This includes the following significant variables (by order of their contribution to the factor): Q9.3—Be more aware of global issues/local issues; Q9.2—Gain up-to-date information; Q9.1—Learn new information and knowledge (all with negative loadings).

Items with factor loadings of 0.5 were retained in this case. From the original 30 negative items for Group Q11, there are five factors extracted on the final run with Kaiser Normalisation (Eigenvalues greater than one).

As demonstrated in the following table, this model of five factors explains a total of 71.18 % of the variation. The Eigenvalues and the amount of variances explained by each of these factors are presented on Table 6 (after rotation).

In Table 7 is presented the Pattern Matrix for Q11—Negative Impact of SN.

The five factors revealed from the Pattern Matrix for Group Q11 are:

- **Factor 1**: This factor has been designated as "Impede to traditional information source, inhibitor to be more sociable and in-person contact and leads to sedentary lifestyle". This includes the following significant variables (by order of their contribution to the factor): Q11.23—Prevents me from watching television; Q11.24—Prevents me from reading the newspapers; Q11.22—Prevents me from shopping in stores; Q11.25—Prevents me from talking on the phone/mobile; Q11.21—Prevents me from participating in physical activities; Q11.19—Prevents me from having face to face contact with my family; Q11.20—Prevents me from having face to face contact with my friends;
- **Factor 2**: This factor has been designated as "Trigger anxiety and losing interest". This includes the following significant variables (by order of their contribution to the factor): Q11.11—Stresses me; Q11.12—Depresses me; Q11.13—Makes me feel lonely; Q11.10—Bores me;

Table 6 Eigenvalues and amount of variances explained by each of the factors—Q11 negative impact of SN

Total variance explained							
Factor	Initial eigenvalues			Extraction sums of squared loadings			Rotation sums of squared loadings[a]
	Total	% of variance	Cumulative %	Total	% of variance	Cumulative %	Total
1	10.440	45.393	45.393	10.170	44.216	44.216	8.499
2	2.913	12.664	58.057	2.651	11.526	55.742	7.126
3	1.751	7.612	65.670	1.472	6.401	62.144	5.322
4	1.536	6.679	72.348	1.282	5.572	67.715	4.530
5	1.043	4.534	76.882	0.797	3.465	71.180	6.571

Extraction method: principal axis factoring

[a]when factors are correlated, sums of squared loadings cannot be added to obtain a total variance

Table 7 Patter matrix for Q11—negative impact of SN

Pattern matrix[a]					
	Factor				
	1	2	3	4	5
Q11_23 Prevents me from watching television	0.904				
Q11_24 Prevents me from reading the newspapers	0.904	−0.185	0.124		
Q11_22 Prevents me from shopping in stores	0.888	0.102			
Q11_25 Prevents me from talking on the phone/mobile	0.853				
Q11_21 Prevents me from participating in physical activities	0.795				
Q11_19 Prevents me from having face to face contact with my family	0.728	0.175	−0.141		0.102
Q11_20 Prevents me from having face to face contact with my friends	0.703	0.200			
Q11_15 Makes me addict	0.396		0.195	0.158	0.119
Q11_11 Stresses me		0.907			
Q11_12 Depresses me		0.888			
Q11_13 Makes me feel lonely		0.840			
Q11_10 Bores me		0.715		0.127	
Q11_6 Distracts me easily		−0.282	0.806		
Q11_1 Prevents me from concentrating more on writing and reading skills		0.113	0.770		−0.142
Q11_3 Scatters my attention	−0.111		0.632	0.125	0.168
Q11_5 Decreases my deep thinking	0.108		0.617		
Q11_4 Decreases my grammar and proofreading skills		0.380	0.570		−0.218
Q11_28 Increase privacy concerns	−0.110			0.955	
Q11_29 Increase security concerns				0.952	
Q11_30 Increase intellectual property concerns	0.141			0.769	
Q11_26 Prevents me from completing my work on time			−0.101		0.905
Q11_27 Prevents me from completing my study on time	0.125				0.865
Q11_8 Prevents me from completing my work/study on time	−0.124	0.140	0.378	−0.110	0.582

Extraction method: principal axis factoring
Rotation method: promax with Kaiser normalization
[a]Rotation converged in 6 iterations

- **Factor 3**: This factor has been designated as "Inhibitor on developing literacy skills, reduce further thinking capability and unable to focus on one matter for longer time". This includes the following significant variables (by order of their contribution to the factor): Q11.6—Distracts me easily; Q11.1—Prevents me from concentrating more on writing and reading skills; Q11.3—Scatters my attention; Q11.5—Decreases my deep thinking; Q11_4—Decreases my grammar and proofreading skills;
- **Factor 4**: This factor has been designated as "Increasing privacy, security and intellectual property concerns". This includes the following significant variables (by order of their contribution to the factor): Q11.28—Increase privacy concerns; Q11.29—Increase security concerns; Q11.30—Increase intellectual property concerns;
- **Factor 5**: This factor has been designated as "Inhibitor to accomplish higher priority as scheduled". This includes the following significant variables (by order of their contribution to the factor): Q11.26—Q11_26 Prevents me from completing my work on time; Q11.27—Prevents me from completing my study on time; Q11.8—Prevents me from completing my work/study on time.

5 Discussion

The results have demonstrated that the respondents understand that the use of social networks is associated with positive and negative aspects. Both the descriptive statistics and the exploratory factor analysis highlighted communication, information, participation and collaboration as central benefits and distraction, security, privacy and intellectual property concerns and inhibition of non-digital literacy skills were mentioned as the core challenges.

The respondents' viewpoints in terms of the positive impact of using social networks can be divided into four main concepts: communication, information, participation and collaboration. The advantages for communication became evident in item *Q9.5 Communicate with my peers frequently* (M = 4.15; SD = 0.772); item *Q9.8 Communicate with my different communities* (M = 3.80; SD = 0.884); and in factor 1—*As a tool to study or work independently and support personal or professional network*. Communication as also been highlighted by Lawler, Molluzzo [13], whose research concludes that social networks are often used by students to communicate with their family and friends, and by abundant research on this topic [15, 17–19]. Information also played an important role in the responses of the students as can be seen in item *Q9.2 Gain up-to-date information* (M = 4.06; SD = 0.842); item *Q9.1 Learn new information and knowledge* (M = 3.85; SD = 0.867); and factor 4—*Updated information and knowledge*. This is coherent with the fact that in general, students use social networks to share information and to disseminate events and/or causes [13]. With regards to participation, its significance was illustrated by item *Q9.3 Be more aware of global issues/local issues*

(M = 3.85; SD = 0.846) and factor 3—*Towards being a "Green" user*, which corroborated current studies [18]. Finally, in terms of collaboration, the results are coherent with the belief that social networks are key elements for the creation of web based communities and that they represent an important medium for connection [11]. This was visible in item *Q9.6 Collaborate with my peers frequently* (M = 3.99; SD = 0.849) and factor 2—*Teamwork building instrument.*

From the perspective of the negative impacts there are three main factors: distraction, security, privacy and intellectual property concerns and inhibition of non-digital literacy skills. Studies have reported the distracting effects of social networks [19], which was confirmed by the students' responses in item *Q11.6 Distracts me easily* (M = 3.52; SD = 1.101), item *Q11.3 Scatters my attention* (M = 3.44; SD = 1.004) and factor 5—*Inhibitor to accomplish higher priority as scheduled.* The students displayed concerns in terms of privacy, security and intellectual property concerns in item *Q11.29 Increase security concerns* (M = 3.33; SD = 1.157); item *Q11.28 Increase privacy concerns* (M = 3.31; SD = 1.167); item *Q11.30 Increase intellectual property concerns* (M = 3.08; SD = 1.035); and in factor 4—*Increasing privacy, security and intellectual property concerns.* These issues are among the most cited disadvantages of social networks in general [1] and of their use in education [13]. To conclude, the inhibition of non-digital literacy skills became apparent in item *Q11.1 Prevents me from concentrating more on writing and reading skills* (M = 3.23; SD = 1.023); factor 1—*Impede to traditional information source, inhibitor to be more sociable and in-person contact and leads to sedentary lifestyle*; factor 2—*Trigger anxiety and losing interest*; and factor 3—*Inhibitor on developing literacy skills, reduce further thinking capability and unable to focus on one matter for longer time.*

6 Conclusion

This chapter's main research question intended to define the positive and negative effects of using social networks, according to Portuguese higher education students. The results of the online questionnaires addressed this question and revealed the students' clear understanding of the advantages and disadvantages of using social networks. As reported by the students, social networks are beneficial in terms of communication, information, participation and collaboration, but they constitute a distraction, they create security, privacy and intellectual property concerns and they can work as inhibitors of non-digital literacy skills. The main limitations of this research, which will be the focus of future research, include the narrow scope of the questions, the use of a non-representative sample and the fact that it was restricted to the opinion of students.

The panoply of advantages and disadvantages that both the respondents and the relevant literature stated are an important reminder of the significance of exploring the concept of online social network in its entirety. The questionnaires had a limited scope and the debate of the pertinence of applying social networks involves multiple variables and it is moving towards the question of what strategies to use to implement them successfully in education. Hence, examining these strategies is an important research endeavour for future work. Moreover, the fact that the sample was not representative, poses an important limitation. Moving forward it is imperative to thoroughly examine specific national realities and different educational systems. This chapter provided a depiction of higher education Portuguese students' perceptions about the use of social networks. Their responses were illustrative of the pervasiveness of social networks in several areas of society and the importance that they have been acquiring in educational settings. Solely the opinions of the students were surveyed, which provided only a constricted perspective. Future research should focus on collecting the viewpoints of the remaining stakeholders, more specifically, the teaching community and academic institutions. The successful application of social networks in education and other sectors is dependent on being aware of the global picture that includes all participants.

References

1. Boyd DM, Ellison NB (2007) Social network sites: definition, history, and scholarship. J Comput Mediated Commun 13(1):210–230
2. Cardoso G, Mendonça S, Lima T, Paisana M, Neves M (2014) A internet em Portugal: Sociedade em Rede 2014. OberCom, Lisbon
3. Eurostat (2014) Individuals using the internet for participating in social networks (Code: tin00127). Unit G4: Innovation and information society, Luxembourg
4. Eurostat (2014) Internet use by individuals (Code: tin00028). Unit G4: Innovation and information society, Luxembourg
5. Friesen N, Lowe S (2012) The questionable promise of social media for education: connective learning and the commercial imperative. J Comput Assist Learn 28(3):183–194
6. Greenhow C, Robelia B, Hughes JE (2009) Learning, teaching, and scholarship in a digital age: Web 2.0 and classroom research: what path should we take now? Educ Researcher 38(4):246–259
7. Marktest G (2014) Os Portugueses e as redes sociais em 2014. Análise sobre o comportamento dos portugueses nas redes sociais, Lisbon
8. Guille A, Hacid H, Favre C, Zighed DA (2013) Information diffusion in online social networks: a survey. SIGMOD Rec 42(2):17–28
9. Isaias P, Miranda P, Pífano S (2013) The impact of Web 2.0 adoption in higher education. In: Kommers P, Kasparova E, Bessis N (eds) IADIS international conference web based communities and social media. Prague, Czech Republic, pp 65–73
10. Isaías P, Pífano S, Miranda P (2012) Social network sites: modeling the new business-customer relationship. In: Social networking and community behavior modeling: qualitative and quantitative measures. IGI Global, Hershey, pp 248–265. doi:10.4018/978-1-61350-444-4.ch014
11. Isaías P, Pífano S, Miranda P (2012) Web 2.0: Harnessing democracy's potential. In: Ed D, Matthew AJ (eds) Public service, governance and Web 2.0 technologies: future trends in social media. IGI Global, Hershey, pp 223–236
12. Isaías P, Pífano S, Miranda P (2014) Higher education and web 2.0: theory and practice. In: Pelet J-E (ed) E-Learning 2.0 technologies and web applications in higher education Hershey. IGI Global, Hershey. doi:10.4018/978-1-4666-4876-0

13. Lawler JP, Molluzzo JC (2010) A study of the perceptions of students on privacy and security on social networking sites (SNS) on the internet. J Inf Syst Appl Res 3(12):1–18
14. Marder B, Joinson A, Shankar A (2012) Every post you make, every pic you take, I'll be watching you: behind social spheres on Facebook. In: 45th Hawaii International Conference onSystem Science (HICSS). IEEE, Hawaii. pp 859–868
15. Minhoto P, Meirinhos M (2012) As redes sociais na promoção da aprendizagem colaborativa: um estudo no ensino secundário. Educação, Formação & Tecnologias 4(2):25–34
16. Park SY, Cha SB, Lim K, Jung SH (2014) The relationship between university student learning outcomes and participation in social network services, social acceptance and attitude towards school life. Br J Educ Technol 45(1):97–111
17. Patrício MR, Gonçalves V (2010) Facebook: rede social educativa? In: de UdL-I, Educação (eds) I Encontro Internacional TIC e Educação—I International Meeting on ICT and Education. Lisbon, pp 593–598
18. Rennie F, Morrison T (2013) E-learning and social networking handbook: resources for higher education. Routledge, New York
19. Tess PA (2013) The role of social media in higher education classes (real and virtual)—a literature review. Comput Hum Behav 29(5):A60–A68
20. Thelwall M, Kousha K (2014) Academia. edu: social network or academic network? J Assoc Inf Sci Technol 65(4):721–731

An Examination of Greek College Students' Perceptions of Positive and Negative Effects of Social Networking Use

Thomas Kitsantas, David S. Chirinos, Suzanne E. Hiller and Anastasia Kitsantas

Abstract The vast array of social media network sites provide individuals with the opportunity for communication based on similar interests, occupations, events, or political views while integrating additional features such as mobile accessibility, video and photo sharing, and blogging. The benefits and drawbacks of social media networking vary depending on cultural and societal constructs. The purpose of the present chapter is to examine Greek college students' perceptions (N = 258) of the positive and negative aspects of social networking. It also examines gender and age differences in these perceptions. Findings show that social networking has a positive effect on student learning, communication, and motivation. However, social networking can also lead to feelings of isolation and concerns about academic performance and privacy. Implications for practice are discussed.

Keywords Social networking · College students · Greece

1 Introduction

Social discourse is fundamental for gathering, sharing, and diffusing knowledge [2]. Over the course of the last two decades, online social media networks have influenced diverse facets of the global population in terms of forming personal relationships and accessing resources [16]. Online social media network is a term that extends to a variety of services in which individuals develop personal connections through informal network applications [35] such as wikis, blogs, podcasts and vodcasts as well as websites including Facebook, Bebo, Twitter, and Friendster. By definition, social media networks provide users with the ability to post publicly available profiles, maintain a list of connections, and create pathways to relate with new individuals through their contact list [5, 10].

T. Kitsantas (✉) · D.S. Chirinos · S.E. Hiller · A. Kitsantas
Technological Institute of Epiros, 1, Irinis & Filias Street,
46100 Igoumenitsa, Thesprotia, Greece

T. Issa et al. (eds.), *Social Networking and Education*,
Lecture Notes in Social Networks, DOI 10.1007/978-3-319-17716-8_9

Research conducted throughout Spain, Italy, and the United States indicates that the most frequent users of social media are between the ages of 16 and 18, followed by 13–15 year olds [1]. Given these findings, a number of research studies have focused on the impact of technologically enhanced social media interactions on academic achievement in terms of an increase in collegiate students' grade point averages, self-regulation strategies, and self-efficacy development [20, 29, 34, 35]. As such, online social media tools like Facebook and Twitter afford innovative opportunities for collegiate instructors to enhance student learning through modelling, mentoring, assessments, and promoting self-regulation strategies [9, 12], However, a limited number of studies have been conducted to document the negative and positive effects of social media including the examination of gender and age differences. The aim of this study was to uncover how the use of social networking is perceived among college students. Below, we review research on (a) the positive effects of social networking (b) negative effects of social networking, and (c) present research on gender difference and perceived uses of social networking.

2 Research on Social Networking

One of the benefits of social media networks within educational settings is that they support student goal-setting, self-monitoring and self-reflection during knowledge acquisition [11, 23]. Through technological frameworks, learners connect with peers and instructors to receive assistance and feedback so as to evaluate their performance and refine skills. The computer generated interactions during self-reflection are crucial in developing self-motivation and improving academic achievement. Feedback from peers and instructors within this context promotes higher levels of self-efficacy, performance satisfaction, and contentment with the university [35]. As a result, individuals are more likely to persist in a task until the establishment of a high level of knowledge and skill development [24, 36].

Social media use occurs across academic spheres and cultural contexts in universities globally. A number of studies have been conducted to determine how social media tools impact student learning and motivation. For example, [29] tested a model fit of academic performance with the predictors of academic capabilities, goal orientation, technological use, and the level of social networking interactions. Participants (N = 349) were undergraduate students taking an introductory psychology course which incorporated education information technologies within the course structure. Results indicated that academic ability was the greatest predictor of academic performance. However, social networking had a significant and unique contribution to overall academic performance, greater than goal orientation and education information technology usage combined. The implications of this study were that social networking resources augment effective course infrastructure by providing students with accessibility to individuals with similar performance goal orientations, as well as to accommodate mentoring support [29].

Social media has also been shown to increase students' motivation, particularly students' self-efficacy beliefs. Self-efficacy is defined as the degree to which a learner feels capable of performing a task under specified conditions [2]. Wang and Wu [34] examined the role of self-efficacy, feedback behaviour, and learning strategies on academic performance within a web-based learning environment. The results revealed that feedback through the Netports system increased student performance on content knowledge particularly if peer critiques centered on elaboration of content information rather than on specific item responses [34]. Similarly, [35] assessed the impact of student online social networking engagement with cognitive, affective, and skill-based learning outcomes. Their findings showed that Facebook usage had a positive effect on social acceptance and acculturation, which in turn positively influenced self-esteem, satisfaction with the university experience, and improved performance outcomes [35].

In addition to enhancing student motivation and learning through peer interactions and mentoring, another compelling use for online instruction is to promote information gathering and help seeking. The online component for technologically supported classrooms has been shown to encourage students to ask for assistance. Kitsantas and Chow [22] found that students in distance and distributed learning courses were more likely to use help seeking strategies via technological tools as compared to their counterparts in traditional classrooms. Cheng et al. [7] examined the use of self-regulation strategies to promote online help seeking via informational technologies. Specifically, this study targeted the interaction of student self-regulation, student evaluative strategies for filtering information, and accessing information online. Findings indicated that students with more advanced self-regulation skills and technology commitments were able to utilize online tools for help seeking to a greater extent. Further, self-regulation strategies served as a mediator between technological skills and online help seeking. Despite a variety of options for locating academic information, students tended to avoid using self-regulation strategies to request instructional support. To improve academic performance, results from this study suggested that students require guidance on how to apply social networks to develop self-regulation skills [7]. Concurrently, [9] examined the impact of a 2 week collegiate self-regulation training period prior to a semester long course. Students who received specific training on how to apply self-regulation strategies within a social media network platform were more likely to continue using these types of skills to complete course work while peers without this training did not demonstrate advanced levels of self-regulatory skills. Overall, a growing body of studies show that social networking has a positive impact on student learning, motivation, information gathering, and communication.

Albeit the positive aspects of integrating online social media networks within course instruction, some researchers have concluded that there are drawbacks to online social media networks when focusing on maintaining privacy, credibility of information, and ethical concerns [27]. Individuals may be willing to post personal information on network sites due to peer pressure, indifference to protecting privacy, trust in the network or other users, and an unawareness of risks [15]. For teens, the types of information disclosed and personal setting choices give rise to privacy concerns [33]. In terms of academic achievement, several studies cite a detrimental relationship between time management and scholastic progress [18, 28, 30].

For example, in order to assess the factors which influence undergraduate students enrolled in business courses, [28] studied the amount of time and level of focus on social media platforms. Three hundred forty (N = 340) participants from a variety of courses completed a survey targeting the constructs of student characteristics, academic competence, attention span, predictors of behaviour, time spent on online social networking, time management, and academic performance. Structural equation modelling results revealed significant direct effects between time management, network duration, and student characteristics with student achievement. Time spent for social networking as well as a high attention deficit had a negative impact on student achievement. In conjunction, higher levels of attention deficit had a direct effect on the time individuals spent on social network platforms. These findings suggest that although students feel confident in their capabilities to use online social media networks to support learning, the tendency is to use these resources for social purposes instead [28].

Similarly, [18] focused on the relationship between time, activity choices on Facebook, and academic achievement. Undergraduate students from a northeastern United States college (N = 1839) completed an online survey targeting the time spent on Facebook and common activities which were used in conjunction with GPA scores. Findings from hierarchical regression indicated that there was a negative association between time spent on Facebook and GPA. An increase of one standard deviation of time spent on Facebook totalling 93 min, decreased overall GPA by 0.189. Further, the use of Facebook to prepare for course work did not influence GPA. As a result, encouraging social discussions on course content requires well-defined interventions and facilitation from the instructor [18].

Another aspect considered by [19] regarding students' time spent on Facebook and academics examined the potential for discrepancies between actual Facebook usage and self-reported usage. Forty five college students (N = 45) completed survey measures regarding their Facebook use as well as installed monitoring software on their computers. The monitoring application recorded the participants' computer use (websites, programs, documents, applications) for a total of 1 month. Correlational and inferential statistics (paired t-tests) showed positive correlations between self-reported and actual usage—although there were significant overestimations between student self-reports and actual Facebook use. This finding raises the possibility that students may have difficulties gauging their actual social networking use, which could complicate efforts in studying these factors.

As time management and social distractions have been negatively correlated with academic achievement, a Swedish study examined the impact of social networking on student achievement, personality traits, trust, and self-regulation with 239 Swedish undergraduate students (N = 239). The data showed that spending 5–10 h on Facebook hindered student achievement. Additionally, those participants with higher levels of self-regulation spent less time on Facebook and demonstrated greater academic progress [30]. In closing, research studies indicate that social networking may have a negative impact on student achievement when time management is askew.

Self-regulation training and support through online social media networks enhances self-efficacy and academic performance [7, 9, 29, 35] yet there are disparities on the connection between online social media and learning based on gender. Even more so, there is limited work related to gender differences and online social media networks overall [32].

When considering gender, there are inconsistencies in the potential for fostering academic achievement via technological interactions. Demographic research on online social media network users highlight differences based on gender. According to a survey of 2,261 adults (N = 2261) conducted by the Pew Research Center's Internet and American Life Project [13] social networking sites such as Facebook, Pinterest, and Instagram are popular with women, and that overall, females subscribe to online social network platforms (71 %) to a greater extent than men (62 %). Furthermore, female undergraduate students use social media to stay connected and navigate technological tools to a greater extent than males [21]. Female undergraduate students spend more time on Facebook than males and self-report higher levels of anxiety if they are not able to access the platform [32].

With the recent surge in online social media networks over the past 10 years, and even less time relating this phenomenon to academics, sparse information exists on gender differences, academic achievement, and online social media. In an exploratory Nigerian collegiate study of gender, academics, and self-efficacy, Nigerian males were more likely to use online social media for academic pursuits as compared to females [25]. In contrast [26] cite the use of online platforms as a viable forum to close gender achievement gaps for females in science oriented careers. Specifically, the mentoring component of technologically supported communication enhances occupational identity formation through discourse related to securing and maintaining scientific roles in the labor force for women.

The benefits and disadvantages of social media networking vary throughout the world due to cultural distinctions [30]. For this reason, an examination of the impact of online social media networks within a variety of societal constructs, particularly related to academic applications, is a relevant consideration. The aims of the present chapter are twofold: (1) to examine Greek college students' perceptions of the positive and negative aspects of social networking and (Gordon, #1706) to determine whether there were any significant gender and age differences in these perceptions.

3 Methods

3.1 Research Questions

The present study employed a survey research design to examine the following two research questions:

What are Greek college students' positive and negative perceptions of social networking?

Are there significant gender and age differences in how Greek college students perceive the positive and negative aspects of social networking?

3.2 Participants

A total of 258 undergraduate and graduate students participated in this survey. The students were recruited from five classrooms from a public university in Greece. Participants were 75 % female (N = 194) and 25 % male (N = 64) and ranged in age from 18 to 42 years. No ethnic composition was recorded for this sample. The majority of the participants (49 %) reported to spend up to 5 h social networking per day while 23 % of the participants reported to spend less than 1 h social networking per day.

Technological Institute of Epirus is a public institution, which is part of the Greek tertiary education. It functions under the auspices of the Minister of Education and Religious Affairs. Students for the present study were recruited by the Department of Applied Foreign Languages in Management and Economy which is one of the 14 departments in the Institution. The mission of this department is to offer students the opportunity to acquire knowledge and skills by combining the study of foreign languages and business and management issues. Graduates are able to acquire a multifaceted education and develop their intercultural and business awareness in an increasing globalized world.

3.3 Data Collection Instrument

In addition to capturing the student demographics, the survey assessed the amount of time participants spend social networking, amount of time spent on email, and types of activities performed online (e.g. games, shop, chat, study, work, banking, etc.). It also included two scales on the positive and negative effects of social networking.

Positive Effects of Social Networking. A 25-item scale was developed to assess students' use of social networking and its potential positive effect on students' ability to organize and maintain their work, studies, and social life. For example, students were asked how the use of social networking allowed them to "collaborate with my peers frequently" or to "develop my personal and communication skills". Items followed a 5-point Likert-type scale ranging from 1 = *strongly disagree* to 5 = *strongly agree*.

Negative Effects of Social Networking. A 30-item scale was developed to assess students' use of social networking and its potential negative effect on student's ability to organize and maintain their work, studies and social life. Items followed a

5-point Likert-type scale ranging from 1 = *strongly disagree* to 5 = *strongly agree*. Sample items include: the use of social networking "scatters my attention" and the use of social networking "depresses me".

3.4 *Procedure*

Instructors were asked to forward an email to their students asking them to complete the online survey regarding their use of social networking. The response rate was 58 %.

4 Results

Survey data collected were analyzed in three steps. First, an exploratory factor analyses was conducted in order to examine underlying latent structures and relationships among the survey items. Both positive and negative survey items were factor analyzed separately. Second, Pearson's product-moment correlation coefficient analysis were conducted to examine possible relationships among identified components. Third, independent sample *t*-tests were conducted to examine significant differences among the responses in terms of gender and age.

4.1 *Factor Analyses*

An exploratory factor analysis was conducted on the survey items using varimax rotation. Positive items (N = 25) and negative items (N = 30) were examined separately. Items with factor loadings of 0.6 were retained. From the original 25 positive items, five components emerged with Eigenvalues = 5.39, 1.53, 1.30, 1.16 and 1.04 (respectively), which accounted for 74.4 % of the variance in the items. The first component, "professional skills" (n = 5 items) yielded a Cronbach's α reliability coefficient of 0.85, followed by "information" (n = 2 items) yielded $\alpha = 0.82$, "communication" (n = 2 items) yielded $\alpha = 0.77$, "academic skills" (n = 3 items) yielded $\alpha = 0.76$, and "relationships" (n = 2 items) yielded $\alpha = 0.72$ (see Table 1).

From the original 30 items examining the negative effects of social networking, five components emerged with Eigenvalues = 6.59, 2.18, 1.64, 1.61, and 1.29 (respectively), which accounted for 73.92 % of the variance in the items. The first component, "emotional health" (n = 6 items) yielded a Cronbach's $\alpha = 0.87$, followed by "academic performance" (n = 3 items) yielded $\alpha = 0.80$, "privacy" (n = 3 items) yielded $\alpha = 0.87$, "isolation" (n = 4 items) yielded $\alpha = 0.87$, and "limited exposure to other media" (n = 2 items) yielded $\alpha = 0.81$ (see Table 1).

Table 1 Positive and negative effects of social networking

Positive effects	M	SD	FL	Alpha
Professional skills				0.85
Develop my personal and communication skills	3.37	1.09	0.61	
Concentrate more on my reading and writing skills	3.12	1.08	0.85	
To prepare my professional attitude toward study and work	3.28	1.01	0.78	
Be more sustainable person	3.11	0.95	0.79	
Provide reliable and scalable services	3.08	0.92	0.61	
Information				0.82
Learn new information and knowledge	3.93	1.0	0.82	
Gain up-to-date information	3.80	0.95	0.90	
Communication				0.77
Communicate with my peers frequently	3.80	0.96	0.81	
Collaborate with my peers frequently	3.66	0.90	0.85	
Academic skills				0.76
Overcome study stress	3.21	1.10	0.78	
Complete my study more quickly	3.46	1.10	0.91	
Scrutinize my research study more easily	3.51	0.93	0.71	
Relationships				0.72
Communicate with my peers frequently	3.62	0.89	0.80	
Develop intercrossing relationships with my peers	3.36	0.96	0.77	
Negative effects				
Emotional health				0.87
Bores me	2.62	1.04	0.81	
Stresses me	2.50	1.06	0.81	
Depresses me	2.60	1.04	0.78	
Makes me feel lonely	2.70	1.18	0.76	
Makes me lazy	3.04	1.18	0.63	
Makes me more gambler	2.59	1.16	0.60	
Academic performance				0.80
Prevents me from concentrating on writing and reading skills	3.28	1.05	0.92	
Prevents me from remembering the fundamental knowledge and skills	3.08	0.97	0.82	
Scatters my attention	3.38	0.95	0.75	
Privacy				0.87
Increase privacy concerns	3.39	0.89	0.90	
Increase security concerns	3.35	0.95	0.92	
Increase intellectual property concerns	3.25	1.02	0.78	
Isolation				0.87
Prevents me from having face to face contact with my family	2.89	1.22	0.86	
Prevents me from having face to face contact with my friends	2.82	1.21	0.88	
Prevents me from participating in physical activities	3.00	1.21	0.68	

(continued)

Table 1 (continued)

Positive effects	M	SD	FL	Alpha
Prevents me from shopping in stores	2.79	1.19	0.65	
Limited exposure to other media				0.81
Prevents me from watching television	3.24	1.15	0.90	
Prevents me from reading the newspapers	3.15	1.21	0.84	

4.2 Descriptive and Correlational Analyses

Correlations were performed to examine relationships among all the variables, (see Table 2). Several significant correlations emerged between various components. For the positive components, "professional skills" was significantly correlated to "information", *r*(Gordon, #1706) = 0.36, $p = 0.01$, to "communication", *r*(Gordon, #1706) = 0.39, $p = 0.01$, and to "relationships", *r*(Gordon, #1706) = 0.42, $p = 0.01$. "Information" was significantly correlated to "communication", *r*(Gordon, #1706) = 0.33, $p = 0.01$ and to "academic skills", *r*(Gordon, #1706) = 0.37, $p = 0.01$. Lastly, "academic skills" was significantly correlated to "relationships", *r* (Gordon, #1706) = 0.35, $p = 0.01$.

Within the negative components, "emotional health" was significantly correlated to "privacy", *r*(Gordon, #1706) = 0.34, $p = 0.01$ and to "isolation", *r*(Gordon, #1706) = 0.56, $p = 0.01$. "Academic performance" was significantly correlated to "privacy", *r*(Gordon, #1706) = 0.32, $p = 0.01$. "Privacy" was significantly correlated to "isolation", *r*(Gordon, #1706) = 0.41, $p = 0.01$. Lastly, "isolation" was significantly correlated to "limited exposure to other media", *r*(Gordon, #1706) = 0.38, $p = 0.01$.

4.3 Gender and Age Differences

Independent samples *t*-tests were conducted to compare gender and age differences among the 10 composites formed (see Table 3). A number of significant differences were found among the composite variables in terms of gender and age. It was revealed that females ($M = 3.30$, $SD = 0.71$) had significantly higher scores than males ($M = 2.84$, $SD = 0.95$) on "professional skills", $t(241) = 3.47$, $p = 0.001$. Females ($M = 3.97$, $SD = 0.74$) also reported significantly higher perceptions than males ($M = 3.54$, $SD = 1.22$) on "Information", $t(241) = 2.50$, $p = 0.02$. Finally, females ($M = 3.51$, $SD = 0.81$) reported significantly higher perceptions than males ($M = 3.03$, $SD = 0.92$) on "academic skills", $t(241) = 3.52$, $p = 0.001$ and on "relationships" ($M = 3.59$, $SD = 0.95$) versus ($M = 3.16$, $SD = 0.95$), $t(241) = 3.21$, $p = 0.01$.

Table 2 Zero-order correlations among all variables

Variables	1	2	3	4	5	6	7	8	9	10
1.Professional skills	1.00	0.36**	0.39**	0.52**	0.42**	0.17	−0.01	0.11	0.11	0.13*
2.Information		1.00	0.33**	0.37**	0.41**	−0.19**	0.06	0.04	−0.11	0.09
3.Communication			1.00	0.30**	0.37**	0.06	0.15*	0.09	0.09	0.06
4.Academic skills				1.00	0.35**	−0.06	0.10	0.09	0.10	0.16*
5.Relationships					1.00	0.03	0.15*	0.05	0.16*	0.20**
6.Emotional health						1.00	0.27**	0.34**	0.56**	0.29**
7.Academic performance							1.00	0.32**	0.27**	0.27**
8.Privacy								1.00	0.41**	.26**
9.Isolation									1.00	.38**
10.Limited exposure to other media										1.00
Mean	3.19	3.87	3.73	3.39	3.49	2.68	3.25	3.33	2.88	3.19
SD	0.80	0.89	0.84	0.86	0.82	0.87	0.84	0.85	1.03	1.08

*significant at the 0.05 **significant at the 0.01 level

Table 3 Positive and negative effects based on age and gender

Variables	Female		Male		*t*-test	*p*
	M	SD	M	SD		
1. Professional skills	3.30	0.71	2.84	0.95	3.47	0.001
2. Information	3.97	0.74	3.54	1.22	2.50	0.02
3. Communication	3.80	0.78	3.53	0.99	1.92	0.06
4. Academic skills	3.51	0.81	3.03	0.92	3.52	0.001
5. Relationships	3.59	0.76	3.16	0.92	3.21	0.001
1. Emotional health	2.68	0.88	2.66	0.83	0.13	0.90
2. Academic performance	3.38	0.78	2.82	0.89	4.37	0.001
3. Privacy	3.39	0.80	3.12	0.96	1.96	0.05
4. Isolation	2.88	1.07	2.87	0.89	0.04	0.97
5. Limited exposure to other media	3.22	1.06	3.10	1.16	0.69	0.49
Variables	18–22		22–32		*t*-test	*p*
	M	SD	M	SD		
1. Professional skills	3.18	0.78	3.23	0.89	−.33	0.74
2. Information	3.90	0.82	3.61	1.25	1.30	0.20
3. Communication	3.72	0.86	3.87	0.75	−1.11	0.27
4. Academic skills	3.42	0.84	3.17	0.93	1.46	0.15
5. Relationships	3.49	0.84	3.44	0.70	0.38	0.71
1. Emotional health	2.66	0.88	2.78	0.86	−0.75	0.46
2. Academic performance	3.26	0.83	3.23	0.91	0.19	0.85
3. Privacy	3.31	0.84	3.43	0.90	−0.78	0.44
4. Isolation	2.85	1.07	3.16	0.63	−2.45	0.02
5. Limited exposure to other media	3.20	1.10	3.24	0.92	−0.25	0.80

Within the negative components of the scale, only one significant difference emerged with females ($M = 3.38$, $SD = 0.78$) reporting more negative perceptions than males ($M = 2.81$, $SD = 0.89$) on "academic performance", $t(241) = 4.37$, $p = 0.001$. Finally, in terms of age differences, one significant difference was found with students between the ages of 18–22 ($M = 2.85$, $SD = 1.07$) reporting lower perceptions on "isolation", $t(241) = -2.45$, $p = 0.02$, than students between the ages of 22–32 ($M = 3.16$, $SD = 0.63$).

5 Discussion

Across varied geographical regions and subject domains, previous studies cite social influence and social relations as strong motivational factors for student participation in online social media networks [31, 35]. This study adds to this knowledge by providing an understanding of how Greek college students perceive the positive and negative aspects of social media and by examining these perceptions in terms of gender and age differences. In alignment with past research, the Greek participants viewed the positive aspects of social networking in terms of five different areas. The largest composite of professional skills described the use of social networking as a way to develop skills—personal, communicative, and academic. Participants also viewed social networking as a valuable form of information. Two items with the largest means both belonged to the information composite indicating the strong preference for social networking as a means towards learning new information and staying up-to-date on information. Other positive effects of social networking included its facilitative role in developing and maintaining relationships, as well as in aiding the development of academic skills.

Studies on gender differences are limited and inconsistent, although in science occupational domains, online social media networks via mentoring relationships positively influence identity formation [26]. Within the current study, the positive effects of social networking were more pronounced for female students than male students as females reported significantly higher scores on four out of the fives scale composites. This finding suggests that females may benefit more from social networking than males within this population. No differences were found on positive composites between the two age groups.

Congruent with prior research throughout the world, current findings show that students engaged in the use of social media form relationships and maintain expedient personal contact with friends [3, 8, 16, 28]. In addition, students reported utilizing this type of media for instructional practices. For the participants in this study, online social media networking as a source of knowledge development was a particularly potent reason to utilize this technological platform [4, 31]. As the current generation of collegiate students is adept at the use of online social media, the focus of effective instruction in academia has adjusted to group projects, self and peer reflection, and an array of online formal and informal tools to facilitate student learning by capitalizing on networking social structures [6]. These research findings suggest that aside from extending personal contacts, students in Northern Greece recognize the benefits of online social media networks in supporting educational development.

Past research has indicated that social networking is associated with negative effects on student academic achievement [18, 28]. However, in the present study, there were some striking variations in negative effects related to emotional well-being, isolation, and security concerns. Although, online social media networks have been found to promote acculturation, positive relationship building, and psychological well-being within college students [7, 31, 35], findings from current research identified negative aspects of social networking including stress, depression, compulsion, loneliness and boredom.

In addition, students described negative effects in terms of isolation. This perception stemmed from the role of social networking in preventing students' face to face contact with friends and family. Students also described an increased concern with privacy and social networking. In contrast, studies with young students show a tendency to be less concerned with security risks or have an inflated trust of people through online platforms [15], and that trust is not a primary inhibitor of online social media use [30]. Some students were also interested in finding time to engage with more traditional media. Further, significant differences in social networking between gender and age revealed that older students reported a heightened sense of isolation as a result of social networking.

6 Implications and Conclusions

There are several implications associated with the present findings in terms of providing support to augment the benefits of social networking for this sample. First, it seems that females tended to benefit more from the use of social media than males. This finding could indicate that classes with higher percentages of females (e.g. education classes, nursing classes) which incorporate social networking into their courses, best support student needs. Furthermore, the only non-significant gender difference on the positive composites was communication, indicating that all students consider social networking as a viable source of communication. Second, the highest rated item, using social networking to "learn new information and knowledge" ($M = 3.93$), possibly indicates that social networking could be used in courses to promote task interest by providing a vehicle for learning new information. Finally, from an age perspective, the discovery that the "older" group reported higher isolation is an illuminating finding. Perhaps younger students are more accustomed to these types of learning technologies which also has implications for instruction.

In an effort to counter the negative effects of social networking on academic achievement, instructors should teach students how to use self-regulation strategies to deal with social distractions [18]. Promoting self-regulation strategies through modelling is particularly crucial in online settings where students are inherently self-directed as compared to traditional classroom forums [7, 9, 23, 29]. Previous findings indicate that students with low self-regulation skills or high levels of distractedness tend to perform at lower levels than their peers [30].

Further, the results of the present study should be interpreted with caution because the impact of social networking does not necessarily transcend across cultural contexts [30]. According to [14], rather than creating homogeneity across geographical and cultural backgrounds, regional differences create distinctive uses for social media networking sites and foster intertwined differentiated groups. For example, research in the United States and the United Kingdom tend to describe the development of individual relationships; however, in other parts of the world the family unit and cultural experiences steer interactions as a cohesive group rather than on an individual basis. Further, members of collectivist societies may be less likely to participate in online social media network systems due to the overarching importance of family, close friends, and group goals [17]. Thus, research interpretations centred on the impact of social media networks should be extended to account for diverse cultural backgrounds and academic disciplines. In fact, more studies are needed to assess the impact of online social media networks on achievement through a lens which accounts for cultural variations. Finally, due to a small sample size, more research should be conducted to establish the psychometric properties of the scales across cultures.

References

1. Altuna J, Aydin H, Burham O, Amenabav N (2013) The digital user of social networks: a comparative, transcultural and intergenerational study. Int Online J Educ Sci 5(3):598–610
2. Bandura A (1997) Self-efficacy: the exercise of control. Freeman, New York
3. Bernal C, Angulo F (2012) Interactions of young Andalusian people inside social networks. Dossier, pp 25–30. doi:10.3916/C40-2013-02-02
4. Bosch TE (2009) Using online social networking for teaching and learning: Facebook use at the University of Cape Town. Commun S Afr J Commun Theor Res 35(Gordon, #1706):185–200. doi:10.1080/02500160903250648
5. Boyd DM, Ellison MB (2008) Social network sites: definition, history, and scholarship. J Comput Mediat Commun 13:210–230. doi:10.1111/j.1083-6101.2007.00393.x
6. Cadima R, Ojeda J, Monguet JM (2012) Social networks and performance in distributed learning communities. Educ Technol Soc 15(Gordon, #1706):296–304
7. Cheng K-H, Liang J-C, Tsai C-C (2013) University students' online academic help seeking: the role of self-regulation and information commitments. Internet High Educ 16:70–77. doi:10.1016/j.iheduc.2012.02.002
8. Cheung CMK, Chiu P-Y, Lee MKO (2011) Online social networks: why do students use facebook? Comput Hum Behav 27:1337–1343. doi:10.1016/j.chb.2010.07.028
9. Cho K, Cho MH (2013) Training of self-regulated learning skills on a social network system. Soc Psychol Educ 16:617–634. doi:10.1007/s11218-013-9229-3
10. Clafferty EM (2011) Facilitating social networking within the student experience. Int J Electr Eng Educ 48(3):245–251
11. Dabbagh N, Kitsantas A (2012) Personal learning environments, social media, and self-regulated learning: a natural formula for connecting formal and informal learning. Internet High Educ 15:3–8. doi:10.1016/j.iheduc.2011.06.002
12. Dabbagh N, Kitsantas A (2013) The role of social media in self-regulated learning. Int J Web Based Communities (IJWBC) (Special Issue, Social Networking and Education as a Catalyst Social Change) 9(Gordon, #1706):256–273. doi:10.1504/ijwbc.2013.053248
13. Duggan M, Brenner J (2013) The demographics of social media users-2012. Pew research center website. http://pewinternet.org/~/media//Files/Reports/2013/PIP_SocialMediaUsers.pdf. Accessed 19 May 2014
14. Global social media impact study (2013) ERC project 2011-AdG-295486 social network sites and social media. http://gsmis.org/. Accessed 19 May 2014
15. Gross R, Acquisti A (2005) Information revelation and privacy in online social networks. In: Proceedings of WPES'05, pp 71–80. ACM, Alexandria, VA. http://www.heinz.cmu.edu/~acquisti/papers/privacy-facebook-gross-acquisti.pdf. Accessed 19 May 2014
16. Hew KF (2011) Students' and teachers' use of Facebook. Comput Hum Behav 27:662–676. doi:10.1016/j.chb.2010.11.020
17. Jackson LA, Wang J-L (2013) Cultural differences in social networking site use: a comparative study of China and the United States. Comput Hum Behav 29:910–921. doi:10.1016/j.chb.2012.11.024
18. Junco R (2012) Too much face and not enough books: the relationship between multiple indices of Facebook use and academic performance. Comput Hum Behav 28:187–198. doi:10.1016/j.chb.2011.08.026

19. Junco R (2013) Comparing actual and self-reported measures of Facebook use. Comput Hum Behav 29:626–631. doi:10.1016/j.chb.2012.11.007
20. Junco R, Heibergert G, Loken E (2011) The effect of Twitter on college student engagement and grades. J Comput Assist Learn 27:119–132. doi:10.1111/j.1365-2729.2010.00387.x
21. Kimbrough AM, Guadagno RE, Muscanell NL, Dill J (2013) Gender differences in mediated communication: women connect more than do men. Comput Hum Behav 29:896–900. doi:10.1016/j.chb.2012.12.005
22. Kitsantas A, Chow A (2007) College students perceived threat and preference for seeking help in traditional, distributed, and distance learning environments. Comput Educ 48:383–395. doi:10.1016/j.compedu.2005.01.008
23. Kitsantas A, Dabbagh N (2010) Learning to learn with integrative learning technologies. Information Age Publishing, Inc, Charlotte
24. Kitsantas A, Reiser RA, Doster J (2004) Developing self-regulated learners: goal setting, self-evaluation, and organizational signals during acquisition of procedural skills. J Exp Educ 72(Gordon, #1706):269–287. doi:10.3200/JEXE.72.4.269-287
25. Oladejo MA, Adelua OO, Ige NA (2013) Age, gender, and computer self-efficacy as correlates of social media usage for scholarly works in Nigeria. In: Proceedings of the international conference on e-Learning, Cape Town, South Africa, pp 316–320
26. Murthy D, Rodriguez A, Kinstler L (2013) The potential for virtual communities to promote diversity in the sciences. Curr Sociol 61(7):1003–1020. doi:10.1177/0011392113502994
27. Myers SB, Endres MA, Ruddy ME, Zelikovsky N (2012) Psychology graduate training in the era of online social networking. Train Educ Prof Psychol 6(1):28–36. doi:10.1037/a0026388
28. Paul JA, Baker HM, Cochran JD (2012) Effects of online social networking on student academic performance. Comput Hum Behav 28:2117–2127
29. Rizzuto TE, LeDoux J, Hatala JP (2009) It's not just what you know, it's who you know: testing a model of the relative importance of social networks to academic performance. Soc Psychol Educ 12:175–189. doi:10.1007/s11218-008-9080-0
30. Rouis S, Limayem M, Salehi-Sangari E (2011) Electron J Res Educ Psychol 9(3):961–994
31. Sánchez RA, Cortijo V, Javed U (2014) Students' perceptions of Facebook for academic purposes. Comput Educ 70:138–149. doi:10.1016/j.compedu.2013.08.012
32. Thompson SH, Lougheed E (2012) Frazzled by Facebook? An exploratory study of gender differences in social network communication among undergraduate men and women. Coll Student J 46(1):88–98
33. Vanderhoven E, Schellens T, Valcke M (2013) Exploring the usefulness of school education about risks on social network sites: a survey study. J Media Literacy Educ 5(1):285–294
34. Wang S-L, Wu P-Y (2008) The role of feedback and self-efficacy on web-based learning: the social cognitive perspective. Comput Educ 51:1589–1598
35. Yu AY, Tian SW, Vogel D, Kwok RC-W (2010) Can learning be virtually boosted? An investigation of online social networking impacts. Comput Educ 55:1494–1503
36. Zimmerman BJ, Kitsantas A (1997) Developmental phases in self-regulation: shifting from process goals to outcome goals. J Educ Psychol 89(1):29–36. doi:10.1037/0022-0663.89.1.29

Effects of Social Networking on Learning: The Opinions of Italian University Students

Donatella Persico, Carlo Chiorri, Maria Ferraris and Francesca Pozzi

Abstract While the use of social networks (SNs) and social media is increasingly permeating all sectors of the global society, in Italy there is an ongoing debate about its advantages and drawbacks for learning, especially within formal educational contexts. In order to contribute to such a debate, a study has been conducted, aimed to investigate the Italian university students' beliefs about the positive and negative effects of social networking on their learning and to identify any correlation between such beliefs and the students' characteristics. This chapter reports and discusses the results of the study, which was based on the data collected through a survey to 336 Italian university students (F = 63.6, 83.8 % aged below 32). Results revealed that Italian university students perceive social networks as useful tools for both improving their learning and connecting with their peers, but also that they are aware of their undesirable consequences, such as experiencing negative emotions, losing concentration and being prevented from engaging in extra-academic activities.

Keywords Social networking · Social networks · Social media · Web 2.0 · Learning · Perceived effect · University students · Higher education

---

D. Persico (✉) · M. Ferraris · F. Pozzi
Istituto Per Le Tecnologie Didattiche, Consiglio Nazionale Delle Ricerche, Genoa, Italy
e-mail: persico@itd.cnr.it

M. Ferraris
e-mail: ferraris@itd.cnr.it

F. Pozzi
e-mail: pozzi@itd.cnr.it

C. Chiorri
Dipartimento Di Scienze Della Formazione, Università Di Genova, Genoa, Italy
e-mail: carlo.chiorri@gmail.com

T. Issa et al. (eds.), *Social Networking and Education*,
Lecture Notes in Social Networks, DOI 10.1007/978-3-319-17716-8_10

1 Introduction

This chapter, as the whole of this book, addresses a controversial issue, namely, the effects of the use of social networks on learning, and it does so by investigating Italian students' perceptions about this issue.

Before getting to the heart of the matter, some clarifications about the terminology that will be used in this contribution are needed. First of all, the term 'social networking', in the following, is used to indicate the use of the internet from PCs and mobile devices to create and share content within communities of people with similar interests. This can be done primarily by using one or many of the well-known social network or social media systems such as Facebook, Twitter, Instagram, Linked-In, Google+, Flickr, SlideShare, Delicious, YouTube. These are web-based applications through which users can create a personal profile and build a network of peers with whom such exchanges are privileged. Alternatively, social networking can take place through one or more internet communication and sharing services such as wikis, blogs, podcasts, clouds, etc., that are often referred to as 'Web 2.0' tools. All of these tools are believed to offer users' unprecedented affordances to research, create, communicate, share and thus learn. The underlying assumption for this belief is that online collaboration and virtual communities make constructivist and connectivist learning processes possible, thus enabling deep understanding and problem solving of complex matters [6, 24] and enhancing the social component of learning, which is an essential aspect for a community of inquiry to be effective [22, 26, 35].

Consistent with these assumptions, a large body of literature indicates that social networks are not only leisure environments, but they also allow learning processes [18, 30], although often informally and incidentally. As a matter of fact, the intertwining of informal, online learning with formal learning processes is becoming a frequent scenario, often considered desirable [23]. As a consequence, many researchers and practitioners [18, 21, 31] claim that teachers in schools and lecturers in universities should learn how best to take advantage of this scenario, in which social media play an essential role to enhance the learning experiences of their students. However, in many schools and universities mobile devices and their use are still banned [29]. Winters [36] maintains that one of the main reasons why the benefits of the new media are not yet manifesting themselves in educational systems, is that most attempts to promote them are not involving teachers, i.e. the main agents of change in any educational system.

On the other hand, there are also authors who point out important drawbacks of the use of these tools [1, 2, 4, 15, 33]. Among these shortcomings, the most commonly cited are their distractive power, the fact that they may induce reading habits that hinder prolonged concentration and focus, the risks of addiction, of privacy infringements and non-desired neglection of other interests.

The purpose of this chapter is to contribute to this debate, assuming that there may be both positive and negative influences of social networks on learning. The study belongs to a wider, international investigation, whereby different researchers in different countries have used the same survey to collect the opinions of a sample of students about the pros and cons of the use of social networks with regard to their study skills and their ability to achieve their learning objectives. In particular, the aim of this chapter is to investigate the opinions of Italian university students who completed the survey on the perceived effects of the use of social networks on their learning as well as to identify possible correlations of the main positive and negative factors and students' background characteristics, such as age, gender, field of study, etc.

In particular, our research questions were:

- What are the beliefs of the Italian university students about the (positive and negative) effects of social networking on learning?
- Is there any correlation between the effects identified (both positive and negative) and the students' characteristics and social networking habits?

2 Use of Social Media: The Current Landscape

Studies concerning the use of social media and their impact in various sectors of life show that internet and social networks are increasingly permeating the society.

A literature review concerning social media technologies in U.S. higher education [5] provides a clear, though geographically limited picture of this phenomenon. Among others, it cites a national poll by the Harvard Institute of Politics [12], according to which over 90 % of students at 4 year colleges reported having Facebook profiles. College students' use of Facebook mostly reflects a one-to-many style, in which students create content and share it with others. Students interacted more frequently with existing friends than with new connections and were more likely to observe content than to produce it [20]. As for teachers, Seaman and Tinti-Kane [28] examined the impact of social media sites on personal, professional, and instructional use by higher education faculty members in the U.S. They reported that "[…] a clear pattern has emerged from this series of reports—faculty are much more willing to embrace social media in their personal lives than they are to use it for professional or teaching purposes." [28], p. 3.

As for the alleged positive impact of social networks in education, Tess [32] underlines that empirical evidence, so far, is missing.

Indeed, a few studies have investigated the students' opinions about social networks use, with special emphasis on negative aspects. An Australian study on adolescents showed that primary reasons for the non-use of these sites were "lack of motivation, poor use of time, preference for other forms of communication, preference for engaging in other activities, cybersafety concerns, and a dislike of self-presentation online" [2], p. 396. Another study [33] investigated the reasons why some university students decided not to use social network sites, finding that these students perceive them as a potentially addictive waste of time, which might violate privacy. Many of them also claimed that they did not trust virtual friendships and did not like sharing personal ideas and photos online. A survey addressing students of four Spanish universities [3] investigated various aspects concerning the use of Web 2.0 tools for collaborative learning and group work among university students. The authors concluded that, apart from Facebook and Twitter, students still do not feel comfortable enough with uses of Web 2.0 tools for learning. However, as pointed out by Gewerc et al. [9], the choice of the tools is not the key problem: student-centred pedagogical approaches should promote the ecological framework within which collaborative learning processes are to take place. On the same vein, Gikas and Grant [10] used focus groups to investigate students' opinions about the use of social media and Web 2.0 tools on mobile devices. Among the advantages, they mentioned the affordances of technology for 'anywhere-anytime interaction', as well as collaboration and engagement in content creation. Among the disadvantages, frustration due to fear of failure of technology, to the small size of the devices used and to the tools' distractive power were the most mentioned.

To the best of our knowledge, only a few studies about the impact of social networks on education and, more broadly, on daily life, were carried out on Italian students. Among these, a recent study [34] highlighted that while 35 % of the world population is connected, and 26 % has an account on at least one social network, in Italy, 58 % of the population is connected (around 35 million people), while 42 % (that is around 26 million people) has an account on a social network. Besides, the penetration of mobile technology in Italy is considerably high (158 %, that is, more than 1,5 device per person). Another study [11] pointed out that in Italy (as all over the world) there are differences in the kinds of devices and use of social networks across generations: the so-called 'Millennials' (born approximately between early '80s and early 2000s) prefer smartphones and visual-oriented social networks (such as Instangram), the GenX (born between mid-'60s and early '80s) prefer tablets, the Baby Boomers (born between 1946 and mid-'60s) still opt for PCs and laptops. Facebook seems to be the most used social network in Italy, regardless of the users' age. Furthermore, two other studies [14, 27] reported and analyzed data about some of the most important variables affecting the digital divide, which still characterizes this country.

However, the studies addressing the impact of social media in Italy rarely focused on learning at university. For example, Milan [19] focused on the way this phenomenon is affecting the Italian market while Gatti Casati and Salsa [8] investigated the impact on people behavior in the work place. Actually, there are a few reports about single experiences/practices of use of social networks in specific educational contexts or general reviews about the potentialities offered by these technologies (see, e.g., [25]). For instance, Mazzoni and Iannone [17] investigated the way in which social network sites are used by "emerging adults", defined as "young people in the transition from adolescence to adulthood, and particularly those in their last year of high school or at university", to support their transition between adolescence and adulthood. However, no systematic study has been carried out so far in Italy with the aim of addressing the issue of how learners in higher education use social networks and what is the perceived impact of these tools on their learning. Thus, this chapter fills a gap in research by presenting evidence about the opinions of Italian university students on the pros and cons of social networking with regard to their study habits and, more generally, their learning.

3 Research Method, Data Collection and Sampling Technique

In order to investigate students' perceptions about advantages and disadvantages of social networking on learning, a web survey was designed. It comprised three sections: (1) background information about the respondents (age, gender, field of study, daily hours spent on social networks and using e-mail, whether the internet was used for specific tasks or activities such as studying, playing games, connecting with acquaintances, etc.); (Gordon, #1706) positive effects of social networking on study activities (25 items, see Table 1) and (3) negative effects of social networking on study activities (30 items, see Table 2). Both Sects. 2 and 3 items required participants to rate the extent to which each effect of social networking was true of them on a 5-point, Likert-type scale. After each of these two sections, additional open-ended questions allowed participants to enter their comments. Both positive

Table 1 Positive aspects investigated by the survey

	Social networking allows me to:
Pos 1	Learn new information and knowledge
Pos 2	Gain up-to-date information
Pos 3	Be more aware of global issues/local issues
Pos 4	To remember facts/aspects of the past
Pos 5	Communicate with my peers frequently
Pos 6	Collaborate with my peers frequently
Pos 7	Communicate with my peers from different universities
Pos 8	Communicate with my different communities
Pos 9	Develop intercrossing relationships with my peers (i.e. Artistic talents, sport and common interests)
Pos 10	Study independently
Pos 11	Overcome study stress
Pos 12	Complete my study more quickly
Pos 13	Understand and solve study problems easily
Pos 14	Scrutinize my research study more easily
Pos 15	Develop my personal and communication skills
Pos 16	Concentrate more on my reading and writing skills
Pos 17	To prepare my professional attitude toward study and work
Pos 18	Be more sustainable person
Pos 19	Provide reliable and scalable services
Pos 20	Become more "Greener" in my activities
Pos 21	Reduce carbon footprint in my activities
Pos 22	Acquire new acquaintances—work related
Pos 23	Acquire new acquaintances—friendship relationship
Pos 24	Acquire new acquaintances—romance relationship
Pos 25	Do whatever I want, say whatever I want, and be whoever I want

Table 2 Negative aspects investigated by the survey

	The use of social networking:
Neg 1	Prevents me from concentrating more on writing and reading skills
Neg 2	Prevents me from remembering the fundamental knowledge and skills
Neg 3	Scatters my attention
Neg 4	Decreases my grammar and proofreading skills
Neg 5	Decreases my deep thinking
Neg 6	Distracts me easily
Neg 7	Prevents me from participating in social activities
Neg 8	Prevents me from completing my work/study on time
Neg 9	Makes me sick and unhealthy
Neg 10	Bores me
Neg 11	Stresses me
Neg 12	Depresses me
Neg 13	Makes me feel lonely
Neg 14	Makes me lazy
Neg 15	Makes me addict
Neg 16	Makes me more gambler
Neg 17	Makes me insecure to release my personal details from the theft of personal information
Neg 18	Makes me receive an immoral images and information from unscrupulous people and it is difficult to act against them at present
Neg 19	Prevents me from having face to face contact with my family
Neg 20	Prevents me from having face to face contact with my friends
Neg 21	Prevents me from participating in physical activities
Neg 22	Prevents me from shopping in stores
Neg 23	Prevents me from watching television
Neg 24	Prevents me from reading the newspapers
Neg 25	Prevents me from talking on the phone/mobile
Neg 26	Prevents me from completing my work on time
Neg 27	Prevents me from completing my study on time
Neg 28	Increase privacy concerns
Neg 29	Increase security concerns
Neg 30	Increase intellectual property concerns

and negative effects concerned cognitive (e.g. "social networking scatters my attention"), social (e.g. "social networking allows me to communicate with my peers frequently"), organizational (e.g. "social networking prevents me from completing my study on time") and security (e.g. "social networking increase my privacy concerns") aspects. The full range of items is reported in Tables 1 and 2.

The survey design was coordinated by the editors of this book, and the development of the items was the result of a negotiation with the authors of the various chapters. The survey was delivered in English, assuming that most of the Italian university students would be able to understand it, but answers to open-ended questions were accepted in Italian.

The survey was administered in Italy in 2013. A snowball sampling was used to reach the highest possible number of university students of all grades (undergraduate, graduate, master and PhD students). the use of this sampling technique prevented us to control the total number of the students reached by the survey, but the total number of respondents was 553. However, 217 cases were discarded because they were largely incomplete. Subsequent analyses were therefore carried out on 336 cases. Multiple imputation was used to handle missing values, which never exceeded 3 % in any of the variables considered. Results reported below are thus based on pooled statistics.

4 Data Analysis and Results

We used factor analysis to synthesize the information provided by the items of positive and negative effects of using social networks, derived factor scores and used them as criteria in a multivariate general linear model that specified background variables as predictors. This analysis allowed us to test how items of Sects. 2 and 3 could be grouped into a smaller set of latent variables grounding on their pattern of correlations and how the scores on these latent variables were associated to demographic and networking habits of the respondents.

In the following sections, we first provide data about the main features of the sample, then we provide a bird's eye on the positive and negative aspects of social networking and finally we report on the results of the factor analysis.

4.1 Sample Features

Participants were mostly females (63.6 %) and younger than 32 years (Table 3).

The field of study of participants was mainly humanities, followed by science and engineering (Table 4).

The majority of the respondents reported to devote less than an hour per day to social networking, while most of the remaining people reported spending between 1 and 5 h on this activity (Table 5). As for e-mail, an even larger proportion of the respondents reported using it only for less than an hour per day (Table 5). These

Table 3 Age of participants

Age range	Percentage
18–22	32.8
22–32	51.0
32–42	7.8
42–52	6.9
Over 52	1.5

Table 4 Field of study of participants

Field of study	Percentage
Humanities	40.0
Science and engineering	20.9
Health sciences	14.3
Economic and law	13.4
Information technology	6.3
Art and design	3.3
Others please specify	1.8

Table 5 Time spent on social networking and e-mail

Time spent	Social networking (%)	E-mail (%)
Less than an hour	53.4	71.6
Up to 5 h	40.6	23.9
5–10 h	4.8	4.2
10–20 h	0.6	0.3
Over 20 h	0.6	0.0

results suggest that very few of the respondents seem to be addicted to the use of these tools. In order to deal with sparse data in some categories of the two variables, in subsequent analyses these variables were dichotomously recoded as "less than one hour" and "more than one hour".

Participants reported that they use the internet for e-mailing (84.4 %), studying (78.8 %), seeking travel information and reservations (50.1 %) and chatting (48.5 %) (Fig. 1). Nobody reported using the internet for buying stocks or investing online, hence we did not report this category. Further uses, as reported in the open-ended questions, were "listening to music", "watching films", "information searching", "social network usage", "news reading", "practicing a hobby".

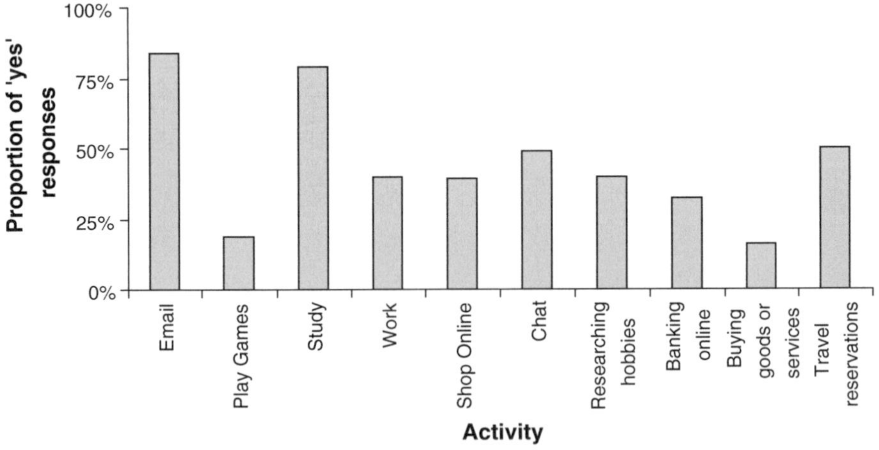

Fig. 1 Uses of the internet (respondents could choose more than one option)

5 Positive and Negative Aspects of Social Networking

5.1 Positive Aspects

As shown in Fig. 2, the highest mean ratings for positive effects were those of items 5 ("Communicate with my peers frequently"), 2 ("Gain up-to-date information") and 1 ("Learn new information and knowledge"), while the lowest ratings where those of items 16 ("Concentrate more on my reading and writing skills"), 24 ("Acquire new acquaintances—romance relationship") and 12 ("Complete my study more quickly"). Most of the open-ended answers stressed the importance of communication with peers, including appreciation for practical aspects like speed, ease and low-cost of contacts, as well as democracy of relationships.

5.2 Negative Aspects

The highest mean ratings for negative effects were those of items 6 ("Distracts me easily"), 3 ("Scatters my attention") and 1 ("Makes me lazy"), while the lowest were those of items 16 ("Makes me more gambler"), 22 ("Prevents me from shopping in stores") and 19 ("Prevents me from having face to face contact with my family") (Fig. 3). These data are consistent with answers to the open-ended questions, which include many references to the risk of dependence and/or addiction; loss of contact with real life, loss of concentration and risk of distraction from study.

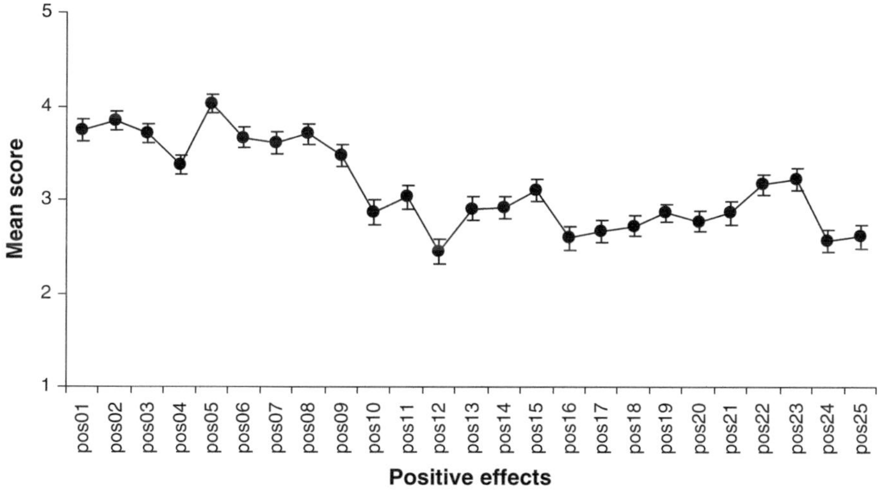

Fig. 2 Mean level of agreement with the positive and negative aspects of social networking (*1* strongly disagree; *5* strongly agree)

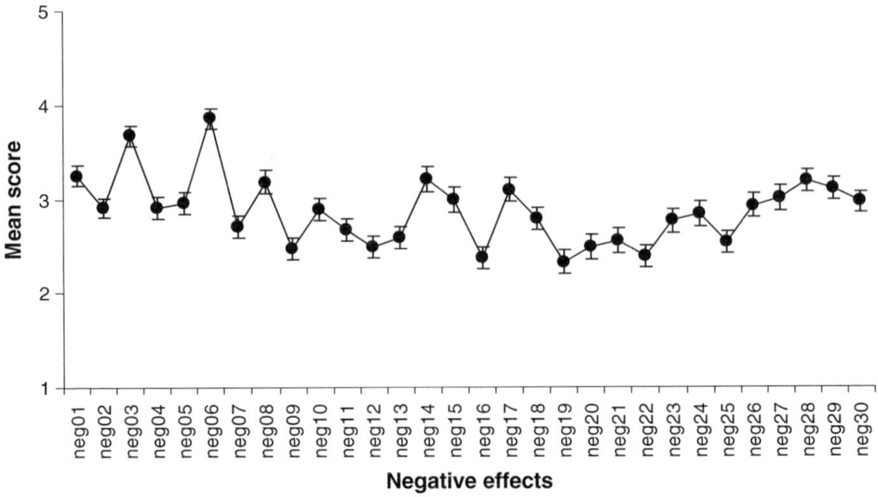

Fig. 3 Mean level of agreement with the positive and negative aspects of social networking (*1* strongly disagree; *5* strongly agree)

5.3 *Factor Analysis of Positive and Negative Aspects of Social Networking*

The simple inspection of item mean scores does not allow a parsimonious interpretation of results. Hence, we performed a factor analysis to synthesize the information and group items in a smaller set of composite variables.

As a first step in factor analyzing the students' positive and negative ways to use the social networking, we examined the item score distributions. As pointed out by Muthén and Kaplan [1985], item score distributions can be considered as substantially non-normal when their skewness and kurtosis are out of the [−1; +1] range. Actually, some items had skewness and/or kurtosis out this range, but since the departure from normality appeared to be modest (highest absolute skewness and kurtosis were 1.14 and 1.26, respectively) we decided to consider items as continuous indicators and to use Principal Axis Factoring in subsequent analyses.

The next step was to identify possible redundancies among the items, i.e., couples or groups of items whose correlation was high enough (i.e., >|0.65|) to suggest that they were basically mapping the same content, and thus that their composite score (i.e., the mean of scores of too much correlated items) could be used instead. We inspected the item correlation matrix and identified some couples or groups of items with high intercorrelations (Table 6). For these couples/groups of items a composite score (i.e., mean of item scores) was computed and used in subsequent analyses.

Items neg26 and neg27 ("Prevents me from completing my work on time" and "Prevents me from completing my study on time") were excluded since, as also

Table 6 New variables generated after screening for redundant items of positive and negative ways to use the social networking

Original items	Original content	New items	New content
pos01, pos02	Learn new information and knowledge Gain up-to-date information	pos0102	Get new information
pos05, pos06	Communicate with my peers frequently Collaborate with my peers frequently	pos0506	Communicate/collaborate with my peers frequently
pos07, pos08	Communicate with my peers from different universities Communicate with my different communities	pos0708	Communicate with my peers from different universities/communities
pos12, pos13, pos14	Complete my study more quickly Understand and solve study problems easily Scrutinize my research study more easily	pos121314	Studying more easily
pos20, pos21	Become more "Greener" in my activities Reduce carbon footprint in my activities	pos2021	Be environment-friendly
pos23, pos24	Acquire new acquaintances —friendship relationship Acquire new acquaintances —romance relationship	pos2324	Acquire new acquaintances
neg10, neg11, neg12, neg13	Bores me Stresses me Depresses me Makes me feel lonely	neg10111213	Feel bored, stressed, depressed or lonely
neg19, neg20, neg21	Prevents me from having face to face contact with my family Prevents me from having face to face contact with my friends Prevents me from participating in physical activities	neg192021	Prevents engagement in physical and social activities
neg28, neg29, neg30	Increase privacy concerns Increase security concerns Increase intellectual property concerns	neg282930	Raise confidentiality concerns

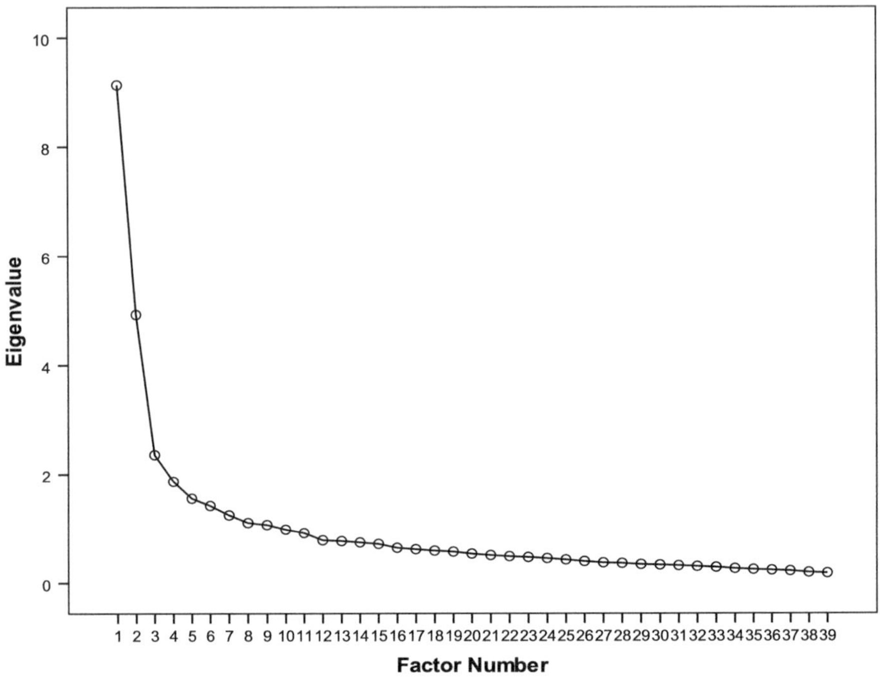

Fig. 4 Scree-plot for the factor analysis carried out on positive and negative ways to use the social networking

shown by their high intercorrelations, they were overlapping with the content of item neg08 ("Prevents me from completing my work/study on time").

We then factor analyzed the pooled correlation matrix using Principal Axis Factoring and Promax rotation. The scree-plot (Fig. 4) suggested that at least four factors should be extracted, as the line begins to level off after the fourth component.

However, we examined 4-, 5- and 6-factor solutions, and we found that the 5-factor solution most approached a simple solution (i.e., each item having a substantial [>0.30] loading on only one factor, with small/negligible loadings on the other factors) while accounting for a substantial amount of variance (50.88 %) (Table 7 Pattern matrix from the exploratory factor analysis on positive and negative ways to use the social networking7).

According to the content of the items with the highest loadings on each factor, factors were labelled as:

- F1: Widening learning opportunities and enhancing autonomy (WLO)
- F2: Causing negative emotions (NE)
- F3: Hindering concentration and study effectiveness (HCE)
- F4: Limiting extra-study activities (LESA)
- F5: Improving social interactions and global awareness (ISA)

Table 7 Pattern matrix from the exploratory factor analysis on positive and negative ways to use the social networking

	Factor				
Item	1	2	3	4	5
pos0102_Get new information	**0.42**	0.02	−0.05	−0.15	0.29
pos03_Be more aware of global issues/local issues	**0.34**	0.07	−0.08	−0.09	**0.35**
pos04_To remember facts/aspects of the past	0.24	0.05	−0.05	−0.06	**0.35**
pos0506_Communicate/collaborate with my peers frequently	0.16	−0.09	0.06	0.07	**0.71**
pos0708_Communicate with my peers from different universities or communities	0.16	0.16	−0.05	0.05	**0.67**
pos09_Develop intercrossing relationships with my peers (i.e. Artistic talents, sport and common interests)	0.27	−0.03	0.02	0.11	**0.47**
pos10_Study independently	**0.74**	0	0.04	−0.05	−0.04
pos11_Overcome study stress	**0.37**	0.04	−0.06	0.09	0.19
pos121314_Studying more easily	**0.8**	−0.05	0.03	0.06	−0.03
pos15_Develop my personal and communication skills	**0.44**	−0.02	−0.19	0.17	0.21
pos16_Concentrate more on my reading and writing skills	**0.62**	0.14	−0.23	0.03	−0.03
pos17_To prepare my professional attitude toward study and work	**0.82**	−0.01	−0.01	0.06	−0.02
pos18_Be more sustainable person	**0.72**	−0.02	0.08	−0.11	0.1
pos19_Provide reliable and scalable services	**0.65**	−0.1	0.12	−0.04	0.14
pos2021_Be environment-friendly	**0.58**	0.06	0.11	−0.13	0.11
pos22_Acquire new acquaintances—work related	**0.5**	0	0.11	−0.09	0.21
pos2324_Acquire new acquaintances	0.27	0.06	0.03	0.07	**0.41**
pos25_Do whatever I want, say whatever I want, and be whoever I want	**0.3**	−0.09	−0.02	0.09	0.11
neg01_Prevents me from concentrating more on writing and reading skills	−0.02	−0.15	**0.8**	−0.01	0.12
neg02_Prevents me from remembering the fundamental knowledge and skills	0.06	−0.11	**0.82**	−0.06	−0.13
neg03_Scatters my attention	−0.27	0.11	**0.49**	−0.06	0.27
neg04_Decreases my grammar and proofreading skills	0.08	0.06	**0.62**	−0.04	−0.15
neg05_Decreases my deep thinking	0.05	0.18	**0.55**	0.03	−0.14
neg06_Distracts me easily	−0.26	0.2	**0.3**	0.06	**0.34**
neg07_Prevents me from participating in social activities	0.21	0.14	**0.48**	0.09	−0.19

(continued)

Table 7 (continued)

Item	Factor				
	1	2	3	4	5
neg08_Prevents me from completing my work/study on time	−0.02	0.15	**0.5**	0.17	0.11
neg09_Makes me sick and unhealthy	0.09	**0.51**	0.05	0.12	−0.16
neg10111213_Feel bored, stressed, depressed and lonely	−0.06	**0.62**	0.03	0.03	−0.17
neg14_Makes me lazy	−0.12	**0.74**	0.01	−0.1	0.15
neg15_Makes me addict	−0.04	**0.72**	−0.01	0.04	0.18
neg16_Makes me more gambler	0.01	**0.53**	0	0.18	−0.08
neg17_Makes me insecure to release my personal details from the theft of personal information	0.01	**0.81**	−0.13	−0.2	0.06
neg18_Makes me receive an immoral images and information from unscrupulous people and it is difficult to act against them at present	0.04	**0.65**	0	−0.08	−0.11
neg192021_Prevents engagement in physical and social activities	0.07	**0.32**	−0.01	**0.55**	−0.09
neg22_Prevents me from shopping in stores	0.05	0.04	−0.07	**0.75**	−0.07
neg23_Prevents me from watching television	−0.07	−0.05	−0.03	**0.71**	0.22
neg24_Prevents me from reading the newspapers	−0.08	−0.16	0.09	**0.79**	0.14
neg25_Prevents me from talking on the phone/mobile	0	−0.08	−0.01	**0.74**	−0.05
neg282930_Raise confidentiality concerns	0.06	**0.42**	0	0.01	0.16
Correlation with 2	−0.20	–	–	–	–
Correlation with 3	0.44	0.59	–	–	–
Correlation with 4	−0.02	0.54	0.42	–	–
Correlation with 5	0.29	−0.29	−0.24	−0.29	–

We then computed factor scores and used them as criterion variables in a main-effects-only multivariate analysis of variance (MANOVA) model, followed by Sidak-corrected post hoc comparisons. Demographic variables, education background and networking habits were the predictors. Box's test for the equality of covariance matrices was not significant ($M = 288.875$, $F(210,6836.535) = 1.042$, $p = 0.327$), suggesting that MANOVA could be applied. After controlling for multiple comparisons we found significant multivariate effects of age (Pillai's Trace = 0.113, $F(15,771) = 2.005$, $p = 0.032$), daily hours spent on social networks (Pillai's Trace = 0.102, $F(5,255) = 5.768$, $p < 0.001$), using the internet for studying (Pillai's Trace = .089, $F(5,255) = 4.988$, $p = 0.001$) and using the internet for chatting (Pillai's Trace = 0.069, $F(5,255) = 3.805$, $p = 0.008$)

The multivariate effect of age was due to significant differences among age groups in WLO ($F(3,259) = 4.784$, $p = 0.003$), since the 42–52 year group scored significantly higher than the 22–32 year group ($p = 0.002$). The multivariate effect of daily hours spent on social networks was due to higher scores on WLO ($F(1,259) = 13.052$, $p < 0.001$) and ISA ($F(1,259) = 23.685$, $p < 0.001$) for those who use social networks more than one hour per day and to higher scores in HCE ($F(1,259) = 6.331$, $p = 0.012$) for those who use social networks less than hour per day. The multivariate effect of using the internet for studying was due to higher scores on ISA ($F(1,259) = 5.030$, $p = 0.026$) of those who do use the internet for studying. The multivariate effect of using the internet for chatting was due to higher scores on ISA ($F(1,259) = 15.665$, $p < 0.001$) of those who use the internet for chatting.

Although the multivariate effect of the variable was not significant, we also found significant univariate effects for gender in ISA ($F(1,259) = 5.758$, $p = 0.017$; females > males), for field of study in WLO ($F(6,259) = 2.523$, $p = 0.022$; Economics and Finance > Science and Engineering), for using internet for e-mailing in LESA ($F(1,259) = 5.371$, $p = 0.021$; No > Yes), and for using the internet for shopping in WLO ($F(1,259) = 5.640$, $p = 0.018$; Yes > No).

6 Discussion

The aim of this study was to survey the opinions of Italian university students on the pros and cons of social networking and find possible correlations with their profile (age, gender, background and social networking habits).

Participants were asked to rate their agreement with each of 55 items mapping positive and negative effects of social networking. After screening the items for redundancies, a factor analysis suggested that items could be grouped into five latent variables that we named (1) Widening learning opportunities and enhancing of autonomy, (Gordon, #1706), Causing negative emotions, (3) Hindering concentration and study effectiveness, (Gordon, #1706) Limiting extra-study activities and (5) Improving social interactions and global awareness.

Together with the inspection of single items mean scores, the results of this study provide interesting answers to our first research question (i.e. what are the beliefs of the Italian university students about the effects of social networking on learning?), by suggesting that students perceive social networking as useful tools for widening their learning opportunities through connections to peers and access to information, but also that they are aware of their undesirable consequences, such as experiencing negative emotions, losing concentration and being prevented from engaging in extra-academic activities.

In addition, further statistics were conducted to address the second research question (i.e. "is there any correlation between the effects identified and the students' characteristics?"). The multivariate analysis of variance showed that widening of learning opportunities and enhancing of autonomy was more appreciated by older participants, somewhat contradicting the common belief that younger people should be more positive towards social networking. Not surprisingly, respondents who use social networks more than 1 h per day scored higher on both widening learning opportunities and enhancing autonomy and improving social interactions and global awareness; while respondents who use social networks less than 1 h scored higher on hindering concentration and study effectiveness. Therefore, students' beliefs about the effects of social networking seem to be related to the amount of use they make of its tools: the more they believe in their benefits, the more they use them, the more they believe in their distractive power, the less they use them. However, since this was a cross-sectional study, it is not possible to determine whether a student spends less time on social networks because she/he experienced their negative effects, or the other way around. The same argument applies in explaining why those who do not use the internet for e-mailing scored higher on the belief that social networking limits their extra-study activities than those who do.

Students that spend more than 1 h per day on social networks and that use internet for studying, chatting and shopping reported higher scores on two positive factors such as widening learning opportunities and enhancing autonomy and improving social interactions and global awareness. They also reported lower scores on a negative factor such as hindering concentration and study effectiveness than students who spend less time on social networks. These results suggest that frequent users of social networks may tend to appreciate their advantages more than they acknowledge their disadvantages, but it should be noted that it is possible that the time spent using these tools cuts into time normally spent on other activities including studying, and hence might undermine academic achievement [13].

We also found that females and economics and finance students appreciate the opportunity to widen their learning opportunities and enhance their autonomy more than males and science and engineering students, respectively. These results are consistent with the well-known gender differences in academic motivation and achievement (for a review, see, e.g., [7]) and with studies that report that engineering students are less likely to be heavy social network users (see, e.g., [16]).

As for the study limitations, there are at least two aspects that deserve being mentioned. The first is the sampling method used: it is well known that the snowball sampling technique does not guarantee representativeness of the sample obtained. While the demographic features of the sample used appear to be in line with the official data about previous academic years,[1] carrying out a rigorous check of representativeness was not possible due to lack of updated data about the distribution of the real population. The second limitation is that, since the survey questions and answer options were prepared for an international target, they do not fit the Italian target as well as they would if they were prepared for especially for it. However, this limitation is counterbalanced by the advantage that the results obtained in all of the other countries and illustrated in the other chapters of this book will allow to get an international panorama on the study theme.

[1]http://statistica.miur.it/ustat/Statistiche/IU_home.asp.

7 Conclusions

The attitude towards social networking that emerges from the results presented in this chapter is twofold. The positive effects are widely recognized, and those that are mostly appreciated concern the possibility to access information and communicate and collaborate with peers. On the other hand, the negative aspects, and specifically, the risks of becoming addict and to be distracted by the virtual world so to lose concentration, are also clearly perceived by the respondents. As it could be expected, the students who use these tools more tend to appreciate their advantages more than the others, while the students who use them less are those who fear their interference with concentration and attention more.

While researchers appear to be inclined to emphasize the importance of the advantages of social networking tools for education and thus advocate the need for a bidirectional contamination of formal and informal learning [23, 28], the Italian higher education students involved in this survey tend to see both the positive and the negative aspects of the use of these tools as of equal importance. Therefore, a crucial issue to be addressed by future research appears to be whether the perceived risks make students more cautious than researchers towards the use of these tools in learning and teaching activities.

References

1. Andersson A, Hatakka M, Grönlund Å, Wiklund M (2014) Reclaiming the students—coping with social media in 1:1 schools. Learn Media Technol 39(1):37–52. doi:10.1080/17439884.2012.756518
2. Baker R, White K (2011) In their own words: why teenagers don't use social networking sites. Cyberpsychol Behav Soc Netw 14(Gordon, #1706):395–398. doi:10.1089/cyber.2010.0016
3. Cabero-Almenara J, Marín-Díaz V (2014) Educational possibilities of social networks and group work. Univ Stud Percept Comunicar 21(42):165–172. doi:10.3916/C42-2014-16
4. Carr N (2008) Is Google making us stupid? Yearb Natl Soc Study Educ 107:89–94. doi:10.1111/j.1744-7984.2008.00172.x
5. Davis III CHF, Deil-Amen R, Rios-Aguilar C, González Canché M (2012) Social media and higher education: a literature review and research directions. University of Arizona and Claremont Graduate University. http://works.bepress.com/hfdavis/2/. Accessed 10 Oct 2014
6. Dillenbourg P (ed) (1999) Collaborative learning: cognitive and computational approaches. Elsevier, Oxford
7. DiPrete TA, Buchmann C (2013) The rise of women. Russell Sage Foundation, New York
8. Gatti Casati A, Salta G (2012) L'impatto dei social network sul mondo del lavoro: problemi e prospettive. Bollettino ADAPT 42, November 26th, 2012. http://www.bollettinoadapt.it/old/files/document/19561gatti_salta_26_1.pdf. Accessed 10 Oct 2014
9. Gewerc A, Montero L, Lama M (2014) Collaboration and social networking in higher education. Comunicar 21(42):55–63. doi:10.3916/C42-2014-05
10. Gikas J, Grant M (2013) Mobile computing devices in higher education: student perspectives on learning with cellphones, smartphones & social media. Internet High Educ 19:18–26. doi:10.1016/j.iheduc.2013.06.002

11. Globalwebindex (2014) Generations Audience Report Q2 2014. http://insight.globalwebindex.net/gwi-generations-audience-report. Accessed 10 Oct 2014
12. HIOP (2011) IOP youth polling: Spring 2011 survey. Harvard Institute on Politics. University J. F. Kennedy School of Government, Cambridge, MA. http://www.iop.harvard.edu/spring-2011-survey Accessed 10 Oct 2014
13. Junco R (2012) Too much face and not enough books: the relationship between multiple indices of Facebook use and academic performance. Comput Hum Behav 28(1):187–198. doi:10.1016/j.chb.2011.08.026
14. Laforenza D, Martinelli M, Serrecchia M (2012) Il fenomeno Internet. In: Avveduto S (ed) Scienza connessa – Rete, media e social network. Gangemi, Roma, pp 17–34
15. Madge C, Meek J, Wellens J, Hooley T (2009) Facebook, social integration and informal learning at university: "It is more for socialising and talking to friends about work than for actually doing work". Learn Media Technol 34(Gordon, #1706):141–155. doi:10.1080/17439880902923606
16. Martin C (2014) Social networking usage and grades among college students. Whittermore School of Business & Economics. University of New Hampshire. http://www.unh.edu/news/docs/UNHsocialmedia.pdf. Accessed 10 Oct 2014
17. Mazzoni E, Iannone M (2014) From high school to university: impact of social networking sites on social capital in the transitions of emerging adults. British J Educ Technol 45(Gordon, #1706):303–315. doi:10.1111/bjet.12026
18. Mcloughlin C, Lee MJW (2008) Future learning landscapes: transforming pedagogy through social software. Innovate 4(5). doi:10.1.1.186.6097
19. Milan L (2012) Impatto dei social media: mercato e trend. http://www.slideshare.net/leonardo.milan/limpatto-dei-social-media. Accessed 10 Oct 2014
20. Pempek TA, Yermolayeva YA, Calvert SL (2009) College students' social networking experiences on Facebook. J Appl Dev Psychol 30(3):227–238. doi:10.1016/j.appdev.2008.12.010
21. Persico D, Pozzi F (2013) The role of representations for the development of a participatory culture of Learning Design among educators. In: Parmigiani D, Pennazio AY V (eds) Learn Teach Media Technol. AISBL Brussels, Belgium, pp 365–372
22. Persico D, Pozzi F, Sarti L (2010) Monitoring collaborative activities in computer supported collaborative learning. Distance Educ 31(1):5–22. doi:10.1080/01587911003724603
23. Pettenati MC, Cigognini ME (2007) Social Networking Theories and Tools to Support Connectivist Learning Activities. Int J Web-Based Learn Teach Technol (IJWLTT) 2(3):42–60. doi:10.4018/jwltt.2007070103
24. Pozzi F, Persico D (Karlsson, #1577) (2011) Techniques for fostering collaboration in online learning communities. Theoretical and practical perspectives. Information Science Reference, Hershey
25. Ranieri M, Manca S (2013) I social network nell'educazione. Erickson, Trento
26. Rourke L, Anderson T, Garrison DR, Archer W (2007) Assessing social presence in asynchronous text-based computer conferencing. J E-Learn Distance Educ 14(Gordon, #1706):50–71
27. Sartori L (2012) Il ritardo degli italiani nella società dell'informazione. In: Avveduto S (ed) Scienza connessa—Rete, media e social network. Gangemi Editore, Roma, pp 35–44
28. Seaman J, Tinti-Kane H (2013) Social media for teaching and learning. Pearson Learning Solutions and the Babson Survey Research Group. http://www.pearsonlearningsolutions.com/assets/downloads/reports/social-media-for-teaching-and-learning-2013-report.pdf#view=FitH,0. Accessed 10 Oct 2014
29. Sharples M (2006) How can we address the conflicts between personal informal learning and traditional classroom education. In: Sharples M (ed) Big issues in mobile learning. University of Nottingham, pp 21–24. http://www.cin.ufpe.br/~mlearning/intranet/m-learning/Big%20Issues%20in%20Mobile%20Learning.pdf#page=21. Accessed 10 Oct 2014
30. Siemens G (2005) Connectivism: A learning theory for the digital age. Int J Instr Technol Distance Learn 2(1):3–10

31. Smith F (2007) How to use social-networking technology for learning. Why teachers should embrace networking, and how they can use it to improve education. http://www.edutopia.org/how-use-social-networking-technology. Accessed 10 Oct 2014
32. Tess P (2013) The role of social media in higher education classes (real and virtual)—a literature review. Comput Hum Behav 29(5):A60–A68. doi:10.1016/j.chb.2012.12.032
33. Turan Z, Tinmaz H, Goktas Y (2013) The reasons for non-use of social networking websites by university students. Comunicar 21(41):137–145. doi:10.3916/C41-2013-13
34. Wearesocial (2014) Social, digital and mobile in Europa 2014. http://www.slideshare.net/wearesocialit/social-digital-mobile-in-europa-2014. Accessed 10 Oct 2014
35. Wegerif R (1998) The social dimension of asynchronous learning networks. J Asynchron Learn Netw 2(1):34–49
36. Winters N (2013) How teachers in Africa are failed by mobile learning. http://www.scidev.net/global/education/opinion/how-teachers-in-africa-are-failed-by-mobile-learning.html. Accessed 10 Oct 2014

Part IV
Mediterranean, Turkey

Social Networking in Higher Education in Turkey: Students' Use and Perceptions

Sehnaz Baltaci Goktalay and Zehra Ozdilek

Abstract The proliferation of social networking sites (SNSs) has created a phenomenon that engages millions of Internet users around the world, especially young people. Given the popularity of these sites and their importance in young people's lives to facilitate communication and relationships, it is important to understand the factors influencing SNS use and explore perceptions of the young generation about the effects of SNS on their daily life. The SNS trend is a relatively new one in Turkey and little research has been reported on its acceptance and use in education. This research was designed to gather preliminary evidence of the current adoption of SNSs by higher education students. The study was conducted in a public university in Turkey with 180 participants. The purposes of using the Internet and the positive effects of using the SNSs were studied. The results show that students are using the Internet for email, playing games, studying, working, and for communication purposes. Results of this small-scale study in one location indicate that students differ somewhat in their current and anticipated uses of SNSs such as the currently-popular Facebook. It also showed that the young generations are using SNSs for learning new information, collaboration, and communication purposes. While both males and females were equally positive of using the SNNs, males were more negative on the dimensions of cognitive and emotional effects of SNNs.

Keywords Internet · Social networking sites · Higher education · Facebook · Turkey · Social media

---

S.B. Goktalay (✉) · Z. Ozdilek
Faculty of Education, Uludag University, 16059 Bursa, Turkey
e-mail: sehnazbg@uludag.edu.tr

Z. Ozdilek
e-mail: zozdilek@uludag.edu.tr

T. Issa et al. (eds.), *Social Networking and Education*,
Lecture Notes in Social Networks, DOI 10.1007/978-3-319-17716-8_11

1 Introduction

1.1 Growth of Social Networking

Recent developments in Internet technologies cause people to integrate new technologies into their daily life. Around 40 % of the world population has Internet connection today. The number of Internet users has increased more than tenfold from 2000 to 2014. Turkey's Internet use rank is on the average with 46.62 % of the population using the Internet [12]. Figure 1 shows the number of global Internet users per year since 1993.

Especially young generation communicate and form their social relationships through Social Networking Sites (SNSs) [15, 27]. SNSs are the fastest-growing and most popular form of the Internet-based technologies used by young people. SNSs are one of the latest examples of communications technologies that have been widely-adopted by higher education students, and thus have the potential to become a valuable resource for supporting students' communication and collaboration with faculty.

SNSs such as Friendster, MySpace, and Facebook allow individuals to present themselves, create their social networks, and establish/maintain connections with others. These sites can be categorized as work-related contexts (e.g., LinkedIn.com), relationship initiation (the original goal of Friendster.com), connecting those with shared interests (e.g., MySpace.com), or the university student population (the original goal of Facebook.com). SNSs began with the launch of SixDegrees.com. It allowed users to create profiles, have a friends list and surf the friends. Recently, MySpace and Facebook in particular have become very popular. They both are SNSs that provide personalized and interactive services based on users' interest and activities on the web. Especially Facebook is one of the most popular SNSs for higher education students [8, 13, 18].

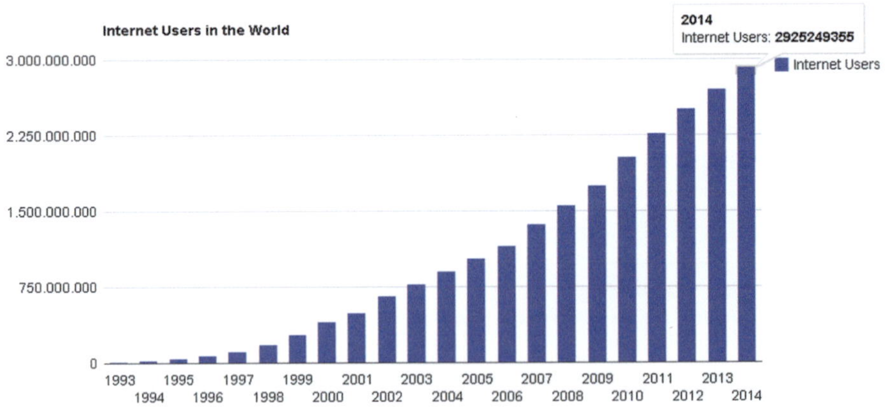

Fig. 1 Internet users in the world. *Source* Internet Live Stats

In early 2004, Facebook was created by a 23 year-old Harvard student Mark Zuckerberg. The general concept was to digitize the Harvard freshman-year to see each other's photos, flirt, network, and interact. At first, Facebook.com was limited to students at Harvard with a university email address [2]. Later, the Facebook phenomenon spread worldwide but still required users to have university email addresses associated with supported institutions to keep the site as an intimate and private community. In 2005, Facebook was open outside the university network.

With over 1,184 million subscribers worldwide (according to Facebook.com statistics retrieved in June, 2014), Facebook, now has a diverse community of users at all levels. The users can create a profile and provide such information as personal interests, education, photos, create/join groups and pages based on their interests, and create events. The messages and chat are also used frequently.

1.2 Current Uses of Social Networking Sites Among Young People

According to the Pew Internet & American Life Project Report results in 2007, 93 % of teens not only use the Internet, and but also treat it as a venue for social interaction. The report also found that use of Instant Messaging (IM) dropped from 75 % in 2004 to 68 % in the 2007 study, since IM functionality has been integrated into most social networking and gaming applications.

The 2013 report from the Pew Internet & American Life Project [9] shows that 73 % of online adults use SNSs, 42 % of them use multiple SNSs, but Facebook remains the dominant platform for users. While Facebook is popular across the population, other SNSs have also developed their own users. When asked how often they visit the SNSs they use, Facebook, Instagram, and Twitter users have the highest rates of engagement. Facebook users are the most engaged with 63 % visiting the site at least daily. Only 14 % of Facebook users report that they visit the site less than once a week. Instagram users follow Facebook users with 57 % daily uses. Twitter users are also frequent visitors to the site with 46 % daily visits. LinkedIn and Pinterest users are the least engaged with 13 and 23 % respectively.

Another research [16] investigated the views of university students from European countries such as Lithuania, Romania, Ukraine, Czech Republic, and Turkey regarding the use of SNSs. Their results show that majority of the participants visit SNSs a few times a day. Interestingly, SNSs are the most popular among Turkish students. According to the responses, easier communication with many people at once, getting in touch with friends and family living abroad, possibility to find new information and share it were the reported advantages of using SNSs. They also indicated few disadvantages as well. These include lack of privacy, deceptions, and false information. Özmen and Atıcı [21] have recently examined the use of learning management systems supported by SNSs in distance education in Turkey. The researchers investigated the views of fifteen participants regarding these platforms. While the participants stated that possibility of easy exchange of available information as a benefit, the distraction of excessive use of chatting was the most negative aspects of SNSs.

According to the Pew Internet & American Life Project Report results in 2007, 93 % of teens use the Internet, and they were treating it as a venue for social interaction. The report also found that use of Instant Messaging (IM) dropped from 75 % in 2004 to 68 % in the 2007 study, since IM functionality has been integrated into so many social networking and gaming applications.

The 2013 report from the Pew Internet & American Life Project [10] shows that 73 % of online users use SNSs, 42 % of them use multiple SNSs, but Facebook remains the dominant platform. While Facebook is popular across the population, other SNSs have also developed their own users (Fig. 2).

When asked how often they visit the SNSs they use, Facebook, Instagram, and Twitter users stand out as having the highest rates of engagement (Fig. 3). Facebook users are the most engaged with 63 % going on the site at least daily. Only 14 % of Facebook users report that they visit the site less than once a week. Instagram users follow Facebook users with 57 % daily uses. Twitter users are also frequent visitors to the site with 46 % daily visits. LinkedIn and Pinterest users are the least engaged with 13 and 23 % respectively.

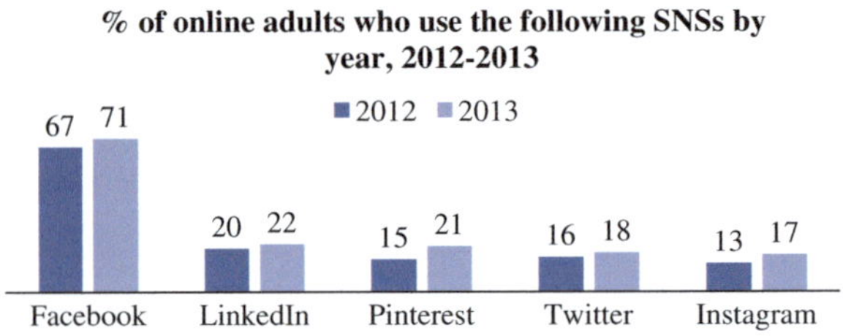

Fig. 2 Pew Research Center's Internet Project Tracking Surveys, 2012–2013. N = 1445

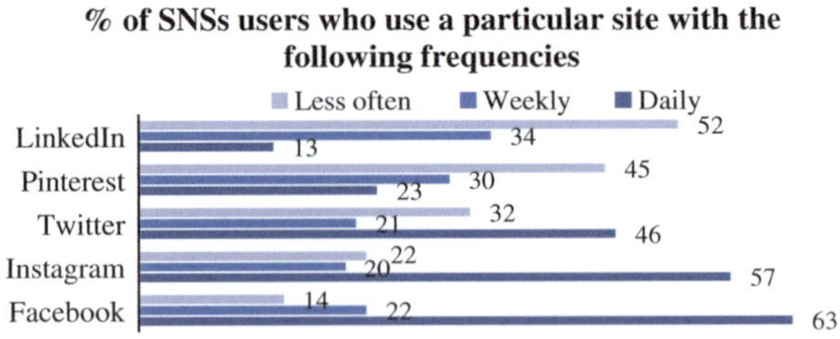

Fig. 3 Pew Research Center's Internet Project Tracking Surveys, 2012–2013. N = 1445

1.3 Why Youth Use Social Networking Sites

Although some of the ways that youth spend their time have changed recently, the main developmental tasks of youth have remained the same. Key characteristics of adolescent development comprise identity development, intimacy development, and peer interaction. SNSs are designed to support social interaction. Users post some information in her/his profile (photograph, video, interests, etc.) to communicate and that information is about one's identity. Users can communicate through various applications and those interactions address many concerns of adolescence, such as the need for friendship and peer feedback [23]. Like personal websites, SNSs provide an easy way to interact with peers and gather peer feedback to self-validation or the formation of relationships [19, 28].

1.4 Study Purpose and Research Questions

The proliferation of social networking sites (SNSs) has created a phenomenon that engages millions of Internet users around the world, especially young people. Given the popularity of these sites and their importance in young people's lives to facilitate communication and relationships, it is important to understand the factors influencing SNS use and explore perceptions of young generation about positive and negative effects of SNS [11, 19]. The SNS is a relatively new trend in Turkey and little research has been reported on its acceptance and use in education. This research was designed to gather preliminary evidence of the current adoption of SNSs by higher education students. The research is explored to answer the following questions:

- For what reasons do students use the Internet?
- What do students think about the positive effects of using the SNSs?
- What do students think about the negative effects of using the SNSs?
- Are there any gender differences with respect to positive and negative effects of using the SNSs?

2 Methodology

2.1 Study Procedure and the Instrument

This study was conducted in a public university in Turkey during 2013–2014 academic year. Research suggests that university students form suitable samples for studies dealing with Internet or SNSs, since they tend to be frequent users of several SNSs [24]. Students were invited to participate in the study through Facebook pages/groups, provided with information about the aim of the study and informed that the participation to the study was voluntary and confidential. The study was conducted in compliance with the relevant laws and institutional guidelines. The participants were given a URL through which the survey was conducted as an online questionnaire. As a result, 254 university students answered the online questionnaire. The students age ranged from 18 to 42, with 129 males (46 %) and 150 females (54 %). Questionnaires with missing data were eliminated from the dataset and the remaining 180 questionnaires were analyzed.

The questionnaire had three parts: the first part gathered background information (7 items), the second part was on the positive effects of social networking (25 items), and the third part asked the negative effects of social networking (30 items). Part 1 asked about participants' age, gender, field of study, highest education level, time spent on SNSs daily, time spent on the Internet for email, and what else they perform on the Internet. Part 2 asked about how they used the social networking in positive ways to organize and maintain their work, study, and social life. Part 3 asked about negative effects of social networking on students' life. A five-point Likert-type scale was used where 1 was "strongly disagree", 2 was "disagree", 3 was "Neutral", 4 was "agree", and 5 was "strongly agree." In addition, two open-ended questions were added to ask the participants to provide comments on the positive and negative effects of using social networking. The English version of the questionnaire was translated into Turkish and back translated into English to check the translation inconsistency [4]. Different translators were used in these stages. The precise wording of the questionnaire was de-centered [4] away from the original language version and adjusted so that it was smooth and natural sounding, as well as equivalent, in both languages.

2.2 *Data Analysis*

The first step of the quantitative analysis was to test the precision of the questionnaire. The coefficient alpha was calculated. The overall reliability of the instrument (0.88) reached the widely advocated level of Cronbach's alpha 0.70 [7, 20]. The exploratory factor analysis was applied for the questionnaire. An independent sample t-test, descriptive statistics including mean average, standard deviation, frequencies and percentages were used to analyze the quantitative data using SPSS 20.0. The qualitative data from the survey were analyzed using a content analysis method [29]. Content analysis is a process of determining a set of concepts and relationships within which the data can be analyzed. It is used in revealing the concepts and themes that could not be formed as a result of descriptive analysis. For this purpose, the data were firstly conceptualized, then the occurring concepts were arranged in a systematic way and, finally, the themes explaining the data were formed and the process was completed [29].

Within the 180 survey responses, overall 152 statements were identified as relevant to the second research question and relevant statements were then gathered under six dimensions of the positive effects of using the SNSs. These statements were used as the coding categories for the participants' responses. The data were independently coded by both authors using the identified elements and categories to increase inter-coder reliability. The percentage of the agreement between the coding sets for the quotes was 84 and 88 % with a Cohen Kappa inter coder agreement coefficient.

3 Key Findings

3.1 Background Information of the Participants

After the missing data were eliminated, the remaining 180 participants ranged in age from 18 to 42 and 50 % were male and 50 % were female. The majority of the participants were between ages of 18 and 22 (60 %), while 38.9 % were between 22 and 32, and only 1.1 % was between 32 and 42. It is reported that 73.89 % of them were full-time students, 15 % were teachers and 11.11 % were among other professions such as engineers, nurses, technicians, self-employed, civil servants. When asked "How many hours do you spend on the social networking daily, not including email?", 47 participants (26.1 %) answered less than an hour, 104 participants (57.8 %) answered up to 5 h, and 25 (13.9 %) answered 5–10 h. Only 2.2 % of the participants chose over 10 h (Fig. 4). When asked about time spent on the Internet for email use, 148 participants (82.2 %) answered less than an hour, 23 participants (12.8 %) answered up to 5 h, and only 9 (5 %) answered over 5 h (Fig. 5).

Another question asked for the participants' preferences on what they accessed while on the Internet. Some Yes/No questions were answered as shown in Fig. 6. While 158 participants (87.8 %) answered Yes to email use, 144 (80 %) were using the Internet for studying and only 58 (32.2 %) for working purposes. Chatting also featured highly with 143 (79.4 %) participants. Some participants also stated that

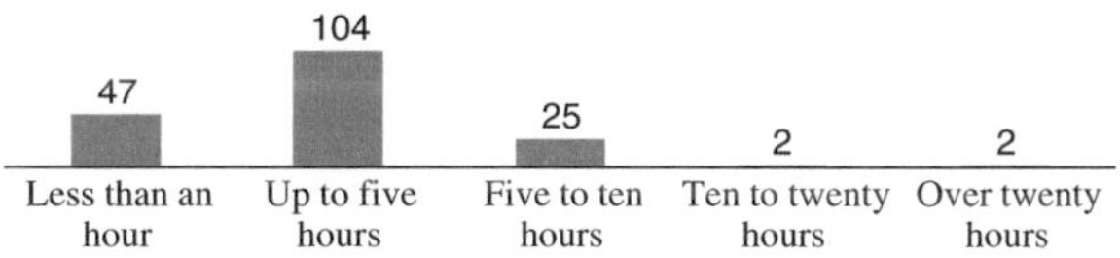

Fig. 4 Time spent on the Internet for email use per day

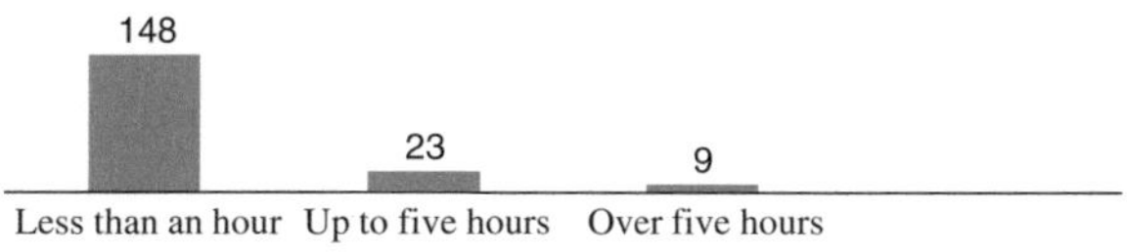

Fig. 5 Time spent on the social networking daily, not including email

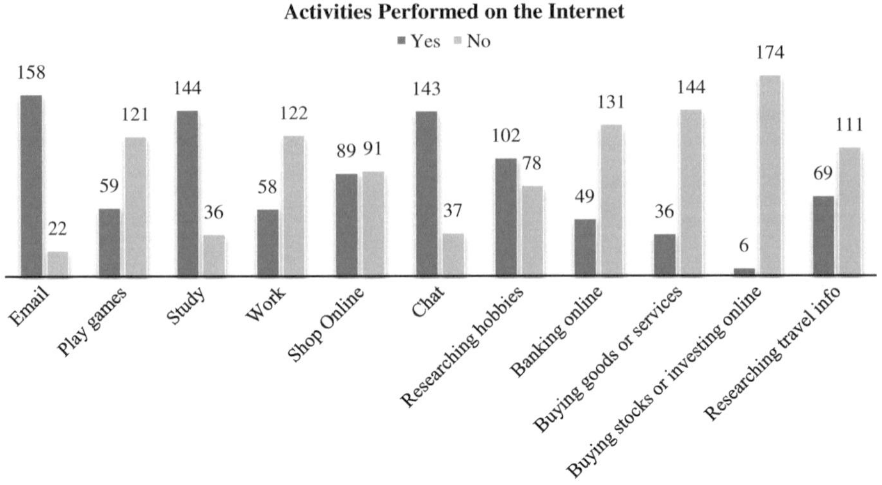

Fig. 6 Activities performed on the Internet

they used the Internet for watching movies, TV series, reading newspapers, listening to music, downloading music/movie, social networking, and following sports news.

3.2 *Factor Analysis*

To test the psychometric properties of the questionnaire, various analyses were conducted. First, principal components analysis (PCA) with a varimax rotation was used to determine whether items grouped themselves into factors. Second, an internal consistency analysis using Cronbach's (1951) coefficient alpha was used to determine reliability of the subscales. Bartlett's test of sphericity [1] was statistically significant ($p < 0.001$), suggesting that the data were appropriate for factor analysis and no evidence of multicollinearity or singularity was found [30]. The Kaiser-Meyer-Olkin [14] measure of sampling adequacy was 0.88, indicating that the sample size was appropriate for factor analysis.

To determine the optimal factor solution, we used two methods: the eigenvalue greater than one rule [14] and the scree analysis [6]. When PCA was run followed by varimax rotation, five-factor solution accounted for 62.79 % of variance for positive effects subscale. The loadings of all items on each of the five factors for positive effects of SNSs subscale are displayed in Table 1. Coefficients smaller than 0.330 were suppressed [5]. Only one item (Q31) failed to reach a 0.40 level of correlation with any of the five factors. Items (Q31, Q32, Q33, Q34, and Q35) with equivalent loadings on multiple factors (Thompson 2004) were removed from the subscale, and the factor analysis was repeated with remaining 20 items (Table 2).

Table 1 Item loadings on five factors for positive effects of SNSs subscale (25-item)

Positive effects subscale items	Factors				
	1	2	3	4	5
Q38—Be more sustainable person	**0.808**				
Q37—To prepare my professional attitude toward study and work	**0.773**				
Q39—Provide reliable and scalable services	**0.763**				
Q40—Become more "Greener" in my activities	**0.714**				
Q36—Concentrate more on my reading and writing skills	**0.692**				
Q41—Reduce carbon footprint in my activities	**0.601**				0.412
Q35—Develop my personal and communication skills	0.513	0.437			
Q30—Study independently	**0.434**				
Q31—Overcome study stress	0.376	0.330	0.367		−0.338
Q23—Be more aware of global issues/local issues		**0.789**			
Q22—Gain up-to-date information		**0.788**			
Q21—Learn new information and knowledge		**0.737**			
Q24—To remember facts/aspects of the past		**0.629**			
Q34—Scrutinize my research study more easily	0.542	0.571			
Q33—Understand and solve study problems easily	0.503	0.554			
Q32—Complete my study more quickly	0.509	0.517			
Q27—Communicate with my peers from different universities			**0.784**		
Q26—Collaborate with my peers frequently			**0.685**		
Q29—Develop intercrossing relationships			**0.677**		
Q28—Communicate with my different communities			**0.662**		
Q25—Communicate with my peers frequently		0.434	**0.620**		
Q44—Acquire new acquaintances—romance relationship				**0.835**	
Q45—Do whatever I want, say whatever I want, and be whoever I want				**0.834**	
Q43—Acquire new acquaintances—friendship relationship				**0.653**	0.446
Q42—Acquire new acquaintances—work related				0.428	**0.595**

Table 2 Item loadings on 20-item four factors for positive effects of SNSs subscale

Positive effects of SNSs subscale items	Factors			
	1	2	3	4
Q38—Be more sustainable person	**0.824**			
Q39—Provide reliable and scalable services	**0.767**			
Q37—To prepare my professional attitude toward study and work	**0.752**			
Q40—Become more "Greener" in my activities	**0.710**	0.334		
Q36—Concentrate more on my reading and writing skills	**0.700**			
Q41—Reduce carbon footprint in my activities	**0.669**			
Q30—Study independently	**0.412**			
Q22—Gain up-to-date information		**0.844**		
Q23—Be more aware of global issues/local issues		**0.767**		
Q21—Learn new information and knowledge		**0.696**		
Q24—To remember facts/aspects of the past	0.359	**0.625**		
Q25—Communicate with my peers frequently		**0.604**	0.508	
Q27—Communicate with my peers from different universities			**0.778**	
Q28—Communicate with my different communities			**0.707**	
Q29—Develop intercrossing relationships			**0.684**	
Q26—Collaborate with my peers frequently		0.448	**0.610**	
Q43—Acquire new acquaintances—friendship relationship				**0.811**
Q44—Acquire new acquaintances—romance relationship				**0.787**
Q45—Do whatever I want, say whatever I want, and be whoever I want			0.335	**0.769**
Q42—Acquire new acquaintances—work related				**0.607**

After removing five items from the subscale, four-factor solution was emerged with remaining 20 items. The four-factor solution accounted for 60.4 % of variance. Factor 1, Being Environment-Friendly, included seven items and accounted for 31.8 % of variance. Factor 2, Gaining Knowledge, contained five items and accounted for 43.5 % of variance. Factor 3, Communication, contained four items and accounted for 53.7 % of variance. Factor 4, Acquiring Acquaintances, included four items and accounted for 60.4 % of variance.

Another PCA was run in order to check the optimal factor solution for negative effects of SNSs subscale. The loadings of all items on each of the seven factors are displayed in Table 3.

Only one item (Q62) failed to reach a 0.40 level of correlation with any of the seven factors. Some items did not fit conceptually with the primary concerns of the factor. We therefore decided to reduce the number of items to (a) eliminate those items with low loadings, (b) include only those items that were theoretically

Table 3 Item loadings on seven factors for negative effects of SNSs subscale (30-item)

Negative effects of SNSs subscale items	Factors						
	1	2	3	4	5	6	7
Q75—Increase security concerns	**0.876**						
Q74—Increase privacy concerns	**0.856**						
Q76—Increase intellectual property concerns	**0.776**						
Q63—Makes me insecure to release my personal details from the theft of personal information	**0.745**						
Q70—Prevents me from reading the newspapers		**0.828**					
Q71—Prevents me from talking on the phone/mobile		**0.748**					
Q69—Prevents me from watching television		**0.695**					
Q68—Prevents me from shopping in stores		**0.674**					
Q58—Depresses me			**0.812**				
Q57—Stresses me			**0.804**				
Q56—Bores me			**0.731**				
Q59—Makes me feel lonely			0.579		0.343	0.413	
Q55—Makes me sick and unhealthy			**0.525**				
Q66—Prevents me from having face to face contact with my friends				**0.793**			
Q65—Prevents me from having face to face contact with my family				**0.726**			
Q67—Prevents me from participating in physical activities				**0.707**			
Q53—Prevents me from participating in social activities			0.343	**0.549**			
Q64—Makes me receive an immoral images and information from unscrupulous people and	0.502			0.527			

(continued)

Table 3 (continued)

Negative effects of SNSs subscale items	Factors						
	1	2	3	4	5	6	7
it is difficult to act against them at present							
Q54—Prevents me from completing my work/study on time					**0.675**		
Q61—Makes me addict					**0.661**		
Q73—Prevents me from completing my study on time		0.495		0.344	0.584		
Q72—Prevents me from completing my work on time		0.490			0.552		
Q60—Makes me lazy					**0.544**		0.337
Q50—Decreases my grammar and proofreading skills						**0.730**	
Q49—Scatters my attention					0.402	**0.668**	
Q52—Distracts me easily					0.442	**0.633**	
Q51—Decreases my deep thinking			0.348			**0.583**	
Q62—Makes me more gambler			0.331			0.392	
Q47—Prevents me from concentrating more on writing and reading skills							**0.819**
Q48—Prevents me from remembering the fundamental knowledge and skills						0.394	**0.587**

consistent with the factor, and (c) equalize the number of items within each factor. Related items (Q48, Q50, Q51, Q54, Q55, Q59, Q62, Q64, Q72, and Q73) were removed from the subscale, and the factor analysis was repeated with remaining 25 items (Table 4).

After removing ten items from the subscale, five-factor solution was emerged with remaining 20 items. The five-factor solution accounted for 60.4 % of variance. Factor 1, Security, included four items and accounted for 36.7 % of variance. Factor 2, Social Effects, contained four items and accounted for 47.6 % of variance. Factor 3, Cognitive Effects, contained five items and accounted for 56.2 % of variance. Factor 4, Physical Effects, included four items and accounted for 63.1 % of variance. Factor 5, Emotional Effects, contained three items and accounted for 68.8 % of variance.

Table 4 Item loadings on 20-item five factors for negative effects of SNSs subscale

Negative effects of SNSs subscale items	Factors				
	1	2	3	4	5
Q75—Increase security concerns	**0.901**				
Q74—Increase privacy concerns	**0.886**				
Q76—Increase intellectual property concerns	**0.808**				
Q63—Makes me insecure to release my personal details from the theft of personal information	**0.718**				
Q70—Prevents me from reading the newspapers		**0.841**			
Q71—Prevents me from talking on the phone/mobile		**0.752**			
Q68—Prevents me from shopping in stores		**0.735**			
Q69—Prevents me from watching television		**0.719**			
Q49—Scatters my attention			**0.760**		
Q52—Distracts me easily			**0.734**		
Q61—Makes me addict			**0.693**		
Q60—Makes me lazy			**0.687**		
Q47—Prevents me from concentrating more on writing and reading skills			**0.529**		
Q66—Prevents me from having face to face contact with my friends				**0.825**	
Q67—Prevents me from participating in physical activities				**0.789**	
Q65—Prevents me from having face to face contact with my family				**0.693**	
Q53—Prevents me from participating in social activities				**0.671**	
Q57—Stresses me					**0.824**
Q58—Depresses me					**0.813**
Q56—Bores me					**0.750**

3.3 *Positive Effects of Using the SNSs*

Results are organized according to the categories corresponding to the dimensions of positive effects of using the Social Networking survey. The categories and sub-categories, frequencies, and illustrative quotations are presented in Table 5. The frequencies of the statements indicating the priorities of participants can be summarized as gaining knowledge, communication, acquiring acquaintances, and being environment-friendly as we now discuss.

Table 5 Categories, sub-categories, frequencies and illustrative quotes of the participants' responses

Category	F	Sub-category	f	Illustrative quote
Gaining knowledge	59	Learn new information and knowledge	5	I am learning some information that I don't know through social networks
		Gain up-to-date information	31	I immediately informed of everything happening up to date through social networks
		Be more aware of global issues	5	It enables us to realize what is happening in the world
		Communicate with my peers frequently	2	Even though your best friends are away from you, SNSs gives you a chance to get in touch. It gives possibility of frequent communication
		Easy access to information	16	Provides easy access to what I need to learn or curious about
Communication	56	Communicate with my different communities	14	It makes it easier to communicate with friends that I can't talk on the phone
		Ease of communication	28	It is the easiest way of communicating my friends
		Collaborate with my peers	8	Allows me to act simultaneously. It helps me to exchange files with my peers
		Develop my communication skills	6	It helps me overcome my difficulty in communicating people
Acquire acquaintances	22	Work related	8	It allows emergence of new ideas that normally doesn't come up
		Do whatever I want, say whatever I want, and be whoever I want	9	If there are things I can't say with confidence to face to face, I'm more comfortable expressing them on SNSs
		Develop relationships with my peers	5	SNSs strengthen our communication with our friends
Be environment-friendly	2	Study independently	2	I can easily do homework alone

3.3.1 Gaining Knowledge

It can be said that the *gaining knowledge* dimension was taken into more consideration for the participants as the majority (f = 59) of statements related to this category. The sub-categories showed that the ability to 'gain up-to-date information' (f = 31) was more prevalent than other aspects such as 'learn new information and knowledge' (f = 5), 'be more aware of global issues' (f = 5), and 'communicate with my peers frequently' (f = 2). Although not included in the questionnaire, a new sub-category of 'easy access to information' (f = 16) emerged from our analyses of the open ended answers. None of the participants addressed the sub-category of 'to remember facts/aspects of the past' within the category.

3.3.2 Communication

The second highest consideration as measured by the frequency of statements addressing the category was *communication* (f = 56). 'Ease of communication' (f = 28) and 'to collaborate with my peers frequently' (f = 8) gained more attention than the other sub-categories such as 'to communicate with my different communities' (f = 7) and 'to develop my communication skills' (f = 6). The 'ease of communication' and 'to develop my communication skills' sub-categories were not found on the items of the original survey. None of the participants referred to the sub-categories of 'to develop intercrossing relationships with my friends' and 'to communicate with my peers from different universities'.

3.3.3 Acquiring Acquaintances

It is clear that this category was a relatively low priority for these participants with only 22 statements coded in this area. 'Do whatever I want, say whatever I want', and 'be whoever I want' (f = 9) and 'work related' (f = 8), and 'develop relationships' (f = 5) appeared within this category. 'Acquire friendship and romance relationships' was not stated by any participants.

3.3.4 Being Environment-Friendly

The analysis indicated that there were fewest statements related to this category as only 2 statements were coded within 'study independently' sub-category.

The participants did not provide any comments regarding other items such as 'to concentrate more on my reading and writing skills', 'to prepare my professional attitude toward study and work', 'to be more sustainable person', 'to provide reliable and scalable services', 'to become more greener in my activities', and 'to reduce carbon footprint in my activities' that is found in the questionnaire.

3.4 Negative Effects of Using the SNSs

The following section introduces and describes the categories that emerged from the content analysis. Participants' responses were organized according to categories corresponding to the dimensions of negative effects of using the SNSs on the questionnaire (Table 6).

Table 6 Categories, sub-categories, frequencies and illustrative quotes of the participants' responses

Category	F	Sub-category	f	Illustrative quote
Physical effects	94	Waste of time	36	It takes a lot of time in front of the computer or cell phone because of the social media
		Prevents me from face to face contacts with friends	11	Instead of coming together, I prefer to communicate through Internet
		Prevents me from participating physical activities	4	I go to gym less. SNSs prevent me from participating active life
		Makes me sick and unhealthy	12	Since I am on the computer or with my cell phone all the time, it affects my health in a negative way a lot
		Prevents me from participating in social activities	31	SNSs use degenerates my relationships with others
Cognitive effects	52	Scatters my attention	9	I frequently need to check my Facebook account to see what others are sharing. It distracts me easily
		Prevents me from concentrating more on writing and reading skills	2	I read books less since I use Facebook
		Makes me lazy	7	I don't want to do anything else when I am online
		Makes me addict	26	I feel like I need to check my Facebook account all the time. I am always online
		Distracts me easily	6	When I join a group, it distracts me from concentrating to complete my work
		Prevents me from thinking creatively	2	Prevents me of thinking creatively since everything is on the SNSs or on the Internet
Security	28	Privacy issues	19	I feel insecure. People are so curious about private lives
		False information	9	There is so much false information, so it is hard to trust anybody
Social effects	10	Prevents me from talking on the phone	3	I prefer to send a message instead of calling my friends
		Show off	7	People are posting every minute of their lives online to show off. Nobody is able to enjoy the moment
Emotional effects	2	Depresses me	2	Following people on Facebook depresses me

3.4.1 Physical Effects

As seen in Table 2, the most frequently occurring negative category was *physical effects*. The sub-category of 'waste of time' (f = 36), which was not a part of the original questionnaire and 'prevents me participating in social activities' (f = 31) was mostly observed statement from the open-ended responses. 'Prevents me from face to face contacts with friends' (f = 11), 'prevents me from participating physical activities' (f = 4), and 'prevents me from talking to phone' (f = 3) gained less attention than the first two sub-categories. The sub-category of 'makes me sick and unhealthy' (f = 12) also emerged from the open-ended responses unlike the items of the questionnaire.

3.4.2 Cognitive Effects

The data analysis showed that *cognitive effects* category (f = 52) has the second highest statements. While 'makes me addict' (f = 26) received the highest priority by the participants, they also stated that SNSs 'scatter their attention' (f = 9), 'makes them lazy' (f = 7), 'distracts them easily' (f = 6), and 'prevent from concentrating more on writing and reading' (f = 2). A new sub-category, 'prevents creativity' (f = 2) emerged from the analysis of open-ended responses of the participants.

3.4.3 Security

This sub-category gained significant attention from the participants (f = 28). Especially, students were complaining about being insulted through social media, 'receiving false information' (f = 9) through the SNSs, and 'feeling insecure' (19).

3.4.4 Social Effects

While 'show off' (f = 7) sub-category had the highest score, participants also reported that SNSs 'prevent them from talking on the phone' (f = 3). Make people show off, which was not found on the original questionnaire, was coded within the category.

3.4.5 Emotional Effects

The data analysis showed that *emotional effects* category (f = 2) has the lowest statements. Participants stated that SNSs 'depresses them. This sub category has also emerged from the analysis of open-ended responses out of the questionnaire.

3.5 Gender Differences on Students' SNSs Use

An independent sample t-test was performed to test if there was a gender difference with students' use of SNSs. Table 7 shows that there was no gender differences between the being environment friendly ($t_{178} = -1.264$, $p > 0.05$), gaining knowledge ($t_{178} = -1.033$, $p > 0.05$), communication ($t_{178} = -0.493$, $p > 0.05$), acquiring acquaintances dimensions ($t_{178} = 3.347$, $p > 0.05$) and with the total test scores ($t_{178} = 0.332$, $p > 0.05$). Therefore, it can be said that both females and males think equally about positive of using the SNNs.

An independent sample t-test was run to determine if there were any differences between the males' and females' test scores on the negative aspects of SNSs. Results showed that there were no statistically significant differences on the *security* ($t_{178} = -0.745$, $p > 0.05$), *social effects* ($t_{178} = 3.145$, $p > 0.05$), and *physical effects* dimensions ($t_{178} = 0.776$, $p > 0.05$) between males and females. On the other hand, there was a significant difference on the *cognitive effects* dimension ($t_{178} = 0.000$, $p < 0.05$), *emotional effects dimension* ($t_{178} = 1.312$, $p \leq 0.05$), and total mean average scores ($t_{178} = 1.131$, $p \leq 0.05$) between male and female participants. These results indicated that males ($x = 3.16$, $sd = 0.75$) think more negatively about the *cognitive effects* dimension than the females do ($x = 3.16$, $sd = 0.98$). In addition, male participants' *emotional effects* dimension scores ($x = 2.35$, $sd = 0.99$) were higher than the female participants' ($x = 2.17$, $sd = 0.78$) which means that males hold more negative views on the *emotional effects* dimension as seen in Table 8.

Table 7 Results of the independent sample t-test analysis for positive effects of SNSs using

Dimension	Gender	N	Means	SD	df	t	p
Being environment-friendly knowledge	Female	90	3.45	0.64	178	−1.264	0.057
	Male	90	3.31	0.78			
Gaining knowledge	Female	90	4.22	0.59	178	−1.033	0.190
	Male	90	4.12	0.71			
Communication	Female	90	3.80	0.73	178	−0.492	0.282
	Male	90	3.74	0.86			
Acquire acquaintances	Female	90	2.85	0.85	178	3.347	0.139
	Male	90	3.30	0.94			
Total	Female	90	3.07	0.41	178	−0.332	0.081
	Male	90	3.10	0.51			

Table 8 Results of the independent sample t-test analysis for negative effects of SNSs using

Dimension	Gender	N	Mean	SD	df	t	p
Security	Female	90	3.10	0.97	178	−0.745	0.172
	Male	90	2.84	0.89			
Social effects	Female	90	2.29	0.95	178	3.145	0.205
	Male	90	2.79	1.01			
Cognitive effects	Female	90	3.16	0.75	178	0.000	0.014*
	Male	90	3.16	0.98			
Physical effects	Female	90	2.44	0.93	178	0.776	0.158
	Male	90	2.56	1.03			
Emotional effects	Female	90	2.17	0.78	178	1.312	0.010*
	Male	90	2.35	0.99			
Total	Female	90	2.68	0.62	178	1.131	0.051*
	Male	90	2.80	0.77			

4 Conclusions

This study has gained a preliminary insight into university students' usage of Internet and social media and their perceptions of the effects of SNSs. Results of this small-scale survey in one location indicate that students differ somewhat in their current and anticipated uses of SNSs such as the currently-popular Facebook. Our first question focused on the purpose of using the Internet. Students reported approximately an hour daily. This result is similar to the results reported by [22] and [3], both of whom used multiple-choice questions to index daily time spent on the ınternet use. These results show that the Internet has been integrated into students' daily life. Our second question focused on the positive effects of using SNSs. Roblyer et al. [25] stated that SNSs may have great potential for improving the higher education experience. Our study also agreed with this statement showing that 80 % of the participants are using SNSs for studying. Our results also support Pempek et al.'s [22] study showing that students are using SNSs to communicate with friends and to collaborate. Students seem open to the idea of using SNSs both for personal and academic purposes (i.e. studying). As Schwartz [26] reported the potential of Facebook and similar SNSs for communication in real-time, the results of this study also showed that the young generation are using SNSs for learning new information, collaboration, and communication purposes. The third question focused on the negative effects of using SNSs. According to participants' responses the most negative effects of using SNNs are waste of time, addiction, preventing from participating in social activities, and security issues. The fourth research question was about any gender differences between users of SNSs. Our results showed that the only significant difference between males and females was with the negative effects of SNSs usage on cognitive and emotional effects dimensions. Although other research in Turkey [32, 33] and in other countries [17, 31] found significant gender differences on the usage of social networks that females are more likely to use social networks to keep in touch with friends either living nearby or in other schools while males are more likely to use social networks to find potential friends and find people with similar interests, our study showed no difference either in communication or in maintaining relationships.

This chapter contributes to efforts to document the usage purpose of social networking by university students. Since the higher education sector has to catch up with advancements in new information and communication technologies, it becomes fundamental to conduct more research on the value of social networking. Further research efforts should focus on the usage patterns of social networking among university students. The more researchers understand the importance of SNSs and their impact on students' academic behaviors, the more they will be able to effectively integrate SNSs into higher education in a successful deployment.

There are several limitations of this study. First, the perceptions of university students may be different than younger students or non-university young adults. Second, this study assesses a specific group, attending one public university in western Turkey, who may differ from other students in terms of accessing Internet connection. Third, this study is descriptive. Experimental studies may allow for deeper analysis and more meaningful information about students' use of social networking sites. Further research may be conducted to explore online privacy concerns. Genders differences may also need further inquiry with a different sample.

References

1. Bartlett MS (1954) A note on the multiplying factors for various chi square approximations. J Roy Stat Soc 16:296–298
2. Boyd DM, Ellison NB (2007) Social network sites: definition, history and scholarship. J Comput Mediat Commun 13(1):article 1
3. Boyd DM, Ellison NB (2007) Social network sites: definition, history, and scholarship. J Comput Mediat Commun 13(1):210–230
4. Brislin RW (1980) Translation and content analysis of oral and written material. In: Berry HCTaJW (ed) Handbook of cross-cultural psychology, vol 2. Allyn and Bacon, Boston, pp 389–444
5. Can A (2014) SPSS ile Bilimsel Araştırma Süresince Nicel Veri Analizi, vol 2. Pegem, Ankara
6. Cattell RB (1966) The scree test for the number of factors. Multivar Behav Res 1(2):245–276. doi:10.1207/s15327906mbr0102_10
7. Crocker L, Algina J (1986) Introduction to classical and modern test theory. Holt, Rinehart, & Winston, New York
8. Davenporta SW, Bergmanb SM, Bergmanc JZ, Fearringtond ME (2014) Twitter versus Facebook: exploring the role of narcissism in the motives and usage of different social media platforms. Comput Hum Behav 32:212–220
9. Duggan M, Smith A (2013) Social media update 2013. Pew Internet and American Life Project
10. Duggan M, Smith A (2014) Social Media Update 2013. Pew Research Center
11. Eberhardt DM (2007) Facing up to Facebook. About Campus 12(4):18–26

12. Internet Live Stats (2014). http://www.internetlivestats.com/internet-users/#trend. Accessed October 2014
13. Junco R (2013) Comparing actual and self-reported measures of Facebook use. Comput Hum Behav 29(3):626–663
14. Kaiser HF (1974) An index of factorial simplicity. Psychometrika
15. Kert SB, Kert A (2010) The usage potential of social network sites for educational purposes. Int Online J Educ Sci 2(2):486–507
16. Lamanauskas V, Šlekienė V, Ragulienė L, Iordache D, Pribeanu C, Bilek M, Cavas B, Mazurok T (2013) Social networking websites from the point of view of university students: a comparative analysis. Probl Educ 21st Cent 57:61–78
17. Lenhart A, Madden M (2007) Social networking websites and teens: an overview. Pew/Internet
18. Madge C, Meek J, Wellens J, Hooley T (2009) Facebook, social integration and informal learning at university: 'It is more for socialising and talking to friends about work than for actually doing work'. Learn Media Technol 34(2):141–155
19. Mazer JP, Murphy RE, Simonds CJ (2007) I'll see you on "Facebook": the effects of computer-mediated teacher self disclosure on students motivation, affective learning, and classroom climate. Commun Educ 56(1):1–17
20. Nunnally JC (1978) Psychometric theory, vol 2. McGraw-Hill, New York
21. Özmen B, Atıcı B (2014) Learners' views regarding the use of social networking sites in distance learning. Int Rev Res Open Dist Learn 15(4)
22. Pempek TA, Yermolayeva YA, Calvert SL (2009) College students' social networking experiences on Facebook. J Appl Dev Psychol 30(3):227–238. doi:10.1016/j.appdev.2008.12.010
23. Pempek TA, Yermolayeva YA, Calvert SL (2009) College students' social networking experiences on Facebook. J Appl Dev Psychol 30:227–238
24. Pornsakulvanich V, Haridakis P, Rubin AM (2008) The influence of dispositions and Internet motivation on online communication satisfaction and relationship closeness. Comput Hum Behav 24(5):2292–2310
25. Roblyer M, McDaniel M, Webb M, Herman J, Witty JV (2010) Findings on Facebook in higher education: a comparison of college faculty and student uses and perceptions of social networking sites. Internet High Educ 13(3):134–140
26. Schwartz H (2009) Facebook: the new classroom commons? Chron High Educ 56(6):B12–B13 doi:citeulike-article-id:6130861
27. Steinfield C, Ellison NB, Lampe C (2009) Social capital, self-esteem, and use of online social network sites: A longitudinal analysis. J Appl Dev Psychol 29:434–445
28. Stern SR (2004) Expressions of identity online: prominent features and genders differences in adolescent World Wide Web home pages. J Broadcast Electron Media 48(2):218–243
29. Strauss AL, Corbin J (1990) Basics of qualitative research: grounded theory procedures and techniques. Sage, Newbury Park
30. Tabachnick BG, Fidell LS (2001) Using multivariate statistics, vol 4. Allyn & Bacon, Upper Saddle River
31. Thelwall M (2008) Social networks, gender, and friending: an analysis of MySpace member profiles. J Am Soc Inform Sci Technol 59(8):1321–1330
32. Tufekci Z (2008) Gender, social capital and social network (ing) sites: women bonding, men searching. In: Annual Meeting of the American Sociological Association
33. Usluel Y, Mazman S (2009) Sosyal Ağların Benimsenmesi Ölçeği. Eğitim Bilimleri ve Uygulama 8(15):139–160

Effects of Social Media on Students: An Evaluation Approach in Turkey

Utku Köse

Abstract Today, social media has a great impact on people's daily life. At this point, it can be said that social media enables people to ensure a practical communication channel with other people all over the world and perform many other information-related activities like reaching to the desired information, editing it or sharing it with other clients over the Internet—web environment. Because their highly interactive using features and functions, social media services are widely used by people, over computers or computer related systems like mobile devices. In time, communication and interaction related benefits of social media have enabled this approach to be used within different fields of the modern life. The education field is one of these fields in which social media has a remarkable popularity. In the sense of the related explanations, objective of this work is to evaluate effects of social media on students. At this point, effects of social media on students have been examined by using a student survey tool. In this sense, a total of 102 university students (from different departments—study areas) have been enabled to fill different survey sections in order to receive responses for especially some statements regarding to effects of social media over students' general activities. In order to ensure a specific evaluation perspective, the work has been done in Turkey and in this way; positive and negative effects of social media over Turkish students have been analyzed briefly. The work has been done because evaluating both positive and negative effects of social media on students makes it possible to analyze better importance of social media within students' life and obtain some certain ideas about effects of the social media on improving students' knowledge and abilities or just limiting them. Obtained findings with this work show that the social media affects (Turkish) students generally in a positive manner. But it can also be said that negative use of social media can prevent students from improving their cognitive level and affects their social and physical aspects in a negative manner.

U. Köse (✉)
Computer Sciences Application and Research Centre, Usak University, Usak, Turkey
e-mail: utku.kose@usak.edu.tr

T. Issa et al. (eds.), *Social Networking and Education*,
Lecture Notes in Social Networks, DOI 10.1007/978-3-319-17716-8_12

Keywords Social media · Internet · Web · Effects of social media · Turkey · Turkish students · Education

1 Introduction

Nowadays, the world is under the influence of rapidly changing technologies including computer and communication technologies as the most remarkable ones. When we consider the function of both computer and communication technologies in forming living style and the form of the society, it can be understood that today's many daily activities are done highly based on computer related devices and improved communication technologies and the importance of reaching to the desired information, editing it, and also sharing it over the world become an important problem among people, who are members of the changing world. At this point, developments and improvements within computer technology and its effects on improving the other associated technologies has a given a great impact on shaping the humankind's living style and enabling them to adapt to a world supported with a digital power. As a result of developments in time, an important communication technology called as Internet has appeared and taken an active role within people's life rapidly. With mutual improvements in software and hardware technologies, Internet and the Web (the logical interface of the Internet) have been being employed in almost every activity in our modern life. All of these changes can be also connected with needs of the information society and the improving importance of information (or data in a digital manner within computer related devices) as a mutual change trend for years. Needs on reaching to the desired information, editing it, and sharing it over the world with other people have made it necessary to design and develop Web tools employing interactive features and functions and finally, a new concept, which is called as social media, has appeared.

Today, social media has a great impact on people's daily life. At this point, it can be said that social media enables people to ensure a practical communication channel with other people all over the world and perform many other information-related activities like reaching to the desired information, editing it or sharing it with other clients over the web environment. Because their highly interactive using features and functions, social media services are widely used by people, over computers or computer related systems like mobile devices. In time, communication and interaction related benefits of social media have enabled this approach to be used within different fields of the modern life. The education field is one of these fields in which social media have a remarkable popularity. When we examine the associated literature in detail, it can be seen that researchers and scientists are focused highly on usage of interactive tools for improving educational processes and the social media is one of the most important interactive tools that are widely taken into consideration. Especially function of social media to reach to the desired information, edit the information or share it with other clients over the web is too important in educational manner [4, 10]. Eventually, it is clear that popularity of the social media will be last for long time because of the momentum in developments and improvements within social media world.

In the sense of the related explanations, objective of this work is to provide an evaluation approach for effects of social media on students. In order to ensure a specific evaluation perspective the work has been done in Turkey and in this way, positive and negative effects of social media over Turkish students have been analyzed briefly. It is known that when the social media is used in a beneficial way, many advantages to improve especially teaching—learning perspectives can be gained. So, it has been firstly focused on positive effects of social media over the related students. After that, negative effects have been examined in the sense of students' cognitive development, social development, physical development, and also their security perceptions. It is believed that the work will be remarkable research approach because of its subject focused on effects of social media and the objective group in a specific country.

Remaining content of this paper is organized as follows: Next section is devoted to the social media concept in order to enable readers to have enough information and idea about the social media, which is the key subject of the work. After this section, the third section explains today's popular social media services. In this sense, it focuses on some recent, popular services to provide enough information about features and functions of the foremost social media services—tools. Following to that, the fourth section provides the necessary explanations regarding to the evaluation—research aspects of the work. At this point, the related section focuses on evaluation—research method, research questions, the evaluation—research tool, and details regarding to the students—participants, who have taken part within the evaluation approach. Next, the fifth section provides findings obtained via the related student survey sections and the sixth section discusses about all of these findings in order to reach to some certain results. Finally, the paper ends with conclusions and some additional discussions on possible future works.

2 What is Social Media?

Before examining the effects of social media over students, it is a better approach to define the social media concept briefly and give enough information about it in order to enable readers to have idea about the fundamentals of the work subject. Simply, the social media is a concept, which can be used for defining the digital social interaction and information sharing, editing platform over which people can also communicate with each other by using special interactivity tools. Social media is originally associated with especially computer technologies including computer—based communication technologies. When we look at to the literature, we may also encounter with some more definitions. For example, Ahlqvist et al. defines it as a social interaction among people which allows them to create, share or exchange information, ideas, and images or videos over virtual communities and networking systems [1]. On the other hand, Kaplan and Haenlein define it as "a group of Internet-based applications that build on the ideological and technological foundations of Web 2.0, and that allow the creation and exchange of user-generated content" [6, p 61]. The term of Web 2.0 over here is used for defining the generation of Web platform and technologies, which provides the function of sharing, creating information and ensuring interactive communication and collaboration-based activities over the Web. Especially social media services—technologies are typical Web 2.0 technologies.

In the sense of today's technological conditions, it can be expressed that social media services are useful tools for creating Web-based communities where people can communicate and interact with other people by using Web interfaces and tools. Today's popular social media services employ different approaches, methods, or technologies for enabling people—users to experience interactive communication and different ways of sharing, creating, and also exchanging the information. It has been expressed in the literature that social media services have encouraged new ways to communicate and share information and they are used regularly by millions of people with a rapidly improving popularity in time [7–9].

2.1 Advantages and Disadvantages of Social Media

A good way to understand importance of social media in today's world is explaining its essential advantages. In this way, it can be more possible to think better about communication and information sharing oriented features and functions, which take users' attention and keep an improving popularity among them. But except from the related advantages, social media services also employ some disadvantages, which may cause negative effects from different perspectives. Before focusing more on research story of the work, it is a better idea to express briefly both advantages and disadvantages of social media.

As it is also reported commonly in the related literature, essential advantages of social media can be expressed as follows [2, 3]:

- Social media and the related services enables users to benefit from a worldwide communication channel, which includes different types of communication approaches, methods, and techniques to improve Internet based communication among people, who are in distance places.
- Social media provides an improved interaction for users and make it possible to ensure improved, Web oriented socialization via computer based tools. In this way, people—users, who are in common interests, have possibility to contact with each other even they live in different, distance areas of the world.
- One of the most important advantages of social media is that it allows users to reach to the desired information rapidly, edit any information collaboratively, and also share information with other users over the Web easily. In this way,

social media enables people—users to improve their effectiveness and productivity in works or studies.
- Global interactivity and sophistication of social media services make it easier to apply them in different fields of modern life. Thus, a global, digital socialization networking is ensured in the sense of business, academic environments, and public or private communities.
- Social media enables people—users to express them in a multimedia supported, interactive environment and learn something from other people's—users' posts, shares…etc. From this perspective, the social media is also an effective channel that enables communities to announce their problems, needs with a high voice.
- Real-time updates and non-stop information flow within social media services enable people—users to always keep themselves informed about the world. It also makes it very easy to keep in touch with the family, friends or any other close people.

Especially interactive using features and functions of social media are important factors keeping the related services always popular. But improved interactive using features and functions may also cause some kind of disadvantages, because they make people addicted to the digital environment. Disadvantages of social media generally appear when it is used in a negative way. At this point, it is possible to express some important disadvantages as follows [2, 3]:

- When it is thought in the sense of physical activities or socialization, the social media may reduce face-to-face interaction and become just a waste of time over the Internet—web.
- The social media may cause false or harmful information to be shared along the Internet—web rapidly.
- Because of its simple and effective features and functions to ensure an interactive communication environment, the social media may cause cyber-bullying and also some crimes against people.
- Sharing information mechanism of social media improves risks of fraud and identity theft. In this sense, the social media comes with important disadvantages causing the private life to become public unlawfully.
- Because of its highly interactive communication features and functions, the social media may also become a good, secure communication channel for especially crime organizations.

3 Today's Popular Social Media Services

When we take today's Web environment into consideration, it can be said that there are many different kinds of social media platforms in order to ensure the related communication and information usage mechanisms and features explained for the social media generally within the previous section. In order not affect the flow of the paper negatively; it has explained some popular social media services as follows [11]:

- **Facebook:** Facebook is one of the most important social media environment, which employs many different sides of the social media concept/environment. Currently it is the most popular social media environment for users all over the world. In this social media environment, it is possible to prepare a profile for yourself and ensure contacts via this profile by adding your friends to your friend list, or making any other Facebook related activities like creating pages, joining to groups, playing games or using applications, which are provided over the Facebook platform, and perform any other things related to information modification and share. Generally, Facebook is a wide social media platform for sharing the information in different forms like text-based, image-based, or video-based. When you reach such information over the Facebook platform, it is possible to make comments over it, or perform any other activities like sharing it over your profile, or page, groups…etc. and liking it in order to make it a trending share. Facebook includes all kinds of communication ways including Web-cam contact.
- **Twitter:** Twitter is a revolutionary social media service in which users can type and share a 140-word text (Tweet) by using the related controls. In this sense, it is possible to use some special syntax to share your text with defined groups—topics. Like Facebook, Twitter also has a typical profile-based account for each user and it is possible for each user to follow other ones in order to receive their shares instantly over the Twitter interface. Twitter is also a very strong media tool, which has been effective on sharing information with other users or communicating with each other during especially communal events, or riots.
- **Wikipedia:** Wikipedia is a free Web-based encyclopedia in which users can have a collaboration to prepare pages providing information for any specific subject—item. It is also the origin of the Web technology Wiki, which defines the social media approach of creating and updating a Web-based knowledge collaboratively. Today, there are many similar forms of such technology for enabling users to work collaboratively for creating knowledge related contents over the Web.
- **LinkedIn:** LinkedIn is a social media platform, which is related to mostly business-based social interaction. At this point, LinkedIn uses the profile-based account system and users on LinkedIn can create their own profiles by indicating their jobs, working experiences, abilities… etc. and contact with other people providing their own business-based profiles. Over the platform, it is possible to join groups of specific companies or search for job announcements or take part in announcing job opportunities in order to reach more people over the Web.
- **Tumblr:** Tumblr is a typical social media service, which allows users to create their own blog pages in a shorter form. Briefly, the service makes it possible for users to follow other users' blog pages, share their media over their own blog environments and keep in touch with updates come from the followed blog pages. All of these activities regarding to posting new content or following updates can be done easily by also using a common Web interface provided over the platform (Fig. 1).

Fig. 1 Communication in today's modern world is greatly based on social media [5]

- **Google Plus:** Google Plus is the social media environment provided by the Google Company. This service is similar to other wide social media services like Facebook or LinkedIn and uses the same approach of user profile in order to enable users to share information and have social interaction with other users over the Web/social media environment.
- **MySpace:** MySpace, is a popular social media service, which allows users to create their own profiles and perform the related activities on information obtaining, sharing or ensuring interactive communication sessions like many other popular social media services allow. As different, additional functions, the MySpace also enables users to create music band pages for their groups and share their albums or records via Web platform. In this sense, it is possible to share different kinds of media including sounds, videos or images and also provide contents within specific blog pages.
- **Academic Social Media Services:** Over the Web, there are also academic-oriented social media services that academicians, researchers and scientists can use to create their own profile and share academic works, ideas over specially designed Web interfaces. Some popular versions of such services are Mendeley, Academia, and ResearchGate. All of these services aim to provide an effective information sharing and communication platform for especially people from academic and scientific fields.
- **Foursquare:** Foursquare is a social media service, which is based on discovering places and sharing or gaining information—suggestions about popular places all over world. In this sense, users can make check-in when they visit a place and perform many different social interaction activities like contacting with active visitors—users, making comments about the place. It is also possible to have information about the place by reading comments or any other

information shared over the Foursquare page of the place visited. Generally, users over the Foursquare are focused on places like restaurants, cafes, shopping places—malls or any other places regarding to entertainment.

- **YouTube:** YouTube is a social media service for sharing videos over the Web. In time, YouTube has improved and gained many features and functions for being a more effective social media platform, which focuses on videos. Over this platform, it is possible to create user accounts, which also include profile-oriented features and also channel feature in which you can share your videos over the YouTube and with users, who are following your channel. It is possible for YouTube-users to like your video and/or make comments under it in order to form a social environment.
- **Instagram:** Instagram is a social media environment in which users can share pictures—photos or videos over their account. Like other social media services, it is possible for Instagram users to like and make comment on other users' photos shared over their pages. Instagram is also actually a mobile application connected with the Web interface so users can use the application to take pictures, record videos and share them over the Web.
- **Pinterest:** Pinterest is a social media service, which allows users to share their media about an interest subject over user based created, visual boards. At this point, the Pinterest allows users to pin their visual objects over boards and in this way, it is allowed to share information regarding to common interests with other users over the platform. Like other services, Pinterest also has some similar functions like liking or making comments. Briefly, it is a different social media service, which is also a visual discovery, collection, sharing, and storage tool [12].

Except from the explained services above, there are many different kinds of social media services over the Web. With changing popularities, they provide the mechanism of social media concept and enable users to experience Web-based interactivity and communication. Current power of these services also comes from increasing usage of especially mobile devices. Because people generally use their mobile devices like smart phones or tablets in order not to cut their connection with the social media over the live Web. From this perspective, it is clear that these services are good tools for performing many communication and information related works included within different fields. Education is one of these fields in which both teachers and students can benefit from highly interactive multimedia tools, communication techniques, and many other thing aiming to enable people for reaching to the desired information, editing it or sharing it over the Web.

4 Evaluating Effects of Social Media on Students

In this study, effects of social media on students have been examined in order to have some remarkable findings on what is the role of social media within students' life. At this point, it has been believed that evaluating both positive and negative effects of social media on students makes it possible to analyze better importance of social media within students' life and obtain some certain ideas about effects of the social media on improving students' knowledge and abilities or just limiting them.

4.1 Evaluation—Research Method

In the sense of the work concept, the research has been done by focusing on students' ideas—experiences on using the social media in their daily life or works—studies. At this point, it can be said that evaluation—research method is based on receiving feedbacks from objective participants of this study and reaching to some results—ideas by analyzing the findings. As it can be understood, research questions of the work are mostly based on role of social media within students' life and its effects in this manner.

4.2 Research Questions

As associated with the objective of this work, the foremost research questions can be listed briefly as follows:

- What are positive and negative effects of social media on students?
- How do a social media affect students' life in a positive or negative manner?
- How do a social media affect students' cognitive, social, and physical development?
- How do a social media affect students' security anxiety level—status in the sense of Internet—web environment?
- As a general perspective, do a social media affect students and their life positively or negatively?

4.3 Evaluation—Research Tool

Within the evaluation approach of this work, a student survey tool has been employed in order to receive some findings for having better idea about effects of social media on students. In this sense, a total of 102 university students (from different departments—study areas) have been enabled to fill different survey sections in order to receive responses for especially some statements regarding to effects of social media over students' general activities. The survey consists of different sections in order to take enough information about students' features but in order not to affect the flow of the paper, only two essential sections including statements about positive and negative effects of social media over students and received feedbacks for these statements are provided in detail within this work.

In order to have enough idea on positive effects of social media on the related students, a total of 25 statements have been asked for receiving feedbacks. It has been wanted the students to give their responses to each statement by using the Likert Scale. Generally, the statements are in the form of 'thanks to the social media I can/do…' On the other hand, negative effects of social media on students have been tried to be evaluated via a total of 30 statements, which aim to ask students to figure out how they use the social media in a negative way. It has been wanted the students to give their responses to each statement by using the Likert Scale. Generally, the statements are in the form of 'the use of the social media…'.

4.4 Information About Participants

As it was expressed before, a total of 102 university students have been taken active part within the evaluation approach of this work. At this point, some brief information obtained about the related students—participants via some other survey sections can be explained as follows:

- A total of 69 male (about 68 %) and a total of 33 female (about 32 %) students have filled the related survey.
- Age intervals regarding to the students are:
  - 18–22 → 53 students (about 52 %)
  - 22–32 → 39 students (about 38 %)
  - 32-42 → 9 students (about %9)
  - 42–52 → 1 student (about 1 %)
- The students' departments—study areas are generally:
  - Computer Technologies (about 32 %)
  - Mathematics (about 22 %)
  - Foreign Trade (about 15 %)
  - Business (about 11 %)
  - Turkish Language and Literature (about 10 %)
  - Office Management (about 7 %)
  - Logistics (about 3 %)

- All students, who have taken the survey, were able to use social media for remarkable time periods within their daily life and they were also authority enough on computer usage.

5 Findings Obtained via Evaluation Approach

According to the general structure of the student survey(s), it is possible to focus on obtained findings in the sense of two different perspectives: positive and negative effects of social media.

5.1 *Findings Obtained for Evaluating Positive Effects of Social Media*

Within the filled survey on positive effects of social media on students, the statements and also received feedbacks for them are presented under Table 1.

In the sense of factor analysis of the related survey, also descriptive statistics are given in the Table 1. Also, Tables 2, 3, and 4 present statistics respectively for

Table 1 Survey on positive effects of social media on students (statements and received responses)

St. No	Statement ('Thanks to the social media, I can/do…')	Responses for[a]					Mean	Var.[b]	St. Dev.[c]
		1	2	3	4	5			
1	Learn new information and knowledge	2	2	9	54	35	4.16	0.67	0.82
2	Gain up-to-date information	1	2	2	55	42	4.32	0.50	0.71
3	Be more aware of global issues/local issues	2	1	14	57	28	4.06	0.63	0.79
4	Remember facts/aspects of the past	6	1	19	48	28	3.89	1.03	1.01
5	Communicate with my peers frequently	1	6	7	52	36	4.14	0.73	0.86

(continued)

Table 1 (continued)

St. No	Statement ('Thanks to the social media, I can/do…')	Responses for[a]					Mean	Var.[b]	St. Dev.[c]
		1	2	3	4	5			
6	Collaborate with my peers frequently	3	6	27	38	28	3.80	1.01	1.01
7	Communicate with my peers from different universities	3	10	14	49	26	3.83	1.03	1.02
8	Communicate with my different communities	3	14	18	48	19	3.65	1.06	1.03
9	Develop intercrossing relationships with my peers (i.e. Artistic talents, sport and common interests)	3	9	15	55	20	3.78	0.92	0.96
10	Study independently	5	9	20	50	18	3.66	1.06	1.03
11	Overcome study stress	12	5	13	47	25	3.67	1.53	1.24
12	Complete my study more quickly	6	12	22	40	22	3.59	1.27	1.13
13	Understand and solve study problems easily	7	10	18	43	24	3.66	1.32	1.15
14	Scrutinize my research study more easily	7	8	10	49	28	3.81	1.28	1.13
15	Develop my personal and communication skills	4	12	16	48	22	3.71	1.12	1.06
16	Concentrate more on my reading and writing skills	11	22	28	28	13	3.10	1.44	1.20
17	Prepare my professional attitude toward study and work	9	16	25	38	14	3.31	1.35	1.16

(continued)

Table 1 (continued)

St. No	Statement ('Thanks to the social media, I can/do…')	Responses for[a]					Mean	Var.[b]	St. Dev.[c]
		1	2	3	4	5			
18	Be more sustainable person	9	21	23	35	14	3.24	1.41	1.19
19	Provide reliable and scalable services	7	19	26	35	15	3.31	1.31	1.14
20	Become more "Greener" in my activities	7	12	24	38	21	3.53	1.32	1.15
21	Reduce carbon footprint in my activities	10	21	26	27	18	3.22	1.54	1.24
22	Acquire new acquaintances—work related	7	13	17	47	18	3.55	1.28	1.13
23	Acquire new acquaintances—friendship relationship	6	11	13	49	23	3.71	1.24	1.11
24	Acquire new acquaintances—romance relationship	22	30	24	16	10	2.63	1.58	1.26
25	Do whatever I want, say whatever I want, and be whoever I want	16	13	14	39	20	3.33	1.83	1.35

[a]Likert Scale: 1 → 'I strongly disagree'; 2 → 'I disagree'; 3 → 'I'm neutral'; 4 → 'I agree'; 5 → 'I strongly agree'
[b]Variance
[c]Standard Deviation
Total Responders: 102

Table 2 Statistics for 'Kaiser-Meyer-Olkin (KMO) and Bartlett's Test' regarding to the survey evaluating positive effects of social media

Kaiser-Meyer-Olkin measure of sampling adequacy		0.878
Bartlett's test of sphericity	Approx. Chi-Square	1995.927
	df	300
	Sig.	0.000

Table 3 Statistics for 'Communalities' regarding to the survey evaluating positive effects of social media

Statement	Initial	Extraction
Learn new information and knowledge	1.000	0.808
Gain up-to-date information	1.000	0.769
Be more aware of global issues/local issues	1.000	0.854
To remember facts/aspects of the past	1.000	0.702
Communicate with my peers frequently	1.000	0.768
Collaborate with my peers frequently	1.000	0.764
Communicate with my peers from different universities	1.000	0.601
Communicate with my different communities	1.000	0.769
Develop intercrossing relationships with my peers…	1.000	0.731
Study independently	1.000	0.620
Overcome study stress	1.000	0.742
Complete my study more quickly	1.000	0.840
Understand and solve study problems easily	1.000	0.880
Scrutinize my research study more easily	1.000	0.792
Develop my personal and communication skills	1.000	0.503
Concentrate more on my reading and writing skills	1.000	0.810
To prepare my professional attitude toward study and work	1.000	0.847
Be more sustainable person	1.000	0.776
Provide reliable and scalable services	1.000	0.799
Become more "Greener" in my activities	1.000	0.827
Reduce carbon footprint in my activities	1.000	0.766
Acquire new acquaintances—work related	1.000	0.674
Acquire new acquaintances—friendship relationship	1.000	0.550
Acquire new acquaintances—romance relationship	1.000	0.789
Do whatever I want, say whatever I want, and be whoever I want	1.000	0.769

'KMO and Bartlett's Test', 'Communalities', and 'Total Variance Explained' regarding to the survey on positive effects of social media.

5.2 *Findings Obtained for Evaluating Negative Effects of Social Media*

In the sense of the other filled survey, which is for evaluating negative effects of social media on students, the statements and also received feedbacks for them are presented under Table 5.

Table 4 Statistics for 'Total Variance Explained' regarding to the survey evaluating positive effects of social media

C.[a]	Initial Eigenvalues			Extraction sums of squared loadings		
	Total	% of Variance	Cu. %[b]	Total	% of Variance	Cu. %[b]
1	11.481	45.923	45.923	11.481	45.923	45.923
2	2.222	8.886	54.810	2.222	8.886	54.810
3	1.649	6.598	61.407	1.649	6.598	61.407
4	1.199	4.797	66.204	1.199	4.797	66.204
5	1.186	4.745	70.949	1.186	4.745	70.949
6	1.014	4.055	75.005	1.014	4.055	75.005
7	0.807	3.230	78.234			
8	0.699	2.797	81.031			
9	0.668	2.674	83.705			
10	0.555	2.221	85.925			
11	0.505	2.019	87.944			
12	0.446	1.785	89.729			
13	0.362	1.449	91.178			
14	0.336	1.345	92.523			
15	0.297	1.187	93.710			
16	0.262	1.050	94.760			
17	0.236	0.944	95.704			
18	0.226	0.903	96.607			
19	0.179	0.716	97.322			
20	0.168	0.672	97.994			
21	0.141	0.563	98.557			
22	0.127	0.507	99.063			
23	0.087	0.348	99.411			
24	0.077	0.309	99.720			
25	0.070	0.280	100.000			

[a]Component
[b]Cumulative %

Table 5 also includes descriptive statistics related to the survey. In the sense of factor analysis, Tables 6, 7, and 8 provide other statistics.

Table 5 Survey on negative effects of social media on students (statements and received responses)

St. No	Statement ('The use of the social media…')	Responses for;[a]					Mean	Var.[b]	St. Dev.[c]
		1	2	3	4	5			
1	Prevents me from concentrating more on writing and reading skills	11	17	22	41	11	3.24	1.39	1.18
2	Prevents me from remembering the fundamental knowledge and skills	13	28	30	26	5	2.82	1.22	1.10
3	Scatters my attention	12	18	15	44	13	3.27	1.53	1.24
4	Decreases my grammar and proofreading skills	16	32	17	32	5	2.78	1.42	1.19
5	Decreases my deep thinking	15	29	20	31	7	2.86	1.45	1.20
6	Distracts me easily	9	23	13	46	11	3.26	1.40	1.19
7	Prevents me from participating in social activities	11	28	26	29	8	2.95	1.31	1.15
8	Prevents me from completing my work/study on time	13	27	21	36	5	2.93	1.33	1.15
9	Makes me sick and unhealthy	20	26	22	28	6	2.75	1.50	1.22
10	Bores me	16	34	17	29	6	2.75	1.43	1.20
11	Stresses me	18	38	22	21	3	2.54	1.20	1.10
12	Depresses me	17	40	22	18	5	2.55	1.24	1.11
13	Makes me feel lonely	15	41	18	24	4	2.62	1.25	1.12
14	Makes me lazy	9	11	20	41	21	3.53	1.42	1.19
15	Makes me addict	6	12	14	50	20	3.65	1.22	1.10
16	Makes me more gambler	23	30	20	24	5	2.59	1.47	1.21
17	Makes me insecure to	13	20	24	33	12	3.11	1.50	1.23

(continued)

Table 5 (continued)

St. No	Statement ('The use of the social media…')	Responses for;[a]					Mean	Var.[b]	St. Dev.[c]
		1	2	3	4	5			
	release my personal details from the theft of personal information								
18	Makes me receive an immoral images and information from unscrupulous people and it is difficult to act against them at present	18	29	19	26	10	2.81	1.62	1.27
19	Prevents me from having face to face contact with my family	14	35	14	28	11	2.87	1.60	1.26
20	Prevents me from having face to face contact with my friends	13	29	17	30	13	3.01	1.61	1.27
21	Prevents me from participating in physical activities	11	27	20	30	14	3.09	1.55	1.24
22	Prevents me from shopping in stores	17	42	18	22	3	2.53	1.20	1.10
23	Prevents me from watching television	15	33	18	27	9	2.82	1.51	1.23
24	Prevents me from reading the newspapers	15	29	19	30	9	2.89	1.52	1.23
25	Prevents me from talking on the phone/mobile	14	40	16	24	8	2.73	1.43	1.20
26	Prevents me from completing my work on time	12	27	21	34	8	2.99	1.40	1.18

(continued)

Table 5 (continued)

St. No	Statement ('The use of the social media…')	Responses for;[a]					Mean	Var.[b]	St. Dev.[c]
		1	2	3	4	5			
27	Prevents me from completing my study on time	10	27	29	30	6	2.95	1.20	1.09
28	Increase privacy concerns	11	17	20	33	21	3.35	1.64	1.28
29	Increase security concerns	11	13	20	37	21	3.43	1.57	1.25
30	Increase intellectual property concerns	10	17	20	36	19	3.36	1.54	1.24

[a]Likert Scale: 1 → 'I strongly disagree'; 2 → 'I disagree'; 3 → 'I'm neutral'; 4 → 'I agree'; 5 → 'I strongly agree'
[b]Variance
[c]Standard Deviation
Total Responders: 102

Table 6 Statistics for 'Kaiser-Meyer-Olkin (KMO) and Bartlett's Test' regarding to the survey evaluating negative effects of social media

Kaiser-Meyer-Olkin measure of sampling adequacy		0.863
Bartlett's test of sphericity	Approx. Chi-Square	2512.458
	df	435
	Sig.	0.000

Table 7 Statistics for 'Communalities' regarding to the survey evaluating negative effects of social media

Statement	Initial	Extraction
Prevents me from concentrating more on writing and reading skills	1.000	0.545
Prevents me from remembering the fundamental knowledge and skills	1.000	0.688
Scatters my attention	1.000	0.766
Decreases my grammar and proofreading skills	1.000	0.717
Decreases my deep thinking	1.000	0.744
Distracts me easily	1.000	0.651
Prevents me from participating in social activities	1.000	0.532
Prevents me from completing my work/study on time	1.000	0.666
Makes me sick and unhealthy	1.000	0.661

(continued)

Table 7 (continued)

Statement	Initial	Extraction
Bores me	1.000	0.706
Stresses me	1.000	0.844
Depresses me	1.000	0.842
Makes me feel lonely	1.000	0.493
Makes me lazy	1.000	0.734
Makes me addict	1.000	0.669
Makes me more gambler	1.000	0.446
Makes me insecure to release my personal details from the theft of personal information	1.000	0.709
Makes me receive an immoral images and information from unscrupulous people and it is difficult to act against them at present	1.000	0.636
Prevents me from having face to face contact with my family	1.000	0.705
Prevents me from having face to face contact with my friends	1.000	0.736
Prevents me from participating in physical activities	1.000	0.666
Prevents me from shopping in stores	1.000	0.746
Prevents me from watching television	1.000	0.615
Prevents me from reading the newspapers	1.000	0.657
Prevents me from talking on the phone/mobile	1.000	0.723
Prevents me from completing my work on time	1.000	0.783
Prevents me from completing my study on time	1.000	0.807
Increase privacy concerns	1.000	0.825
Increase security concerns	1.000	0.819
Increase intellectual property concerns	1.000	0.722

Table 8 Statistics for 'Total Variance Explained' regarding to the survey evaluating negative effects of social media

C.[a]	Initial Eigenvalues			Extraction sums of squared loadings			Rotation sums of squared loadings		
	Total	% of Variance	Cu. %[b]	Total	% of Variance	Cu. %[b]	Total	% of Variance	Cu. %[b]
1	12.327	41.089	41.089	12.327	41.089	41.089	5.462	18.208	18.208
2	3.037	10.123	51.212	3.037	10.123	51.212	4.659	15.530	33.738
3	2.357	7.855	59.067	2.357	7.855	59.067	4.165	13.883	47.621
4	1.890	6.300	65.367	1.890	6.300	65.367	3.720	12.401	60.022
5	1.242	4.142	69.509	1.242	4.142	69.509	2.846	9.486	69.509
6	0.992	3.306	72.815						
7	0.913	3.043	75.857						
8	0.809	2.698	78.555						
9	0.705	2.350	80.905						

(continued)

Table 8 (continued)

C.[a]	Initial Eigenvalues			Extraction sums of squared loadings			Rotation sums of squared loadings		
	Total	% of Variance	Cu. %[b]	Total	% of Variance	Cu. %[b]	Total	% of Variance	Cu. %[b]
10	0.647	2.158	83.063						
11	0.569	1.898	84.961						
12	0.545	1.816	86.777						
13	0.465	1.548	88.325						
14	0.438	1.460	89.785						
15	0.387	1.290	91.075						
16	0.371	1.237	92.312						
17	0.332	1.105	93.417						
18	0.305	1.017	94.434						
19	0.274	0.912	95.347						
20	0.244	0.812	96.159						
21	0.210	0.700	96.859						
22	0.171	0.571	97.430						
23	0.139	0.463	97.893						
24	0.129	0.431	98.324						
25	0.113	0.377	98.701						
26	0.098	0.328	99.029						
27	0.093	0.311	99.339						
28	0.079	0.264	99.603						
29	0.063	0.211	99.814						
30	0.056	0.186	100.000						

[a]Component
[b]Cumulative %

6 Discussion

After focusing on the related findings and analyzing them from different perspectives, it has been possible to reach to some key points—discussions regarding to effects of the social media on students. As it can be understood, the related key points—discussions can be expressed under two different perspectives, which are positive and negative effects.

6.1 *Positive Effects of Social Media*

According to the obtained responses, it is possible to express following findings in the sense of positive effects of social media on students:

- Thanks to the social media, students can ensure more interactive communication with their near or far peers/friends.
- With the social media, students rarely acquire new acquaintances–romance relationships. It can be said that the communication effects of social media is based on only new friendships and communication with peers.
- The social media is good at enabling students to study their lessons, focus on reaching to the desired information and make it easier to reach to new information and improve their knowledge.
- Thanks to the social media, students can be more aware of global /local issues and remember facts/aspects regarding to the past.
- With the social media, students can perform collaborative works easier and develop intercrossing relationships.
- The social media helps students for improving their study time and problem understanding/solving abilities.
- The social media is not good enough for enabling students to concentrate more on their own reading and writing skills.

6.2 Negative Effects of Social Media

As it was expressed before, negative effects of social media can be examined in the sense of four different perspectives regarding to students. At this point, it is clear that the related negative effects are related to the situations when the social media is used by students in a negative way. Using the social media in a positive manner is an important research question that belongs to wider future research works.

According to the responses to the related survey statements, remarkable findings about negative effects of social media on students can be expressed as follows:

- **Negative effects on cognitive development:** When it is evaluated in the sense of cognitive development, students think that social media prevents them from concentrating more on their writing and reading skills. It is also important that the social media distracts students easily and scatters their attention. When it is evaluated in the sense of effects of social media on deep thinking, remembering knowledge or skills and also completing studies in time, students' responses are not clear in order to have a certain idea if usage of social media causes negative effects on these situations. It is also not clear if social media prevents students from reading newspapers.
- **Negative effects on social development:** Negative effects of social media on social development are generally because of addiction. Most of students think that social media makes them addict and affect their social situations in a negative manner. In this sense, generally students think that social media makes them to feel lonely. When it is asked if the social media depresses the students, they think that it does not depress them but they are not clear if the social media bores or stresses them. When the situation is evaluated in the sense of face to

face interaction, it is not possible to have a certain idea because some students think that the social media prevents them having face to face interaction while some students do not agree. Students do not think that the social media prevents them from shopping in stories or talking on the phone. But it is still not clear if social media prevents students from watching television or completing their works or studies in time (There are more students thinking that social media prevents them from completing their works or studies in time; but there are also remarkable amount of responses for counter ideas, which makes it not clear to have certain evaluation).

- **Negative effects on physical development:** Students generally think that the social media makes them lazy, which may cause physical development in a negative manner. It can also be said that social media generally does not make students sick or unhealthy; but some students are not certain about this situation. On the other hand, it is not clear that if the social media prevents students from participating in physical activities but findings regarding to this situation does not match with the findings explaining that social media may make students lazy. This may be because the students feel themselves lazy in a psychological perspective.
- **Negative effects regarding to security:** Clear findings found for negative effects of social media are generally regarding to the perspectives about security anxiety. It can be said that the social media cause increasing concerns on privacy, security and also intellectual property.

According to the findings obtained via the evaluation process and the ideas that have been reached thanks to the findings show that the related research questions, which have been indicated before, have been answered properly with the performed work. On the other hand, it is also possible to focus on some limitations that are related to the work and also explain some future work ideas in order to enable readers to know the potentials that can be activated in similar future works.

6.3 Limitations and Future Work

In the sense of the subject, research area, and any other characteristics of the work, important limitations can be expressed briefly as follows:

- This work has been performed in Turkey and the objective group of the evaluation process has included Turkish students. From this perspective, the work is a remarkable, specific research approach because it focuses on a report that includes ideas to analyze status within a specific country. But in order to reach to a global evaluation on effects of social media over students, realizing a more comprehensive project is a better idea.
- Regarding to the effects of the social media, the objective group of the evaluation process includes only students. If it is wanted to reach to ideas about what are effects of the social media on people—users generally, a similar work

employing people—users from different sides of the life to be analyzed should be performed.

- There are many different factors (number of students, each student's characteristics, general features of the environment in which the research takes place… etc.) that may affect the results of the work. It is clear that all of the related factors cannot be controlled via any alternative work, but this situation gives good ideas on alternative research works controlling specific factors.

Obtained findings, reached results, and also limitations regarding to the current work allow thinking about future potentials. When it is discussed in the sense of future works, it can be said that more comprehensive research works on evaluating effects of social media can be performed by designing different surveys analyzing the problem from different perspectives. At this point, it is also a good idea to apply different kinds of surveys in order to have more detailed findings about different effects of social media on students. Also, designing some applied evaluation approaches rather than using only a survey tool can be a remarkable evaluation approach for similar works. In this way, it will also be possible to evaluate better both usage of social media and characteristics—physiological aspects of objective groups taking part in such research works.

7 Conclusions

In this study, effects of social media on students have been examined in both positive and negative perspectives. In order to ensure a research method, a survey tool has been applied for Turkish students and in this way, it has been also aimed to have idea about what we can say about effects of social media in especially Turkish students. It is though that the survey group formed via university students from different departments is a good enough objective environment to obtain objective ideas about both positive and negative effects of social media. As general, the work is also a remarkable reference for having idea about Turkish students' perspectives on the social media, which is the most powerful communication and interaction tool of today's modern world.

Obtained findings show that the social media affects Turkish students generally in a positive manner. But it can also be said that negative use of social media can prevent students from improving their cognitive level and affects their social and physical aspects in a negative manner. It is also clear that there is only a thin line that enables students to benefit from advantages of social media or have some disadvantages caused by generally social media addiction. According to the findings, we can say that positive usage of social media is not a difficult thing to do; even social media addictions can be transformed into a totally improvement in the sense of knowledge and skills if the social media can be used more in a good way and disadvantages regarding to decreases on social and physical activities can be eliminated with different solutions.

Eventually, the performed work is a remarkable reference in the sense of effects of social media on especially students. Also, focusing on Turkey is a unique characteristic of the work and this feature is an important gain for the associated literature. In addition to the current work, there will be also some future works, which are thought while focusing on limitations. In this sense, there will be works, which are based on applying different types of surveys, focusing on different aspects to evaluate effects of social media, and also performing improved evaluation approaches including both applied processes and surveys.

References

1. Ahlqvist T, Bäck A, Halonen M, Heinonen S (2008) Social media road maps exploring the futures triggered by social media. VTT Tiedotteita – Valtion Teknillinen Tutkimuskeskus (2454):13
2. Asia-Pacific Economics Blog (2014) Advantages and disadvantages of social networking. http://apecsec.org/advantages-and-disadvantages-of-social-networking/. Accessed 16 Dec 2014
3. BBC (2013) The positives and negatives of using social networking sites (News School Report —Student Reports). http://www.bbc.co.uk/schoolreport/22065333. Accessed 16 Dec 2014
4. Chung L-Y (2011) Web 2.0-based e-learning: a probe into the application of online social networking in college freshman English curriculum. Adv Mat Res (403–408):1240–1243
5. Get5ocial (2015) Social media landscape (image). http://get5ocial.com. Accessed 5 Jan 2015
6. Kaplan AM, Haenlein M (2010) Users of the world, unite! The challenges and opportunities of social media. Bus Horiz 53(1):61. doi:10.1016/j.bushor.2009.09.003
7. Köse U (2013) A sociologic evaluation: effects of social networking caused e-learning on university students. Int J Web Based Commun 9(2):274–290
8. Ortutay B (2009) Fast-growing Facebook's user base hits 200 million. Yahoo! Finance
9. Owyang J (2009) A collection of social network stats for 2009. Web Strategy by Jeremiah Owyang. http://www.web-strategist.com/blog/2009/01/11/a-collection-of-soical-network-stats-for-2009/. Accessed 29 May 2014
10. Rožac J, Buendía F, Ballester J, Kos A, Pogačnik M (2012) Integration of learning management systems with social networking platforms: E-learning in a Facebook supported environment. In: International Conference on Mobile, Hybrid, and On-line Learning, Valencia, Spain, 30 January–4 February, 2012
11. Sert S, Köse U (2014) Impact of social media on marketing: a view on success stories. In: International conference on knowledge, economy and management, Antalya, Turkey, 27–30 November 2014
12. Wikipedia (2015) Pinterest. http://en.wikipedia.org/wiki/Pinterest. Accessed 3 Jan 2015

Social Network Usage

Yasemin Koçak Usluel

Abstract The purpose of this study is to overview the general use of social net-work sites (SNs) in Turkey in higher education students, and to examine how this usage relates positively and negatively to their work, study, social life, cognitive development, social development, physical development and sense of security. The study is designed with a descriptive approach to display current situation of SNs usage in Turkey. The data is collected through an online survey. The results highlighted that "gaining up-to date information" and "learning new information and knowledge" are the most positive ways to organize their work, study and social life in participants' SNs usage. It is also remarkable that the average scores for positive aspects of SNs have on students' lives, is higher than the negative aspects that SNs have, according to the opinion of the students. But, it is clear that results of negative effects showed that "increasing privacy concerns" is the most important security factor.

Keywords Social network · Usage · Internet activities · Positive way · Negative effect · Higher education

1 Introduction

Studies on the change in technology and the effect of this on lives of individuals, has been subject to a vast number of research in different context and frequency, based on the quality of technology, the characteristics of individuals and the structure and dynamics of societies. It could easily be stated that social networks have differentiated themselves from other technologies. The rate of adoption in particular, in diffusion of social networks to a large users` mass, is the most striking

Y.K. Usluel (✉)
Hacettepe University, Ankara, Turkey
e-mail: kocak@hacettepe.edu.tr

T. Issa et al. (eds.), *Social Networking and Education*,
Lecture Notes in Social Networks, DOI 10.1007/978-3-319-17716-8_13

among its qualities. In fact, Facebook, for example, is visited by 900,000,000 persons per month [8, 9].

It has been reported that Social Network (SN) statistics provide current snapshots of social media trends [5]. According to his report; users between the age of 18–29 have a usage of 89 %; and 72 % of all internet users are now active on social media.

Social networks (SNs) such as Facebook, Twitter, LinkedIn, …etc. became an important component in daily life across the world and in all ages groups. According to [8, 9], in terms of usage, Facebook comes first, Twitter second, while LinkedIn comes third.

Nowadays, individuals generally use more than one social network for different purposes, such as; providing rich sources, sharing information, joining or creating groups, meeting with new people, communicating with others, being visible [4, 6, 14, 17, 19, 20, 27]. Various factors such as number of following peers, enjoyment, usefulness can affect a user's SNs usage [22]. It is also stated that ease of use, usefulness, social influence, community identification, facilitating conditions could also have an effect in usage of SNs in educational context [23]. Users who create a personal network, in which they can share ideas, information, stories, pictures, sounds, videos, …etc. and thereafter they connect with others who have similar interests and learn more about occurrences such as events, studies, …etc. [6, 18, 20, 24]. SNs not only increase social interaction and communication among users but also shape their behavior and provide forum for the spread of information, ideas, and influences [2, 28].

It is noteworthy that the research on SNs, recently is regarding, the approach of students and teachers on the usage of SNs [10, 26]; the support of academic activity [3, 13, 15, 17]; determining the educational usage of SNs amongst students [1, 11, 16, 23]. The findings show that SNs provide a platform for sharing of information, and ease informal learning. It was also concluded that students' experiences in SNs are positive and using SNs improves quality of learning in higher education. It could further be stated that Facebook was found to be a highly convenient tool for academic advising, in higher education.

Although, the purpose of usage of SN can differentiate, several studies, have found that SN usage by means of production and collaboration is limited; and within the educational context, the advantage of networks is not sufficiently being taken. [21, 27].

Since, the social network sites can be used for any number of purposes, and their diffusion is rapid, cross cultural analysis becomes a necessity. Defining the existing situation is the first step in this analysis.

1.1 Purpose

The purpose of this study is to overview the general use of SNs in Turkey among higher education students, and to examine how this usage relates positively and negatively to their work, study, social life, cognitive development, social development, physical development and security.

In order to investigate the usage of SNs of higher education students in Turkey, the following research questions were explored.

Research Questions

1. How is the general internet usage tendency of participants?
2. What are the possible positive effects of the usage of SNs?
3. What are the possible negative effects arising from usage of SNs?

2 Method

The study is designed with a descriptive method to display current situation of SNs usage in Turkey.

2.1 Study Group

The study group consists of 173 participants who have answered an online survey. 64 (37 %) of the participants were male and 109 (63 %) of them were female. The age of the participants ranged from 18 to 51, though 77.5 % were between 18–22 and 21.4 % were between 22 and 32.

2.2 Materials

The data is collected though an online survey, which consists of three parts. This survey was developed within the scope of a project under the coordinator ship of Tomayess Issa. In the first part, there were questions for demographic information (age, gender, job, study field, education level) and general information about the usage of internet (daily time spent on social networking, daily time spent on internet for e-mail, online activities on the internet). The second part of survey consisted of 5-likert type (strong disagree to strongly agree) questions to examine how students use social networking in a positive way to organize their work, study and social life. The third part of the survey consisted of 5-likert type (strong disagree to strongly agree) questions that examined negative effects of social network usage from the perspectives of cognitive development, social development, physical development and security.

3 Results

The results of the study are to be reported under three sections; (1) results on general internet usage tendency of participants, (2) results on positive way of social networking usage and (3) negative effects of social networking usage from different perspectives.

3.1 Descriptive Statistics of Internet Usage of Participants

Table 1 display the number of hours that participants spend on SNs daily, not including email.

According to Table 1, the majority of the participants (56 %) spend up to five hours of their time on SNs per day, followed by nearly 36 % who use SNs less than an hour per day.

When the same users were asked how many hours they spent using the internet for e-mails, 78 % of the users stated that they use the internet for less than an hour.

As seen Table 2 most of the participants spent less than an hour per day on the internet for e-mails. In this case, it will be beneficial to define the users internet usage, besides emails. Table 3, shows the students' internet activities.

As seen on Table 3, internet was being used most heavily for studying (93 %) and emailing (90 %) by the participants. "Buying stocks or investing online" was

Table 1 Reported number of hours spent per day using social network

	Answer	N	%
1	Less than an hour	62	35.8
2	Up to five hours	98	56.6
3	Five to ten hours	11	6.4
4	Ten to twenty hours	1	0.6
5	Over twenty hours	1	0.6
	Total	173	100

Table 2 Reported number of hours spent per day using internet for email

	Answer	N	%
1	Less than an hour	134	77.5
2	Up to five hours	26	15
3	Five to ten hours	6	3.5
4	Ten to twenty hours	5	2.9
5	Over twenty hours	2	1.2
	Total	173	100

Table 3 Reported activities on the internet

Activity	N	%
Study	161	93.1
E-mail	156	90.2
Chat	111	64.2
Researching hobbies	93	53.8
Shop online	83	48.0
Making or researching travel information or reservations	73	42.2
Work	70	40.5
Play games	66	38.2
Banking online	57	32.9
Buying goods or services	56	32.4
Others—please specify	15	8.70
Buying stocks or investing online	8	4.60

the least used activity. It could be claimed that, the main reason for these results could be fact that most of the participants are university students. For example, using internet for studying is at 93 % while for work purposes is at 40 %. It could be thought that, if a similar study was to be conducted within a different occupation group, the results might differ accordingly.

3.2 *Results on Use of Social Network in a Positive Way*

Participants were asked to indicate their level of agreement to statements about the use of social networking in a positive way of organizing and maintaining their work, study and social life. In Table 4, descriptive statistics about each of the statements in the questionnaire are provided below.

As seen in Table 4, "gaining up-to date information" was found to be a leading item having the highest mean score that students reports as a positive way to organize their work or study. While similar items that "learning new information and knowledge" and "be more aware of global issues/local issues" followed this as having high mean scores, "acquiring new acquaintances-romance relationship" item has the lowest mean score. However, this could be because it may be perceived to be humiliating when people use the internet to acquire a romantic relationship. This possible setback was attempted to be minimized through making the survey anonymous. Another, more plausible reason so as to why acquiring new acquaintances is least used could be rooted in the essence of the Turkish culture. A cross cultural study could reveal different results, and this usage of SNs could rank higher in a more individualistic culture.

Table 4 Descriptive statistics of use of social networking in positive way

Question	N	Min	Max	Mean	sd
Gain up-to-date information	173	2	5	4.37	0.66
Learn new information and knowledge	173	1	5	4.35	0.77
Be more aware of global issues/local issues	173	1	5	4.26	0.83
Communicate with my peers frequently	173	1	5	4.21	0.88
Collaborate with my peers frequently	173	1	5	3.99	0.94
To remember facts/aspects of the past	173	1	5	3.85	0.89
Communicate with my different communities	173	1	5	3.83	0.96
Communicate with my peers from different universities	173	1	5	3.78	1.00
Study independently	173	1	5	3.68	1.14
Scrutinize my research study more easily	173	1	5	3.60	1.09
Complete my study more quickly	173	1	5	3.58	1.23
Acquire new acquaintances—work related	173	1	5	3.58	1.02
Acquire new acquaintances—friendship relationship	173	1	5	3.55	1.02
Develop intercrossing relationships with my peers (i.e. Artistic talents, sport and common interests)	173	1	5	3.53	0.94
Understand and solve study problems easily	173	1	5	3.51	1.11
Develop my personal and communication skills	173	1	5	3.46	1.09
Overcome study stress	173	1	5	3.29	1.19
Reduce carbon footprint in my activities	173	1	5	3.17	1.10
Be more sustainable person	173	1	5	3.14	0.93
To prepare my professional attitude toward study and work	173	1	5	3.13	1.11
Become more "Greener" in my activities	173	1	5	3.13	1.10
Provide reliable and scalable services	173	1	5	3.12	0.95
Do whatever I want, say whatever I want, and be whoever I want	173	1	5	3.09	1.30
Concentrate more on my reading and writing skills	173	1	5	2.97	1.15
Acquire new acquaintances—romance relationship	173	1	5	2.80	1.17

3.3 Results on Negative Effects of Social Networking

In this section, results of negative effects of social networking on the cognitive development, social development, physical development and security will be reported.

Table 5 presents the descriptive statistics of each item which indicate negative effects of social networking form different perspectives.

As seen from Table 5.negative effects of social networking were examined in four different perspectives as cognitive development, social development, physical development and security. The most important negative effect of social networking

Table 5 Descriptive statistics of negative effects

Question	N	Min	Max	$\overline{\chi}$	sd
Cognitive development					
Distracts me easily	173	1	5	3.55	1.13
Scatters my attention	173	1	5	3.45	1.05
Prevents me from concentrating more on writing and reading skills	173	1	5	3.17	1.03
Decreases my deep thinking	173	1	5	2.76	1.08
Prevents me from remembering the fundamental knowledge and skills	173	1	5	2.71	0.99
Decreases my grammar and proofreading skills	173	1	5	2.54	0.96
Social Development					
Prevents me from completing my work/study on time	173	1	5	3.05	1.25
Makes me lazy	173	1	5	3.24	1.27
Makes me insecure to release my personal details from the theft of personal information	173	1	5	3.17	1.15
Prevents me from participating in social activities	173	1	5	2.51	1.05
Makes me addict	173	1	5	3.12	1.22
Makes me receive an immoral images and information from unscrupulous people and it is difficult to act against them at present	173	1	5	2.92	1.17
Makes me feel lonely	173	1	5	2.49	1.14
Bores me	173	1	5	2.47	1.07
Makes me sick and unhealthy	173	1	5	2.38	1.1
Depresses me	173	1	5	2.35	1.06
Stresses me	173	1	5	2.34	1.04
Makes me more gambler	173	1	5	2.10	1.01
Physical development					
Prevents me from completing my study on time	173	1	5	3.02	1.32
Prevents me from completing my work on time	173	1	5	2.94	1.27
Prevents me from reading the newspapers	173	1	5	2.87	1.33
Prevents me from watching television	173	1	5	2.88	1.34
Prevents me from participating in physical activities	173	1	5	2.81	1.25
Prevents me from having face to face contact with my friends	173	1	5	2.61	1.14
Prevents me from having face to face contact with my family	173	1	5	2.47	1.2
Prevents me from talking on the phone/mobile	173	1	5	2.42	1.12
Prevents me from shopping in stores	173	1	5	2.25	1.09
Security					
Increase privacy concerns	173	1	5	3.56	1.12
Increase security concerns	173	1	5	3.50	1.08
Increase intellectual property concerns	173	1	5	3.34	1.13

Table 6 Descriptive statistics of negative effect of social networking factors

Factors under the negative effect	N	Min	Max	$\overline{\chi}$	SD
Security	173	1.00	5.00	3.47	1
Cognitive Development	173	1.00	5.00	3.03	0.77
Physical development	173	1.00	5.00	2.70	0.84
Social development	173	1.00	5.00	2.68	0.72

was found as "increasing privacy concerns" ($\bar{X}$ = 3.56, sd = 1.12) and "increase intellectual property concerns" ($\bar{X}$ = 3.34, sd = 1.13); both items under the security title. Following that, "distracts me easily" ($\bar{X}$ = 3.55, sd = 1.13) under the cognitive development were found to be important negative effects of social networking that participants reported. "Makes me gamble more" under the social development was considered as the least important negative effect of social networking by the participants.

In Table 6 general descriptive statistics of each negative effect factor is presented.

As seen in Table 6, security was the most important factor as a negative side of social networking while social development was the least; reported by participants.

4 Conclusion

This study has examined general use of SNs in Turkey among higher education students and how this usage relates positively and negatively to their work, study, social life, cognitive development, social development, physical development and security. It was found that almost all of the users use the internet for studying and more than half of the participants use SNs up to five hours per day. Whereas the usage of internet for emails is less than an hour per day. This finding showed that individuals spent hours of their time, as a part of their daily routines, on SNs.

The results also highlighted that "gaining up-to date information" and "learning new information and knowledge" are the most positive ways to organize their work, study, and social life in participants' SNs usage.

In conclusion, the students have reported that the positive effects of SNs in their lives is higher than the negative effects. However, it is clear the predominant reason behind the negative effects arises from the lack of security the students feel when using SNs. Research has stated that SNs can pose privacy concerns such as accessing or giving away personal information, safety of users and negative effects of possible fake users. [4, 7, 12].

It is not possible to find the reasons behind the positive and negative effects, in such a descriptive study.

4.1 Limitations and Future Research

This study, regarding the description of an existing situation, is limited to the students' opinions on the usage of SNs. Therefore the answers to "why" and "how" cannot be obtained from this study.

In order to provide for a deeper analysis on the opinions of students, for future research; the answer to the question "why" and "how" can be obtained through focus group discussion based on the findings of this study. Furthermore, a correlation between the real situation and the perception of the student could be observed through log data.

Another important limitation of the study is the lack of a validity and reliability of the questionnaire. Therefore, each item presented in the results have been obtained through mean calculations.

A more comprehensive understanding of SNs can be reached when future research based on the theoretical framework, using a mix method is conducted.

References

1. Amador P, Amador J (2014) Academic advising via Facebook: Examining student help seeking. Internet High Educ 21:9–16. doi:10.1016/j.iheduc.2013.10.003
2. Anagnostopoulos A, Kumar R, Mahdian M (2008) Influence and correlation in social networks. In: Proceedings of the 14th ACM SIGKDD international conference on knowledge discovery and data mining. Las Vegas, Nevada, USA
3. Arquero JL, Romero-Frias E (2013) Using social network sites in higher education: an experience in business studies. Innovations Educ Teach Int 50(3):238–249
4. Boyd D, Ellison NB (2008) Social network sites: definition, history, and scholarship. J Comput Mediated Commun 13(1):210–230. doi:10.1111/j.1083-6101.2007.00393.x
5. Bullas J (2014) 22 Social media facts and statistics you should know in 2014. http://www.jeffbullas.com/2014/01/17/20-social-media-facts-and-statistics-you-should-know-in-2014/
6. Cheung CMK, Chiu P-Y, Lee MKO (2011) Online social networks: why do students use facebook? Comput Hum Behav 27(4):1337–1343. doi:10.1016/j.chb.2010.07.028
7. Çimen A, Yılmaz MB (2014) Which content is appropriate for instructional based social network? Opinions of K12 Teachers in Turkey. Procedia Soc Behav Sci 116:2338–2343. doi:10.1016/j.sbspro.2014.01.569
8. Forkosh-Baruch A (2014) eBizMBA Top 15 most popular social networking sites. http://www.ebizmba.com/articles/social-networking-websites
9. Hew KF (2011) Students' and teachers' use of Facebook. Comput Hum Behav 27(2):662–676. doi:http://dx.doi.org/10.1016/j.chb.2010.11.020
10. Falahah RD (2012) Study of social networking usage in higher education environment. Procedia Soc Behav Sci 67:156–166. doi:10.1016/j.sbspro.2012.11.316
11. Forkosh-Baruch A, Hershkovitz A (2012) A case study of Israeli higher-education institutes sharing scholarly information with the community via social networks. Internet High Educ 15(1):58–68. doi:10.1016/j.iheduc.2011.08.003
12. George A (2006) Living online: the end of privacy? http://www.newscientist.com/article/mg19125691.700-living-online-the-end-of-privacy.html

13. Gewerc A, Montero L, Lama M (2014) Collaboration and social networking in higher education. Communicar 42(21):55–62. doi:10.3916/C42-2014-05
14. Hew KF (2011) Students' and teachers' use of Facebook. Comput Hum Behav 27(2):662–676. doi:10.1016/j.chb.2010.11.020
15. Hung H-T, Yuen SC-Y (2010) Educational use of social networking technology in higher education. Teach High Educ 15(6):703–714
16. Hurt NE, Moss GS, Bradley CL, Larson LR, Lovelace M, Prevost LB, Camus MS (2012) The 'Facebook'effect: college students' perceptions of online discussions in the age of social networking. Int J Scholarsh Teach Learn 6(2):10
17. Irwin C, Ball L, Desbrow B, Leveritt M (2012) Students' perceptions of using Facebook as an interactive learning resource at university. Australas J Educ Technol 28(7):1221–1232
18. Işık F (2013) Comparison of the use of social network in education between North and South Cyprus. Procedia Soc Behav Sci 103:210–219. doi:10.1016/j.sbspro.2013.10.328
19. Karal H, Kokoç M (2010) Üniversite öğrencilerinin sosyal ağ siteleri kullanım amaçlarını belirlemeye yönelik bir ölçek geliştirme çalışması. Turk J Comput Math Educ 1(3):251–263
20. Kwon O, Wen Y (2010) An empirical study of the factors affecting social network service use. Comput Hum Behav 26(2):254–263. doi:10.1016/j.chb.2009.04.011
21. Lampe C, Wohn D, Vitak J, Ellison N, Wash R (2011) Student use of Facebook for organizing collaborative classroom activities. Comput Support Learn 6(3):329–347. doi:10.1007/s11412-011-9115-y
22. Lin K-Y, Lu H-P (2011) Why people use social networking sites: an empirical study integrating network externalities and motivation theory. Comput Hum Behav 27(3): 1152–1161. doi:10.1016/j.chb.2010.12.009
23. Mazman SG, Usluel YK (2010) Modeling educational usage of Facebook. Comput Educ 55 (2):444–453. doi:10.1016/j.compedu.2010.02.008
24. Murray KE, Waller R (2007) Social networking goes abroad. Int Educ 16(3):56–59
25. Özmen B, Atıcı B (2014) The effects of social networking sites in distance learning on learners' academic achievements. Eur J Open Distance e-Learn 17(2):60–74
26. Roblyer MD, McDaniel M, Webb M, Herman J, Witty JV (2010) Findings on Facebook in higher education: a comparison of college faculty and student uses and perceptions of social networking sites. Internet High Educ 13(3):134–140. doi:10.1016/j.iheduc.2010.03.002
27. Usluel YK, Atal D (2013) Students' approach to social network in educational context. Int J Web Based Communities 9(2):188–198
28. Zhu T, Wang B, Wu B, Zhu C (2014) Maximizing the spread of influence ranking in social networks. Inf Sci 278:535–544. doi:10.1016/j.ins.2014.03.070

Part V
Social Networking in North America

College Students' Perceptions of Positive and Negative Effects of Social Networking

Anastasia Kitsantas, Nada Dabbagh, David S. Chirinos and Helen Fake

Abstract The aim of this study was to examine college students' perceptions of social networking in the United States. A secondary purpose was to determine whether differences in gender and age were prevalent. One hundred and twenty eight (N = 128) students were surveyed online. Data showed that social networking was helpful for communication, information gathering, and that it positively influenced their academic work. However, students also reported that social networking had a negative impact on their social interactions, emotional health and work completion, with younger participants reporting greater negative effects of social networking on work completion. Students also reported that social networking can be addictive, distractive, and a threat to their privacy. Although no significant gender differences emerged in students' perceptions, numerically females viewed social networking in more positive terms. Educational implications and future directions for research are discussed.

Keywords Social networking · Social media · U.S. college students · Higher education · Web 2.0 · Pedagogical affordances · Computer-Mediated communication

A. Kitsantas (✉) · N. Dabbagh · D.S. Chirinos · H. Fake
George Mason University, Fairfax, USA
e-mail: akitsant@gmu.edu

N. Dabbagh
e-mail: ndabbagh@gmu.edu

D.S. Chirinos
e-mail: dchirino@gmu.edu

H. Fake
e-mail: hfake@gmu.edu

T. Issa et al. (eds.), *Social Networking and Education*,
Lecture Notes in Social Networks, DOI 10.1007/978-3-319-17716-8_14

1 Introduction

Social networking has its roots in early forms of computer-mediated communication (CMC) and collaboration tools such as groupware, virtual communities, and instant messaging, and can best be understood by tracing the socio-technological evolution of social software from the pre-Internet era (pre 1969) to the Web 2.0 era (post 2000) and beyond [7]. Before Web 2.0 enabled social media technologies such as Facebook and Twitter became popular, the terms "social software" and "social computing" were being used interchangeably to describe information and communication technologies (ICT) that supported networked learning environments such as Ted Nelson's 1963 concept of a hypertext document system and Engelbart's 1962 concept of how an "integrated domain" called oNLineSystem (NLS) could augment collaborative activities [7]. The pre-Internet era set the stage for CMC and group collaboration but it was not until the Internet era (1969–1992) that network-enabled social interactions or what we have come to know as social networking began in earnest. The Internet era ushered in communication systems such as Usenet, a global Internet discussion board-like system, BITNET, an electronic mailing list or listserv that enabled early social networks, and The WELL, a virtual networked community that used computer conferencing and email for communication. These virtual communication groups or systems were the precursor of social networking that would become ubiquitous in the Web 2.0 era.

As CMC tools began to connect people around the globe, Internet technologies became more social, [1, 20] however it was not until the emergence of Web 2.0 social media technologies in 2005 that new patterns of social networking were realized. Specifically, a core set of social networking tools emerged, such as Friendster (2002), MySpace (1999), LinkedIn (2003), and Facebook (2003), that collectively changed the rules of social networking because of their user-centricity, user friendliness, wide availability, socially connective technology platform, and resource sharing and tagging capabilities [7, 8]. While this brief overview of social networking underscores its evolutionary nature from a socio-technological perspective, there is no doubt that Web 2.0 social media technologies have dramatically changed the nature of social networking resulting in potentially consequential implications on teaching and learning in higher education contexts [1, 8, 14, 16]. Hence, there is a dire need to understand how social networking is impacting student behavior from a social, cognitive, and emotional perspective, in order to inform the pedagogical design of social networking experiences for learning.

2 Research on Social Networking

Research on the negative and positive effects of social networking on college students is steadily growing. There is evidence that students may respond positively to the use of social networking in higher education contexts and that social networking can make learning more attractive, collaborative, and meaningful, by integrating formal and informal learning opportunities and by fostering a closer relationship between educational institutions and the social environment [5, 6, 11, 12]. In contrast, there is also evidence regarding the negative effects of social networking such as feelings of alienation, distraction, privacy issues, superficiality of communication, the low value that university faculty place on interpersonal relationships, and the lack of evidence regarding the impact of social networking on academic achievement [12, 23, 24].

In a correlational study, Barker [3] examined how 734 freshmen enrolled in a communications course used Social Networking Sites (SNS) in order to understand the relationships between gender, high and low levels of group identification, collective self-esteem, and usage purposes (i.e. social gratification or social compensation). Barker [3] hypothesized that certain groups would exhibit particular behaviors depending on an individual's sense of belonging in their group, their current level of collective self-esteem, and their gender. While few of the variables examined exhibited significant correlational values, the findings revealed that females and males use SNS with different goals in mind. Specifically, males were more likely to use SNS for educational and gaming purposes whereas females were more likely to use SNS to cultivate and maintain relationships. Implications of this study suggest more research is needed to understand user behaviors in SNS in order to ensure better user experiences and enhanced learning opportunities.

A literature review aimed at examining the benefits and disadvantages of integrating social media tools in schools was conducted by Blazer [4]. Benefits included offering students 21st century collaborative learning experiences enabled by newer tools and technologies that are already omnipresent in their day to day life experiences and providing more digital literacy to students. Disadvantages included fears stemming from cyberbullying, threat of inappropriate student—teacher relationships, and the inability to filter content which could potentially expose children to inappropriate and unsanctioned imagery. Additionally, the review revealed that no study has been able to demonstrate a correlation between social media use and increases or decreases in a student's G.P.A. Implications suggested establishing mechanisms to train parents and teachers on social media use, cyberbullying, and best practices in integrating technology in schools as well as developing policies and rules surrounding social media use in educational contexts.

Furthermore, Lui and Yu [15] used several wellness and social support measurements to identify whether there was a relationship between an individual's well-being and Facebook use by examining correlations between wellness, social support, online social support, gender, and intensity of Facebook use. Participants were a convenience sample of 400 college students with 330 students completing all survey information. Findings revealed a strong correlation between higher use of Facebook and high online social support. Online social support was also found to be a high predictor of general social support allowing Facebook to be an extension of general social support. The researchers argued that while SNS like Facebook offered a mechanism for online support, they do not substitute day to day human relationships. Specifically, the findings demonstrated that social media affordances could only provide certain types of social support due to the nature of the tools. For instance, within SNS, students can receive support from an emotional, informational, and companionship standpoint. On the other hand, SNS do not offer tangible support (i.e. financial or physical). The researchers suggest examining the conditions and factors that support the cultivation of online friendships and learning relationships without initial contact outside social networks.

Rambe [19] investigated the role of social media in the classroom using a virtual ethnography. The researcher accomplished this by observing student interaction on a Facebook page designed for 450 Information Systems students (organized academically into two "clusters") at a South African University. The goal was to examine whether student appropriation of social media in university contexts constitute or manifest constructive disruptions and how Community of Inquiry (COI) components were articulated on Facebook. Rambe analyzed data collected from the wall posts, message boards, and private message spaces, and found that Facebook groups offered a safe space for students to complain, challenge "hegemonic" control by authorities, and seek help for "unsophisticated" questions. The researcher claimed that this "third space" offered a more "democratic" classroom wherein the teachers' roles were "innovatively transformed to that of dialogue facilitators, information managers, knowledge brokers, and knowledge management consultants" (Rambe 2012, p. 142). Further, Rambe considered three components of Garrison and Cleveland-Innes COI framework, social presence, cognitive presence, and teacher presence, and found that social presence was the most represented. Despite the asymmetrical representation of social presence in the Facebook group, the researcher concluded that the collective identity and the democratization of the space was beneficial to the overall community, though, Rambe suggested that more teacher scaffolding is needed in order to increase cognitive and teacher presence.

From an educational perspective, Okoro [17] examined the benefits and disadvantages of integrating social media technologies into the classroom. The author argues, referencing literature and his experiences teaching classes at Howard University, for the use of social media in the classroom citing their collaborative and constructivist affordances as well as an ability to provide just-in-time student assessment. Showing statistics that demonstrate the prevalence of use from an international and demographic standpoint, Okoro highlights the ubiquitous nature of these tools for purposes other than learning. However, Okoro suggests best practices for integrating social media in higher education contexts to include assigning small group work, assigning points for pertinent comments in online discussions, and offering feedback. He also suggests that the benefits of using social media include prevalence in the day to day lives of the audience, increased assessment opportunities, enabling student communication, supporting team efforts and team development, increased interest due to real world applications, and expansion of support systems. Okoro cites the disadvantages of using social media to include group think rather than self-reliance, lack of critical thinking skills, and potentially increased absenteeism.

Jenkins-Guarnieri, Wright and Johnson [13] examined relationships between the Five-Factor Model (FFM) [9] (i.e. extraversion, agreeableness, conscientiousness, openness, and neuroticism), social competence, and Facebook use. The study sought to make the associations between these variables explicit through the development of a working model. Participants were 17–22 year olds at Rocky Mountain University. The final sample included 617 individuals who self-reported their Facebook use using the Ellison Scale. The only factor found to be highly correlated with increased Facebook use was extraversion. All other variables had weak correlations. It is important to note that the diagnostics focused on self-reporting. The researchers argue that further investigation is needed to understand the impacts of social networking behavior on the individuals who utilize the systems the most. By having a better understanding of the characteristics of SNS users, designers can optimize user experiences and mitigate potential obstacles that could get in the way of the designer's ultimate objectives. Similarly, college instructors will also be better positioned to design learning activities that support SNS user characteristics and scaffold learning experiences.

The research summarized revealed that social networking has both positive and negative effects on students. Positive effects or benefits included increased collaboration and communication, digital literacy, social and emotional support, democratization of learning, increased assessment and feedback opportunities, and support for team efforts. Negative effects or disadvantages included fears from cyberbullying or inappropriate teacher-student relationships, increased absenteeism, decreased self-reliance, and lack of critical thinking skills. Additionally, the research revealed that there are several factors that impact student use of social networks such as gender and personality traits. The purpose of this chapter is to further our understanding of these factors in order to leverage the pedagogical affordances of social networking in higher education contexts.

3 Methods

3.1 Research Questions

Two overarching research questions guided the present study. The first one focused on uncovering U.S. college students' positive and negative perceptions of social networking. The second research question explored whether any gender and age differences exist in how U.S. students view social networking.

3.2 Participants

A total of 128 undergraduate and graduate students participated in this study. The students were recruited from 16 classrooms from the university's college of education. The students were 77 % female (N = 98) and 23 % male (N = 30) and ranged in age from 18 to 52+ years. No ethnic composition was recorded for this sample. The majority of the participants (56 %) reported to spend less than one hour social networking per day while 34 % of the participants reported to spend up to five hours social networking per day.

3.3 Data Collection Instrument

Positive Effects of Social Networking Survey. A 25-item scale was developed to assess students' use of social networking and its potential positive effect on students' ability to organize and maintain their work, studies, and social life. For example, students were asked how the use of social networking allowed them to: "collaborate with my peers frequently" or "develop my personal and communication skills". Items followed a 5-point Likert-type scale ranging from 1 = *strongly disagree* to 5 = *strongly agree.*

Negative Effects of Social Networking Survey: A 30-item scale was developed to assess students' use of social networking and its potential negative effect on students' ability to organize and maintain their work, studies and social life. Items followed a 5-point Likert-type scale ranging from 1 = *strongly disagree* to 5 = *strongly agree*. Sample items include: the use of social networking "scatters my attention" and the use of social networking "depresses me".

The survey also assessed the amount of time participants spend social networking, amount of time spent on email (not considered social networking), and other types of activities performed online (e.g. playing games, shop, chat, study, work, etc.).

3.4 Procedure

This survey was administered at a large public university located in the Mid-Atlantic region of the United States. Sixteen instructors from the College of Education were asked to forward an email to their students asking them to complete an online survey regarding their use of social networking.

4 Results

4.1 Factor Analyses

An exploratory factor analysis was conducted on the survey items using varimax rotation. Positive items (N = 25) and negative items (N = 30) were examined separately. Items with factor loadings of 0.6 were retained. From the original 25 positive items, three components emerged with an Eigenvalues = 7.54, 2.34, and 1.33 (respectively), which accounted for 75 % of the variance in the items. The first component, "information" (N = 3 items) yielded a Cronbach's α reliability coefficient of 0.92, "communication" (N = 4 items) yielded α = 0.87, and "academic performance" (N = 8 items) yielded α = 0.94 (see Table 1).

From the original 30 negative items, six components emerged with Eigenvalues = 9.15, 2.73, 1.90, 1.53, 1.31, and 1.04 (respectively), which accounted for 76.77 % of the variance in the items. The first component, "social interaction" (N = 6 items) yielded a Cronbach's α = 0.87, "privacy" (N = 3 items) yielded α = 0.92, "distraction" (N = 6 items) yielded α = 0.85, "emotional health" (N = 3 items) yielded α = 0.91, "work completion" (N = 2 items) yielded α = 0.92, and "addiction" (N = 3 items) yielded α = 0.80 (see Table 2).

4.2 Descriptive and Correlational Analyses

Descriptive statistics, means, standard deviations, and correlations among the variables are presented in Table 3. Several significant correlations emerged between various components. For the positive components, "information" was significantly correlated to "communication", $r(128) = 0.50$, $p = 0.01$, to "academic

Table 1 Benefits of social networking

	M	SD	FL	Alpha
Information				0.92
Learn new information and knowledge	3.93	1.06	0.91	
Gain up-to-date information	4.19	1.03	0.88	
Be more aware of global issues/local issues	3.91	1.15	0.89	
Communication				0.87
Communicate with my peers frequently	4.17	0.95	0.72	
Communicate with my peers from different universities	3.68	1.16	0.89	
Communicate with my different communities	3.93	1.02	0.87	
Develop intercrossing relationships with my peers	3.46	1.07	0.83	
Academic Performance				0.94
Study independently	3.15	1.20	0.63	
Complete my study more quickly	2.64	1.19	0.86	
Understand and solve study problems easily	2.95	1.11	0.78	
Scrutinize my research study more easily	2.91	1.14	0.86	
Concentrate more on my reading and writing skills	2.69	1.13	0.89	
To prepare my professional attitude toward study and work	2.80	1.18	0.93	
Be more sustainable person	2.85	1.14	0.81	
Provide reliable and scalable services	2.92	1.12	0.78	

Table 2 Negative effects of social networking

	M	SD	FL	Alpha
Social interaction				0.87
Prevents me from having face to face contact with my family	2.08	0.98	0.68	
Prevents me from having face to face contact with my friend	2.13	1.01	0.65	
Prevents me from participating in physical activities	2.45	1.22	0.55	
Prevents me shopping in stores	2.21	1.05	0.76	
Prevents me from watching television	2.17	1.06	0.71	
Prevents me from reading the newspapers	2.57	1.30	0.65	
Privacy				0.92
Increase privacy concerns	3.57	1.12	0.95	
Increase security concerns	3.58	1.12	0.96	
Increase intellectual property concerns	3.25	1.15	0.88	
Distraction				0.85
Prevents me from remembering the fundamental knowledge and skill	2.56	0.93	0.69	
Scatters my attention	3.57	1.17	0.61	
Decreases my grammar and proofreading skills	2.78	1.17	0.88	
Decreases my deep thinking	2.72	1.16	0.85	
Distracts me easily	3.67	1.21	0.58	
Emotional Health				0.91
Stresses me	2.33	1.11	0.94	
Depresses me	2.32	1.11	0.83	
Makes me feel lonely	2.25	1.15	0.77	
Work Completion				0.92
Prevents me from completing my work/study on time	2.61	1.17	0.63	
Prevents me from completing my work on time	2.40	1.15	0.75	
Prevents me from completing my study on time	2.44	1.19	0.74	
Addiction				0.80
Makes me sick and unhealthy	1.89	0.936	0.67	
Makes me addict	2.17	1.14	0.64	
Makes me more gambler	1.66	.767	0.77	

performance", $r(128) = 0.53$, $p = 0.01$, to "social interactions", $r(128) = 0.22$, $p = 0.05$, and to "privacy", $r(128) = 0.28$, $p = 0.01$. "Communication" was significantly correlated to "academic performance", $r(128) = 0.40$, $p = 0.01$ and to "distraction", $r(128) = 0.18$, $p = 0.05$. "Academic performance" was significantly and negatively correlated to "distraction", $r(128) = -0.22$, $p = 0.05$.

For the negative components, "social interactions" was significantly correlated to "privacy", $r(128) = 0.25$, $p = 0.01$, to "distraction", $r(128) = 0.42$, $p = 0.01$, to "emotional health", $r(128) = 0.56$, $p = 0.01$, to "work completion", $r(128) = 0.63$,

Table 3 Zero-order correlations and means and standard deviations among all variables

	Correlations								
Variables	1	2	3	4	5	6	7	8	9
1. Information	1.00	0.50**	0.53**	0.22*	0.28**	0.17	0.16	0.16	0.11
2. Communication		1.00	0.40**	0.12	0.09	0.18*	0	0.11	0.09
3. Academic Performance			1.00	0.17	−0.02	−0.22*	−0.04	−0.16	0.04
4. Social Interactions				1.00	0.25**	0.42**	0.56**	0.63**	0.63**
5. Privacy					1.00	0.35**	0.32**	0.14	0.16
6. Distraction						1.00	0.44**	0.51**	0.37**
7. Emotional Health							1.00	0.49**	0.52**
8. Work Completion								1.00	0.53**
9. Addiction									1.00
Mean	4.01	3.81	2.87	2.27	3.47	3.06	2.30	2.48	1.91
SD	1.00	0.89	0.96	0.87	1.06	0.90	1.03	1.09	0.81

*correlation is significant at the 0.05 level (two-tailed); **correlation is significant at the 0.01 level (two-tailed)

$p = 0.01$, and to "addiction", $r(128) = 0.63$, $p = 0.01$. "Privacy" was significantly correlated to "distraction", $r(128) = 0.35$, $p = 0.01$, and to "emotional health", $r(128) = 0.32$, $p = 0.01$. "Emotional health" was significantly correlated to "work completion", $r(128) = 0.49$, $p = 0.01$, and to "addiction", $r(128) = 0.52$, $p = 0.01$. "Work completion" was significantly correlated to "addiction", $r(128) = 0.53$, $p = 0.01$.

4.3 Gender and Age Differences

At a descriptive level, there appears to be variation in social networking among the participants by age group (see Table 4). For instance, younger participants tended to report higher means (M = 4.11) in the information subscale compared to older participants (M = 3.89). This finding could be indicative of a likely generational shift in how people receive and keep up with information. The privacy subscale also shows an interesting trend as older participants report higher concern (M = 3.70) with privacy compared to younger participants (M = 3.17). Younger participants report higher agreement of social networking as a distracter (M = 3.23) compared to older participants (M = 2.90).

Independent samples *t*-tests were conducted to compare gender differences among the nine components formed (see Table 4). No significant differences were observed. A one-way ANOVA was conducted to compare age differences among the nine components (see Table 5). One significant difference was observed on "work completion" among the age groups, $F(4, 112) = 3.73$, $p < 0.01$, with 18–22 year old students reporting significantly higher negative effects on "work completion" ($M = 3.14$, $SD = 1.11$) compared to 22–32 group ($M = 2.39$, $SD = 1.06$), 32–42 group ($M = 2.61$, $SD = 1.09$), 42–52 year olds ($M = 2.11$, $SD = 0.88$), and over 52 group ($M = 1.85$, $SD = 0.97$).

Table 4 Positive and negative effects of social networking based on gender

Positive effects	Female		Male		*t*-test	*p*
	M	SD	M	SD		
1. Information	4.06	0.90	3.86	1.28	0.79	0.43
2. Communication	3.92	0.76	3.46	1.18	1.97	0.06
3. Academic performance	2.88	0.96	2.83	0.98	0.19	0.85
Negative effects						
1. Social interaction	2.21	0.88	2.44	0.83	−1.24	0.22
2. Privacy	3.55	1.04	3.20	1.07	1.51	0.14
3. Distraction	3.13	0.92	2.83	0.81	1.67	0.10
4. Emotional Health	2.29	1.10	2.33	0.77	−0.22	0.83
5. Work completion	2.41	1.09	2.71	1.08	−1.31	0.20
6. Addiction	1.85	0.78	2.08	0.88	−1.26	0.22

Table 5 Positive and negative effects of social networking based on age

Positive effects	18–22		22–32		32–42		42–52		Over 52		F	*p*
	M	SD	M	SD	M	SD	M	SD	M	SD		
1. Information	4.11	0.93	4.06	0.93	4.03	1.15	3.89	0.94	3.78	1.39	0.26	0.90
2. Communication	4.10	0.85	3.87	0.85	3.65	0.97	3.83	0.74	3.22	1.16	1.78	0.14
3. Academic performance	3.00	1.07	2.75	0.76	2.89	1.21	3.10	0.95	2.57	0.98	0.76	0.55
Negative Effects												
1. Social interaction	2.38	0.86	2.24	0.92	2.44	0.79	2.13	0.88	1.98	0.87	0.71	0.59
2. Privacy	3.17	1.11	3.47	1.05	3.65	0.98	3.70	1.00	3.19	1.26	0.97	0.43
3. Distraction	3.27	0.97	3.13	0.93	3.10	0.81	2.91	0.74	2.44	1.00	1.58	0.19
4. Emotional health	2.54	1.17	2.32	1.07	2.25	0.95	2.16	0.96	2.11	0.90	0.46	0.76
5. Work completion	3.14	1.11	2.39	1.06	2.61	1.09	2.11	0.88	1.85	0.97	3.73	0.01
6. Addiction	2.25	0.91	1.84	0.74	1.99	0.90	1.75	0.77	1.52	0.50	1.83	0.13

5 Discussion

In terms of research question 1, the findings of the present study clearly showed that students perceived that there are positive and negative effects associated with social networking. Positive effects included using social networking to gather information, communicate, and engage in studying which in turn leads to academic success. The participants also mentioned several negative aspects related to social networking including being distractive, addictive, and interfering with work completion.

Furthermore, some interesting findings emerged when examining research question 2. In regards to the positive effects of social networking, female participants reported numerically higher perceptions on all three factors that emerged: communication, information, and academic achievement. This may be an indication that females (at least in this sample), view social networking in more positive terms. In terms of age differences, the 42–52 year old group reported the highest perceptions as to the beneficial aspects of social networking in relation to the academic performance factor. Also, both females and males were identical in viewing the worth of social networking in the following order: information, communication, academic performance. Perhaps this group of students viewed social networking as a tool for learning rather than a means of communication or information. Other researchers [21] have found that students were more open to the idea of using Facebook as an instructional tool as well as a social forum. The 18–22 group of students viewed "information" and "communication" in nearly identical terms, but they reported noticeably lower perceptions for "academic performance". It seems like this group has a distinct understanding as to the positive aspects of social networking, favoring its communication and informational value.

Turning now to the negative effects of social networking, distraction and emotional health factors were the only two components that held a linear digression in terms of age and means, indicating that the younger groups of students were more susceptible to social networking's negative aspects on these two factors. This difference may be indicative of younger participants spending more time social networking thus, having more opportunities for distraction or it could be that older participants are more disciplined in their social networking. Correlations analyses also revealed that the emotional health subscale showed an interesting trend as there is an inverse relationship between scores on this subscale and age. In addition younger participants reporting greater and statically negative effects of social networking on work completion than the older participants. Finally, females reported higher negative perceptions for only two out of the six factors, providing more evidence that females perhaps value social networking more than males.

6 Implications, Limitations, and Future Directions

The penetration of social networking in today's societies is unprecedented however its adoption in the field of education continues to be controversial [11, 23]. Duggan and Brenner [10] reported that 67 % of internet users in the U.S. whose age ranges between 18 and 29 use social networking sites (SNS) such as Facebook, Twitter, Pinterest, Instagram, and Tumblr, while only 44.1 % of faculty members in higher education use social media in their teaching with a higher percentage in the Humanities and Arts disciplines [22]. Additionally, these faculty (N = 8,016) are mostly using blogs and wikis rather than SNS to support their teaching. Research also suggests that college students whose age ranges between 18 and 34 are using SNS for long hours and that the adoption of mobile devices and mobile apps is the driving force for the increase in social networking and social media use [2]. The results of this study demonstrate that U.S. college students have positive perceptions of social networking particularly as this relates to information gathering, communication, and academic performance. The findings also indicate that gender and age plays a role in impacting student perceptions with females having more positive views of social networking than males and the older age group reporting higher benefits of social networking when it comes to academic performance.

In terms of limitations, the relatively small sample size used to obtain these results should be considered when interpreting the findings. Further, the gender imbalance of the participants, a common occurrence in U.S. colleges of education, should also be considered as these students may behave differently than students from other colleges and disciplines.

In summary, the research suggests that students are more open to using social networking as a teaching and learning tool than faculty, hence the challenge is to support faculty in leveraging the pedagogical affordances of social networking and minimize its negative effects in order to provide a more attractive and innovative learning experience and break the boundaries between formal and informal learning [6]. Meeting these challenges will require future researchers to address these contemporary and fast evolving issues. In particular, future research should strive to keep up with students' social networking use as the adoption of new platforms (e.g. Snapchat) and new generation learning environments (e.g., Personal Learning Environments or PLEs) may offer insights as to how students are using (and perceiving) social networking functionality. As Erik Qualman, author of *Socialnomics*, *Digital Leader* and *Crisis*, puts it, "we don't have a choice on whether we DO social media, the question is how well we DO it" [18].

References

1. Alexander B (2006) Web 2.0: a new wave of innovation for teaching and learning? EDUCAUSE Rev 41(2):32–44

2. Bannon D (2012) State of the media: the social media report 2012, Nielson. http://www.nielsen.com/us/en/reports/2012/state-of-the-media-the-social-media-report-2012.html. Accessed 18 May 2014
3. Barker V (2009) Older adolescents' motivations for social network site use: the influence of gender, group identity, and collective self-esteem. CyberPsych Behav 12(2):209–213. doi:10.1089/cpb.2008.0228
4. Blazer C (2012) Miami-Dade County Public Schools.: social networking in schools: Benefits and risks; Review of the research; Policy considerations; and Current practices. Info: Capsule: Research Services, Miami-Dade County Public Schools 1109
5. Bugeja M (2006) Facing the Facebook. Chron High Educ 52(21):C1–C4
6. Dabbagh N, Kitsantas A (2012) Personal learning environments, social media, and self-regulated learning: a natural formula for connecting formal and informal learning. Internet High Educ 15(1):3–8. doi:10.1016/j.iheduc.2011.06.002
7. Dabbagh N, Reo R (2011) Back to the future: tracing the roots and learning affordances of social software. In: Lee MJW, McLoughlin C (eds) Web 2.0-Based e-Learning: applying social informatics for tertiary teaching. IGI Global, Hershey, pp 1–20
8. Dabbagh N, Reo R (2011) Impact of Web 2.0 on higher education. In: Surry DW, Stefurak T, Gray R (eds) Technology Integration in higher education: social and organizational aspects. IGI Global, Hershey, pp 174–187
9. Digman JM (1990) Personality structure: emergence of the five-factor model. Annu Rev Psychol 41:417–440
10. Duggan M, Brenner J (2013) The demographics of social media users-2012: PewResearch internet project. http://pewinternet.org/Reports/2013/Social-media-users.aspx. Accessed 18 May 2014
11. Gewerc A, Montero L, Lama M (2014) Collaboration and social networking in higher education. Comunicar 42:55–63. doi:10.3916/C42-2014-05
12. Gomez-Aguilar M, Roses S, Farias P (2012) The academic use of social networks in college. Report 38:131–138. doi:10.3916/C38-2012-03-04)
13. Jenkins-Guarnieri MA, Wright SL, Johnson BD (2013) The interrelationships among attachment style, personality traits, interpersonal competency, and Facebook use. Psychol Pop Med Cult 2(2):117–131. doi:10.1037/a0030946
14. Kesim E, Agaoglu E(2007) A paradigm shift in distance education: Web 2.0 and social software. Turk Online J Dist Educ 8(3):66–75
15. Lui CY, Yu CP (2013) Can Facebook use induce well-being? Cyberpsychol Behav Soc Networking 16(9):674–678. doi:10.1089/cyber.2012.0301
16. McLoughlin C, Lee MJW (2008) Future learning landscapes: transforming pedagogy through social software. Innovate J Online Educ 4(5):1–9
17. Okoro E (2012) Integrating social media technologies in higher education: costs-benefits analysis. J Int Educ Res 8(3):255–262
18. Qualman E (2013) Socialnomics: how social media transforms the way we live and do business. Wiley & Sons Inc, Hoboken
19. Rambe P (2012) Constructive disruptions for effective collaborative learning: navigating the affordances of social media for meaningful engagement. Electron J E-Learn 10(1):132–146
20. Rheingold H (1993) The virtual community. Addison-Wesley, Reading
21. Roblyer MD, McDaniel M, Webb M, Herman J, Witty JV (2010) Findings on Facebook in higher education: a comparison of college faculty and student uses and perceptions of social networking sites. Internet High Educ 13(3):134–140. doi:10.1016/j.iheduc.2010.03.002
22. Seaman J, Tinti-Kane H (2013) Social media for teaching and learning: Pearson learning solutions. http://www.pearsonlearningsolutions.com/assets/downloads/reports/social-media-for-teaching-and-learning-2013-report.pdf#view=FitH,0. Accessed 18 May 2014
23. Selwyn N (2009 Faceworking: exploring students' education-related use of Facebook. Learn Med Technol 34(2):157–174. doi:10.1080/17439880902923622
24. Zaidieh A (2012) The use of social networking in education: challenges and opportunities. World of Comput Sci Inf Technol J 2(1):18–21

How American Students Perceive Social Networking Sites: An Application of Uses and Gratifications Theory

Rowena L. Briones and Melissa Janoske

Abstract A survey of 467 U.S. college students provided insight into the positive and negative gratifications of using social networking sites. Results corroborate and move forward extant research on how participants use social networking to share information, build community, and engage with people and news that they might not otherwise access. Participants also acknowledged the negatives of social networking, particularly for college students, including a lack of focus on work and concerns for privacy and the decrease in face-to-face interaction as it is replaced with putting forward the "great, exciting lives" they feel they need to keep up with others online. This brings forth the idea of social surveillance, a distorted reality stemming from comparison of the self with others, and the need to compete in order to build the community they desire through social networking sites.

Keywords Social networking · Uses and gratifications · College students · Online community · Social media · Social surveillance · Online engagement

1 Introduction

According to the Pew Internet and American Life Project, 86 % of undergraduate students use social networking sites [46]. Of these sites, Facebook is the most widely used, with 96 % of college students being active users [14]. Students have found the groups feature of Facebook to be particularly helpful, as they are used for team projects and keeping tabs with on-campus organizations [36]. Twitter has also been especially useful for college students, who take advantage of the site's easy search

R.L. Briones (✉)
Virginia Commonwealth University, Richmond, USA
e-mail: rlbriones@vcu.edu

M. Janoske
University of Memphis, Memphis, USA
e-mail: melissa.janoske@memphis.edu

T. Issa et al. (eds.), *Social Networking and Education*,
Lecture Notes in Social Networks, DOI 10.1007/978-3-319-17716-8_15

function to network and make professional contacts [41]. However, in spite of this anecdotal evidence, very few empirical studies have explored the motivations and challenges behind social media use among the college population [16, 40]. Therefore, with the uses and gratifications theory as a guiding framework, this book chapter presents survey results among college students at a large US public university to determine the positive and negative effects of using social networking sites.

2 Theoretical Framework and Background on Social Networking

2.1 Uses and Gratifications Theory

Although traditionally understood and studied through television-watching patterns, uses and gratifications theory has more recently been studied within social media [1, 2, 28, 32]. Uses and gratifications theory states that people choose different forms of mass media in order to fulfill different needs, including surveillance, information learning, entertainment, personal identity, parasocial interaction, companionship, and escape [8, 26]. Making online communities the medium of choice can help fulfill these needs in a specific manner and through interaction with other people, based on the Internet's focuses on interactivity, responsiveness, spontaneity, dialogue, and propinquity [29]. Gratifications fulfilled easily and more frequently by Internet-based communication include convenient information seeking, guidance and opinion seeking, seeking a variety of opinions, and specific inquiry [28].

There is a distinction within uses and gratifications theory between gratifications sought and gratifications obtained [20, 27, 39]. Gratifications sought are those the user expects to obtain before utilizing the specific medium; gratifications obtained are those that the user actually experiences through the use of the medium. The difference between gratifications sought and obtained can predict the amount of satisfaction felt by the user [38, 39]. Media that fulfill sought gratifications are more likely to help users form habits and thus maintain a user base; those that do not provide those gratifications often lead users to try other media instead [38, 39]. Gratifications obtained are frequently the focus of research in order to understand the continued use of a medium [2, 9, 44].

The ability for interactivity within social media changes the user from mere recipient of information into potential producer of knowledge, often referred to as a prosumer [48]. With this extended control over creation, it is even more important to understand how publics are using different forms of social media to engage with others, gratify needs, and fulfill goals. The potential for the Internet to improve a person's life has also emerged as a large motivating factor in favor of using the medium [32].

Interactivity also has other dimensions that impact how social media is utilized, including increasing factors like playfulness, connectedness, information collection, and reciprocal communication [21]. Users of social communication sites find obtained gratifications such as having fun, killing time, and relaxing or escaping from daily responsibilities [44], as well as bond-based functions like interacting with like-minded individuals and information seeking [1]. Parasocial interaction online can also help decrease social loneliness [50].

This ability to understand the variety of gratifications available specifically through online communication makes uses and gratifications a sound theoretical base for looking at how college students choose social networking sites and what those sites allow them to accomplish.

2.2 *Social Networking and Online Communities*

Most of the research about online social communities started in a wide variety of areas, but has lately focused in the health-related arena [4]. Research on health-based communities has found an existing dual function provided to users: task-oriented or technical information used to increase initial membership, and socio-emotional support, or bond-based commitment, receive from other community members used to maintain membership [11, 18, 52]. Community in this sense is often defined as a concept that includes elements of bonding, commonality, reciprocity, and identity [51].

These online communities are often characterized by specialized relationships and weaker ties, or a select few people to whom one is especially close, and a general knowledge of and connection to a much larger section of the greater community [30]. Online communities often suffer from membership instability due to their ability to be left at any point in time [31, 34]. Insufficient member stability decreases the development of trust, reducing active knowledge sharing [34].

According to boyd [10], organizations active on social networking sites need to be aware that some people are becoming "friends" to express ideas about themselves, not out of desire to interact or communicate with the organization itself, or to make meaning of interacting with an organization, which organizations can then use to gather information about publics. Phillips [43] found that publics choose to maintain relationships that do not require extra attention while still allowing belongingness.

Individuals are increasingly turning to social media to search for and/or share information about a big event, causing the creation of a new catch phrase: "if it doesn't spread, it's dead" [23, para 1], where spreadability is a more conscious choice on the part of the public than simply letting something go viral. Going viral within social media means something that is highly and continuously spread among individuals, typically over a short period of time [35]. The item is passed from one social media platform to the next, provoking discussion, or at least acknowledgement, from around the globe [35]. Viral also means the number of individual people who see the content, but there is no real agreement on the threshold of when content has been seen by enough people to be considered viral [3]. Generally, positive content is more likely to be shared, and content that evokes strong positive or negative emotion is more likely to go viral than weaker emotions [6].

Individuals are also using social media to make more traditional content more engaging, in a playful or entertaining way to interact [17]. However, Carpentier [12] stressed that while new platforms may offer additional opportunities, organizations must maintain professional quality and social relevance in order to properly engage with their publics and stakeholders. Individuals looking to put emphasis on their own ideas and thoughts might include information from an organization, but are not likely to stop there, thwarting organizational attempts to control or moderate social media channels [29]. Using an individual social media platform to establish a stance on an issue can be a risky move, even as it broadens our understanding of social stake and how to use social media to engage with organizations and with one another [47]. Messages are often seen to be personally legitimate if action is taken to spread the message (i.e., retweeting or sharing) [47]. These ideas help communicators understand who is engaged, how they are engaged, and how social media connections are improved and best utilized.

3 Research Questions

Based on the review of the literature and extant research on this topic, the following research questions were asked in this study:

RQ1: What is the overall social networking site usage among US college-aged students?
RQ2: What are the positive uses and gratifications of social networking sites for US college-aged students?
RQ3: What are the negative uses and gratifications of social networking sites for US college-aged students?

4 Method

An online survey was sent to undergraduate students at a large US public university to gather data on motivations, benefits, and limitations of using social networking sites. More specific information on the survey sample, procedure, and design follows in the sections below.

4.1 Survey Sample and Procedure

Participants $N = 467$) were recruited via an online participant pool designed to offer extra credit opportunities to undergraduate students currently enrolled in communication courses (see Table 1 for demographic information). Students signed up to

Table 1 Demographics of study participants

Characteristic	Number of participants	%
Sex		
Male	171	37
Female	296	63
Field of study		
Other	169	37
Humanities	73	16
Health sciences	44	10
Economics and science	40	9
Accounting	38	8
Science and engineering	34	7
Marketing	25	5
Computer science	10	2
Management	10	2
Art and design	7	2
Information systems	3	1
Business law	2	0
Information technology	1	0
Age		
18–22	444	95
22–32	22	5
Education level		
Primary education	51	11
Higher secondary/pre-university	193	42
Professional certificate	1	0
Diploma	115	25
Advanced/higher/graduate diploma	21	5
Bachelor's degree	71	16
Master's degree	1	0

participate in the survey and were directed to a webpage with an introductory message and an electronic link to the online survey. This research was approved by the university's institutional review board (IRB) and participants were asked to provide consent before proceeding to answer the survey questions.

4.2 Survey Design

The survey was comprised of three parts. The first part asked participants for demographic information, including age, gender, field of study, and education level. In addition, the first part of the survey asked participants the number of hours spent on social networking, email, and their preferred activities on the Internet. The second part of the survey focused on the positive effects of social networking. Participants were asked on a 5-point Likert scale (from strongly disagree to strongly agree) whether social networking allows them to do various activities, such as *learn new information and knowledge*, *gain up-to-date information,* and *communicate with my peers frequently.* Participants were also given the opportunity through an open-ended question to offer additional comments on the positive effects of using social networking. The third and final part of the survey focused on the negative effects of social networking in relation to four areas: (1) cognitive development (i.e., *prevents me from concentrating more on writing and reading skills)*; (Gordon, #1706) social development (i.e., *prevents me from participating in social activities)*; (3) physical development (i.e., *prevents me from having face-to-face contact with my family*); and (Gordon, #1706) security (i.e., *increases privacy concerns)*, which were also asked on a 5-point Likert scale. Participants were also given the opportunity through an open-ended question to offer additional comments on the negative effects of using social networking.

4.3 Survey Analysis

The survey results were analyzed in order to understand the most common and average responses, while paying attention to the potential for outliers. Questions were analyzed for means and the separation of individual responses along the Likert scales provided. Qualitative responses were comparatively coded in order to find themes and broader understandings of the data [13]. Coding began with open coding to find initial themes, and then axial coding allowed for themes to be merged into like categories [13]. Codes were reviewed multiple times to ensure consistency, and were revised accordingly to determine the final codes that would be presented as categories in the analysis.

5 Results

This survey allowed for insight into how US college-aged students are using social networking sites, and what they perceived to be the benefits and drawbacks of those sites, and their interactions with others through them. Results will be discussed via research question, first looking at the positive uses and gratifications, then the negative uses and gratifications, and finally, a brief discussion of the overall social networking site usage of participants.

5.1 RQ1: What Is the Overall Social Networking Site Usage Among US College-Aged Students?

This study provided some general information about how US college-aged students are using social networking sites. One of the most interesting findings was in how much of a typical day was taken up by interacting via these sites. 61 % (N = 276) of respondents reported spending up to five hours per day on social networking sites, with 4 % (N = 16) indicating that they spent ten to twenty hours daily on sites such as Facebook and Twitter.

In addition to social networking sites, participants also noted spending significant amounts of time on the Internet in order to use email (86 %; N = 389), where again, more than one-quarter of respondents reported using for up to five hours per day (28 %; N = 125). Other uses of the Internet included studying (78 %; N = 354), shopping online (66 %; N = 298) and chatting with others (63 %; N = 287). While these uses were not discussed as part of the uses and gratifications framework, it is useful to see what other needs were being met when students go online.

5.2 RQ2: What Are the Positive Uses and Gratifications of Social Networking Sites for US College-Aged Students?

The three strongest results for why participants utilized social networking sites were to communicate with peers frequently (M = 4.53, SD = 0.67), to communicate with friends and family outside of their college institution (M = 4.39, SD = 0.81), and to gain up to date information (M = 4.39, SD = 0.73). Additionally, participants did not believe that engaging with social networking sites made them sick or unhealthy (M = 1.90, SD = 0.92), or that it increased unhealthy behaviors such as gambling (M = 1.86, SD = 0.94), or prevented them from having face to face interactions with others (M = 2.12, SD = 1.02).

Qualitative responses to the question of the positive effects of social networking sites can be grouped into a number of general themes, including *keeping in touch with others, help with work,* and *improving general knowledge.*

5.2.1 Keeping in Touch with Others

Participants were particularly clear about this benefit, noting that social networking sites were a “great way to keep in contact with people who live far away” and “to engage in dialogue with people outside of my normal community.” Social networking sites were also repositories for memories, according to a participant who used them to “see all my current pictures.” One participant noted that this also allowed her to “reach people in multiple communities at the same time,” a major benefit for college students who are juggling various social groups and commitments. Another participant continued that idea by saying that "you can get knowledge of certain events through Facebook and be able to participate in more activities." This was echoed with another participant saying social networking brought her "together with people I have not seen in a long time." Thus, the social networking sites were beneficial not just for staying in touch online, but for continuing to build those relationships offline as well.

5.2.2 Help with Work

Beyond general connections with others, social networking allowed the participants to build those relationships toward the greater good, by noting the benefit of getting "homework help from my friends if I am struggling in a class or assignment," or by letting them "multitask with my work." These relationships had broader expectations as well, where one participant used social networking to "spread a new business idea without it costing a lot." Entrepreneurs could use social networking, according to another participant, to "network starting from a very young age where you can set yourself up for possible business ventures later in life." This was helpful from a relational perspective, but using social networking sites also made it easier to "complete work with the help of internet sources."

5.2.3 Improving General Knowledge

Social networking was seen by participants as "extremely helpful to keep one socially aware," where even seeing information on the sites allowed for an increase in general knowledge. Others believed that "news articles on Twitter educate people. People that do not keep up with the news are forced to see these articles pop up and see others tweet and discuss the events and then they are almost forced to be educated on important and worthwhile events." Additional participants believed that "social media sites, such as Twitter, provide up to date information on breaking news" and thus "people are generally more informed about the world around them because they stumble upon this information when using social media."

5.3 RQ3: What Are the Negative Uses and Gratifications of Social Networking Sites for US College-Aged Students?

Participants in the study believed that using social networking sites made it more difficult for them to study quickly (M = 2.64, SD = 1.38), concentrate on reading skills (M = 2.65, SD = 1.13), and improve their professional attitudes (M = 2.75,

SD = 1.14). They also felt that social networking scattered their attention (M = 4.02, SD = 0.89), distracted them easily (M = 4.14, SD = 0.91), and increased their privacy (M = 3.37, SD = 1.09) and security (M = 3.31, SD = 1.11) concerns. Generally, the results about negative uses and gratifications had more variance among participants than the positive uses and gratifications; in other words, people seemed to find the same things to be beneficial, while they were slightly more split on the gratifications that were seen as negative.

General themes based on the qualitative responses to negative uses and gratifications of social networking sites include *increasing distractions, concern for privacy,* and *negative interpersonal ramifications,* each of which will now be discussed in turn.

5.3.1 Increasing Distractions

Participants were commonly grouped in their belief that social networking sites "becomes a mindless habit," which then is "really distracting if you don't know how to control your use of it." Participants did not elaborate on what allowed someone to control that usage. Additional description did come from one participant, who said that "social networking tends to distract me when I'm trying to get work done because its something I can turn too when I am feeling lazy and trying to avoid homework." Another participant concurred, noting that "I am often tempted to check social sites, even if I had previously checked them within the half hour." One participant talked about their struggle with keeping that in check, where social networking sites are "not a priority and should be a fun activity to do AFTER everything else (school, work, etc.)." The final word appeared to belong to the participant who noted that "social networking is like everything else in life, it's great in moderation but if you let it, it can take over your life and for the bad."

5.3.2 Concern for Privacy

A number of participants were concerned about how expressing so much of themselves through social networking sites would affect them, both in the current moment and in the future. One participant generalized the concerns by saying "it increases my concern for privacy, and my concern for what others think about me because if you want to maintain a certain image to family members on Facebook, it is hard to do so without offending them (blocking them) or releasing personal information and pictures." Another participant was more concerned about how they couldn't "protect myself from fraudulent users," similar to the idea that "social networks can give people a little too much insight into my life, that is, if it were ever to get hacked." Finally, some participants noted that social network sites could "cause people to say bad things because they think they won't get caught" or that "people's lives are put out there and they may not realize that it could harm them or be used against them."

5.3.3 Negative Interpersonal Ramifications

Finally, participants were concerned that social networking sites were changing communication, where they "take away the beauty of communicating to people in person and timeless hobbies like reading a book or newspaper." One participant said that "I get bored of it but cannot stop browsing the web." This lack of control speaks to the potential for addiction, and certainly to the idea that some relationships may be impacted due to the reliance on mediated interaction. In seeing what others are doing in such intimate detail, one participant said that social networking can "create jealousy by viewing other people's appearance of having great, exciting lives." This is also seen as "a large distraction to many people and prohibits them from focusing enough attention on more important activities."

6 Discussion

The findings from surveying 467 US college students have answered the research questions by demonstrated that using social networking sites are used fairly frequently by these students and provide both positive and negative uses and gratifications; however, it is definitely a balancing process that is ongoing and ever changing, especially as the amount of time that is spent on these sites continues to grow. Comparing these results to Pew data collected in 2009, it appears as though US college students today spend more time on social networking sites. In the Pew study, 85 percent of college students spent an average of 19.6 h a week on social networking sites [33]—the data we've collected here shows that the number has jumped to over 30 h a week. Overall, positive uses of social media found in this study include keeping in touch with others, help with work, and improving general knowledge.

With this said, the positive uses and gratifications found in this study align with what has been found in extant research. The fact that US college students utilize social networking sites to keep in touch with friends and stay connected was found in Walther and colleagues' [49] study, where 90 % of the Facebook users they surveyed used the platform to stay in touch with long-time acquaintances. Other studies found that social media can be useful in establishing multiple networks that span the globe, as well as further strengthening community relations [21, 44]. Furthermore, the results of this study are in line with Pew's survey data regarding using social media for social awareness and civic engagement, as 19 % of users in the Pew survey posted content relating to some social or political issue [45]. The use of the online space for spreading knowledge and awareness of issues ties into the rise of digital activism, which Joyce [24] broadly defines as using digital technologies in campaigning activities to enable the scope and reach of contemporary activism. The students in this study saw the benefits of utilizing social networking sites to spread the word about some sort of mission or cause they were passionate about, engaging in information sharing with like-minded individuals [1].

It should be noted, however, that these positive uses and gratifications can also be seen from a negative angle. In this study, negative uses of social media included increased distractions, a concern for privacy, and negative interpersonal ramifications. In terms of digital activism, though individuals are encouraged to take their online actions offline [42], the practice has been criticized as not being true or sustaining activism, being given labels such as 'slacktivism' or 'clicktivism' [5, 19, 37]. Beyond activist behavior, keeping in touch with others, which was the number one positive gratification found in this study, is an important use for social media. Our findings support Walther and colleagues' work [49], which found that 50 % of the Facebook users surveyed also reported that they found out important information about their friends via the social networking site. As noted in our results, this has the potential to be both a positive and negative gratification, as information is shared, but in a way that demonstrates the decline of sharing important news face-to-face. Interpersonal communication has been suffering as a result of increasing social networking activity, as Turnbull [48] found that young people are more likely to miss out on in-depth, quality face-to-face conversations due to their growing reliance on short and to-the-point emails and text messaging. She argues that online communication causes messages to lose "richness" and come off "leaner"—meaning that messages shared online are more ambiguous and vague, leading to a greater likelihood of miscommunication (p. 6).

These concerning aspects of social networking sites play into another use and gratification found in previous literature: identity formation, where users digest qualities of their online experience into their own individual identity [15]. This is complicated by our findings where college students express concerns for privacy and problems with interpersonal interactions. A recent phenomenon has occurred where young people compare themselves to others based on their social networking posts and profiles; instead of catching up with friends, users are more likely to feel as though they are *keeping up* with the so-called "perfect" lives of their peers [23, 32]. Keeping up with their peers means decreasing their level of privacy with others, in addition to trying to improve their interpersonal interactions, all of which require increased time and energy spent on identity formation and maintenance. Pempek and colleagues [41] found that Facebook users are more likely to spend time on other people's pages for judgment and evaluation versus maintaining their own content, engaging in what Jay [22] coins as "social surveillance" (p. 44). Therefore, because of the open nature of social media, as well as the fact that people tend to inflate their experiences and share only good news, college students may believe that they are failing or are not good enough in comparison to their peers [7]. This intriguing finding in particular, therefore, can add a unique extension to uses and gratifications theory.

The phenomenon of social surveillance can be seen as a combination of two previously addressed needs, namely, personal identity and surveillance [8, 25]. This study demonstrated that when surveillance is conducted in terms of figuring out one's own personal identity in comparison to others, it can produce a distorted reality that is in definite need of further study and exploration.

7 Limitations and Future Research

A limitation of this study is that it relied on the students' self-reports in their survey responses. Future research can use additional methods, such as experiments or participant observation, to further examine the phenomenon of social surveillance for young adults, and how it affects how they create identities both online and offline. Another limitation is that the data was collected from one university in one geographic location of the US. With this said, because this study's findings cannot be made generalizable to the entire US student population, it is imperative to continue conducting studies such as these to determine the true ramifications of social networking use and online activity, both within the US and around the world.

8 Conclusion

This book chapter discussed the results of a survey given to college-aged students in the US that asked them how they perceived the positive and negative uses and gratifications of social networking sites. The results demonstrated several over-arching themes that coincided with previous research, as the participants turned to these sites for information, community, and engagement, with interpersonal and media sources that they might not have had access to before these channels became readily available. Study findings also described the negatives of social networking, particularly for US college students, where concerns over distractions that take away from schoolwork and more face-to-face interactions as well as privacy/confidentiality concerns can create issues in their personal and professional relationships. Additionally, anxiety over the need to keep up with others' "perfect lives" online brings forth the need of social surveillance, as a distorted reality stems from comparing self to others, leading to feelings of competition and inadequacy in college students. Therefore, as social networking sites continue to shift and change, and the rate of online activity continues to grow, current and future researchers both in the US and abroad can further explore how these platforms impact young adults' knowledge, attitude, and behaviors, and how these tools and technologies work to make the global online space seem not as small.

References

1. Ancu M, Kozma R (2009) MySpace politics: uses and gratifications of befriending candidate. J Broadcast Electron Media 53(4):567–583. doi:10.1080/08838150903333064
2. Anderson IK (2011) The uses and gratifications of online care pages: a study of CaringBridge. Health Commun 26(6):546–559. doi:10.1080/10401236.2011.558335

3. Andrews M, Murakami H (2011) Defining viral: insights into Facebook's new analytics development. http://www.conecomm.com/defining-viral
4. Arduser L (2011) Warp and weft: weaving the discussion threads of an online community. J Techn Writ Commun 41(1):5–31
5. Badger E (2011) Are Facebook, Twitter fostering civic engagement? http://www.millmccune.com/politics/are-facebook-twitter-fostering-civic-engagement-33060/
6. Berger J, Milkman KL (2012) What makes online content viral? J Mark Res 49(2):192–205. doi:10.1509/jmr.10.0353
7. Blog HP (2013) Why generation Y yuppies are unhappy. http://www.huffingtonpost.com/wait-but-why/generation-y-unhappy_b_3930620.html
8. Blumler JG (1979) The role of theory in uses and gratifications studies. Commun Res 6(1):9–36. doi:10.1177/009365027900600102
9. Blumler JG, Katz E (1974) The uses of mass communications: current perspectives on gratifications research. Sage Publications, Beverly Hills
10. Boyd D (2007) Friends, Friendsters, and Top 8: writing community into being on social network sites. First Monday 11(12):13–20. doi:10.5210/fm.v11i12.1418
11. Buis L (2007) Social support provision within online health-focused support group. Paper presented at the international communication association, San Francisco, CA
12. Carpentier N (2009) Participation is not enough: the conditions of possibility of mediated participatory practice. Eur J Commun 24(4):407–420. doi:10.1177/0267323109345682
13. Corbin J, Strauss A (2008) Basics of qualitative research: techniques and procedures for developing grounded theory. Sage Publications, California
14. Derickson (2012) How college students use social media
15. Drussell J (2012) Social networking and interpersonal communication and conflict resolution skills among college freshmen. http://sophia.stkate.edu/msw_papers/21
16. Ellison NB, Steinfield C, Lampe C (2007) The benefits of Facebook "friends": social capital and college students' use of online social network site. J Comput Mediated Commun 12(4):1143–1168
17. Enli GS (2009) Mass communication tapping into participatory culture: exploring strictly come dancing and Britain's Got Talen. Eur J Commun 24(4):481–493. doi:10.1177/0267323109345609
18. Finn J (1999) An exploration of helping processes in an online self-help group focusing on the issues of disability. Health Soc Work 24(3):220–231
19. Gladwell M (2010) Small change: why the revolution will not be tweeted. http://www.newyorker.com/reporting/2010/10/04/10100fa_fact_gladwell?currentPage1
20. Greenberg BS (1974) Gratifications of television viewing and their correlates for British children. In: Blumler JG, Katz E (eds) The uses of mass communications: current perspectives on gratifications research. Sage, Thousand Oaks, California, pp 195–233
21. Ha L, James EL (1998) Interactivity reexamined: a baseline analysis of early business websites. J Broadcast Electron Media 42:457–474
22. Jay M (2012) The defining decade: why your twenties matter—and how to make the most of them now. Hatchet Book Group, New York
23. Jenkins H (2009) If it doesn't spread, it's dead. http://henryjenkins.org/2009/02/if_it_doesnt_spread_its_dead_p.html
24. Joinson A (2008) Looking at, looking up, or keeping up with people? Motives and uses of Facebook. Paper presented at the 26th annual SIGCHI conference on human factors in computing systems, Florence, Italy
25. Joyce M (2010) Digital activism decoded: the new mechanics of change. Internation Debate Education Association, New York

26. Katz E, Blumler JG, Gurevitch M (1974) Utilization of mass communication by the individual. In: Blumler JG, Katz E (ed) The use of mass communications: current perspectives on gratifications research. Sage, Thousand Oaks, California, pp 19–32
27. Katz E, Gurevitch M, Haas H (1973) On the use of mass media for important things. Am Sociol Rev 38:164–181
28. Kaye BK (2010) Going to the blogs: toward the development of a uses and gratifications measurement scale for blogs. Atlantic J Commun 18(4):194–210
29. Kent ML (2010) Directions in social media for professionals and scholars. In. In: Heath RL (ed) The Sage handbook of public relation. Sage, Thousand Oaks, California, pp 643–656
30. Kobayashi T (2010) Bridging social capital in online communities: Heterogeneity and social tolerance of online game players in Japan. Hum Commun Res 36:546–569. doi:10.1111/j.1468-2958.2010.01388.x
31. Komito L (1998) The Net as a foraging society: flexible communities. Inf Soc 14(2):97–106
32. LaAmanda R, Eastin MS (2004) A social cognitive theory of internet uses and gratifications: toward a new model of media attendance. J Broadcast Electron Media 48(3):358–377
33. Lenhart A, Purcell K, Smith A, Zickhur K (2010) Social media and young adults. Pew Charitable Trusts, Philadelphia. Document4
34. Matzat U (2010) Reducing problems of sociability in online communities: Integrating online communication with offline interaction. Am Behav Sci 53(8):1170–1193. doi:10.1177/0002764209356249
35. Mckee D (200) Going viral, part 1: a definition. http://www.sparkplugdigital.com/blog/going-viral-part-1-a-definition/
36. Miller L (2013) Reasons college student use social media. http://memarketingservices.com/2013/06/11/reasons-college-students-use-social-media/
37. Morozov E (2009) The brave new world of slacktivism. http://neteffect.foreignpolicy.com/posts/2009/05/19/the_brave_new_world_of_slacktivism
38. Palmgreen P, Rayburn JD (1979) Uses and gratifications and exposure to public television: a discrepancy approach. Commun Res 6:155–180
39. Palmgreen P, Wenner LA, Rayburn JD (1980) Relations between gratifications sought and obtained: a study of television news. Commun Res 7:161–192
40. Park N, Kee K, Valenzuela S (2009) Being immersed in social networking environment: Facebook groups, uses and gratifications, and social outcomes. CyberPsychol Behav 12(6):729–733
41. Pempek TA, Yermolayeva YA, Calvert SL (2009) College students' social networking experiences on Facebook. J Appl Dev Psychol 30:227–238
42. Petray TL (2011) Protest 2.0: online interactions and aboriginal activists. Media Cult Soc 33(6):923–940
43. Phillips D (2008) The psychology of social media. J New Commun Res 3(1):79–85
44. Quan-Haas A, Young AL (2010) Uses and gratifications of social media: a comparison of Facebook and instant messaging. Bull Sci Technol Soc 30(5):350–361. doi:10.1177/0270467610380009
45. Smith A, Lehman Scholzman S, Verba S, Brady H (2009) The internet and civic engagement. Document4
46. Smith A, Rainie L, Zichuhr K (2011) College students and technology. http://www.pewinternet.org/Reports/2011/College-students-and-technology/Report/Findings.aspx
47. Smith BG (2010) Socially distributing public relations: Twitter, Haiti, and interactivity in social media. Public Relat Rev 36(4):329–335. doi:10.1016/j.pubrev.2010.08.005
48. Turnbull CF (2010) Mom just Facebooked me and dad knows how to tweet: the influences of computer-mediated communication on interpersonal communication and differences through generations. Elon J Undergrad Res Commun 1(1):5–16

49. Walther JB, Van Der Heide B, Kim S-Y, Westerman D, Tong ST (2008) The role of friends' appearance and behavior on evaluations of individuals on Facebook: are we known by the company we keep? Hum Commun Res 34:28–49
50. Wang Q, Fink EL, Cai DA (2008) Loneliness, gender, and parasocial interaction: a uses and gratifications approach. Commun Q 56(1):87–109. doi:10.1080/01463370701839057
51. Willson MA (2006) Technically together: rethinking community within techno-society. Peter Lang, New York
52. Zrebiec JF (2005) Internet communities: do they improve coping with diabetes? Diab Educ 31:825–836

Part VI
Social Networking in Mexico

Impact of Social Networks in Mexican Universities

Ramón Zatarain-Cabada, María Lucía Barrón-Estrada and Rosalío Zatarain-Cabada

Abstract Social networks (SN) have been adopted by university students as a tool to achieve several academic activities like communicate and collaborate with peers, and to keep in touch with distant relatives and friends. However, social networking is a time consuming activity that has some effects in students' life. To determine how social networking is impacting students' life, university students ($n = 150$) at a small northwest university in México were surveyed on their use of social networks. Student responses indicate that social networking support academic activities among peers like communicating, collaborating and learning, but they also show that students get distracted easily and their academic work is not completed in time.

Keywords Social networking · Student activities · Interconnection · Technology adoption · Online communication · Education · Mexican Universities · Online survey

1 Introduction

Internet is one of the technological innovations that have had more impact in the last century into the different economic, political and social activities, and two of its most popular applications are search engines and social networks. Having the internet practically available anytime and anywhere, has impacted us as society by letting us to interconnect in ways that have never been used before.

Social networks sites (SNSs) have become a social revolution within web communities, especially for young users [5]. They are specifically used by user communities for exchanging and sharing information in several formats like videos, text, pictures and more. Boyd and Ellison [2] define the term "social networking" as

R. Zatarain-Cabada (✉) · M.L. Barrón-Estrada · R. Zatarain-Cabada
Instituto Tecnológico de Culiacán, Av. Juan de Dios Bátiz 310 Pte,
Col. Guadalupe, 80220 Culiacán, Sin, Mexico

T. Issa et al. (eds.), *Social Networking and Education*,
Lecture Notes in Social Networks, DOI 10.1007/978-3-319-17716-8_16

web-based services that allow individuals to construct a public or semi-public profile within a bounded system, articulate a list of other users with whom they share a connection, see and traverse their list of connections and those made by others within the system.

Since their appearance, social networking sites like MySpace, Facebook, Cyworld, and Bebo have attracted millions of users, many of whom have integrated these sites into their daily practices. There are hundreds of social networking sites, with technology for a wide range of interests and practices. Some sites are geared to diverse audiences, while others attract people based on common language or racial, sexual, religious or national identities based on affinities. Sites also vary as they incorporate new information and communication tools such as mobile connectivity, blogging and sharing photos and video [2].

Through smart phones, or not so smart, tablets or computers, 85 % of Internet users in Mexico (34.8 millions), have access to social networks. Although there is a clear digital gap in the country, analysts noted that these tools have the ability to democratize Internet. A study of CIU (Competitive Intelligence Unit) named "Mobile Marketing Mexico MX3 2013" reveals that between 2009 and 2013 the use of social networks in the country increased from 69 to 85 %. Socioeconomic status using more this technology is the C + (middle class), with 89 %, followed by the A/B levels, with 86 % usage, while the lowest levels (D/E) penetration is 80 % [3].

1.1 Social Networks in Latin-America and México

According to the Mexican Internet Association [1] Mexico is second among Latin American countries in the use of internet with 19 % [1]. 60 % of the internet users in Latin-American are from Brazil and México and the rest is shared by several countries like Argentina, Colombia, Chile, Peru, and others. 62 % of these users are young people between 15 and 35 years old. In 2011 the number of Internet users worldwide reached 1.374 billion, representing a growth of 10 % while in the same year, Latin-America achieved a growth of 14 %.

In the case of social networks, users in Latin America produced about 115 million visits. The top three more visited social networks were Facebook, Windows Live profile, and Orkut. In Mexico 90 % of internet users have daily access to social networks where the three most popular networks are Facebook, YouTube, and Twitter. It is noteworthy that men in Mexico spend daily an average of 5.76 h connected to social networks, while women do so for 6.13 h, however, it is important to mention that men from 14 to 18 years old spend more time connected to social networks, with an average of 7.12 h, while those who are over 55, spend about 3.13 h.

The average use of social networking sites (e.g. Facebook, Twitter, Youtube, Instagram, Pinterest, Linkedin, Fousquare, and Google+) by gender in Mexico shows that more than 50 % of the users are women. Regarding the electronic media on social networks, users in Mexico are multimedia, because they connect to networks from different devices like tablets, cell phones, desktop computers, or laptops. For example young users (18–24 years old) access networks, more than other age segments through laptops while users aged 25 to 34 year old, make it through cell phone (48.3 %). The device most commonly used to access social networks is the smartphone with Android platform, which is the most used by the segment of 18–24 years, followed by iPhone, which is the most used among consumers who answered a survey between 25 and 34 year old.

1.2 Social Networks in Mexican Universities

From students to parents, from academic members to research personal, everyone is using Facebook, Google+, and other social network sites. Social networks are used in a university environment as a means of interaction and communication between students and teachers. By this means, students share and exchange different elements like notes, school papers, photographs, videos, tasks or projects, etc., and teachers use them to interact with their colleagues and students, as well as support in managing their courses. In some studies made in Mexican universities, results showed that, more than 98 % of students participate in a social network, of which Facebook is by far the most popular [4].

1.3 Study Purpose and Research Questions

The study reported here was designed to gather information about the positive and negative impact of social networking on students' life. We applied a survey to ask students general questions about themselves, their online activities, and their social networking site use. In addition, they were asked more detailed questions regarding their social networking site use and their perceptions about the effects of their social networking site use on their personal relationships.

The study proposed the following questions: (1) Do college students in Mexico have adopted Social Networks as a tool to communicate and collaborate with peers? (2) What portion of students uses social networking sites to gain knowledge? (3) Are there negative effects for the students using social networks? (4) Do students feel comfortable using social networks for any activity?.

2 Method

2.1 Participants

Students from the Computer Science Department at the Instituto Tecnológico de Culiacán (México) participated in this study during Fall 2012 semester. Students who visit the computer lab were randomly chosen to participate in the survey. A total of 151 students answer the survey within 3 days. Only 150 were processed because one has incomplete information in many questions.

2.2 Measures

The survey was divided into three sections: background information, the positive effects of the social networking, and the negative effects of the social networking. Background section presented questions about general personal information like gender, age, field of study, among others; the positive effects of the social networking section was designed to examine how students used the social networking in positive ways to organize and maintain their work, study, and social life, while the negative effects of the social networking section is divided to analyse four perspectives: cognitive development, Social development, Physical Development and Security. In the survey, most items had multiple choice questions using five answer values which are strongly disagree, disagree, neutral, agree and strongly agree, but participants were asked to provide additional information about positive and negative effects of using the social networking.

2.3 Procedure

When participants came to the classroom, the study was explained to them so they can choose to participate or not. We provide some language assistance because the study was written in English and the respondents are native Spanish speakers. Participants completed the hard copy of the survey in about 15–20 min.

3 Results

3.1 Descriptive Statistics

Out of all the participants who took the survey, eighty-one percent of them were male and nineteen percent were female. In this field (computer science) it is common that the student population is male predominant in an 80–20 proportion, that is shown in the sample used in this study. Most students (84 %) ranged in age from 18 to 22 years old and 13 % from 23 to 32 years old. The main field of study was computer science (89 %), with information system having 7 % and information technology 3 %. The highest education level of participants was Higher Secondary/Pre-University with 89 %, Bachelor's Degree 6 %, and Professional Certificate 5 %.

3.2 *Time Spent on the Social Networking and Email Daily*

To get a picture of university students' use of the Internet related to their other activities, participants were asked on the survey about their time spent per day. Table 1 shows information about time spent on social networking and email. Most of the participants (78 %) spent no more than 5 h using social networks every day. While the table shows that 27 % of participants spent less than an hour. Draw our attention that there is a small part of participants (4 %) spending 10 or more hours in the internet (not including the email). With respect to email use, the majority (90 %) report using it up to 5 h daily. The rest (10 %) spent more than 5 h daily.

There were neither significant correlations between gender and time spent on social networking (Pearson's $r = 0.0795$ $p < 0.3334$) nor gender and time spent on email (Pearson's $r = 0.0429$ $p < 0.6024$).

3.3 *Positive Effects of Using the Social Networking*

On the survey, participants were asked about the positive effects of using a social network site. As can be seen from Fig. 1 (using a 5-points Likert scale), "communication with peers", is the most frequent positive activity (4.29) on social networking sites, and "concentrate more on my reading and writing skills", is the least frequent positive activity (3.11). Other activities that according to the students

Table 1 Time spent daily on the social networking and email activities

Hours participants spend on the social networking and email daily					
#	Answer	Responses	SN (%)	Responses	Email (%)
1	Less than an hour	40	27	109	73
2	Up to 5 h	77	51	25	17
3	5–10 h	27	18	11	7
4	10–20 h	4	3	3	2
5	Over 20 h	2	1	2	1
	Total	150	100	150	100

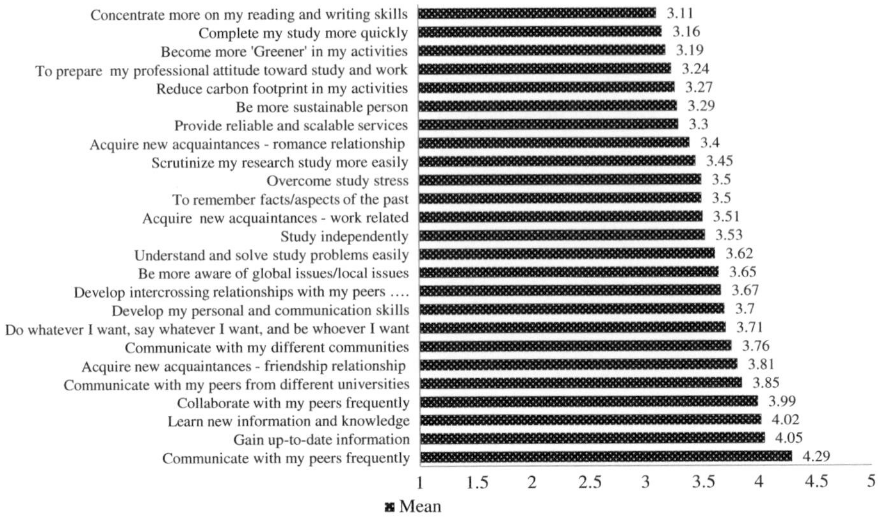

Fig. 1 Positive effects of using social networks

also have very high positive effects are: "Collaborate with my peers frequently" (3.99), "Learn new information and knowledge" (4.02) and "Gain up-to-date information" (4.05).

3.3.1 Perceived Positive Effects of Social Networking Site Use

Table 2 shows that 86 % of participants admit that social networking allowed them to maintain communication with their colleagues ($p = 0.0034$), regardless of the time they spend on social networks but 5 % of the participants disagree with this statement. On the other hand, 148 participants (more than 98 %) use social networks up to 20 h per day. A total of 76 % of participants consider that social networking allows them to gain up to date information regarding important events, but two participants (less than 2 % total) disagree.

We analysed several contingency tables for variable *How many hours do you spend on the internet for email? (Per day)*, and the results show that almost 60 % of participants agree that the use of email help them to understand and solve study problems more easily and also to develop their personal and communication skills ($p = 0.0114$).

On the other hand, there is a strong relation ($p = 0.0063$) between *Gender* and variable *Do whatever I want, say whatever ...* as presented in Table 3. Male participants expressed that one of the positive effects of using social media is that it allows them to express themselves freely and engage with people they wish to. Moreover, the responses of women are evenly distributed over the five options as show in Fig. 2.

Table 2 Contingency table of two variables

How many hours do you spend on the social networking daily, not including email? (Per day)							
Comm. with my peers…		Sample total		Less than an hour		Up to 5 h	
Code	Category	Frequencies	% s/sample	Frequencies	% s/sample	Frequencies	% s/sample
1	Strongly disagree	3	2	1	2.5	0	0
2	Disagree	4	2.67	0	0	2	2.6
3	Neutral	14	9.33	4	10	9	11.69
4	Agree	55	36.67	15	37.5	30	38.96
5	Strongly agree	74	49.33	20	50	36	46.75
	Total	150	100	40	100	77	100

Table 3 Contingency Table of variables *Gender* and *Do whatever I want …*

What is your gender							
Do whatever I want…		Sample total		Male		Female	
Code	Category	Frequencies	% s/sample	Frequencies	% s/sample	Frequencies	% s/sample
1	Strongly disagree	9	6	5	4.1	4	14.3
2	Disagree	12	8	6	4.9	6	21.4
3	Neutral	40	26.7	33	27.0	7	25
4	Agree	41	27.3	35	28.7	6	21.4
5	Strongly agree	48	32	43	35.3	5	17.9
	Total	150	100	122	100	28	100

Fig. 2 Variables *Gender* and *Do whatever I want …* in social networking

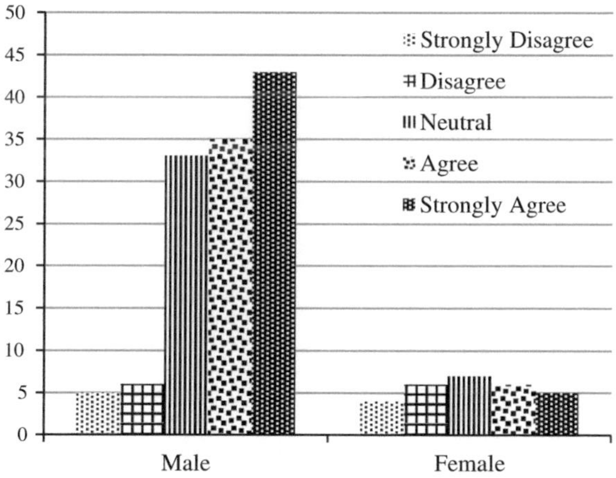

3.4 Negative Effects of Using the Social Networking

On the survey, participants were also asked about the negative effects of using a social networking site. As can be observed from Fig. 3 (with a 5-points Likert scale), "Distracts me easily", is the most frequent negative activity (3.69) and "Depresses me", is the least frequent negative activity (2.32). Other activities that according to the students also have very high negative effects are: "Scatters my attention" (3.53), "Prevents me from completing my work/study on time" (3.27) and "Makes me receive an immoral images and information from unscrupulous people and it is difficult to act against them at present" (3.15).

There were 19 % of respondents that felt that the use of email affects their moods by making them feel lonely. However, for most participants, using the email does not represent changes in their moods.

Analysing a contingency table using variables Age and Makes me more gambler we found that 98 % of students disagree that social networking makes them gamble more, where these students are between 18 and 32 years old. There were three participants (2 %) older than 32 that agree that this is a negative effect of social networking. Students in the age 18–22 do not consider that one of the negative effects of using social networking creates a gambling addiction. This is also the case for student's age 22–32 years, but in a smaller proportion.

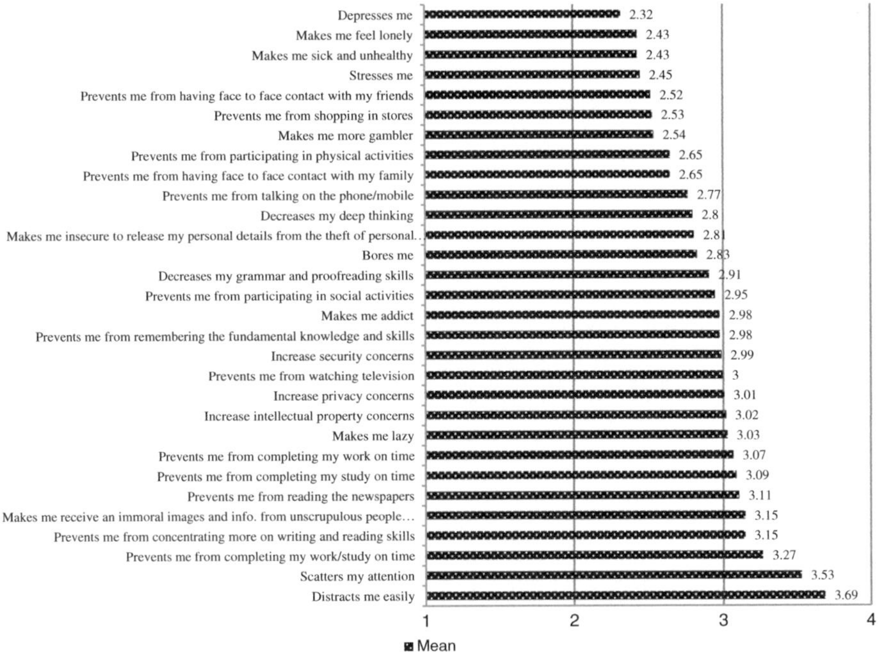

Fig. 3 Negative effects of social networking

Moreover, two of the students older than 32 believe that social networks have a negative effect related to gambling, where this judgment could well be a generational appreciation.

On the other hand, no matter how much time participants use social networks they do not perceive that social networking makes them gamble more. Only 16 % of participants agree with such a perception.

Social networking does not prevent students from shopping in regular stores. More than 50 % of participants disagree that this is a negative effect of social networking and just less than 20 % of participants perceived this as an impediment for regular shopping activities.

4 Discussion

In this section we present our discussion of the results obtained from the surveys of our students. One of the results suggests that there is no difference in the time students use social networks regarding gender. On the other hand, the results confirm that college students in Mexico are using social networks as a mean to communicate and collaborate with peers to solve academics issues. The majority of the students feel that social networking help them to learn and gain knowledge. Besides, students have many concerns about security issues and consider that personal information should be shared with caution.

4.1 Comments on the Positive Effects of Using the Social Networking

The study contains 25 questions about the positive effects of social networking. The results suggest that participants who use social networks observe several positive effects that can be clustered into five groups, these are: (1) Personal development that includes the growth of personal and communication skills, reading and writing proficiency, improving professional attitude toward study, work, and environment. (2) Online Communication that comprises Communication and collaboration with peers in the same university as well as foreign institutions, communication with different groups, and development of intercrossing relationships with peers. (3) Cognitive development that embraces learning new information and knowledge, studying independently, completing study more quickly, understanding and solving study problems easily, and scrutinizing research study more easily. (4) Social commitment that includes skills to be informed of global and local issues, remembering facts/aspects of the past, and overcoming study stress. (5) Eco-friendly that means being friendly with the environment, including reducing carbon copies and become friendlier both at work and personally.

In the survey, participants were asked to add a new comment about the positive effects of using social networks. Next, we list some of the most repeated and peculiar student answers:

To know friends.
To contact distant family.
To bring important information, especially teachers.
To be part of different groups about different interest.
To learn and understand about others cultures.
To realize that Internet is the lifeline of society.
To forget your problems.

4.2 *The Analysis of Negative Effects from Four Perspectives*

On the other hand, there were 30 questions which can be divided in four groups or perspectives to be studied and/or analysed separately. A group of nine questions was directed to aspects of cognitive development, where it seems that the students found that the most negative impact of using social networks is "distraction" (3.69), followed by "Scattering the attention" (3.53). Another group of eight questions was related to aspects of social development (e.g. "prevents me from having face to face contact with my family") and the student did not find a significant impact (negative or positive) on these activities (2.52–3.27). A third group of three questions was associated to physical development (e.g. "prevents me from participating in physical activities") where again student did not find a significant impact on these aspects (2.32–3.03). With respect to security there were five questions like "makes me insecure to release my personal details from the theft of personal information", where again almost half of the students perceive some negative impact (2.81–3.15).

In the survey, participants were also asked to add comments about the negative effects of using social networks. The majority of the participants in our sample reported having serious concerns about privacy and security issues. Next, we list some of the student answers:

It wastes my time.
You may find inappropriate content.
A mental instable person, can make a fake profile, and became a stalker.
People get distracted and that makes them anti-social.
Hasn't enough security.
Sometimes it becomes ′spam′, or just bad information
You can see too much bad grammar.

Our study has some limitations. We have made conclusions from the data collected in the survey, this means that students' answers about the time spent in email and social networking was not verified using real time activity, and students estimated the time spent in these activities. Although students feel they use social networks to learn and gain knowledge, a future study must evaluate what kind of things students are learning and what kind of resources they are using to gain knowledge. Besides that, we also need to explore to which extent teachers are interested in using social networks as a tool in the teaching process.

In conclusion, the results of our study show that most of the Mexican students (78 %) spent no more than 5 h using social networks every day and 90 % used email up to 5 h daily. In relation with positive and negative effects of using social networks "communication with peers", is the most frequent positive activity whereas "Distracts me easily", is the most frequent negative activity. On the other hand, it calls our attention that almost all students (98 %) aged 18–30 years disagree that social networking distract them in activities like gambling.

References

1. AMIPCI (2011) Redes sociales en México y latinoamérica. Asociación Mexicana de Internet. http://octavioislas.files.wordpress.com/2013/04/estudio-amipci-redes-sociales.pdf
2. Boyd DM, Ellison NB (2007) Social network sites: definition, history, and scholarship. J Comput Mediat Commun 13(1):210.230
3. Chávez G (2013) Redes sociales, las preferidas en México. CNN. Accessed 01-02-2014 2014
4. Herrera Batista MA (2012) Cuatro acciones para fortalecer el contacto entre docentes y alumnos universitarios: una propuesta basada en el uso y aplicación de las TIC. In: Congreso Internacional en Educación: Construyendo inéditos viables, Chihuahua, México
5. Lenhart A, Madden M (2007) Social networking websites and teens: an overview. Pew Internet Project
6. Subrahmanyam K, Greenfield P (2008) Communicating online: adolescent relationships and the media. Futur Child 18(1):27

Part VII
Social Networking in Middle East

Social Networking Effects on Jordanian Students

Ibrahim Al-Oqily and Ghazi Alkhatib

Abstract ICT sector is a powerful engine for growth and development of other sectors thus it gains the priority in all life dimensions from economics to social and has further impacted the cultural and political aspects. Social networks bring people together to share ideas, knowledge, and experience. Despite its popularity, Social networks can have positive and negative effects both on its users individually as well as their interactions with others collectively. Other factors analyzed include sustainability awareness and professional attitudes. The authors hope that this study will lead to emphasizing positive effects and reducing negative effects. A survey was published over the Internet and data were collected electronically and analyzed by SPSS using descriptive statistics and factor analysis. Over 750 participated in the survey divided about equally between male and female with the age of vast majority falling between 18–32 years and majoring in IT related fields. The study findings show that male and female young IT students' use of social networking and Internet is limited to rudimentary practices such as email and socialization. This reflected on the negative effects as well on social and physical development and away from the more serious issues of cognitive development and security.

Keywords Social networks · Jordan students · Online communities · Virtual communities · Sustainability · Cognitive development · Social development · Physical development

I. Al-Oqily (✉) · G. Alkhatib
Prince al Hussein bin Abdullah II Faculty for Information Technology, Hashemite University, P. O. Box 150459, Zarqa 13115, Jordan
e-mail: izaloqily@hu.edu.jo

G. Alkhatib
e-mail: g.alkhatib@hu.edu.jo

T. Issa et al. (eds.), *Social Networking and Education*,
Lecture Notes in Social Networks, DOI 10.1007/978-3-319-17716-8_17

1 Introduction

Information and communication technologies [1] became the backbone for the current and future services. In the last decade, we witnessed major changes in methods and operations of everyday life. ICT become the actual measure for progress and success of countries at all levels. The big challenge lies in the speed of the development resulting from the convergence of communications technologies, computer, and information to create value-added communication services; this has contributed to the emergence of new companies that are able to deal with video, audio, images, and data at the same time such as Facebook, Twitter, LinkedIn, Instagram, Pinterest, and Tumblr.

Social networking is basically a website that brings people together. It provides a central location where people can talk and share images and videos. Unlike traditional media that is provided by limited number of users, social networking provide a collaborative and sharing space where everybody can contribute to the content. Usually, these sites provide different services for users where the core is to connect users that share similar interest together by allowing them to create their own profiles and choosing their own friends. Due to the ever increasing development in ICT, the means by which users can access social networks can vary. However, the Internet remains the most widely mean by which people can access such collaborative environments.

Social networks attract users for its simplicity and the functions it provides. Recent studies showed that social networks are the most visited services on the Internet [2]. It requires no special knowledge and even users with little information on how to use computers can use it. However, Social networks can affect our life in many ways. It influences life satisfaction, cognitive ability, quality of life, healthcare, and education [3–8].

Jordan is a developing country with limited resources. Therefore, it invests greatly in education. The number of enrolled students in both public and private universities is estimated at nearly (236) thousand reaching the 4 % of the population. These students are driving force for future and technology revolution. Therefore, in this study we focus on students as the enablers of technology and the seed for our future workforce. We investigate their engagement in social networking and the effect of such environment on them. We studied the positive effects and the social, physical, cognitive development in addition to security. We also measured their sustainability awareness and professional attitude.

The rest of the chapter is organized as follows. Section 2 presents related work, the development of ICT in Jordan is presented in Sects. 3, 4 presents research methodology, Sect. 5 presents the properties of the study sample, conducted survey results and discussion is presented in Sect. 6, and finally in Sect. 7 we conclude the chapter.

2 Related Works

Young Jordanian engagement with social networks and the effects of such environments on Jordanians youth has been studied in [9]. The aim was to identify ways in which social networks can be used creatively in the community. The study shows that the engagement will keep increasing due to the positive effect of its services, and at the same time, the negative effects of social networks will not be a barrier to its expansion. It also reveals that Jordanian youth is not yet ready to use social networks in education but there are chances to enhance education through it. However, Social networks such as Facebook were studied as a learning resource [10] and found to provide a familiar environment for students that can be used to share knowledge. This is not surprising as multimedia elements that constitute the majority of social networks nowadays have a great influence on students and their learning progress [11].

The integration of Web 2.0 technology in higher education was studied in [12]. The study recommends that some Web 2.0 application might contribute to reduce the gender dissimilarity in college students‘ intentions to accept certain ICT for educational purposes. Understanding gender dissimilarity is essential to develop a successful learning environment. However, in [4, 13] students were found to have not enough knowledge with relevant technologies which will influence the values of Web 2.0 technologies.

The authors in [13] compares between faculty and students in terms of use and perception of social networks. The study focuses on the use of Facebook as a well-known social network. Their results show that students are greatly accepting the use of Facebook to support classroom activities than faculty members. Faculty members, on the other hand, prefer the use of email.

The effect of instructor's self-disclosure on Facebook on student motivation, effective learning, and classroom climate was studies in [14]. The study suggest that instructors self-disclosure on social networks have a positive effect on students. However, instructor's use of social networks could negatively affect their credibility. Therefore, they should disclose only appropriate information.

The effects of social networks on students' performance in Taiwan were reported in [15]. The study showed that there is a network effects on student performance for both on-line and off-line learning, and network structure are related to student performance both in the classroom and on Web-based forums. However, students in US University showed a negative relationship between academic performance and time spent on social networks [16].

These prior researches evidenced that social networking research is culturally dependent. It is not quite correct to generalize results drawn in a certain environment. Students in Jordan are assumed to behave in a manner that is consistent with the country values. To this end, we conducted this study focusing on Jordanian student's in order to identify the positive and the negative effects of social networks on them. In the negative effects, besides security, we studied the social, cognitive, and physical development. We will also show results for sustainability awareness and professional attitude. The results of the conducted survey will be presented in the subsequent sections.

3 The Development of ICT in Jordan

The world at this time undergoes big and significant changes at all levels, the acceleration of these changes in all areas creates a lot of challenges and difficulties, especially in the ICT sector, in which these changes rapidly appear sharper than other sectors. However, the dynamics of ICT sector makes it a powerful engine for growth and development of other sectors such as economics, educational, etc. thus it gains the priority in all life dimensions from economics to social and has further impacted the cultural and political aspects. ICT that has formed the digital divide plays a positive and effective role to promote development. Therefore, instead of increasing the social and economic gaps, ICT can be used to improve the performance and methods of work and be part of the exchange process and bridge that gap.

After more than six decades of the independence of the Hashemite Kingdom of Jordan, ICT sector shows a great development and spread of its services, along with a noticeable contribution to the economy. The percentage contribution of ICT in the GDP reached the 10 %, and provided a total of 16,000 direct jobs and 60,000 indirect jobs. Currently, there are more than 10.3 million subscribers in the service of mobile phones with a distribution rate of more than 156 %, approximately 400 thousand subscribers in the fixed-line with a distribution rate of more than 5.5 %, as well as the presence of more than 5.3 million Internet users with a distribution rate of more than 73 %. Figure 1 shows the Jordanian subscribers in fixed and mobile phones and the Internet since 2006. The figure clearly shows a noticeable and continuous demand on mobile phone services and the Internet [1]. Therefore, the Ministry of Information and Communications Technology [1] has launched the national ICT strategy for the years 2013–2017 which focuses on plans that will ensure the development of the ICT sector in the coming 3 years [1].The national ICT strategy should also focus on leveraging identified national strengths. Currently general national strengths are university educated labor, high levels of literacy, and

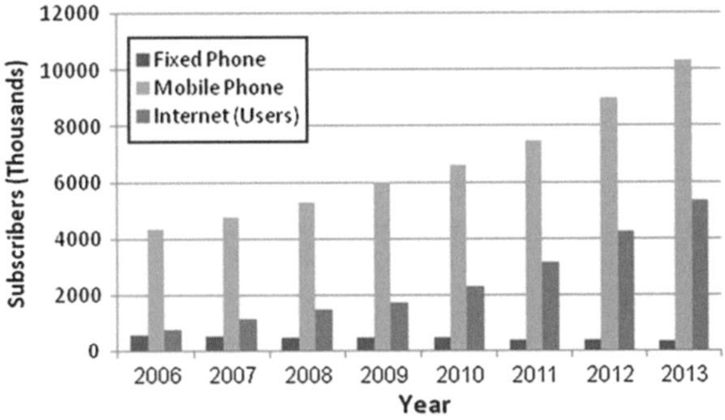

Fig. 1 Jordanian subscribers in fixed and mobile phones and the Internet since 2006 [1]

relatively good ICT infrastructure. To maintain competitiveness in this sector, it is imperative that the public and private sector should work to ensure that education and ICT infrastructure remain internationally competitive.

ICT sector growth and development has affected several other sectors in Jordan. The higher education in Jordan witnessed a significant progress in terms of the diversity of study programs, patterns of teaching, and learning. In the last 20 years, the sector witnessed an outstanding development as well as progress evidenced by the increase of the number of institutions, enrolled students, and administrative and academic members. For instance, the number of public universities has reached 10, in addition to 17 private universities, and 51 community colleges. This increase in educational institutions is accompanied by significant increase in number of enrolled students, with student enrollment reaching 236,000 students in public and private universities [17].

4 Research Methodologies

A questionnaire was developed and published over the Internet. Answers for respondents' background and social network uses were designed with selecting one or more listed options, while factors analyzed used Likert scale. Participants filled in the questionnaire and answers were captured electronically and dumped into spread sheet. The spread sheet was uploaded to SPSS for analysis using descriptive analysis, T-test, and factor analysis. The first method used to classify respondents' background and categorized social networks practices and uses, in addition to ranking uses and practices on social networks. The latter two methods, on the other hand, deployed for factor analysis based on T-test and the Chavat factors.

4.1 Survey Layout and Research Questions

The survey consists of three parts. The first part contains questions related to background information; the second part consists of the positive effects of social networking questions. The last part consists of the negative effects of social networking. It has been further divided into (1) Cognitive development, (2) Social development, (3) Physical development, and (4) Security.

The questionnaire was published over the Internet. Answers for respondents were collected over a period of approximately 12 months. The responses were used to answer the following research questions:

1. What are the positive and negative effects of social-networking usage by students in Jordan?
2. What are the real and potential risks and opportunities through the use of social-networking by gender and age?

3. What are the negative effects of the use of social networking in relationship to the four areas listed in the questionnaire?
4. What is the relationship between the use of social-networking and the notion of sustainability awareness among students in Jordan?
5. What is the relationship between social-networking and the development of professional attitude among students in Jordan?

5 Properties of the Study Sample

The frequencies and the percentages of the population of the study sample are shown in Table 1. It reveals that 52.9 % of the respondents are males while 44.6 % are females. The rest, 2.5 %, have missing information which results in 776 valid respondents. It also shows that the age group (18–22) was the highest in the study sample with 80.2 % followed by 13.8 % for the age group (22–32).

Table 2 shows that more than half of the samples study are students. There were 450 student respondents with 56.5 %. It also shows that 7 % were unemployed while the rest of the respondents are scattered between many jobs, and the computer and engineering fields were the most important.

Table 3 reflects the main fields of study and the education levels. It shows that the highest percentage was 18.8 % for computer followed by information systems and information technology with 13.8 and 12.4 %, respectively. We believe that all these fields are related as they reflect respondents working in the Information Technology (IT) field. The rest of the respondents were scattered between many fields. However,

Table 1 Study sample by gender and age

Gender		Frequency	%	Valid percent	Cumulative %
Valid	Male	421	52.9	54.3	54.3
	Female	355	44.6	45.7	100.0
	Total	776	97.5	100.0	
Missing	System	20	2.5		
Total		796	100.0		
Age		Frequency	%	Valid percent	Cumulative %
Valid	18–22	638	80.2	82.2	82.2
	22–32	110	13.8	14.2	96.4
	32–42	22	2.8	2.8	99.2
	42–52	6	0.8	0.8	100.0
	Total	776	97.5	100.0	
Missing	System	20	2.5		
Total		796	100.0		

Table 2 Study sample by job title

Job title		Frequency	%	Valid percent	Cumulative %
Valid	Physical therapy	6	0.8	0.8	0.8
	Student	450	56.5	63.2	64.0
	Accountant	4	0.5	0.6	64.6
	Android developer	1	0.1	0.1	64.7
	Architecture	1	0.1	0.1	64.9
	Computer	91	11.4	12.8	77.7
	Engineering	29	3.6	4.1	81.7
	Economist	2	0.3	0.3	82.0
	Event coordinator	4	0.5	0.6	82.6
	Programmer	28	3.5	3.9	86.5
	Unemployed	56	7.0	7.9	94.4
	Lecturer	5	0.6	0.7	95.1
	Nurse	6	0.8	0.8	95.9
	Marketing	3	0.4	0.4	96.3
	Information Technology	8	1.0	1.1	97.5
	Business	8	1.0	1.1	98.6
	Director	4	0.5	0.6	99.2
	MIS	3	0.4	0.4	99.6
	Musician	1	0.1	0.1	99.7
	Laboratory	2	0.3	0.3	100.0
	Total	712	89.4	100.0	
Missing	System	84	10.6		
Total		796	100.0		

the table also shows that highest education level among respondents was the bachelor degree with 66.6 % followed by the higher secondary/pre-university with 22.1 %, after adjusting for missing values.

Table 4 reveals that the majority of the respondents spend up to 5 h on social networks with 41 %, while 28.3 % spends less than 1 h and 10.3 % spends from 5 to 10 h. On the other hand, 62.7 % of respondents spends less than 1 h on the email, followed by 12.3 % for those who spends up to 5 h. The table clearly states that social networks are more attractive and respondents spend on it much higher time compared to the Internet uses.

Table 5 demonstrates that using the Internet for study was the most preferred activity among respondents with 0.618 mean followed by using the Internet for chat and email with 0.543 and 0.446 mean respectively. However, the rest of the uses gained lower importance level with a mean less than 0.3.

Table 3 Major field of study and education level for respondents

Main field of study		Frequency	%	Valid Percent	Cumulative %
Valid	Accounting	33	4.1	4.9	4.9
	Business law	4	0.5	0.6	5.5
	Economics and finance	19	2.4	2.8	8.4
	Information systems	110	13.8	16.5	24.9
	Information technology	99	12.4	14.8	39.7
	Computer science	150	18.8	22.5	62.2
	Management	15	1.9	2.2	64.5
	Marketing	4	0.5	0.6	65.1
	Health sciences	19	2.4	2.8	67.9
	Humanities	18	2.3	2.7	70.6
	Science and engineering	57	7.2	8.5	79.2
	Art and design	12	1.5	1.8	81.0
	Others	127	16.0	19.0	100.0
	Total	667	83.8	100.0	
Missing	System	129	16.2		
Total		796	100.0		
Highest education level		**Frequency**	**%**	**Valid percent**	**%**
Valid	Primary education	18	2.3	2.7	2.7
	Pre-university	147	18.5	22.1	24.8
	Professional certificate	5	0.6	0.8	25.6
	Diploma	15	1.9	2.3	27.8
	Advanced/graduate diploma	8	1.0	1.2	29.0
	Bachelor's degree	443	55.7	66.6	95.6
	Post graduate diploma	6	0.8	0.9	96.5
	Master's degree	23	2.9	3.5	100.0
	Total	665	83.5	100.0	
Missing	System	131	16.5		
Total		796	100.0		

Table 4 Hours spent daily by respondents on social networking and email

Hours for social networking daily		Frequency	%	Valid percent	Cumulative %
Valid	Less than an hour	225	28.3	34.6	34.6
	Up to five hours	326	41.0	50.1	84.6
	Five to ten hours	82	10.3	12.6	97.2
	Ten to twenty hours	13	1.6	2.0	99.2
	Over twenty hours	5	0.6	0.8	100.0
	Total	651	81.8	100.0	
Missing	System	145	18.2		
Total		796	100.0		
Hours for the Email daily		Frequency	%	Valid percent	Cumulative %
Valid	Less than an hour	499	62.7	76.8	76.8
	Up to five hours	99	12.4	15.2	92.0
	Five to ten hours	38	4.8	5.8	97.8
	Ten to twenty hours	7	0.9	1.1	98.9
	Over twenty hours	7	0.9	1.1	100.0
	Total	650	81.7	100.0	
Missing	System	146	18.3		
Total		796	100.0		

Table 5 The mean and the standard deviation (STD) for the preferred uses of the Internet. The result is listed in descending order based on its importance

	Statement	Mean	STD
3	Do you prefer using the Internet for: Study	0.618	0.486
6	Do you prefer using the Internet for: Chat	0.543	0.498
1	Do you prefer using the Internet for: Email	0.446	0.497
4	Do you prefer using the Internet for: Work	0.298	0.458
2	Do you prefer using the Internet for: Play Games	0.230	0.421
7	Do you prefer using the Internet for: Researching hobbies	0.211	0.408
5	Do you prefer using the Internet for: Shop Online	0.098	0.297
11	Do you prefer using the Internet for: Making or researching travel information or reservations	0.078	0.268
12	Do you prefer using the Internet for: Others	0.060	0.238
9	Do you prefer using the Internet for: Buying goods or services	0.036	0.187
8	Do you prefer using the Internet for: Banking online	0.033	0.178
10	Do you prefer using the Internet for: Buying stocks or investing online	0.018	0.132

6 Positive and Negative Effects of Social Networking

In this section we will analyze part 2 and part 3 of the survey. Part 2 studies the positive effects of social networks while part 3 studies the negative effects. Part 3 is further divided into cognitive development, social development, physical development, and security.

6.1 *Positive Effects of Social Networking*

Table 6 shows that all survey questions gained a high level of importance with a mean greater than 3.5, except for questions 20, 12, and 21 which gained an intermediate importance with mean less than 3.5 and greater than 3.0. However, the last question "Acquire new acquaintances - romance relationship" gained a low importance level with a mean of 2.899 which is less than 3.0.

Table 7 shows a cross tabulation for the positive effects against gender and age group. It shows that gender is insignificant for the positive effects of social networks as all questions gained a high importance level with mean greater than 3.5 with a slight difference between females and males. The exception is for the question "Reduce carbon footprint in my activities" where females have a different view than males with mean of 2.567 and 3.183 respectively. Table 7 also shows that there is a slight difference in most of the survey questions among different age groups except for questions 4, 11, and 12 for the 42–52 age groups. This age group states that the social networking doesn't allow them to collaborate with their peers frequently, or to remember facts/aspects of the past, or to scrutinize their research study more easily.

6.2 *Negative Effects of Social Networking*

The negative effects have been divided into four categories: (1) cognitive development, (2) social development, (3) Physical development, and (4) security. In this section we will investigate these categories in order to identify the real potential risks and opportunities through the use social-networking by gender and age.

6.2.1 Cognitive Development

The mean and the standard deviation (STD) for the negative effects of social networking based on cognitive development are shown in Table 8. The results indicate that the point number six distracts me easily, has a high importance level with a mean greater than 3.5. However, the points 1 and 2 have low importance

Table 6 The mean and the standard deviation (STD) for the positive effects of social networking. The result is sorted in descending order based on its importance

Sig	No.	Statement	Mean	STD
1	2	Gain up-to-date information	4.110	0.946
2	5	Communicate with my peers frequently	4.095	0.912
3	1	Learn new information and knowledge	4.057	1.009
4	6	Collaborate with my peers frequently	4.004	0.890
5	15	Develop my personal and communication skills	3.935	0.902
6	3	Be more aware of global issues/local issues	3.897	0.924
7	7	Communicate with my peers from different universities	3.872	0.919
8	8	Communicate with my different communities	3.864	0.893
9	22	Acquire new acquaintances—work related	3.826	0.914
10	23	Acquire new acquaintances—friendship relationship	3.805	0.961
11	4	To remember facts/aspects of the past	3.791	0.942
12	14	Scrutinize my research study more easily	3.722	0.947
13	9	Develop intercrossing relationships with my peers (i.e. Artistic talents, sport and common interests)	3.711	0.983
14	16	Concentrate more on my reading and writing skills	3.688	1.020
15	11	Overcome study stress	3.684	1.010
16	25	Do whatever I want, say whatever I want, and be whoever I want	3.667	1.163
17	13	Understand and solve study problems easily	3.628	1.007
18	10	Study independently	3.617	1.056
19	17	To prepare my professional attitude toward study and work	3.613	1.017
20	18	Be more sustainable person	3.544	1.025
21	19	Provide reliable and scalable services	3.535	0.958
22	20	Become more "Greener" in my activities	3.408	0.974
23	12	Complete my study more quickly	3.304	1.162
24	21	Reduce carbon footprint in my activities	3.186	1.182
25	24	Acquire new acquaintances—romance relationship	2.899	1.291

level with mean less than 3.0. On the other hand, Table 9 indicates that there is a difference in cognitive development by gender, for males. It also shows that there is a difference in cognitive development by ages. The age group 32–42 gained the highest followed by (22–32), (18–22), (42–52).

6.2.2 Social Development

Table 10 indicates that the point number 8 " Makes me lazy" was on a high level of importance. However, the points 1, 3, 4, 5, 6, 7, and 10 gained a low importance level with a mean less than 3.0. However, Table 11 indicates that there is a difference in social development by gender, for males. The table indicates that there is

Table 7 The mean and the standard deviation (STD) for the positive effects of social networking according to gender and age group. The sequence field represents the survey question as shown in Table 6 in the Sig field

	Females		Males		18–22	22–32	32–42	42–52
Sequence	Mean	STD	Mean	STD	Mean	Mean	Mean	Mean
1	3.792	0.904	4.076	1.073	4.128	3.909	3.85	4.250
2	4.077	0.866	4.142	0.952	3.910	4.018	3.92	4.000
3	3.993	0.889	3.912	0.941	3.812	3.836	3.85	3.500
4	3.857	0.894	3.792	0.904	4.111	3.727	3.69	2.750
5	3.949	0.926	4.077	0.866	4.009	4.073	3.85	3.500
6	3.788	1.003	3.993	0.889	3.866	3.982	4.08	3.500
7	3.670	1.099	3.857	0.894	3.874	3.909	3.92	3.750
8	3.695	1.009	3.949	0.926	3.719	3.727	4.15	3.750
9	3.363	1.159	3.788	1.003	3.605	3.618	3.77	4.000
10	3.612	1.034	3.670	1.099	3.696	3.673	3.77	3.750
11	3.725	1.015	3.695	1.009	3.290	3.691	3.62	2.500
12	3.905	0.907	3.363	1.159	3.652	3.436	3.38	2.750
13	3.766	1.069	3.612	1.034	3.731	3.473	3.62	3.250
14	3.634	1.066	3.725	1.015	3.947	3.655	3.54	4.250
15	3.546	1.094	3.905	0.907	3.694	3.891	4.00	3.000
16	3.568	0.994	3.766	1.069	3.611	3.655	3.69	3.500
17	3.414	1.019	3.634	1.066	3.531	3.582	4.00	3.000
18	3.169	1.297	3.546	1.094	3.510	3.600	3.92	3.000
19	3.799	0.959	3.568	0.994	3.386	3.618	3.77	4.250
20	3.799	0.955	3.414	1.019	3.139	3.545	3.54	3.500
21	3.183	1.261	3.169	1.297	3.834	3.455	3.62	3.250
22	3.630	1.185	3.799	0.959	3.793	3.727	3.85	4.250
23	3.812	0.971	3.799	0.955	2.899	3.891	3.92	3.500
24	2.567	1.248	3.183	1.261	3.695	2.891	3.15	2.250
25	3.711	1.139	3.630	1.185	4.128	3.436	3.92	3.000

Table 8 The mean and the standard deviation (STD) for the negative effects of social networking based on cognitive development

Sig	No.	Statement	Mean	STD
1	6	Distracts me easily	3.538	1.168
2	3	Scatters my attention	3.242	1.071
3	5	Decreases my deep thinking	3.104	1.175
4	4	Decreases my grammar and proofreading skills	3.002	1.162
5	1	Prevents me from concentrating more on writing and reading skills	2.998	1.239
6	2	Prevents me from remembering the fundamental knowledge and skills	2.911	1.164

Table 9 Cognitive development mean and the standard deviation (STD) according to gender and age

Gender	N	Minimum	Maximum	Mean	Std. deviation
Male	269	1.00	5.00	3.1929	0.92422
Female	230	1.00	5.00	3.1857	0.85393
Age	N	Minimum	Maximum	Mean	Std. deviation
18–22	428	1.00	5.00	3.1666	0.88688
22–32	54	1.00	5.00	3.3413	0.92599
32–42	13	2.14	5.00	3.3626	0.94692
42–52	4	2.14	4.00	3.0357	0.79433

Table 10 The mean and the standard deviation (STD) for the negative effects of social networking based on social development

Sig	No.	Statement	Mean	STD
1	8	Makes me lazy	3.380	1.128
2	11	Makes me insecure to release my personal details from the theft of personal information	3.356	1.138
3	2	Prevents me from completing my work/study on time	3.345	1.199
4	12	Makes me receive an immoral images and information from unscrupulous people and it is difficult to act against them at present	3.320	1.230
5	9	Makes me addict	3.097	1.228
6	4	Bores me	2.988	1.178
7	1	Prevents me from participating in social activities	2.932	1.172
8	3	Makes me sick and unhealthy	2.903	1.204
9	5	Stresses me	2.859	1.094
10	7	Makes me feel lonely	2.829	1.186
11	6	Depresses me	2.790	1.134
12	10	Makes me more gambler	2.504	1.327

Table 11 Social development mean and the standard deviation (STD) according to gender and age

Gender	N	Minimum	Maximum	Mean	Std. deviation
Male	268	1.00	5.00	3.0795	0.87791
Female	230	1.00	5.00	2.9564	0.77604
Age	N	Minimum	Maximum	Mean	Std. deviation
18–22	427	1.00	5.00	3.0261	0.83442
22–32	54	1.00	5.00	3.0021	0.81181
32–42	13	2.00	5.00	3.1090	0.96248
42–52	4	1.50	3.58	2.6458	0.86167

a difference in social development by ages where (32–42) got the highest importance level, followed by (18–22), (22–32), and (42–52).

6.2.3 Physical Development

Table 12 indicates that the point number 9 "Prevents me from completing my study on time" was on a high level of importance. However, the points 1, 2, 4, and 7 gained a low importance level with a mean less than 3.0. However, Table 13 indicates that there is a difference in physical development by gender, for females. The table indicates that there is a difference in social development by ages where (32–42) got the highest importance level, followed by (42–52), (22–32), and (18–22),

Table 12 The mean and the standard deviation (STD) for the negative effects of social networking based on physical development

Sig	No.	Statement	Mean	STD
1	9	Prevents me from completing my study on time	3.245	1.218
2	8	Prevents me from completing my work on time	3.225	1.226
3	6	Prevents me from reading the newspapers	3.213	1.304
4	3	Prevents me from participating in physical activities	3.122	1.200
5	5	Prevents me from watching television	3.116	1.290
6	2	Prevents me from having face to face contact with my friends	2.898	1.188
7	1	Prevents me from having face to face contact with my family	2.893	1.179
8	7	Prevents me from talking on the phone/mobile	2.793	1.249
9	4	Prevents me from shopping in stores	2.740	1.209

Table 13 Physical development mean and the standard deviation (STD) according to gender and age

Gender	N	Minimum	Maximum	Mean	Std. deviation
Male	268	1.00	5.00	3.0141	0.94251
Female	230	1.00	5.00	3.0425	0.90835
Age	N	Minimum	Maximum	Mean	Std. deviation
18–22	427	1.00	5.00	3.0132	0.92677
22–32	54	1.00	5.00	3.1379	0.92910
32–42	13	2.00	5.00	3.2650	0.86844
42–52	4	1.33	3.00	2.2500	0.73912

6.2.4 Security

Table 14 indicates that all the points were on an intermediate level of importance with a mean less than 3.5 and greater than 3. Table 15 has the same indication for gender and age. The exception is for the age group (42–52) that gained a low importance level with mean less than 3.0

6.3 Factor Analysis

Based on the Chavat factors matrix set forth in the Table 16 and the amount of the relative importance of each factor, we conclude the following:

(a) The social development factor has the highest influence in the social networking. It is affected with 81.8 % with saturation reached 0.904. It is noticeable that this effect was higher for males and the age group 32–42.
(b) Physical development factor lies in the second place in terms of its influence in social networking. It is affected with 77.5 % with saturation reached 0.881. This effect was higher for females and for the age group 32–42.

Table 14 The mean and the standard deviation (STD) for the negative effects of social networking based on security

Sig	No.	Statement	Mean	STD
1	1	Increase privacy concerns	3.358	1.051
2	2	Increase security concerns	3.341	1.077
3	3	Increase intellectual property concerns	3.379	1.086

Table 15 Security mean and the standard deviation (STD) according to gender and age

Gender	N	Minimum	Maximum	Mean	Std. deviation
Male	268	1.00	5.00	3.3825	0.92125
Female	231	1.00	5.00	3.3377	1.07877
Age	**N**	**Minimum**	**Maximum**	**Mean**	**Std. deviation**
18–22	428	1.00	5.00	3.3555	0.99835
22–32	54	1.00	5.00	3.4568	1.02033
32–42	13	1.33	5.00	3.3077	0.99500
42–52	4	2.33	3.33	2.9167	0.41944

Table 16 Factor analysis

Factor	Component	(%)
Cognitive development	0.843	711
Social development	0.904	818
Physical development	0.881	775
Security	0.731	535

(c) Cognitive development factor lies in the third place in terms of its influence in social networking. It is affected with 71.1 % with saturation reached 0.843. This effect was higher for males and for the age group 32–42.

(d) The security factor had the least influence in social networking. It is affected with 53.5 % with saturation value 0.731. This effect was higher for males and the age group 32–42.

6.4 Sustainability Awareness and Professional Attitude

One sample T-Test used to explain the relationship between the use of social networking and notion of sustainability awareness. The result is shown in Table 17. It indicates that the calculated T value was (−2.239) which is higher than calculated (1.962) with possibility value (0.026) which is lower than the specific value (0.05). Consequently, a significant negative relationship exists between the use of social networking and the notation of sustainability awareness at significant level ($\alpha \leq 0.05$).

Table 18 shows one sample T-Test used to explain the relationship between the use of social networking and professional attitude among the students. The results indicates that the calculated T value was (4.918) which is higher than calculated (1.962) with possibility value (0.000) which is lower than the specific value (0.05). Therefore, these results indicate a significant positive relationship between the use of social networking and professional attitude among respondents at significant level ($\alpha \leq 0.05$).

Table 17 T-Test for sustainability awareness

Mean	Df	T tabled	T	Sig
3.4181	506	1.962	−2.239	0.026

Table 18 T-Test for professional attitude

Mean	df	T tabled	T	Sig
3.655	506	1.962	4.918	0.000

6.5 *Discussion and Significance Contribution from This Study: Theoretical and Practical*

Our research questions were:

1. What are the positive and negative effects of social-networking usage by students in Jordan?
2. What are the real and potential risks and opportunities through the use of social-networking by gender and age?
3. What are the negative effects of the use of social networking in relationship to the four areas listed in the questionnaire?
4. What is the relationship between the use of social-networking and the notion of sustainability awareness among students in Jordan?
5. What is the relationship between social-networking and the development of professional attitude among students in Jordan?

In relationship to the first question, the preceding discussions highlight the positive and negative effects of social networking. On the positive side, communication and collaboration related issues occupied 7 of the top 10 factors, while the other three went to acquiring information and knowledge. On the negative side, distraction, attention, and deep thinking where the top negative effects on cognitive development. For social development, the top five went to laziness, privacy concerns, and morality concerns. Completing study and work on-time, not reading newspapers, not participating on physical activities, and not watching TV were the top five factors for the physical development. As to the last negative effects, the top three issues for security were privacy, security, and intellectual property concerns. As to research question 2, all the above results experienced no significant variations in relationship to gender and age groups.

Research question poses by number 3, the chapter performed factor analysis on the four negative effects of social networks which resulted of the order of social development, physical development, cognitive development, and Security. For research question number 4 and 5, this chapter performed further analysis of the relationship between social networking in one side and sustainability and professional attitudes from the other side, which revealed a negative effect with first one and a positive effect with the latter one.

In comparison to prior research findings, these results also are in congruence with the previously published results [9]. As to suggested dissimilarity in social networking use between genders in [4, 12], our study showed no differences between female and male respondents in all issues questioned in the survey. As to conclusions reported in [15], our study supported the notion that social networking and the Internet can help in study and collaboration among students, as well gaining information and knowledge from social networks. At the same time, our study found negative effect on performing study and work activities on time.

From these findings, we suggest that Jordan's students should be exposed to an awareness campaign on how to use social networks and the Internet to positively impact their life. In addition, technology-wise, they need to be trained on how to interact with the outside world through the creation of Web pages to propagate their attitudes and preferences freely and improve the overall quality of their life.

7 Conclusions and Future Research

Male and female young IT students' use of social networking and Internet is limited to basic aspects such as email and socialization. This reflected on the negative effects as well on social and physical development and away from the more serious issues of cognitive development and security. Throughout the analysis, gender and age did not portray any significant influence on usage patterns of social networks and Internet except in a couple of issues. However, since the vast majority of the sample survey belong the age group 18–22 (more than 80 %), these variations could not be conclusive because of the small sizes of these age clusters. The young people in the sample felt that social networks and the Internet affect study and work behavior negatively. Psychologically, they felt lazy, bored, becoming less social in off-line activities, developing feeling of being insecure from sharing personal information on social networks, and agonized about their inability to do something about immoral images and information they receive from unscrupulous people. Also, respondents viewed the relationship of social networking to professional attitude more positively than sustainability awareness.

In future research endeavors, we plane to include other stakeholders of social media in these studies, such as teachers and institutions and comparing urban vs. rural areas in Jordan. In addition, we hope to conduct comparisons with other countries as well, both regionally and internationally. The conclusions of this study should be understood within the limitations set forth by the survey tools and the geographical location of respondents in the capital of Jordan, as well as the statistical techniques used in the data analysis.

References

1. Moict (2013) The national ICT strategy. http://www.moict.gov.jo/en-us/homepage.aspx. Accessed 15 May 2014
2. ComScore (2011) Social networking: total time spent online. http://blog.comscore.com/2011/06/. Accessed 15 May 2014
3. Alloway TP, Horton J, Alloway RG, Dawson C (2013) Social networking sites and cognitive abilities: do they make you smarter? Comput Educ 63:10–16. doi:10.1016/j.compedu.2012.10.030
4. Bennett S, Bishop A, Dalgarno B, Waycott J, Kennedy G (2012) Implementing Web 2.0 technologies in higher education: a collective case study. Comput Educ 59(2):524–534. doi:10.1016/j.compedu.2011.12.022
5. Din N, Yahya S, Suzan R, Kassim R (2012) Online social networking for quality of life. Procedia Soc Behav Sci 35:713–718. doi:10.1016/j.sbspro.2012.02.141

6. Oh HJ, Ozkaya E, LaRose R (2014) How does online social networking enhance life satisfaction? The relationships among online supportive interaction, affect, perceived social support, sense of community, and life satisfaction. Comput Hum Behav 30:69–78. doi:10.1016/j.chb.2013.07.053
7. Tess PA (2013) The role of social media in higher education classes (real and virtual)—a literature review. Comput Hum Behav 29(5):A60–A68. doi:10.1016/j.chb.2012.12.032
8. Williams J (2010) Social networking applications in health care: threats to the privacy and security of health information. In: Proceedings of the 2010 ICSE workshop on software engineering in health care, 05/03/2010. ACM, pp 39–49. doi:10.1145/1809085.1809091
9. Al-Oqily I, Alkhatib G, Al-Khasawneh A, Alian M (2013) Social networks impact: the case of Jordan youth. Int J Contin Eng Educ Life-Long Learn 23(1):100–114
10. Ractham P, Firpo D (2011) Using social networking technology to enhance learning in higher education: a case study using Facebook. In: 2011 44th Hawaii international conference on system sciences (HICSS), 4–7 Jan 2011. pp 1–10. doi:10.1109/HICSS.2011.479
11. Srivastava S (2012) A study of multimedia & its impact on students' attitude. In: 2012 IEEE international conference on technology enhanced education (ICTEE), 3–5 Jan 2012. pp 1–5. doi:10.1109/ICTEE.2012.6208606
12. Huang W-HD, Hood DW, Yoo SJ (2013) Gender divide and acceptance of collaborative Web 2.0 applications for learning in higher education. Internet High Educ 16(0):57–65. doi:http://dx.doi.org/10.1016/j.iheduc.2012.02.001
13. Roblyer MD, McDaniel M, Webb M, Herman J, Witty JV (2010) Findings on Facebook in higher education: a comparison of college faculty and student uses and perceptions of social networking sites. Internet High Educ 13(3):134–140. doi:10.1016/j.iheduc.2010.03.002
14. Mazer JP, Murphy RE, Simonds CJ (2007) I'll see you on "Facebook": the effects of computer-mediated teacher self-disclosure on student motivation, affective learning, and classroom climate. Commun Educ 56(1):1–17. doi:10.1080/03634520601009710
15. Yang H-L, Tang J (2003) Effects of social network on students' performance: a web-based forum study in Taiwan | The Sloan Consortium. J Asynchronous Learn Netw 7(3):93–107
16. Paul JA, Baker HM, Cochran JD (2012) Effect of online social networking on student academic performance. Comput Hum Behav 28(6):2117–2127. doi:10.1016/j.chb.2012.06.016
17. Mohe (2013) Higher education sector in Jordan. http://www.mohe.gov.jo/. Accessed 15 May 2014

Effects of Social Networking on Higher Education in Saudi Arabia

Sulaiman Alqahtani

Abstract This chapter investigates the perceptions of a sample of Saudi Arabian adults towards the positive benefits and potential risks of contemporary social networking platforms both in everyday life and in the context of higher education. While many universities world-wide are engaged in harnessing the capacities of social net-working to motivate students, encourage connectivity and support collaboration between students and staff, there is limited evidence that this is the case in Saudi Arabia. As argued in this chapter, Saudi Arabia occupies a unique cultural position in that its strict Islamic lifestyle coincides not only with great enthusiasm for social networking on the part of its younger citizens but also with a current drive for reform in its educational sector in order to produce world standard education with a focus on ICT and blended learning options. The research aimed to more closely examine attitudes towards the potentialities and possible threats of social networking so as to guide future national development in the higher education area. This was carried out through surveying 100 participants and the research findings support the notion that Saudi attitudes towards the benefits and threats of social networking match world-wide trends, suggesting that these technologies might be profitably implemented in higher education without significant obstacle.

Keywords Social networking · Saudi Arabia · Higher education · Positive and negative effects · Web 2.0

1 Introduction

The transition from Web 1.00 to Web 2.0 technologies has unleashed a multitude of possibilities for shared interactive online experiences which are generated, shaped and controlled by ordinary individuals rather than web professionals [1–3]. A number of collaborative social networking services have emerged, allowing for shared

S. Alqahtani (✉)
33/269 Hay Street, Perth, WA 6004, Australia
e-mail: s.alqahtani8@student.curtin.edu.au

T. Issa et al. (eds.), *Social Networking and Education*,
Lecture Notes in Social Networks, DOI 10.1007/978-3-319-17716-8_18

activities such as group production and editing of content, the sharing of ideas, opinions and media items with like-minded others, the building of personal and professional networks and communities, and the creation of customised repositories of digital objects. Due to these capacities, the higher education sector has developed an interest in social networking services, driven by the demand for universities to accommodate the needs and preferences of modern learners who attend tertiary institutions expecting to be "engaged, active, social and networked" [4]. The motivation to produce better teaching and learning mechanisms and, by extension, superior academic results in a global knowledge economy also underlies current investigations into the ways in which students interact with digital technologies, coupled with the feasibility of implementing social networking into higher educational pedagogies. While much is now known about these issues, little research has yet addressed the benefits and risks of social networking in higher education in the absolute monarchy of Saudi Arabia, an extremist Islamic country where social, cultural and gender dynamics are shaped by religious and moral tenets which prescribe the daily practices of its citizens. In parallel to this, Saudi Arabia is currently experiencing a period of unprecedented economic and social growth [5]. This is being fuelled by the rapid diversification of the economy, the growth of the private sector and the need to provide a skilled educated Saudi workforce [6]. Saudi Arabia has embarked on an aggressive investment in its education sector which is undergoing significant reforms in order to bring it into line with global standards. The Ministry of Higher Education, which governs the tertiary sector, has pursued a series of 5-year plans with the aim of enhancing the quality and performance of its institutions. The Ministry is highly in favour of ICT initiatives and the potentialities of e-learning in its reform of the sector and officially adopted blended learning as its preferred approach from 2006 [7]. Indeed, Saudi Arabia is currently in the 9th phase of a series of 5-year reform plans (2010–2014) and has dedicated considerable resources to the implementation of ICT-based teaching and learning. Thusfar, though, there has been limited evidence of usage of more innovative social networking technologies in universities and other higher education institutions. In order to pave the way for assimilation of such platforms for teaching and learning in Saudi Arabia, it is urgent that more becomes known about how ordinary citizens view and engage with such technologies. This chapter briefly reviews current global research on perceptions of positive and negative effects of social networking before explaining the research methodology which was used to investigate the views of Saudi citizens. The outcome of the research is summarised and followed by a discussion of its significance for social networking implementation by Saudi Arabian higher education providers.

2 Literature Review

The evolution of online technologies began with the advent of commercial computers in the late 1930s, followed by The Internet in the 1960s and the invention of the World Wide Web in 1989 by Sir Tim Berners-Lee. As information technology has developed, the technology of the web has changed: generally, this progress is described sequentially as Web 1.0, Web 2.0, and Web 3.0. From these evolutionary paradigm shifts have emerged such crucial technologies as websites, email, and, in turn, social networking sites such as Facebook and Twitter among many others. The initial stage of web technology, Web 1.0, was made up of static pages grouped into websites and connected by hyperlinks [8]. In contrast, Web 2.0, a term attributed to O'Reilly [9], distributes the creation of content to ordinary web users who are able to participate by contributing or amending web material, effectively becoming producers and collaborators in their own right. A new wave of technological development referred to as Web 3.0 seems to encapsulate a more sophisticated level of technologies which have developed beyond Web 2.0, including intelligent and suggestive data searches, collation of data, use of mobile technologies, customisation and localisation capacities.

In contrast with other areas of endeavour such as business and healthcare, the higher education sector has been less welcoming of digital technology [1, 10–13]. In more recent times, though, in seeking to engage with the "Net Generation" [14] on its own terms, universities and other higher education providers have more actively sought to deploy the functionalities of collaborative digital technologies in their teaching and learning methodologies. This has led to a nascent body of research into the perceived positive and negative impacts of social networking with two key pillars: investigation of how students use digital platforms to organise their everyday social and learning experiences, and examination of what faculty inclusion of social networking brings about in terms of its impact on students when they are asked to formally engage with technologies as part of their course performance [15]. The main findings of this body of research are represented in the concept maps below. However, while these studies have yielded a number of useful insights into how social networking is operationalised in everyday life and educational settings, scholarship has not, as yet, addressed practices in more culturally peripheral contexts, an example of which is Saudi Arabia (Figs. 1, 2 and 3).

Current research into usage of web 2.0 technologies in tertiary education in Saudi Arabia is sparse and fragmented. Al-Khalifa, Garcia [16] contend that 80 % of universities and higher education providers in Saudi Arabia use social

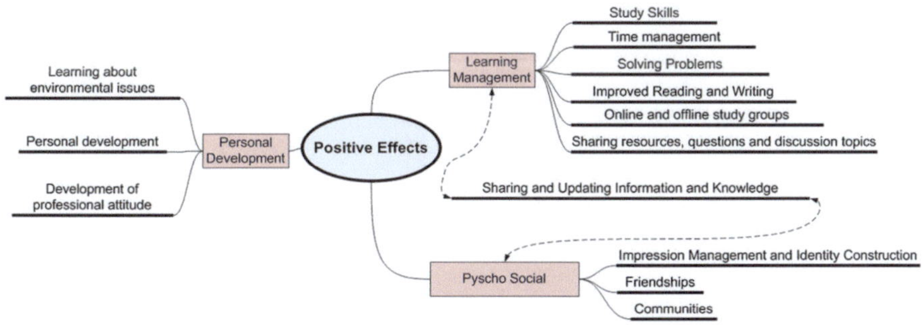

Fig. 1 Positive effects of social networking on students' everyday lives and practices

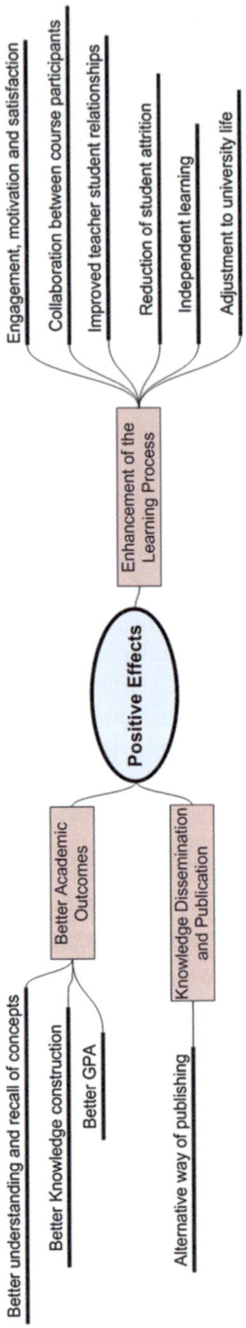

Fig. 2 Positive effects of social networking arising from students' formal engagement with university pedagogies

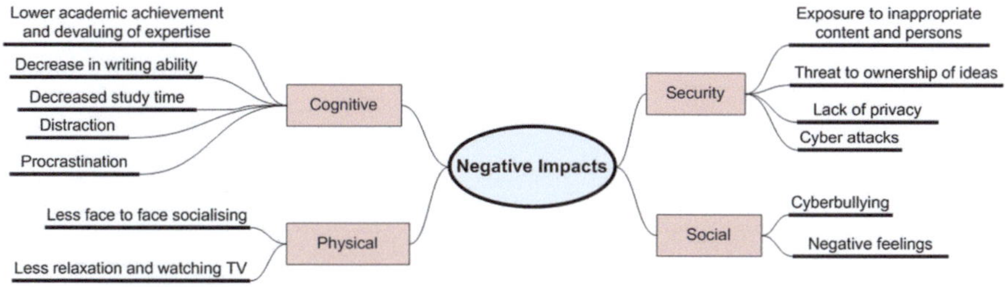

Fig. 3 Negative impacts of social networking in the context of higher education

networking as a way of recruiting students and keeping them updated. However, little published research is available to support enquiry into how Saudi college students perceive and make use of social networking or to what extent faculties incorporate social networking applications into their pedagogical practices [17]. Of the handful of studies that do exist, many focus on "e-learning" technologies and classic LMS tools as opposed to more contemporary Web 2.0 instruments [16, 18–22]. There is also a small amount of usage research into social networking uptake in Saudi Arabia with a focus on barriers such as gender, technical infrastructure issues like internet speeds and lack of Arabic language interfaces, trust and confidentiality issues and culturally engrained rote learning methodologies [16, 17, 22–26].

Thus, the negligible amount of research on social networking usage in Saudi Arabia suggests that implementation of Web technologies in Saudi Arabian universities has not yet reached the level of sophistication of use in other countries, creating fertile ground for further investigation. The goal of this research, then, was to identify prevailing perceptions towards contemporary technologies in Saudi Arabia as a first step.

3 Methodology

The instrument for data collection was a Qualtrics designed online survey which was distributed to 100 adult Saudi participants (aged between 18 and 52) via such media as Facebook and Twitter. Out of the 100 people surveyed, 41 were male and 59 were female. Of the distribution methods used, 29 responses were returned via Twitter, 20 via Facebook and 51 via Whatsapp. (Fig. 4)

The web-based survey was chosen for its advantages over pen and paper-based or email models for a number of reasons: firstly, it offers a low cost, practical option which is highly accessible and easy to disseminate to respondents; moreover, participants can be reminded to submit their responses and be thanked for their participation; data can be downloaded in desired formats; the incidence of error is reduced as responses do not have to be recoded; and finally, the researcher has full control of the survey design and formatting. It is also a highly manageable tool

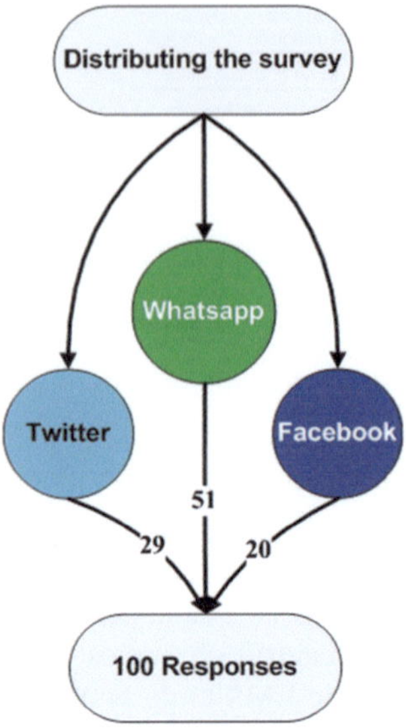

Fig. 4 Data collection methods

which delivers high response rates and swift, easier-to-analyse results, especially when results are downloaded in Excel spreadsheet format [27].

The survey instrument used in this research comprised two sections: closed-ended questions designed to elicit demographic information about the participants and scaled-response questions on the positive and negative effects of social networking using a Likert scale. Respondents were also given the opportunity to express their views in an open-ended section where they could record their comments more anecdotally. The data yielded by the survey was analysed using Social Science Statistics Software (SPSS) and the analysis tools contained in Qualtrics.

4 Data Analysis

In order to augment the currently incomplete picture of social networking in Saudi Arabia, the research developed a conceptual model of positives and negatives of social networking based on a set of survey results and factor analysis (Table 1):

Reliability testing on the data in relation to the positive effects were as follows:

Reliability statistics	
Cronbach's alpha	No. of items
0.897	25

Table 1 Number of responses

Statistic	Value
Min value	1
Max value	2
Mean	1.59
Variance	0.24
Standard deviation	0.49
Total responses	100

There were 25 items evaluated for consistency among the positive effects of social networking. From the results above, it is seen that the model composed of positive attributes is highly consistent (Cronbach's Alpha = 0.897).

Similarly, reliability regarding negative aspects of social networking can be represented as follows:

Reliability statistics	
Cronbach's alpha	No. of items
0.937	30

Thirty components were evaluated to establish the reliability of the negative aspects of social networking chosen for the survey. With a Cronbach's Alpha of 0.937, the model comprising the negative aspects was found to be extremely consistent.

From the two results, that is, for the perceived positive and negative effects of social networking in Saudi Arabia, the choice of aspects of each main effect (positive and negative) was remarkably good.

Factor analysis, a data reduction technique via a group of factors, was used for reduction of the variables for positive and negative effects of social networking.

4.1 *Positive Effects*

From the data analysis, the positive factors that belong to each of the components can be grouped and clearly labelled as follows:

Variable name	Factor loading	Label
Understand and solve study problems easily	0.769	Improvement of study skills
Complete my study more quickly	0.769	
Scrutinize my research study more easily	0.766	
Study independently	0.716	
Overcome study stress	0.506	

Variable name	Factor loading	Label
Acquire new acquaintances—romance relationship	0.755	Relationships and self-expression
Reduce carbon footprint in my activities	0.676	
Do whatever I want, say whatever I want, and be whoever I want	0.663	
Acquire new acquaintances—friendship relationship	0.576	

Variable name	Factor loading	Label
Develop my personal and communication skills	0.772	Personal development
Be more sustainable person	0.765	
To prepare my professional attitude toward study and work	0.719	
Concentrate more on my reading and writing skills	0.701	

Variable name	Factor loading	Label
Communicate with my peers from different universities	0.845	Communication and collaboration
Communicate with my different communities	0.705	
Collaborate with my peers frequently	0.605	

Variable name	Factor loading	Label
Gain up-to-date information	0.824	Improved access to information
Be more aware of global issues/local issues	0.784	
Learn new information and knowledge	0.721	

4.2 Negative Effects

In regard to negative effects, the factors can be grouped and labelled according to the components to which they belong (Fig. 5):

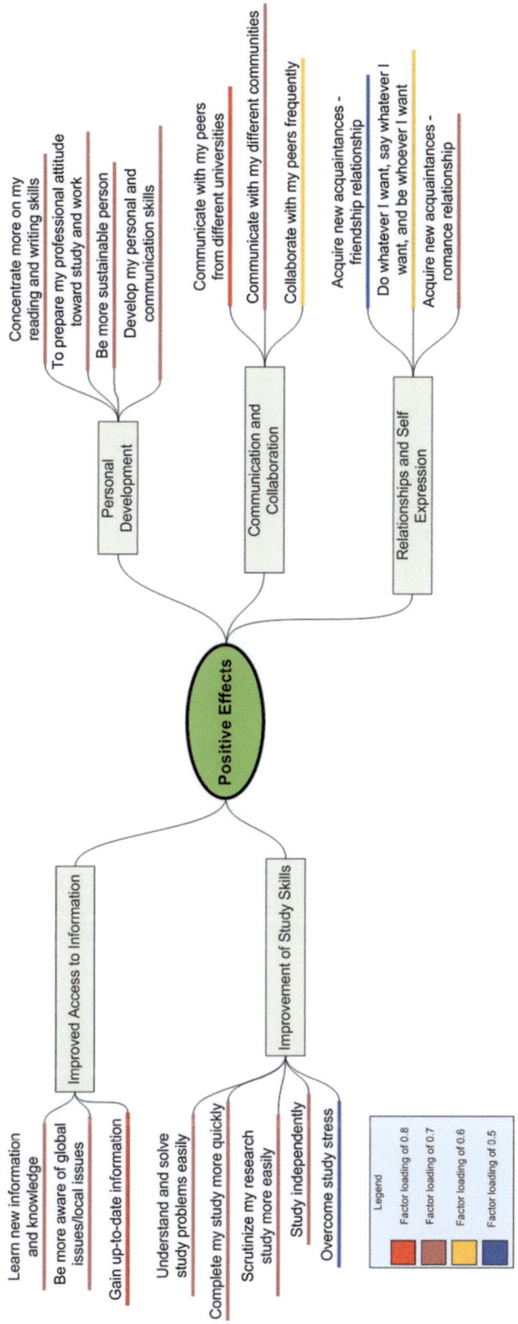

Fig. 5 Positives factors of social networking effects

Variable name	Factor loading	Label
Increase security concerns	0.869	Security
Makes me insecure to release my personal details from the theft of personal information	0.749	
Increase intellectual property concerns	0.736	
Increase privacy concerns	0.734	
Makes me receive an immoral images and information from unscrupulous people and it is difficult to act against them at present	0.507	

Variable name	Factor loading	Label
Prevents me from talking on the phone/mobile	0.745	Decrease in communication through other means
Prevents me from reading the newspapers	0.718	
Prevents me from shopping in stores	0.566	

Variable name	Factor loading	Label
Prevents me from remembering the fundamental knowledge and skills	0.749	Decrease in study skills and concentration/creation of negative emotions
Prevents me from concentrating more on writing and reading skills	0.710	
Depresses me	0.695	
Stresses me	0.689	
Decreases my deep thinking	0.655	
Makes me feel lonely	0.640	
Bores me	0.623	

Variable name	Factor loading	Label
Prevents me from completing my work on time	0.758	Decrease in productivity in study and other life areas
Distracts me easily	0.728	
Makes me lazy	0.707	
Prevents me from completing my study on time	0.692	
Prevents me from participating in physical activities	0.612	

Variable name	Factor loading	Label
Prevents me from participating in social activities	0.737	Poor health
Makes me sick and unhealthy	0.585	

5 Discussion of Findings

Of the positive aspects of social networking enumerated in the survey, the two variables with the highest factor loadings were "Communication with my peers from different universities" and "gain up to date information". These findings are consistent with research into world-wide usages of social networking; for example, a study by Bolar [28] cites the highest motivating factor in using social networking amongst the respondents surveyed as "utility" or network building and communication purposes. A later study by Alkindi and Alhashmi [29] reports that 100 % of respondents used social networking for information gathering with 85 % reporting benefits to their studies. In the Saudi Arabian context, it may be hypothesised that the reason for the high factor loading in "Communicating with peers from different universities" may be due to social restrictions on gender relationships in the country and the limited opportunities for face-to-face social encounters for young people in general. In the case of "Gain up-to-date information", the high loading suggests that Saudi Arabian adults are increasingly reliant on the use of Twitter and other technologies for instant news updates.

Of the factors that receive low loadings, the two lowest were in relation to acquiring new friendship relationships and overcoming study stress. In Saudi Arabia, social networking is not a major mechanism for making new friends, possibly due to issues related to trust. Interestingly, however, the use of social networking for romantic relationships received a relatively high loading of 0.7, suggesting that social networking offers a valued conduit for interaction between males and females to get to know each other within a strictly gender-segregated society. In the case of reduction of study stress, it would appear that few respondents regarded social networking as a useful measure, implying that perhaps it is regarded more as a distractor than a way of ameliorating stress (Fig 6).

The insights that emerge from analysing the negative effects of social networking arising from the survey indicate that the highest area of concern related to security issues in social networking. Other factors which received a relatively high loading were associated with distraction and laziness which may lead to weakening of knowledge and memorization and decreased reading and writing ability. While the concerns about receipt of immoral images, ill-health from using social networking and. not going into physical stores still exist as negative factors, these received a low loading which implies that they are not major negatives for the survey respondents.

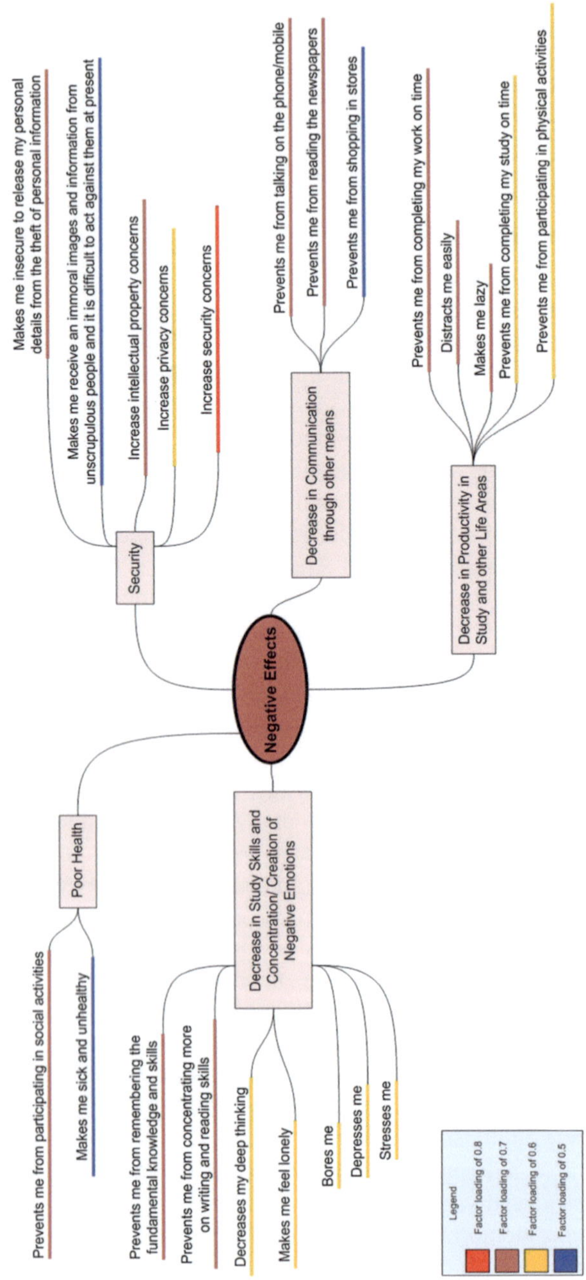

Fig. 6 Negative factors of social networking effects

In general, the survey findings suggest a positive orientation towards social networking on the part of the participants while negative findings about potential threats and harms arising from social networking were relatively minimal and not as pronounced as may have been anticipated in a socially conservative country. Indeed, the conceptual mapping confirms that Saudi Arabian perceptions and attitudes towards social networking are in accord with global patterns, meaning that incorporation could take place without undue or insurmountable barriers to user acceptance on the part of students. In this light, there is scope for further research into what strategies might be used to optimally harness and exploit the opportunities of social networking in education in Saudi Arabia while employing techniques to mitigate the risks. This future research might profitably pinpoint what tools and technologies would best be suited to incorporation into curricula in universities in Saudi Arabia coupled with empirical trials of classroom based adoption of social networking instruments. The ultimate benefit of this would be to provide a set of best practice guiding principles to underpin the assimilation of innovative digital technologies into Saudi higher education.

6 Conclusion

Through examination of this previously neglected area, the research reveals that positive and negative perceptions about social networking in Saudi Arabia are generally in line with global trends based on current research and that there is largely a positive bias towards such technologies. This implies that social networking could offer enormous benefits to teaching and learning in Saudi Arabia as long as the inclusion of such technology is carried out with careful preparation, knowledge, and a degree of caution given the country's socio-cultural and religious distinctions. Larger scale, longitudinal studies and more precise examinations of Web 2.0 technology as it is currently used and may be adapted for usage in Saudi Arabian university curricula and pedagogies are needed so as to confirm and consolidate these tentative findings.

References

1. Thompson J (2007) Is education 1.0 ready for web 2.0 students? Innov J Online Educ 3(4). doi:citeulike-article-id:1205905
2. Kaplan AM, Haenlein M (2010) Users of the world, unite! The challenges and opportunities of social media. Bus Horiz 53(1):59–68. doi:10.1016/j.bushor.2009.09.003
3. Hamid S, Chang S, Kurnia S (2009) Identifying the use of online social networking in higher education. Proc Ascilite Auckland 2009:419–422
4. Baran E (2013) Connect, participate and learn: transforming pedagogies in higher education. Bull IEEE Tech Comm Learn Technol 15(1):10
5. Wynbrandt J (2010) A brief history of Saudi Arabia. Infobase Publishing, New York

6. Ramady MA (2010) Population and demographics: Saudization and the labour market. Springer, New York
7. National Centre for E-learning (Saudi Arabia) (2010). http://www.elc.edu.sa/portal/index.php?mod=content&page=13. Accessed 3 Nov 2013
8. Graham P (2005) Web 2.0: Want to start a startup? 2013
9. O'Reilly T (2004) The open source paradigm shift, 2013
10. Alexander B (2006) Web 2.0: a new wave of innovation for teaching and learning? EDUCAUSE Rev 41(2)
11. Alexander B (2008) Social networking in higher education. In: Katz RN (ed)
12. Gilliam R (2010) Social networking in higher education. Scholar Space
13. Roblyer MD, McDaniel M, Webb M, Herman J, Witty JV (2010) Findings on Facebook in higher education: a comparison of college faculty and student uses and perceptions of social networking sites. The Internet and Higher Education 13(3):134–140. doi:10.1016/j.iheduc.2010.03.002
14. Tapscott D (2009) Grown up digital : how the net generation is changing the world/Don Tapscott. McGraw-Hill, New York. Accessed http://nla.gov.au/nla.cat-vn4546527
15. Boyd DM, Ellison NB (2007) Social network sites: definition, history, and scholarship. Eng Manage Rev IEEE 38(3):16–31. doi:10.1109/EMR.2010.5559139
16. Al-Khalifa HS, Garcia RA (2013) The state of social media in Saudi Arabia's higher education. Int J Technol Educ Market 3(1):65–76. doi:10.4018/ijtem.2013010105
17. Chaurasia M, Asma A, Ahmed A (2011) Opportunities and challenges of Web 2.0 in Arab education. In: Global learn, vol 1, pp 310–315
18. Al Saif AA (2005) The motivating and inhibiting factors affecting the use of Web-based instruction at the University of Qassim in Saudi Arabia
19. Alenezi AR, Abdulkarim A, Veloo A (2010) An empirical investigation into the role of enjoyment, computer anxiety, computer self-efficacy and internet experience in influencing the students' intention to use e-learning: a case study from Saudi Arabian governmental universities. Turk Online J Educ Technol 9(4)
20. Al-Otaibi J (2011) The Saudi Universities students' use of Facebook- an applicable study. College of Arts, Riyadh, King Saud University
21. Al-Saggaf Y (2004) The effect of online community on offline community in Saudi Arabia. Electron J Inf Syst Dev Ctries 16
22. Almalki AM (2011) Blended learning in higher education in Saudi Arabia: a study of Umm Al-Qura University. RMIT University
23. Aljasir SA, Woodcock A, Harrison S (2012) Facebook non-users in Saudi Arabia: why do some Saudi college students not use Facebook? Computer 1:25
24. Binsahl H, Chang S (2012) International Saudi Female students in Australia and social networking sites: what are the motivations and barriers to communication?. ISANA International Academy Association Conference
25. Sultan N, Bunt-Kokhuis S, Davidson C, Sentini A, Weir D (2012) E-Learning in the Arab Gulf: responding to the changing world of education. In: Ramady MA (ed) The GCC economies. Springer, New York, pp 33–48. doi:10.1007/978-1-4614-1611-1_4
26. Alzahrani I, Woollard J (2012) The potential of Wiki technology as an E-learning tool in science and education; perspectives of undergraduate students in Al-Baha University, Saudi Arabia. Online Submission
27. Issa T (2013) Online survey: best practice. In: Information systems research and exploring social artifacts: approaches and methodologies. IGI Global, pp 1–19. doi:10.4018/978-1-4666-2491-7.ch001
28. Bolar K (2009) Motives behind the use of social networking sites: an empirical study. ICFAI J Manage Res 8(1):75–84
29. Alkindi SSA, Alhashmi SM (2012) Use of social networking sites among Shinas College of Technology students in Oman. J Inf Knowl Manage 11(01)

Part VIII
Social Networking in Caribbean

Social Networking by Undergraduate Students at the University of Puerto Rico in Carolina

Noraida Domínguez-Flores

Abstract Considering the growth of social networks and their frequent use by students, a case study was conducted to describe how undergraduate students' use social networking and assess their perception about the positive and negative effects of their use. This chapter presents the results of the study that was conducted with undergraduate students of the University of Puerto Rico. A total of 140 participants completed a questionnaire that was designed to answer the research questions. The results evidenced that the students recognize the positive effects of the use of the social networks in terms of communication and access to information. But, they also recognize the negative effects especially because the use of social networks distracts them from the time they should spend with their class works. After discussing the results, some recommendations are presented that should be considered when integrating the use of social networks in the teaching-learning process.

Keywords Social networking · Undergraduate students · Puerto Rico · Positive and negative effects

1 Introduction

For the past years there has been a great proliferation of the participation of students in social networks. Different social networks, such as Facebook and Twitter, are used to share information, life experiences, and photos, to meet new people, keep in touch with friends, or even play with different games. But, the truth is that the use of these social networks also arises concerns especially when it refers to the time students spend using them, its purposes, and how they are using them. In an article published by Mukherjee and Clark [4], they acknowledge the fact that social workers are concerned by the type of information students share on social networks,

N. Domínguez-Flores (✉)
Graduated School of Information Science and Technologies, University of Puerto Rico, Rio Piedras Campus, San Juan, Puerto Rico
e-mail: noraida.dominguez@upr.edu

T. Issa et al. (eds.), *Social Networking and Education*,
Lecture Notes in Social Networks, DOI 10.1007/978-3-319-17716-8_19

and the impact their actions can have on their relationships and image, which also can impact their future professional life. But, although the possible concerns adults may have about the use of social networks by their adolescents, the reality is that the activity of students through social networks keeps rising. Considering this tendency, a survey was conducted with undergraduate students to identify and describe the use of social networks and the perception of students about the positive and negative effects of social networking.

The survey was conducted with students of the University of Puerto Rico in Carolina. The University of Puerto Rico (UPR) is the largest institution of higher education on the island, having 11 campuses located in different cities. One of these campuses is the University of Puerto Rico in Carolina (UPRC), which is an autonomous unit. UPRC offers bachelors degrees and/or associate degrees in the following academic programs: Business Administration; Hotel and Restaurant Administration; Industrial Automation; Social Sciences; Graphic Arts; Interior Design; Education; and Office Systems. The UPRC community consists of approximately 4,000 students, 250 faculty members, and 230 administrative personnel. This chapter will present and discuss a brief literature about the topic and the results from the collected data, at the end, it will be possible to understand the perception of students about this technology and some recommendations will be shared to promote the effective integration of these technologies into the teaching-learning process.

2 Use of Social Networks

Considering the significant growth of the use of social networks, different authors have developed research in efforts to identify and describe the users behavior through these technologies. Mukherjee and Clark [4] conducted a study with 105 social worker students. The purpose of their study was to examine the participant's attitudes toward the engagement in social networking. To collect the needed data, the researchers administered a questionnaire that included three sections: demographic information, a section where students indicated the type of information they share through social networks and, in the last section, the participants indicated their perception of the people that might visit their social networks profile.

When discussing the results obtained through their study, Mukherjee and Clark [4] concluded that the students are likely to post private information, and that this information can have some type of impact when searching for employment. Because of this, students express that they feel uncomfortable knowing that possible employers may examine their social networks profiles. But, although this possibility, students tend to post private information, without using the privacy options. In general, the study evidenced that students are not fully aware of the possible repercussions on their professional careers of what they post on social networks. On the other hand, the researchers recognize that these social networks may be used to develop new professional networks, but there is a need to educate students about the use of social networks and the consequences of all the information they share.

Valerio and Valenzuela [6] also conducted a study through which they examine the behavior through social networks. The authors conducted a qualitative and ethnographic study with 21 undergraduate students registered in the Information Technologies Program in a private institution in Mexico. This study was conducted for a period of 5 months. As part of the methodology, the researchers used online observations through Facebook and interviews to collect the needed data. In terms of Facebook, they examined this technology as an online culture, considering how the participants use this technology as a complement to their face-to-face activities.

As presented by Valerio and Valenzuela [6] the results of their study evidenced that undergraduate students develop different elements that are part of what social capital is, like identity, sharing of behavior, and trust. These elements are promoted by activities, like the addition of new contacts, communication and sharing of information sources. But, as acknowledge by the authors, how these elements are developed depends on how the user profile is set.

More specifically, Valerio and Valenzuela [6] explained that through the observation that was conducted through Facebook, they were able to identify the type of communication the participants shared through this technology. The authors were able to classify the contacts of the participants as strong links or weak links. Contacts that were classified as strong links are the ones that had close relationship with participants, such as family members, love partners or close friends. On the other hand, the contacts that were classified as weak links, are people that are not close, like classmates, work colleagues, old school friends, old work colleagues, other known people or even unknown, professors and university chancellor.

Another interesting aspect of the observations that were conducted by Valerio and Valenzuela [6] is that they were able to identify the activities that were conducted by participants to share information in different ways with contacts. From the results of this observation, the authors acknowledge that: 10 % of the Facebook status are used to share quotes or songs; 6 % to share a question or doubt; 44 % to share a personal situation, like how they are feeling or what they are doing; 21 % to share jokes; and 8 % to share a personal announcement. But, not only they observed the information that is shared the Facebook status, the authors also identified that participants shared an average of three photos each week, being women the ones that tend to share more photos than men. Also, participants share other type of information, such as links to other webpages, notes, and even the information about applications they use.

One last aspect that was observed as part of the study conducted by Valerio and Valenzuela [6], was the private and public communication that was held by participants. In terms of the public communication, the participants used the Facebook wall to share congratulation, a greeting, a thank you note or a request for information. As explained by the authors, this type of communication promotes the interaction with contacts, which will allow the increase in the social capital.

As part of their conclusions, Valerio and Valenzuela [6] stated that the use of social networks promote the development of the social capital, mainly because it allows effective sharing of personal information, facilitates communication, and the contacts networks can grow. In other words, the use of this social network is beneficial to users, since it will allow sharing with other people and making new connections while sharing personal information and building trust in others.

Educators have also been examining and analyzing the behavior of students through social networks. Singh [5] examined the use of Facebook groups in the classroom. For two semesters, the author compared the use of open groups with close groups with five groups of students. One Facebook group was created for each group of students, through these groups, students completed assed activities to develop different tutorials. The researcher conducted weekly observations and provided needed support. In terms of the open groups, students shared information, while the instructor shared links and answered their questions. At the end of their participation, the students completed a post-study questionnaire to identify how students perceive the student's usefulness of Facebook.

As explained by Singh [5], from the collected data it was evidenced that the structured groups, there were more posts and discussions between students. On the other hand, conversations about different topics were developed in the unstructured groups. In terms of the students' perception about the use of Facebook, they considered that Facebook was useful and that they were able to learn through the group discussions. But, although the positive aspects of this integration, they were "skeptical about the openness of their responses to an entire group" [5]. Also, they still perceive Facebook as a social tool that is best for personal use but, still, Singh indicates that there are pedagogical activities that can be designed and used through these social environments.

Balcikanli [1] presents another example of an educator integrating the use of social networks. The author examined how a group of physical education undergraduate students view the use of social networks. Balcikanli conducted the study with a group of 19 students registered in the course titled "Fair Play Education in Sports". As part of the research, the researcher created a group in Ning, which is a platform that allows users to create their own social network. Throughout the study, the researcher, which was also the professor, shared through the social network all the materials and resources related to the course. The syllabus, discussions questions, relevant information, links and other resources were all shared through Ning. Through interviews, the researcher identified the students' perception about the use social networks as an educational tool. The results evidenced that students considered social networks an effective resource to support the teaching-learning process. They also view Ning as a resource that helps promote the interaction between students and teachers and they enhance the students' motivation towards the course. But, the author acknowledges that "one if the most valuable findings of this research was that students regarded the use of social networking in educational settings as increasing student-student and teacher-student interaction" [1]. In general, it was evidenced that the use of Ning increased the communication, which is an important aspect during the teaching-learning process.

Not only studies have been conducted about social networking, but educators have also integrated activities to compare the use of this technology by gender and promote in students the discussion and reflection about the use of this technology. One example of this type of activity is described by Clipson et al. [2]. The objective of their activity, as explained by the authors, is "to identify specific gender-related differences that affect communication between the sexes while texting, facebooking, or tweeting" [2]. As part of their classroom activity, the authors developed a class assignment that consisted of promoting in students think about specific situations related to the "communication challenges with the opposite sex when texting, facebooking, or tweeting" [2]. As the authors described, the in-class activity consist of arranging male and women students on each side of the classroom, and the purpose if that each genre was asked to make a list about the actions they do not like about how the opposite sex communicates through social network. Then each group presents the list and the other group can respond. At the end of the activity, students may develop a list of rules they may consider to promote an effective communication through social networks between sexes. In general, this type of activity evidences that the discussion about the use of social networking can also be integrated into the teaching-learning process, which may promote a better understanding of its effect on the personal, academic and professional life of users.

3 Methods

Case study is a methodology that is often used to explore an activity or individuals, as explained by Creswell [3], through a case study researchers can describe specific activities and behaviors of a group. This methodology was considered the most appropriate method since it was expected to examine and describe the use of social networks by undergraduate students and their perception about its positive and/or negative effects and use.

The research questions that guided this study were:

1. What is the use of social networks by undergraduate students of the University of Puerto Rico at Carolina?
2. What is the students' perception of the positive effects of the use of Internet and social networking?
3. What is the students' perception of the negative use of social networking?

4 Participants

Participants in this study were 140 undergraduate students of the University of Puerto Rico at Carolina. Fifty-two students (37 %) males, while 88 (63 %) female. In terms of the age range, 136 (97 %) indicated to have between 18–22 years old; two students between 22–32; one student between 32–42; and one student between 42–52.

When identifying the field of study of participants, the responses evidenced that participants represented the different academic programs that are offered in the university. The participants identified the following fields: education, social science, accounting, business law, economics and finance, information systems, management, marketing, health science, humanities, science and engineering, and art and design.

5 Results

Through this study, the researcher examined the perception undergraduate students have related to possible positive and negative effects of social networking. To collect the needed data, a questionnaire was administered to 140 undergraduate students. To facilitate the presentation of results, they are going to be presented according to the research questions that guided the study.

The first research question was: What is the use of social networks by undergraduate students of the University of Puerto Rico at Carolina?

To be able to determine the use of social networks by undergraduate students, the participants were asked to identify how many hours they spend on social networking daily. Figure 1 presents the responses and, as it is evidenced, 57 % of the participants spend up to 5 hours using social networks, while 26 % indicated to spend less than an hour, 14 % 5–10 h, and 4 % 10–20 h.

In terms of the use of social networking, it was considered necessary to compare its use with the time they spend on the Internet to access the email. The results are presented on Fig. 2. The responses evidenced that 127 (92 %) participants use

Fig. 1 Hours spend in social networking

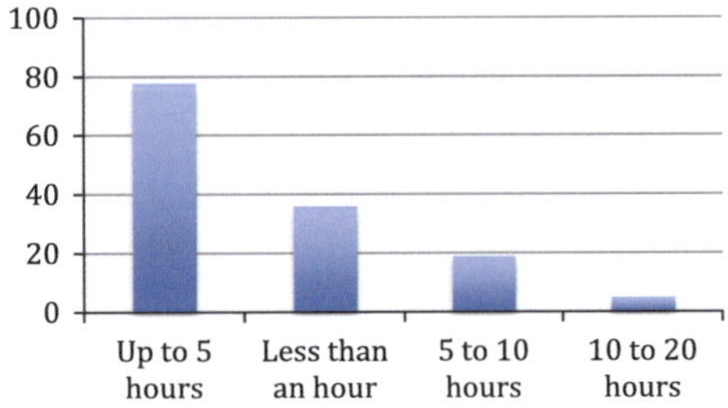

Fig. 2 Hours spend using the email

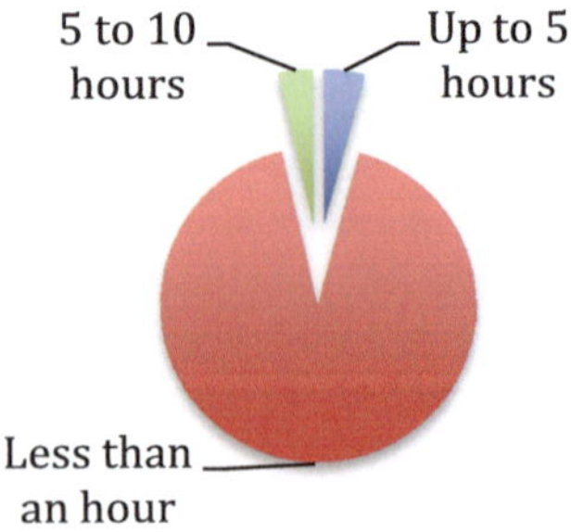

Internet for email less than an hour daily. Only six (4 %) participants indicated to use it for up to 5 h, and five (4 %) for 5–10 h. When comparing these results with the daily use of social networks, it is evident that participants spend more time social networking, than using the email. For the purpose of this study, this result is important since these participants that spend significant time in social networks are the ones that are going to share their perception about its positive or negative effects.

The second research question was: What is the students' perception of the positive effects of the use of Internet and social networking?.

The participants were asked to identify their level of agreement in terms of the positive effects when considering different aspects of the use of the Internet and social networks. The results evidenced that 61 (46 %) participants, from a total of 134, strongly agree that through the Internet they are able to learn new information and gain new knowledge. On the other hand, 43 (32 %) participants indicated they agree with this asseveration, while 26 (19 %) selected to be neutral. Only three students disagree, and only one selected to strongly disagree. With these results, it is evidenced that 78 % of the participants consider they are able to learn new information and gain new knowledge through the use of the Internet. Similar to these results, 75 % of the participants strongly agree that the use of the Internet provides them the opportunity to find up-to date information. On the hand, only 23 % identify their perception as neutral, and only 2 % disagree (Table 1).

In terms of the opportunity Internet and social networking provides to be aware of the global and local issues, 79 % of the participants indicated to strongly agree; 18 % selected to be neutral, and only 3 % indicated to disagree. Similar to this, the participants were asked to indicate their level of agreement when considering how the Internet helps them remember facts or information about the past. For this aspect, 66 % of the participants indicated to strongly agree and agree; 28 % identify to be neutral, and only 6 % indicated to disagree.

At this point, the collected data evidenced that the participants consider the Internet and social networks is positive in terms of accessing current information, which allows them to learn about global and local issues. After considering these aspects of the use of the Internet, the participants were asked to indicate their perception about the positive effects of the Internet to communicate and collaborate with peers.

First, in terms of how the Internet and social networks helps them communicate frequently with peers, 87 % of the participants indicate to strongly agree; 11 % identify their perception as neutral; while 2 % indicated to disagree. Second, the participants were asked to indicate their perception about how the Internet helps them collaborate with their peers. For this question, 70 % of the participants strongly agree that the influence of the Internet is positive, while 27 % stay neutral, and only 3 % indicated to strongly disagree. It is evidenced that students also consider that the Internet is positive to communicate and collaborate with their peers. In this case, when considering peers, it is understood that are students from the same university, this is why participants were also asked to indicate their perception about the positive effect of how the Internet helps them communicate

Table 1 Level of agreement of the positive effects of the use of Internet and social networks

	Strongly agree (%)	Agree (%)	Neutral (%)	Disagree (%)	Strongly disagree (%)
Access to information					
Through Internet I can learn new information and gain knowledge	46	32	19	2	1
Internet provides me with the opportunity to find up-to date information	75	0	23	2	0
Internet and social networking provides me the opportunity to be aware of the global and local issues	79	0	18	3	0
Internet helps me remember facts or information about the past	66	0	28	6	0
Communication and collaboration with peers					
Internet and social networks helps me communicate frequently with peers	87	0	11	2	0
Internet helps me collaborate with my peers	70	0	27	0	3
Internet helps me communicate with peers from other universities	0	69	25	0	6
Internet helps me communicate with other communities	0	67	25	4	4
Internet helps me develop intercrossing relationships with my peers	36	32	28	2	2
Academic works					
Effect of Internet to study independently	31	30	19	15	5
Internet helps to overcome stress	26	30	37	4	3
Internet helps to complete course works more quikly	28	29	20	11	12
Internet helps to complete course works more easily	30	30	23	8	9
Internet helps to scrutinize research more easily	31	32	22	7	8

with peers from other universities. The results evidenced that 69 % of the participants agree, while 25 % identified their opinion as neutral, and only 6 % indicated to strongly disagree. Similar to this question, participants were also asked to indicate their perception about the positive effect of the Internet to help them communicate with other communities. The results of this question were: 67 % indicated to agree, 25 % identified to be neutral, and only 8 % indicated to disagree and strongly disagree.

After considering how the Internet and social networking helps them communicate with others, participants were also asked to indicate their perception when considering the positive effect of the Internet to develop intercrossing relationships with my peers (i.e. Artistic talents, sport and common interests). The results of this question evidenced that 68 % of the participants strongly agree and agree with this asseveration, while 28 % indicated to be neutral, and only 4 % indicated to disagree and strongly disagree.

Other questions were related to the positive effect of the use of Internet with their studies. First, they were asked to indicate their perception in terms of the positive effect of the Internet to study independently. In this question, 61 % indicate to agree and strongly agree; while 19 % stayed neutral, and 20 % disagree and strongly disagree. Also, the students were asked to consider the positive effect of the Internet to help them overcome stress. In this case, 56 % of the participants indicated to agree and strongly agree, 37 % selected to be neutral, and 7 % indicated to disagree and strongly disagree. In terms of this question, it is interesting that, although there is still a greater percentage of participant that agree and strongly agree, when compared with the responses of other questions, there is a greater percentage of students that selected to be neutral.

When considering the resources students have available to locate and access the information they need, the Internet is considered a key to access and share information, and to communicate and collaborate with classmates and educators. Because of the accessibility Internet provides, research process, the learning process and the use of different technologies can be easier to students. Considering this, the students were asked to indicate their perception in terms of the positive effect of the Internet on their activities related to their course works. The first question asked them to indicate their level of agreement in terms of the effect of Internet to overcome their study stress. The results evidenced that 56 % of the participants agree and strongly agree; 37 % answered neutral, and only 7 % answered to disagree and strongly disagree. Considering that more than half of the participants agree with this asseveration, it can be understood that they perceive the Internet as an effective resource to complete their course requirements. This is evidenced in the responses when they were asked in terms of the effect of the Internet to complete their study more quickly. The responses of this question were: 57 % of the participants agree and strongly agree, while 20 % identified as neutral, and 23 % disagree and strongly disagree. Similar responses were obtained when they were asked about how the Internet helps them complete their study more easily. In this case, 60 % agree and strongly agree, while 23 % stayed neutral, and 17 % identified to disagree and strongly disagree. One last aspect related to their course requirements asked participants to indicate their level of agreement in terms of the effect of the Internet to scrutinize their research study more easily. The responses were that 63 % of the participants agree and strongly agree, 22 % answered to be neutral, and 15 % disagree and strongly disagree.

After considering the positive effects of the Internet and social networks related to the academic activities of the students, the students were asked to consider the effects of the Internet to the development of different skills, and the influence on their attitudes. The results are interesting, because the aspects where more percentage of students agree and strongly agree are the ones related to the development of personal and communication skills (60 %), professional attitude toward study and work (40 %), reduce carbon footprint (54 %), acquire new acquaintances—work related (53 %), and acquire new acquaintances—friendship relationship (65 %). But, the one where more percentage of students agree and strongly agree were when they consider that through the Internet they can say and do whatever they want (65 %). On the other hand, the aspects where more percentage of the students stayed neutral were: be more sustainable person (43 %), provide reliable and scalable services (40 %), and become more "Greener" in my activities (43 %).

The third research question was: What is the students' perception of the negative use of social networking?

After considering the positive effects of the Internet and social networks, the participants were asked to indicate their level of agreement when considering negative effects of the Internet. The results evidenced that a significant percentage of the participants agree and strongly agree that the Internet affects the following aspects: Prevents them from concentrating more on writing and reading skills (57 %), scatters their attention (72 %), distracts them easily (65 %), prevents them from completing my work/study on time (44 %), makes them lazy (40 %), makes them insecure to release personal details from the theft of personal information (45 %), and decreases grammar and proofreading skills (39 %).

On the other hand, the participants do not consider that the Internet affects other aspects, such as: preventing from remembering knowledge and skills, decrease deep thinking, preventing from participating in social activities, makes them sick and unhealthy, bores them, stress them, depress them, makes them lonely, makes them addict, gambler, makes them receive immoral images and information from unscrupulous people and it is difficult to act against them at present, prevents them from having face to face contact with their family, contact with friends, participating in physical activities, shopping in stores, watching television, reading the newspapers, talking on the phone/mobile, completing work on time, completing study on time. Also, and it is important to acknowledge, a significant percentage of the participants do not consider that the Internet increase privacy, security, and intellectual property concerns. In general, the percentage that consider negative influence of the use of Internet and social networks in not significant, and this information helps educators to introduce the use of social networks during the teaching-learning process.

6 Discussion

After presenting the results, it can be acknowledge that more than half of the participants agree and strongly agree that the use of the Internet and social networks has a positive effect when accessing information, when they communicate and collaborate with their peers, and when they are completing their academic works. Also, more than 50 % of participants consider the influence of Internet and social networks as a positive one when dealing with different skills, and when considering their attitudes. The fact that the general perception of the students is positive when considering these aspects, then it can be understood that they are not confronting problems, limitations or even negative situations related to the use of these tools. But, it is also important to remember that this is just the students' perception, and that there is the possibility that they are not identifying the effects as negative, just because they ignore them, or they are not aware of the situations.

On the other hand, it is necessary to consider the situations or aspects where more than half of the participants perceive negative effects related to the use of Internet and social networks. First, the fact that the students consider that the Internet and social networks prevents them from concentrating more of writing and reading skills, it can be an opportunity for educators to develop different activities where students can practice these skills through the use of Internet and social networks. Also, through exercises that helps to organize time, exercises that require the use of these tools for specific purposes, could be some of the strategies that can be used to prevent the negative effects of Internet and social networks when dealing with time control.

One of the results that would be important to examine more deeply is the fact that the students do not consider that the use of Internet and social networks increase privacy, security, and intellectual property concerns. This situation could evidence that the students are not aware, they do not know, or they are not educated about the negative effects of sharing personal information, pictures or even commenting about their personal life or the personal life of others through social networks and Internet. In this case, it would be necessary to examine if the students are aware of this type of situation and the security measures they take when using Internet and social networks.

In general, it is evidenced that the students recognize many positive effects of the use of Internet and social networks, especially related to communication and access to information they need to complete their academic works. On the other hand, it is a concern the fact that the students also perceive a negative effect of the use of Internet and social networks related to their writing skills and their distribution of time, both aspects are important not only for academic life, but also for their professional development. The fact that there is a negative effective of the use of these tools, then it can be understood that the way they are using them needs to be evaluated and improved. But, at least they are recognizing a negative influence, which could be the first step to learn on how to use them more positively.

7 Limitations

For the collection of the data, an online survey was used, which included questions that required the participants to identify their perception about the positive and negative effects of the use of Internet and social networks. It is important to consider that the purpose of this study was limited to identify perception only, and that it did not examined or evaluated the possible positive or negative effects that the students could be currently experiencing. On the other hand, the online survey was limited to a specific population, undergraduate students from a campus in the metropolitan area of Puerto Rico, which means that the results could be different in other populations.

One last limitation of this study is the fact that the students were answering this online survey on their own and, maybe, they selected answers that not necessarily represent their current perception. Through the survey they did not had the opportunity to share specific descriptions of the positive or negative effects or influence of the Internet and social networks, which could help to determine if what they consider positive or negative, its really like that.

8 Future Research

Future research could be developed considering the following recommendations:

- Conduct research with other populations, like graduate students, and compare with the perception of undergraduate students.
- Conduct research in other institutions and countries, this could lead to information about the different perceptions and how they change because of culture and/or society.
- Expand the objectives of the study, revise the research questions and the instrument, to include, not only perception, but also the evaluation of what the participants identify as positive or negative effects of the use of Internet and social networks.
- Conduct the research considering specific social networks, and specific tools that are available through the Internet, the results could help to identify which are the specific social networks and online tools that have more positive and negative influence on students.

9 Conclusions

In general, it can be conclude that the participants perceive the effects of the use of the Internet and social networking as positive in many aspects, especially the ones related to the communication and contact with friends, the access to information and their possibility to complete their course works easily, and positive influence to their attitudes. On the other hand, the participants recognize that the use of Internet and social networks also have a negative effect, especially because it affects their concentration on writing and reading skills, distracts them, makes them lazy and makes them insecure about releasing personal information. As a result, it can be conclude that, although the use of Internet and social networks facilitate many of the activities and processes students need to conduct during their academic life, it is also a distraction. In this case, it is necessary to consider the positive effects to develop strategies that can be integrated into the teaching-learning process to promote the positive use of the Internet and social networks. But, since there are also some negative effects, it is also necessary to consider develop different strategies to educate students to help them prevent these negative effects that could affect their academic performance.

References

1. Balcikanli GS (2012) Social networking in physical education: undergraduate students' views on Ning. TOJDE 13(2):277–290
2. Clipson TW, Wilson SA, DuFrene DD (2012) The social networking arena: battle of the sexes. Bus Comm Q 75(1):64–67. doi:10.1177/10805699/1423961
3. Creswell JW (2005) Educational research: planning, conducting, and evaluating quantitative and qualitative research, 2nd edn. Pearson Publication, Upper Saddle River
4. Mukherjee D, Clark J (2012) Students' participation in social networking sites: implications for social work education. J Teach Soc Work 32:161–173. doi:10.1080/08801233.2012.669329
5. Singh L (2013) Guided assessment or open discourse: a comparative analysis of students interaction on Facebook groups. TOJDE 14(1):35–43
6. Valerio G, Valenzuela R (2013) Desarrollo de capital social de los estudiantes universitarios a través de las redes sociales en línea. Itangible Capital 9(4):971–990. url:http://dx.doi.org/10.3926/ic.419

Part IX
Social Networking and Education Model (SNEM)

Social Networking and Education Model (SNEM)

Tomayess Issa, Pedro Isaias and Piet Kommers

Abstract This book examined the influence of the new, revolutionary Social Networking (SN) tool on the education sector nationally and internationally. SN usage by businesses and individuals has become a significant instrument for searching, conducting research, communication, entertainment, commerce and information, as well as teaching. SN was introduced to simplify communication, collaboration, contribution, creativity and interaction among individuals/groups within the same sector worldwide. SN has become an essential part of operations in various sectors including business enterprises, health and education. The use of SN in the education sector can bring diverse opportunities and risks to enhance students' engagement with their colleagues and teachers universally; however, this technology can bring some risks from four perspectives: (1) Cognitive Development, (2) Social Development, (3) Physical Development and (4) Security. This book aimed to explore the opportunities and risks of using SN in relation to various countries from regions including Asia Pacific, Europe, Mediterranean, America, Middle East and the Caribbean. Furthermore, a Social Networking and Education Model (SNEM) is developed to promote and implement Social Networking in the education sector.

Keywords SNEM · Social networking · Risks · Opportunities · Higher education

---

T. Issa (✉)
School of Information Systems, Curtin University, Perth, Australia
e-mail: Tomayess.Issa@cbs.curtin.edu.au

P. Isaias
Palácio Ceia, Rua da Escola Politécnica, Universidade Aberta, n. 141-147, 1269-001 Lisbon, Portugal
e-mail: pisaias@uab.pt

P. Kommers
University of Twente, Enschede, The Netherlands
e-mail: p.a.m.kommers@utwente.nl

T. Issa et al. (eds.), *Social Networking and Education*,
Lecture Notes in Social Networks, DOI 10.1007/978-3-319-17716-8_20

1 Introduction

Social media and new communication technologies are essential for future innovation especially in the education sector as a means of improving and facilitating communication, collaboration, cooperation, involvement, inspiration and interaction among students and students, and students and academics. Currently, there is a shift in the education sector to use numerous and various software besides the home package called World Wide Web or "Web," to enhance communications, collaboration, and interaction among members of the academic community including students. Furthermore, using the web in the education sector will improve data management, support accessibility of the Internet, imitate inspiration and invention, encourage the globalization phenomenon, and enhance students' and teachers' satisfaction via communication and collaboration. The web has evolved into five types, Web 1.0, Web 2.0, Web 3.0, Web 4.0 and Web 5.0 Web 1.0 refers to connecting information and shared read-write hypertext space; while Web 2.0, known as the participative web, allows users to connect via social-networking with more interaction and less external control. Web, 3.0 refers to connecting intelligence and is known as the semantic web. In other words, it is used to identify web-based data so that searches can be more effective, and the information is part of the network. Web 4.0 is a web of integration and Web 5.0 is a web of decentralized smart communicator [5, 50].

In the 21st century, a new technology emerged in various communities to facilitate communication, collaboration, and interaction. This technology is called Social Networking, and is now part of Internet commodities such as email, browsing and blogging. From the 20th century to the present, the Internet has shaped the way in which the education sector interacts, communicates, connects, and exchanges knowledge around the world. Social Networking can reduce operational costs, increase profits, and develop new forms of communication between consumers, stakeholders, vendors, suppliers, universities and health departments. However, this technology can create new challenges for education and its governance and management.

Social Networking or Web 2.0 has brought about an innovative shift in the education sector as it allows students to learn from their lecturers and from each other in a more natural way than ever before. In this particular book, we examine the risks and opportunities associated with the use of Social Networking in the education sector in various regions around the world: Asia-Pacific, Europe, Mediterranean, America, Middle East and the Caribbean. In addition, a Social Networking and Education Model (SNEM) will be developed to promote and implement Social Networking in the education sector.

This book is intended to assist academics, researchers and proponents of online learning and teaching. Academics will be able to share the findings presented in this book, and the Social Networking and Education Model (SNEM), with their students (i.e. Masters and PhD). It is envisaged that this book will assist researchers and anyone interested in online learning to understand the opportunities and risks associated with the use of Social Networking in the education sector, and assist them to implement SN by means of the new SNEM model.

2 Social Networking Opportunities and Risks

Social Networking has become the major component in any business after the Internet, as it links millions of computers and tens of millions of users around the world [63]. In addition, Social Networking usage brings enormous challenges to various sectors including the education sector, as many observers allege that the Social Networking is changing society [15]. The current literature notes that the use of SN in any sector offers new opportunities to become more creative, innovative, unique, more successful and exclusive in the market segment worldwide [69]. However, SN usage can produce significant challenges and threats to users' behaviour, health and social development [44, 55, 61].

Current studies [13, 21, 39, 40, 47, 49, 65, 76] confirm that teaching and learning with SN will create new opportunities for students in terms of cross-sectional relationships, collaboration, real-world connections and the acquisition of different skills. Students will be able to select his/her peers based on the study (or work) experience, research interests, artistic preferences or abilities, talents, sport and others. SN will enhance students' collaboration and communication worldwide and foster students' independent learning, as new skills will be developed from communication, exposure to cutting edge technology and ideas, and research. Students will be able to quickly acquire skills that will benefit them in their current studies and equip them for the real world and their future workplace. By the same token, several studies have affirmed [3, 68, 70] that SN gives students the opportunity to meet new people, establish new networks, and use the second life for learning purposes or entertainment.

On the other hand, SN usage will bring challenges, obstacles, and a growing awareness of the potential negative impacts of the SN on cognitive development, social development, physical development and security [57, 70]. In respect to cognitive development, students may face several problems such as the inability to concentrate on writing and reading, inability to remember [6, 28, 38, 46], inability to think laterally, proneness to distraction and inattentiveness, all of which makes it difficult for them to complete their tasks in school or home and meet deadlines [8]. SN usage may also produce social and physical development problems such as health problems, stress, depression and isolation [2, 9, 53]. These aspects will generate enormous challenges for students and academics. Many academics, supported by the findings of several studies believe that SN will affect students' ability to learn as most will become lazy, lonely, depressed, stressed, and unable to concentrate on reading and searching, and face-to-face social interaction between friends and family will disappear [8, 72]. Finally, security and privacy issues are another concern for students who do not know who will have access to their private information via the Internet. Furthermore, SN will generate new academic problems for students in relation to written reports and essay writing, proofreading and use of correct grammar and vocabulary.

Currently, the majority of students are depending more and more on internet facilities in order to finalize and complete their assessments, and the majority of these websites are lacking the writing and grammar standards and this will influence students ability in his/her assessment presentation. Several studies [34, 37, 42, 54, 60] confirm and posit that these skills are essential not only for university life but for future life as well. Therefore, incorporation in Social Networking principles in teaching will enhance these skills, not decrease them. However, to achieve this in university life, there needs to be strong collaboration between teachers and students to address these concerns, and to understand how the integration of SN in curriculum and units will assist students in their university studies, workplace in the future, and life in general without decreasing their literacy skills. To tackle the above problems, authors developed a new study based on a review of the current literature [3, 8, 9, 12, 23, 28, 33, 34, 38, 40, 46, 47, 53, 57, 60, 65, 68–70, 76] in order to understand the opportunities and risks of adopting SN as a teaching and learning tool in the education sector. The authors developed the following concept figures in relation to the opportunities and risks of SN in the education sector (see Figs. 1, 2).

To confirm the above opportunities and risks (see Figs. 1, 2), an online survey was developed and distributed to 15 countries in the regions of Asia-Pacific, Europe, the Mediterranean, America, the Middle East and the Caribbean, to examine the SN influence on students' behaviour and attitudes especially in teaching and learning. The response rate from all countries has been outstanding. Therefore, the authors are eager to share their perspectives and experiences

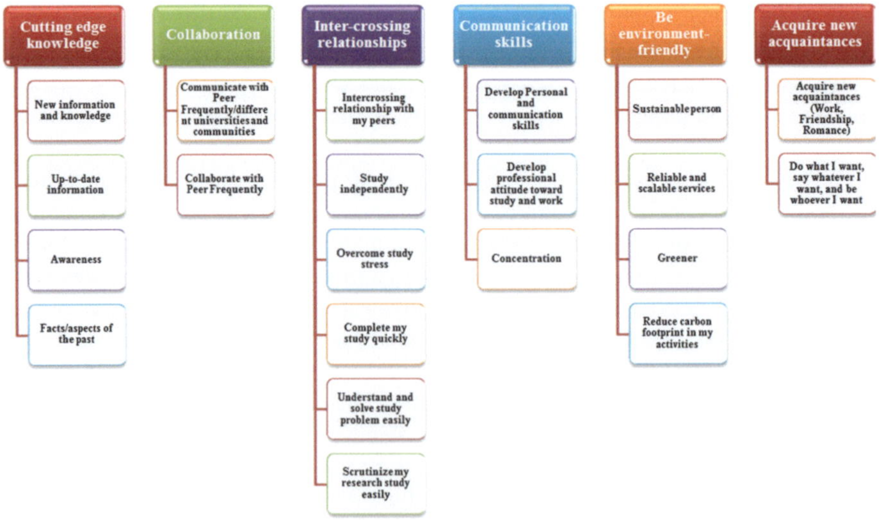

Fig. 1 Students' perspective—opportunities (Prepared by the Authors)

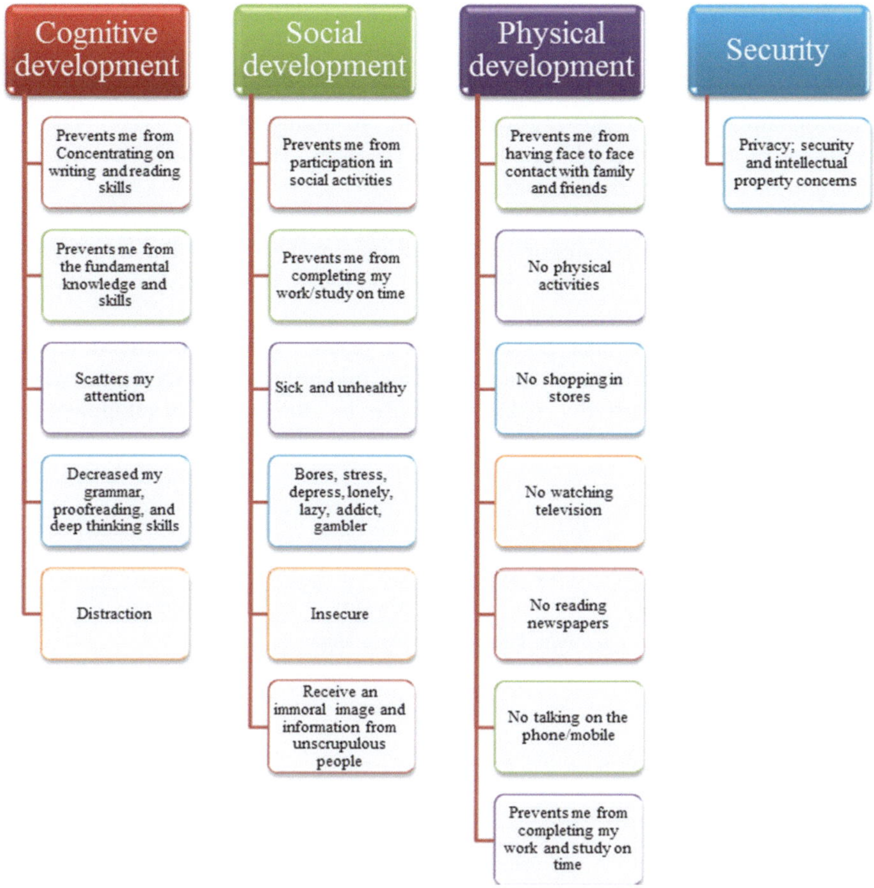

Fig. 2 students' perspective—risks (Prepared by the Authors)

regarding Social Networking usage in the education sector, since it has become an essential tool to improve communication and collaboration among students and teachers, and students and students. However, this tool can bring various problems to students. Hence, this study will examine the problems from three perspectives: (1) Cognitive Development, (2) Social Development, and (3) Physical Development and (4) Security.

Finally, the presentation of Social Networking and Education Model (SNEM) in this chapter will assist the education sector to maximise opportunities and decrease the risks, especially among students, and students and lecturers.

3 Results and Discussion

A total of 3477 participants from 15 countries in six regions responded to the questionnaire, with 46 missing data found, resulting in 3431 valid cases of responses in total for the subsequent Factor Analysis. Table 1 shows the countries of origin of the survey participants.

The analysis was conducted separately for questions from the opportunities and risks groups to assess the opportunities and risks respectively. The opportunities group survey consists of 25 questions while the risks group survey consists of 30 questions.

Based on the Mean and STD Deviation results, it was confirmed that the majority of the respondents agreed toward the opportunities of SN usage, while a mixture reaction toward SN risks especially for the social development (see Tables 2 and 3).

Table 1 Participating country details—(Prepared by the Authors)

Data grouping			
Region	Country	Participants	
Asia Pacific	Australia	153	
	Malaysia	74	
	India	85	
	South Korea	231	
	Pakistan	153	
Total Asia Pacific			696
Europe	Netherlands	135	
	Portugal	130	
	Greece	245	
	Italy	324	
Total Europe			834
Mediterranean	Turkey	457	
		Total Mediterranean	457
America	USA	564	
	Mexico	150	
Total America			714
Middle East	Jordan	495	
	Saudi Arabia	101	
Total Middle East			596
Caribbean	Pueito Rico	134	
Total Caribbean			134
Total all			3431

Table 2 Mean and standard deviation—opportunities—(Prepared by the Authors)

Descriptive statistics		
	Mean	Std. deviation
Q10_l Lear new information and knowledge	4.00	0.952
Q10_2 Gain up-to-date information	4.13	0.879
Q10_3 Be more aware of global issues/local issues	3.91	0.902
Q10_4 To remember facts/aspects of the past	3.67	0.971
Q10_5 Communicate with my peers frequently	4.12	0.909
Q10_6 Collab orate with my peers frequently	3.89	0.933
Q10_7 Communicate with my peers from different universities_l	3.81	1.001
Q10_8 Communicate with my different communities_l	3.80	0.949
Q10_9 Develop intercrossing relationships with my peers_l	3.61	0.970
Q10_10 Study independently_1	3.33	1.169
Q10_l1 Overcome study stress_l	3.38	1.129
Q10_12 Complete my study more quickly_l	3.06	1.261
Q10_13 Understand and solve study problems easily_l	3.34	1.146
Q10_14 Scrutinize my research study more easily_l	3.37	1.121
Q10_15 Develop my personal and communication skills_l	3.48	1.053
Q10_16 Concentrate more on my reading and writing skills_l	3.03	1.134
Q10_17 To prepare my professional attitude toward study and work _1	3.11	1.104
Q10_18 Be more sustainable person_l	3.14	1.027
Q9_19 ftovide reliable and scalable services_l	3.19	0.976
Q10_20 Become more "Greener" in my activities_l	3.10	1.044
Q10_21 Reduce carbon footprint in my activities_l	3.06	1.098
Q10_22 Acquire new acquaintances—workrelared_l	3.50	1.004
Q10_23 Acquire new acquaintances—friendship relationship_1	3.58	1.022
Q10_24 Acquire new acquaintances—romance relationship_1	2.88	1.183
Q10_25 Do whatever I want sary whatever I want and be whoever I want_1	3.21	1.265

Furthermore, the researchers employed principal axis factoring for factor extraction, and to allow the variable to correlate, oblique rotation (rather than orthogonal rotation) was applied using the promax method [12, 24, 25]. To measure the sampling adequacy for the Opportunities and Risks, researchers carried out specific testing using Cronbach's Alpha, Kaiser-Meyer-Olkin and Bartlett's test.

For the Opportunities Group, the Cronbach's Alpha for all 25 variables was 0.918 indicates an excellent internal consistency of the items in the scale [22, 62]. A Kaiser-Meyer-Olkin measure of sampling adequacy of 0.930 indicates a very good sample (Meritorious) size is obtained from the analysis. Finally, the Bartlett's test of sphericity is highly significant, $\chi^2 = 43024.198$, df $= 300$, $p<0.000$, indicating that the items of the scale are sufficiently correlated to factors to be found [1, 14, 18, 27, 67, 75].

Table 3 Mean and standard deviation—risks—(Prepared by the Authors)

Descriptive statistics		
	Mean	Std. deviation
Q12_1 Prevents me from concentrating more on waiting and reading skills_1	3.17	1.101
Q12_2 Prevents me from remembering the fundamental knowledge and skills_1	2.85	1.027
Q12_3 Scatters my attention _1	3.48	1.071
Q12_4 Decreases my grammar and proofreading skills_1	2.88	1.127
Q12_5 Decreases my deep thinking_1	2.89	1.140
Q12_6 Distracts me easily_1	3.58	1.130
Q12_7 Prevents me from participating in social activities_1	2.66	1.136
Q12_5 Prevents me from completing my work study on time_1	3.11	1.157
Q12_9 Makes me sick and unhealthy_1	2.40	1.140
Q12_10 Bores me_1	2.64	1.119
Q12_11 Stresses me_1	2.49	1.080
Q12_12 Depresses me_1	2.42	1.081
Q12_13 Makes me feel lonely_1	2.49	1.141
Q12_14 Makes me lazy_1	3.14	1.190
Q12_15 Makes me addict_1	2.97	1.230
Q12_16 Makes me more gambler_1	2.24	1.141
Q12_17 Makes me insecure to release my personal details from the theft of personal information_1	3.09	1.169
Q12_18 Makes me receive an immoral images and information from unscrupulous people and it is difficult to act against them at present_1	2.85	1.173
Q12_19 Prevents me from having face to face contact with my family_1	2.52	1.180
Q12_20 Prevents me from having face to face contact with my friends_1	2.59	1.186
Q12 21 Prevents me from participating in physical activities_1	2.74	1.229
Q12_22 Prevents me from shopping in stores_1	2.49	1.149
Q12_23 Prevents me from watching television_1	2.78	1.228
Q12_24 Prevents me from reading the newspapers_1	2.94	1.267
Q12_25 Prevents me from talking on the phone/mobile_1	2.60	1.195
Q12_26 Prevents me from completing my work on time_1	2.93	1.196
Q12_27 Prevents me from completing my study on time_1	3.00	1.200
Q12_28 Increase privacy concerns_1	3.33	1.096
Q12 29 Increase security concerns_1	3.29	1.098
Q12_30 Increase intellectual property concerns_1	3.13	1.088

As for the Risks group, the Cronbach's Alpha for all 30 variables from Q12 group was 0.938 indicates an excellent internal consistency of the items in the scale [11, 22]. A Kaiser-Meyer-Olkin measure of sampling adequacy of 0.920 indicates a very good sample (Meritorious) size is obtained from the analysis [27] The

Bartlett's test of sphericity is highly significant, $\chi^2 = 8212.556$, df = 435, $p < 0.000$, indicating that the items of the scale are sufficiently correlated to factors to be found [67].

For Opportunities group, three (3) factors were extracted on the final run with Kaiser Normalisation (Eigenvalues greater than one). As demonstrated in Table 4, this model of three (3) factors accounts for a total of 53.859 % of the variation. The Eigen values and the amount of variance explained by each of these factors are presented below (after rotation).

For the Risks group, five (5) factors were extracted on the final run with Kaiser Normalisation (Eigenvalues greater than one). As demonstrated in Table 5, this model of four factors accounts for a total of 59.983 % of the variation. The Eigen values and the amount of variance explained by each of these factors are presented below (after rotation).

The factor loadings of most of the items are high enough and the one with the cleanest factor is structured to be considered as important [12], and to exclude several items under each factor where the factor loading is below .5 based on the

Table 4 Total variance explained—opportunities (Prepared by the Authors)

Total variance explained							
Factor	Initial eigenvalues			Extraction sums of squared loadings			Rotation sums of squared loadings[a]
	Total	% of variance	Cumulative %	Total	% of variance	Cumulative %	Total
1	6.374	39.837	39.837	5.868	36.674	36.674	5.074
2	2.462	15.387	55.223	2.048	12.797	49.471	3.690
3	1.112	6.950	62.173	0.702	4.388	53.859	4.698

Extraction method: Maximum likelihood

[a]When factors are correlated, sums of squared loadings cannot be added to obtain a total variance

Table 5 Total variance explained—risks (Prepared by the Authors)

Total variance explained							
Factor	Initial eigenvalues			Extraction sums of squared loadings			Rotation sums of squared loadings[a]
	Total	% of variance	Cumulative %	Total	% of variance	Cumulative %	Total
1	8.591	37.351	37.351	7.913	34.405	34.405	6.578
2	2.237	9.727	47.078	1.812	7.880	42.285	5.917
3	1.924	8.365	55.442	1.419	6.171	48.456	4.348
4	1.701	7.394	62.836	1.665	7.238	55.694	3.822
5	1.182	5.141	67.977	0.986	4.289	59.983	4.856

Extraction method: Maximum likelihood

[a]When factors are correlated, sums of squared loadings cannot be added to obtain a total variance

Table 6 Pattern matrix from the opportunities group (Prepared by the Authors)

Pattern matrix[a]	Factor		
	1	2	3
Q10_16 Concentrate more on nay reading and writing skills_1	*0.793*		
Q10_15 Be more sustainable person_1	*0.789*		
Q10_17 To prepare my professional attitude toward study and work_1	*0.785*		0.114
Q10_20 Become more "Greener" in my activities_1	*0.611*		
Q10_15 Develop my personal and communication skills_1	*0.561*	0.148	
Q10_21 Reduce carbon footprint in my activities_1	*0.529*		
Q10_5 Communicate with my peers frequently	−0.139	*0.825*	
Q10_6 Collaborate with my peers frequently		*0.804*	
Q10_7 Communicate with my peers from different universities_1		*0.755*	
Q10_8 Communicate with my different communities_1	0.129	*0.654*	−0.122
Q1Q_2 Gain up-to-date information		*0.500*	0.138
Q10_3 Be more aware of global issues/local issues		*0.424*	0.134
Q10_13 Understand and solve study problems easily_1			*0.913*
Q10_12 Complete my study more quickly_1			*0.807*
Q1014 Scrutinize my research study more easily_1			*0.757*
Q10_10 Study independently_1	0.187		*0.535*

Extraction method: Maximum likelihood. Rotation method: Promaxwith Kaiser normalisation
[a]Rotation converged in 5 iterations

rule of thumb of Stevens [59] for a sample size above 100. In addition, Hair et al. [26] suggested that the sufficient factor loading based on sample size from 350 and more is 0.330. Following is the Pattern Matrix from opportunities group (Table 6):

The three (3) opportunities factors revealed from the Pattern Matrix for opportunities are:

- Factor 1: Assists studying, developing network and professional skills also gaining awareness on environment issues
- Factor 2: Connects me with my peers and helps me to acquire information (local and global)
- Factor 3: Assists me to study or work independently (Table 7)

The five (5) risks factors revealed from the Pattern Matrix for Risks group are:

- Factor 1: Inhibitor in socializing, regular activities and in-person contact
- Factor 2: Trigger anxiety, losing interest and health concern
- Factor 3: Inhibitor on developing literacy and fundamental skills and unable to focus on one matter for a long time

Table 7 Pattern matrix from risks group (Prepared by the Authors)

Pattern matrix[a]					
	Factor				
	1	2	3	4	5
Q12_20 Prevents me from having face to face contact with my friends_1	*0.830*				
Q12_19 Prevents me from having face to face contact with my family_1	*0.794*				
Q12_21 Prevent me from participating in physical activities_1	*0.754*				
Q12_22 Prevents me from shopping in stores_1	*0.714*				
Q 12_23 Prevents me from watching television_1	*0.607*				0.122
Q12_24 Prevents me from reading the newspapers_1	*0.593*	−.0150			0.176
Q12_25 Prevents me from talking on the phone/mobile_1	*0.563*				0.148
Q12_ 12 Depresses me_1		*0.940*			
Q 12_ 11 Stresses me_1		*0.899*			
Q12_13 Makes me feel lonely_1		*0.716*			
Q12_ 10 Bores me_1	−0.108	*0.714*			
Q12_9 Makes me sick and unhealthy_1	0.273	*0.483*			
Q12_1 Prevents me from concentrating more on writing and reading skills_1			*0.799*		
Q12_2 Prevents me from remembering the fundamental knowledge and skills_1	0.194		*0.741*		−0.128
Q12_3 Scatters my attention_1	−0.177		*0.724*		0.122
Q12_6 Distracts me easily_1	−0.152		*0.498*		0.244
Q12_4 Decreases my grammar and proofreading skills_1	0.171	0.106	*0.497*		
Q12_29 Increase security concerns_1				*0.968*	
Q12_28 Increase privacy concerns_1				*0.897*	
Q12_30 Increase intellectual properly concerns_1				*0.712*	
Q 12_27 Prevents me from completing my study on time_1					*0.887*
Q12_26 Prevents me from completing my work on time_1	0.155				*0.838*
Q12_8 Prevents me from completing my work/study on time_1			0.227		*0.567*

Extraction method: Maximum likelihood. Rotation Method: Promax with Kaiser normalization
[a]Rotation converged in 7 iterations

- Factor 4: Cynicism on data security
- Factor 5: Inhibitor to accomplish higher priority as scheduled

A score was calculated for each factor by averaging across each individual item. Table 8 presents the mean and standard deviation of each factor average for the opportunities group:

Table 9 shows the mean and standard deviation of each factor average for risks group:

SN in higher education will assist students to study and to develop a network and professionals skills; furthermore, it will make them more sustainable and more aware of their activities in an effort to reduce paper usage by submitting assessments via the Learning Management Systems and sharing information and data with their colleagues, as this will reduce carbon emissions. Furthermore, from the respondents' feedback it was noted that students consider SN as a useful tool that helps to improve their personal skills (such as Motivation; Leadership; Negotiation, Communication, Problem solving, Time Management, and Reflection) and professional skills (such as Reading. Writing, Research, Information, Critical Thinking, Decision Making Technology, Digital oral presentation, Drawing (i.e. concept maps) and Teamwork) for their current studies study as well as for the workforce in future.

Currently; the higher education sector has started to use and integrate this tool in the curriculum in order to enhance these skills by adding specific assessments and activities in the class. The majority of students confirmed that this tool, particularly the WIKI, is very handy, easy to use, and provides a good platform for analyzing

Table 8 Factor descriptions—opportunities (Prepared by the Authors)

Factor descriptions	Mean	Std deviation
Factor 1: Assists studying, developing network and professional skills also gaining awareness on environment issues	3.16	1.08
Factor 2: Connects me with my peers and helps me to acquire information (local and global)	3.94	0.93
Factor 3: Assists me to study or work independently	3.27	1.17

Table 9 Factor descriptions—risks (Prepared by the Authors)

Factor descriptions	Mean	Std deviation
Factor 1—Inhibitor ill socializing, regular activities and in-person contact	2.66	1.20
Factor 2—Trigger anxiety, losing interest and health concern	2.49	1.11
Factor 3—Inhibitor on developing literacy and fundamental skills and unable to focus on one	3.19	1.09
Factor 4—Cynicism on data security	3.25	1.09
Factor 5—Inhibitor to accomplish higher priority as scheduled	3.02	1.18

different concepts offered by peers; this can lead to more collaboration and communication among peers within and outside the classroom. In particular, WIKI is able to assist students to improve their writing and research skills and the group activities will encourage students to interact and collaborate with their group members and familiarise themselves with the concepts from different perspectives and cultures.

Using SN in higher education does provide opportunities and prospects; however, it can produce several risks and disadvantages to students from lack of social activities and in-person contact and this can lead to anxiety and health concerns. Additionally, frequent use of SN can decrease fundamental skills such as reading and writing and prevent students from being able to focus on one matter for any length of time. However, the disadvantages of this tool are not limited to cognitive, social and physical development problems; security and privacy are major problems for students especially when sharing data and information via the Internet and Social Networking with peer and others, as they become very worried about who will have access to this information now as well as in future.

Our study added new theoretical significance to the current literature, as SN usage in higher education will increase collaboration and communication among students, and will allow students to study and work independently. It is anticipated that these activities will motivate students to improve their professional and personal skills for their current studies and for their future employment. Social Networking has the potential to improve these skills by offering special activities and assessments within and outside the classroom with lecturer moderation and feedback.

Furthermore, one great advantage of using this tool in the higher education sector is it raises awareness of sustainability and the green concept since it encourages students to become 'greener' in their studies and social activities. For example, currently students have begun to submit their assessments via the learning management system. This is appreciated by students since it is cheaper, more sustainable and greener and reduces the carbon footprint. Finally, this tool assists the students to collaborate and interact with other students from overseas in order to share, interact and acquire cutting edge information (see Fig. 3).

In order to tackle the risks and disadvantages of using SN in higher education, a Social Networking and Education Model (SNEM) was proposed to assist academics and researchers to implement Social Networking applications and tools successfully in their classes since applications will undoubtedly assist students in their studies and social activities.

4 Social Networking and Education Model (SNEM)

The online survey results from the regions of Asia-Pacific, Europe, the Mediterranean, America, Middle East and Caribbean assisted the authors to identify new opportunities and risks associated with the implementation of SN in the education sector, and these assisted the authors to develop the Social Networking Education Model (SNEM). The rationale behind the development of the SNEM is to assist academics and researchers to implement SN in the education sector successfully by reducing the risks and increasing the opportunities associated with SN. These were identified after analyzing the online survey, and determining the factors and aspects that address the risks and opportunities.

The SNEM (see Fig. 4) contains the following elements: Teaching Methods, Learning, Technology Design and Psychological Aspects. Each of these contains several sub elements to ensure the successful adoption of SN in the higher education sector.

Teaching methods consist of four elements: learning to learn; blended learning; pedagogy and curriculum [16, 29, 36, 41, 45, 48, 58, 66]. Figure 4 provide the sub factors for each of these. Learning to learn is a method of definition about learning since it involves a set of principles and skills to assist students to learn more effectively and so become learners for life. Blended learning combines face-to-face learning and online learning; these modes are essential in teaching and learning as a means of delivering the materials and knowledge to students. Pedagogy and curriculum are related to teaching principles, professional practice, leading, guiding and methods of teaching; on the other hand, curriculum relates to assessments and activities with which students will complete to achieve educational outcomes.

The learning factor emerges from learning theories, in particular, learning styles and social learning.

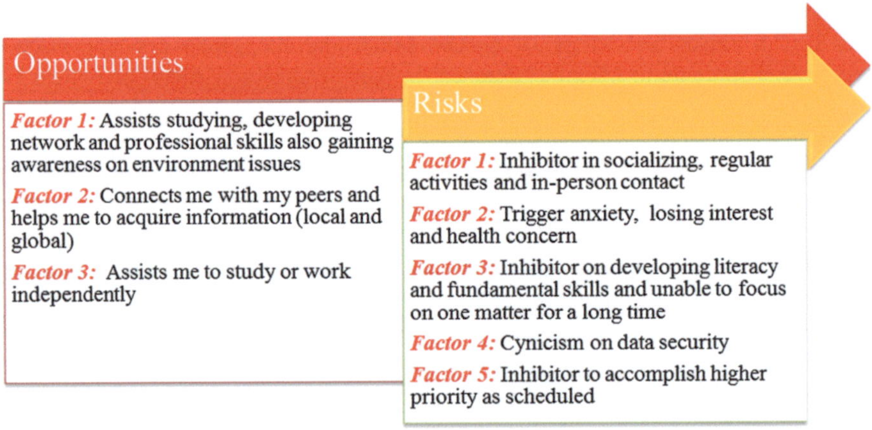

Fig. 3 Summary of the new Opportunities and Risks of SN usage—Global Perspective

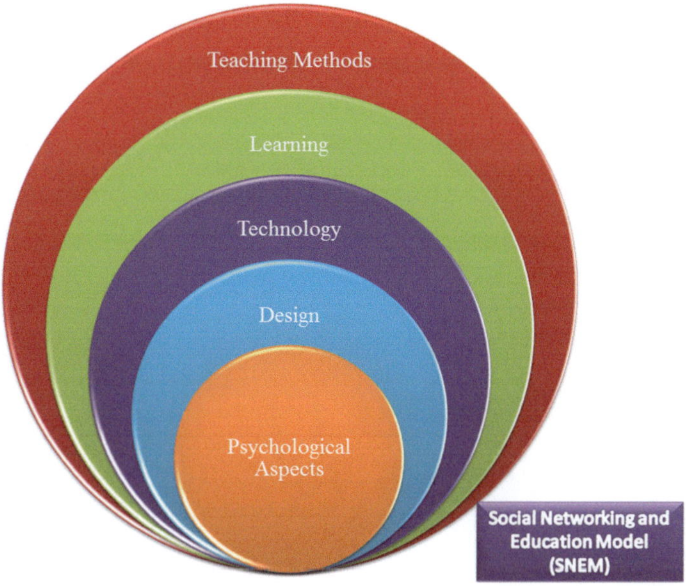

Fig. 4 SNEM—prepared by the authors

Learning theories are divided into two categories: Connectivism and Pragmatism (see Fig. 5). Connectivism is the theory for the digital age; it states simply that knowledge, data and information are disseminated via a network of connections, therefore the learning and teaching process consists the ability to construct and traverse those networks especially by using the latest technology [17, 56]. However, the Pragmatism learning theory is mainly focus on hands-on problem solving; teamwork, experimenting and projects and later the outcomes will be used for decision making [35, 71].

The learning style is based on Neil Fleming's VARK (1988) [19, 20, 45]: visual, auditory, read/write and kinesthetic learning modes (see Fig. 6). Visual learners prefer to use concept maps, drawings, graphs, and flow charts instead of using text and audio. This type of learner relies on visual cues and can better understand the information if it is presented graphically. These visual representations are tools that will help these learners to organize their ideas and understand the concepts being presented. Auditory learners prefer to listen and speak instead of taking notes from the lecturer. This group has the ability to discuss and debate with his/her classmates and lecturers as a means of understanding the concepts of the unit being studied. This group prefers to use the latest auditory technology such as MP3/MP4 audio to pause, forward and rewind, especially for sections that they have difficulty understanding. The read/write learners prefer text, notes and papers as a means of understanding concepts. These types of learners are able to interpret abstract perceptions into arguments and essays. Finally, kinaesthetic learners prefer to learn through experience and practice; this means that they feel and live the experience in order to learn.

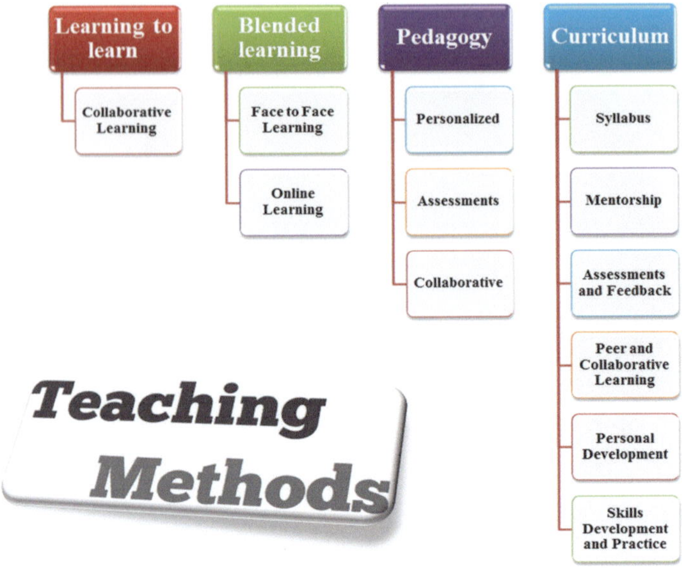

Fig. 5 Teaching methods—prepared by the authors

Social learning consists of attention, retention, reproduction and motivation [4, 10]. Attention: learners need to pay attention in order to obtain the knowledge presented in the unit of study; any interruption or distraction will affect the learning process. Retention: this concept mainly concerns the process of remembering the information that the student has obtained from notes, images, models and others materials and resources. Reproduction: students are required to reproduce the information which they learned during the class, which in turn reflects their level of attention. This behavior will ensure that if students are receptive to information, their skills and observational learning will improve. Finally, students should have the motivation to repeat their performance at the same (hopefully high) standard, and be aware that appropriate performance will be given positive recognition, and conversely, sub-standard performance will have negative consequences.

The technology factor comprises three sub factors namely: system; social and security (see Fig. 7). These sub factors are essential for SNEM to ensure that Social Networking is working and aligned with students' needs especially in terms of security regarding data storage and the user's private information. The system factor relates to the practical implementation of Social Networking in higher education; universities are required to provide hardware, software, databases, internet connectivity and troubleshooting (support and help) for students and lecturers. The final sub-factor is social. For SN implementation to be successful, students need applications and new media such as Blackboard; Moodle and other facilities.

In order to implement Social Networking without any user frustration, design plays an essential role in this model, especially in terms of interface; usability,

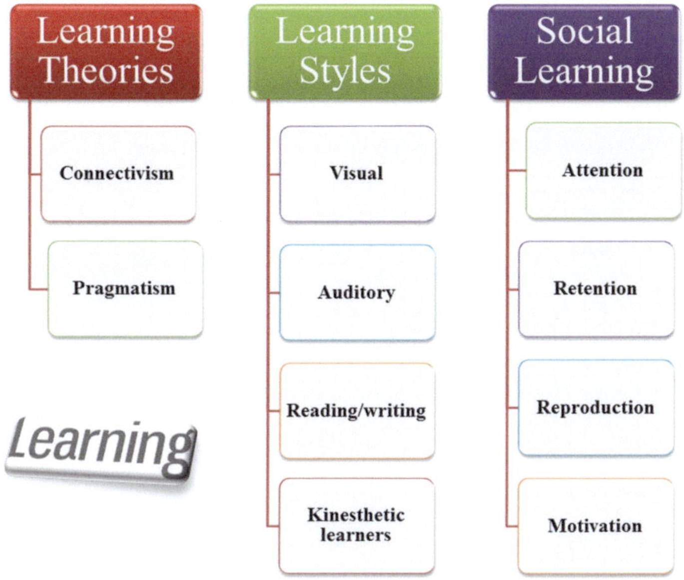

Fig. 6 Learning—prepared by the authors

Human Computer Interaction (HCI), and navigation (see Fig. 8). Attention to these aspects of SN is vital since usability means that the interface is efficient, effective, safe, easy to learn, easy to remember, easy to use and to evaluate, practical, visible, and provides a satisfactory experience. The principles of HCI are intended to ensure that the interface is practical and visually attractive in relation to text, style, fonts, layout, graphics and color [31]. The navigation sub-factor aims to establish communication between the interface and navigation in the hypermedia application [30].

The final factor in SNEM is the psychological aspect (see Fig. 9); this factor will assist teachers to understand students' cognitive and behavioural attitudes toward the use of this technology in the learning and teaching process [36, 43, 52, 73].

Furthermore, this factor will assist students to meet their study needs and requirements, since teachers using the technology play a major role especially in terms of activities and assessments. According to Issa, Issa and Kommers [30, 32] "The constructive feedback is intended to ascertain whether students are on the right track, and to allow students to learn from their mistakes and prevent future repetitions of the same errors. Furthermore, the adoption of this approach in postgraduate and undergraduate units will improve students' confidence and motivate them to complete the assessment tasks on time, and most importantly, align with the unit objectives and aims". The idea of motivation is a process to assist user to move toward a goal or aim; while encouragement is to give courage, hope, and increase confidence among users to achieve their aims. The idea of

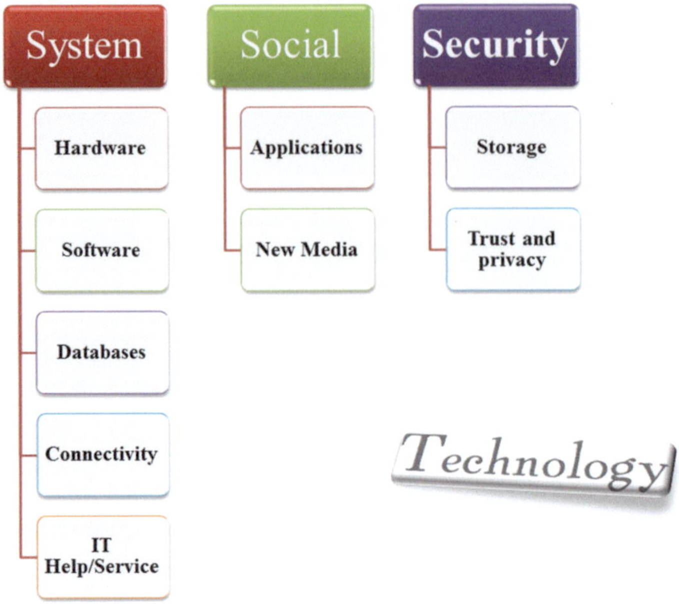

Fig. 7 Technology—prepared by the authors

Fig. 8 Design—prepared by the authors

awareness is to have knowledge or judgment of something, whilst inspiration is a process that takes place when a user sees or hears something that causes them to develop and generate new ideas [7, 51, 64, 74].

Furthermore, this feedback is intended to raise students' awareness and encourage, motivate and inspire them during the learning process, fostering their independent learning and improving their professional and personal skills by using the technology and, in particular, accessing their teachers' regular feedback.

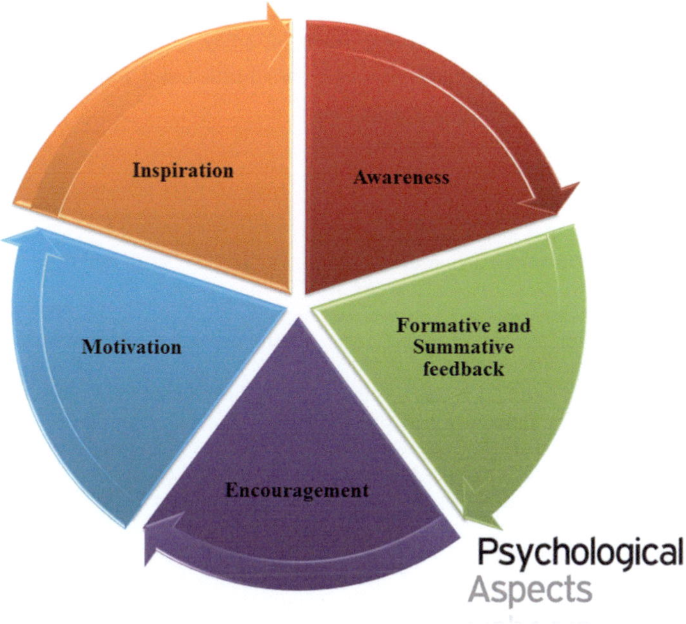

Fig. 9 Psychological aspects—prepared by the authors

5 Conclusion

This chapter discussed the survey results obtained from countries in Asia-Pacific, Europe, Mediterranean, America, Middle East and Caribbean. Moreover, SNEM has been developed in order to reduce the risks and increase the opportunities for students who use SN as an integral part of their studies. The survey results have confirmed the literature review and new factors have emerged namely: developing network and professional skills, sustainability awareness, and interaction between peers locally and globally. Moreover, this tool allows students to work independently. On the other hand, the survey results continue to bring to our awareness new factors in relation to risks, as student use of this tool will displace face-to-face social interaction and the regular activities; and this can lead to anxiety and health concerns. Furthermore, the regular use of this tool in the education sector will erode fundamental skills and prevent students from focusing on one matter for any length of time. Finally, the survey concluded that security and privacy is a major problem for students in terms of the storage and sharing of information. Therefore, SNEM has been developed to reduce risks and increase learning and teaching opportunities for both students and teachers. SNEM comprises: Teaching Methods, Learning, Technology Design and Psychological Aspects. Each factor includes several sub factors to ensure the successful adoption of SN in the higher education sector. In future, further study will be carried out to examine and assess the SNEM in developed and developing countries as a means of meeting the needs of academics and students.

References

1. Aleamoni LM (1976) The relation of sample size to the number of variables in using factor analysis techniques. Educ Psychol Measur 36:879–883
2. Amstadter AB, Broman-Fulks J, Zinzow H, Ruggiero KJ, Cercone J (2009) Internet-based interventions for traumatic stress-related mental health problems: a review and suggestion for future research. Clin Psychol Rev 29(5):410–420
3. Baams L, Jonas K, Utz S, Bos H, Vuurst L (2011) Internet use and online social support among same sex attracted individuals of different ages. Comput Hum Behav 27(5):1–8
4. Bandura A (1977) Social learning theory. Holt Rinehart and Winston, New York
5. Benito-Osorio D, Peris-Ortiz M, Armengot C, Colino A (2013) Web 5.0: the future of emotional competences in higher education. Glob Bus Perspect 1(3):274–287. doi:10.1007/s40196-013-0016-5
6. Bergquist T, Gehl C, Mandrekar J, Lepore S, Hanna A, Osten A, Beaulieu W (2009) The effect of internet-based cognitive rehabilitation in persons with memory impairments after severe traumatic brain injury. Brain Inj 23(10):790–799
7. Business dictionary (2015) Motivation. http://www.businessdictionary.com/definition/motivation.html. Accessed 26 Feb 2015
8. Carr N (2008) Is Google making us stupid? The Atlantic Monthly
9. Casale S, Fioravanti G (2011) Psychosocial correlates of internet use among Italian students. Inte J Psychol 1–11
10. Cheung CM, Liu IL, Lee MK (2015) How online social interactions influence customer information contribution behavior in online social shopping communities: a social learning theory perspective. J Assoc Inf Sci Technol
11. Connelly LM (2011) Cronbach's alpha. Medsurg Nurs 20(1):44–45
12. Costello A, Osborne J (2005) Best practices in exploratory factor analysis: four recommendations for getting the most from your analysis. Pract Assess Res Eval 10(7):1–9
13. Dabbagh N, Kitsantas A (2011) Personal learning environments, social media, and self-regulated learning: a natural formula for connecting formal and informal learning. Internet High Educ 15(1):3–8
14. de Winter JCF, Dodou D, Wieringa PA (2009) Exploratory factor analysis with small sample sizes. Multivar Behav Res 44(2):147–181. doi:10.1080/00273170902794206
15. DiMaggio P, Hargittai E, Neuman R, Robinson J (2001) Social implications of the Internet. Annu Rev Sociol 27:307–336
16. Driscoll M (2002) Blended learning: let's get beyond the hype. E-learning 1(4)
17. Duke B, Harper G, Johnston M (2013) Connectivism as a digital age learning theory. Int HETL Rev 4–13
18. Dziuban CD, Shirkey EC (1974) When is a correlation matrix appropriate for factor analysis? Some decision rules. Psychol Bull 81(6):358
19. Felder RM, Silverman LK (1988) Learning and teaching styles in engineering education. Eng Educ 78(7):674–681
20. Fleming ND (1995) I'm different; not dumb. Modes of presentation (VARK) in the tertiary classroom. In: Research and development in higher education. Proceedings of the 1995 annual conference of the higher education and research development society of australasia (HERDSA), HERDSA. pp 308–313

21. Fox J, Moreland JJ (2015) The dark side of social networking sites: an exploration of the relational and psychological stressors associated with Facebook use and affordances. Comput Hum Behav 45:168–176. doi:10.1016/j.chb.2014.11.083
22. Gliem J, Gliem R (2003) Calculating, interpreting, and reporting Cronbach's alpha reliability coefficient for Likert-type scales. Paper presented at the 2003 Midwest research to practice conference in adult, continuing and community education
23. Griffiths MD, Kuss DJ, Demetrovics Z (2014) Chapter 6—Social networking addiction: an overview of preliminary findings. In: Feder KPRC (ed) Behavioral addictions. Academic Press, San Diego, pp 119–141. doi:http://dx.doi.org/10.1016/B978-0-12-407724-9.00006-9
24. Hair J, Anderson R, Tatham R, Black W (1998) Multivariate data analysis. Prentice Hall, Upper Saddle River
25. Hair J, Black W, Babin B, Anderson R (2009) Multivariate data analysis. Prentice Hall, Upper Saddle River
26. Hair J, Black W, Babin B, Anderson R (eds) (2010) Multivariate data analysis: a global perspective. Pearson Prentice Hall, Upper Saddle River
27. Hill BD (2012) The sequential Kaiser-Meyer-Olkin procedure as an alternative for determining the number of factors in common-factor analysis: a Monte Carlo simulation proquest, Umi Dissertation Publishing, USA
28. Huang F, Lee M (2010) Dynamic treatment effect analysis of TV effects on child cognitive development. J Appl Econom 25:392–419
29. Hughes-Wiener G (1986) The "learning how to learn" approach to cross-cultural orientation. Int J Intercult Relat 10(4):485–505
30. Issa T (2008) Development and evaluation of a methodology for developing websites. PhD thesis, Curtin University, Western Australia. http://espace.library.curtin.edu.au/R/MTS5B8S4X3B7SBAD5RHCGECEH2FLI5DB94FCFCEALV7UT55BFM-00465?func=results-jump-full&set_entry=000060&set_number=002569&base=GEN01-ERA02
31. Issa T, Isaias P (2014) Promoting human-computer interaction and usability guidelines and principles through reflective journal assessment. In: Emerging research and trends in interactivity and the human-computer interface. IGI Global, pp 375–394. doi:10.4018/978-1-4666-4623-0.ch019
32. Issa T, Issa T, Kommers P (2014) Feedback and learning support that fosters students' independent learning: an Australian case study. Int J Learn 19:29–39
33. Issa T, Kommers P (2013) Social networking for web-based communities. Int J Web Based Commun 9(1):5–24
34. Kearns L, Frey B (2010) Web 2.0 technologies and back channel communication in an online learning community. Tech Trends 54(3):41–54
35. Kivinen O, Ristela P (2003) From constructivism to a pragmatist conception of learning. Oxford Rev Educ 29(3):363–375. doi:10.1080/03054980307442
36. Lalonde M, Castro JC (2015) Amplifying youth cultural practices by engaging and developing professional identity through social media. Youth practices in digital arts and new media: learning in formal and informal settings:40
37. Lee S (2009) Online communication and adolescent social ties: who benefits more from Internet use? J Comp-Mediated Commun 14(3):509–531
38. Levy B (2003) Mind matters: cognitive and physical effects of aging self-stereotypes. J Gerontol Psychol Sci 58B(4):203–211
39. Liu D, Brown BB (2014) Self-disclosure on social networking sites, positive feedback, and social capital among Chinese college students. Comput Hum Behav 38:213–219. doi:10.1016/j.chb.2014.06.003
40. Mathew B (2014) Using a social networking tool for blended learning in staff training: sharing experience from practice. J Neonatal Nurs 20(3):90–94. doi:10.1016/j.jnn.2014.03.005
41. Mockler N, Groundwater-Smith S (2015) Curriculum, pedagogy, assessment and student voice. In: Engaging with student voice in research, education and community. Springer, pp 139–150

42. Mokhtari K, Reichard C, Gardner A (2009) The impact of Internet and television use on the reading habits and practices of college students. J Adolesc Adult Literacy 52(7):609–619
43. Monks TG, Kawwa T (1971) Social psychological aspects of comprehensive education. Int Rev Educ 17(1):66–76. doi:10.1007/BF01421371
44. Mueller A, Mitchell JE, Peterson LA, Faber RJ, Steffen KJ, Crosby RD, Claes L (2010) Depression, materialism, and excessive Internet use in relation to compulsive buying (Comprehensive Psychiatry in Press, Corrected Proof)
45. Murphy RJ, Gray SA, Straja SR, Bogert MC (2004) Student learning preferences and teaching implications. J Dent Educ 68(8):859–866
46. Nahl D (2005) Affective and cognitive information behavior: Interaction effects in Internet use In: Gove A (ed) Proceedings of the American society for information science and technology Charlotte (US), vol 1. pp 1–14
47. Oh HJ, Ozkaya E, LaRose R (2014) How does online social networking enhance life satisfaction? The relationships among online supportive interaction, affect, perceived social support, sense of community, and life satisfaction. Comput Hum Behav 30:69–78. doi:10.1016/j.chb.2013.07.053
48. Oliver M, Trigwell K (2005) Can 'blended learning' be redeemed? E-learn Digital Media 2 (1):17–26
49. Pan Y, Xu Y, Wang X, Zhang C, Ling H, Lin J (2015) Integrating social networking support for dyadic knowledge exchange: a study in a virtual community of practice. Inf Manag 52 (1):61–70. doi:10.1016/j.im.2014.10.001
50. Patel K (2013) Incremental journey for World Wide Web: introduced with Web 1.0 to recent Web 5.0–a survey paper. Int J Adv Res Comput Sci Softw Eng 3(10):410–417
51. Psychology dictionary (2015) What is awareness. http://psychologydictionary.org/awareness/. Accessed 26 Feb 2015
52. Safuanov IS (2004) Psychological aspects of genetic approach to teaching mathematics. International group for the psychology of mathematics education
53. Selfhout M, Branje S, Delsing M, Bogt T, Meeus W (2009) Different types of Internet use, depression, and social anxiety: the role of perceived friendship quality. J Adolesc 32:819–833
54. Shaw LH, Gant LM (2002) In defense of the Internet: the relationship between Internet communication and depression, loneliness, self-esteem, and perceived social support. Cyber Psychol Behav 5(2):157–171
55. Shen C, Chiou J (2010) The impact of perceived ease of use on Internet service adoption: the moderating effects of temporal distance and perceived risk. Comput Hum Behav 26:42–50
56. Siemens G (2005) Connectivism: a learning theory for the digital age. Int J Instr Technol Distance Learn 2(1):3–10
57. Sigelman C, Rider E (2012) Life-span human development. WADSWORTH—Cengage Learning, USA
58. Smith A (1983) Learning to Learn W
59. Stevens J (1992) Applied multivariate statistics for the social sciences. Erlbaum, Hillsdale
60. Sun S (2011) The Internet effects on students communication at Zhengzhou institute of aeronautical industry management advances in computer science. Environ Ecoinform Educ 5 (11):418–422
61. Taragola N, Lierde D (2010) Factors affecting the Internet behaviour of horticultural growers in Flanders. Belgium Comput Electron Agric 70:369–379
62. Tavakol M, Dennick R (2011) Making sense of Cronbach's alpha. Int J Med Educ 2:53
63. Teo T, Lim V, Lai R (1997) Users and uses of the Internet: the case of Singapore. Int J Inf Manage 17(5):325–336
64. The Encouragement Foundation (2015) What is encouragement http://encouragementfoundation.org/what-is-encouragement-2/. Accessed 26 Feb 2015
65. Thompson L, Dawson K, Ferdig R, Black E, Boyer J, Coutts J, Paradise N (2008) The intersection of online social networking with medical professionalism. J Gen Intern Med 23 (7):954–957

66. Thrun S (1996) Learning to learn: introduction. In: Learning to learn, Citeseer
67. Tobias S, Carlson JE (1969) Brief report: Bartlett's test of sphericity and chance findings in factor analysis. Multivar Behav Res 4(3):375–377
68. Van Deursen AJAM, Van Dijk JAGM, Peters O (2011) Rethinking Internet skills: the contribution of gender, age, education, Internet experience, and hours online to medium- and content-related Internet skills. Poetics 39(2):125–144
69. Van Dijk JAGM (2006) The network soceity. Sage Publisher India, New Delhi
70. Verdick.org; (2011) Positive effects of Internet usage on child development. http://www.verdick.org/child-development-and-the-internet/child-dev-pos. Accessed 25 Sept 2011
71. Wallace CS, Brooks L (2015) Learning to teach elementary science in an experiential, informal context: culture, learning, and identity. Sci Educ 99(1):174–198
72. Walther J, Van Der Heide B, Tong S, Carr C, Atkin C (2010) Effects of interpersonal goals on inadvertent intrapersonal influence in computer-mediated communication. Hum Commun Res 36(3):323–347
73. Watson AS (1963) Some psychological aspects of teaching professional responsibility. J Legal Educ 1:1–23
74. What is How to Info (2015) What is inspiration. http://www.whatishowtoinfo.com/what-is-inspiration/. Accessed 26 Feb 2015
75. WIlliams B, Onsman A, Brown T (2010) Exploratory factor analysis: a five-step guide for novices. J Emerg Primary Health Care 8(3):1–13
76. Zhu DH, Chang YP, Luo JJ, Li X (2014) Understanding the adoption of location-based recommendation agents among active users of social networking sites. Inf Process Manage 50 (5):675–682. doi:10.1016/j.ipm.2014.04.010

Glossary

Acquire new acquaintance Acquire new acquaintance in work, friendship and romantic relationship.

Addiction Compulsive behaviors that often undermine and interfere with individuals' ability to meet their personal and professional responsibilities.

Adoption The awareness of innovations and beginning the usage of the said innovation.

Blended learning The use of both face to face and computer aided learning methodologies in delivering course content and in student learning.

Carbon Footprint It is the total Carbon dioxide (CO2) emission created by different human activities (such as fuel consumption) in a specific time period.

Cognitive Development A set of factors that influence users' behaviour and attitudes toward social networking usage, i.e. inability to concentrate on writing and reading, inability to remember, and shallow brains.

Collaboration Allow users to collaborate and communicate with their peers, and communities frequently.

Collaborative learning Arranging learners to work and study in teams. Its main success has been that those learners who undertake the role of tutor gain metacognitive understanding, while those in the role of tutee feel supported by getting knowledge from the more gifted students; a win-win situation.

Communication To develop users' reading, writing skills and professional attitude toward study and work.

Critical Thinking The ability of making decision, reasoning, and problem solving.

Cutting edge knowledge Allow users to learn and gain up-to-date news, information and knowledge, and to remember facts/aspects of the past.

Digital activism Using digital technologies (i.e., social media, the Internet, mobile) for campaigning activities related to activist purposes.

T. Issa et al. (eds.), *Social Networking and Education*,
Lecture Notes in Social Networks, DOI 10.1007/978-3-319-17716-8

Education Studying various subjects and courses for the development of individual and for making people earn their livelihood.

Education The transfer of knowledge from one generation to another.

Emotional Health A state of emotional and cognitive wellbeing which facilitates one's functioning in everyday life.

Environment-friendly become greener in their activities to reduce carbon footprint.

Facebook Facebook is the most popular social networking site with more than 1 billion members. Members can connect it through a wide range of applications and mobile devices.

Factor Analysis A data reduction methodology used to uncover statistical relationship patterns.

Factor Analysis a process in which the values of observed data are expressed as functions of a number of possible variables in order to find which are the most important.

Going viral Social media content that is highly and continuously spread among users over a short period of time. Typically viral social content is passed among various channels over this period of time.

Higher Education It refers to the education beyond the secondary level provided by different colleges and universities.

Higher Education Undergraduate or graduate education at universities or similar educational institutions, especially to degree level.

Identity formation Individuals integrate aspects of their online experience into their own identity.

Indian Perspective We find the effect of social networking on education from India's point of view.

Informal learning Any learning that takes place in everyday activities with no specific plans or pre-determined objectives. The World Wide Web and, in particular, social networking through the web provide limitless opportunities for informal learning.

Information behaviour A concept that is used to describe the way any individual behaves when locating and using the information that is accessed through different technologies.

Information Seeking The way people attempt to obtain information.

Interconnection A link between two elements who belong to different networks or groups.

Inter-crossing relationships Allow users to foster independent learning and become more self-regulating learners with the ability to solve their problems easily.

Internet An advanced, computer network based communication technology, which connects different types of devices worldwide via a special protocol suite called as TCP/IP.

Internet-based gratifications Individuals turn to the Internet to fulfill different needs, which can include motivations such as convenient information seeking, guidance and opinion seeking, seeking a variety of opinions, specific inquiry, having fun, killing time, and/or relaxing or escaping from daily responsibilities.

Isolation A lack of contact and connection between individuals and groups of people.

Learning climate despite of group techniques and social methods, students feel if the final assessment evaluates learning achievements as individual or as collective assets. Learning climate is the sense of collaboration versus competition among students.

Learning paradigm The basic view on what really makes the difference in learning. Is it the transfer from experts to novices? Is it mutual help amongst students? Is it the view that acquiring knowledge is essentially a very personal (ideosyncratic) process of constructing and interlinking concepts? Etc.

Mexican universities A set of institutions dedicated to undergraduate and graduate education levels.

Negative effect Distraction, lack of concentration, inability to complete the study on time and privacy concerns on the social networks.

Negative Factors of social networking Negative factors that change students' behaviour and attitudes in negative way. For example, health problems related to prolonged use of computers such as eye diseases, lack of exercises, lack of participating physically in society and waste of time and resources.

Negative Feeling Any feeling which stops individuals from behaving rationally.

Online communication A communication between peers using a web-based system.

Online communities Internet based communities that use social technology to communicate and develop ties around a particular interest or subject.

Online Communities people who interact with each other through the internet.

Online content Content that is created and edited online and can assume a variety of formats (text, video, image). This content can be generated by website providers or more recently, with the emergence of content creation and sharing tools, it can be the result of users' contributions.

Online Social networks Interactive online platforms that are primordially composed of user profile information, a list of contacts and several communication and content generation tools. Social network websites can be of a general nature (Facebook) or gravitate around a specific sector, such as business (LinkedIn) or academia (Academia.edu).

Online survey A web-based survey to collect information about some topic.

Pedagogical Affordances The specific features of a technology that enables teaching and learning processes.

Physical Development Prevents users from having face to face contact with family and friends, and participating in physical activities and watching the traditional media.

Positive factors of social networking Positive factors that influence students' behaviour and attitudes in positive way For example, it enhances communicational skills of the students, provides an access to a universal educational and information system, an opportunity to learn different cultures and to meet different people, making friends of similar interests and fostering collaboration and mutual learning.

Positive way The fast and easy realization of cooperation and communication process on the social networks.

Privacy Concerns The concern for personal information on Social Network Sites.

Privacy Regard and concern for one's private and personal information from undue intrusion.

Professional Networks A specific type of social network that is used to connect with other professionals and share information for professional reasons.

Profile A user's identifying information requested when that user signs up for a social networking site. Profile may include a username, a photo, contact information, personal or professional interests, education, etc.

Prosumer A social media user who actively produces knowledge online versus passively receiving information.

Self-Regulation Self-initiated and self-sustained efforts used to regulate one's actions in the pursuit of a given task.

Social Capital Refers to the specific benefits that are derived from the social interaction that occurs through a social network.

Social Development A set of factors that influence users' behaviour and attitudes toward social networking usage, i.e. health problem, stress and depression and isolation.

Social Interaction Communication, in varying forms, between individuals and groups of people.

Social Isolation A symptom of psychological challenges of inability to interact with society.

Social Media Services Computer applications that employ different type of tools in order to ensure social media oriented virtual platforms.

Social Media A group of networked Internet-based applications that allow people to create, share, and exchange content in a variety of multimedia formats.

Social Media Computer-oriented environments that enable individuals to create, edit, or share different type of information (i.e. texts or digital media) and interact with other individuals in the sense of information share.

Social Media Social media where users create and publish/share their video, audio, text or any kinds of multimedia in a social environment, such as a blog, podcast, forum, wiki, video hosting site, or social networking site.

Social Media Web-based applications allowing the creation and sharing of user-generated content. These include Web 2.0 tools such as blogs, wikis or videosharing sites.

Social Media Web-based platforms and applications which facilitate the creation and dissemination of user generated content.

Social Media Whereas traditional media is based on an information delivery and consumption dynamic, social media employs social technology to empower users to create, edit and exchange information.

Social Network Sites The web-based platforms that allow individuals to interact over the Internet.

Social Network Systems/Sites Web-based applications through which users can create a personal profile and build a network of peers with whom they communicate and share multimedia content. Well-known examples are Facebook, Twitter, Instagram, Linked-In, Google+, Flickr, and Delicious.

Social Networking and Education Model (SNEM) Contains Teaching Methods, Learning, Technology Design and Psychological Aspects.

Social Networking Opportunities Refers to cutting edge knowledge, collaboration, and inter-crossing relationships, communication, environment-friendly and acquire new acquaintance.

Social Networking Risks Refers to cognitive, social, physical developments and security.

Social networking sites Social networking sites (SNS) are communication tools and file sharing tools. Blogs, wikis, YouTube, Facebook, Twitter, and LinkedIn are good examples.

Social Networking Sites An online environment that supports the mutual interaction between persons such as photographs, videos, texts and profile information. For Example, Facebook, YouTube and Twitter …etc.

Social Networking Sites SNSs are interactive websites which allow users to present themselves, create their social networks, and establish/maintain connections with others.

Social networking The use of contemporary web based applications as a means of virtually connecting with other users both personally and professionally.

Social networking A web-based system where a set of people share information about themselves, make connections, and communicate with a group of people to whom they are related.

Social networking in this paper, the meaning of the term is not interpreted in the restrictive sense of using Social Network Systems, but rather in the broader sense of using Internet from PCs or mobile devices to communicate with peers or participate to communities' activities though Web 2.0 tools.

Social Networking is a virtual community for communication, collaboration, connection, cooperation among users to create profiles and exchange information.

knowledge interests, entertainment and global and local news between users.

Social Networking It is the act of socializing in an online environment/social networking sites.

Social Networking Refers to the action of interacting with other individuals through a social network.

Social Networking Social Networking is a network of people who are connected using sites like Facebook, LinkedIn and Google Plus. Social Networking provides them a platform to stay connected and contact each other for social and business purpose.

Social Networking The act of using social networking sites for the purposes of communicating, connecting, sharing, creating, and consuming of information.

Social Networking The practice of using networked websites and applications to make connections and expand social contacts.

Social networking The sum of face-to-face and mediated social contacts. Since the arrival of web-based social media, social networking has become a more explicit effort to build and articulate relational structures, both for professional and for leisure arguments.

Social networking Tools to assist users to search interact and communicate with global and local people to interchange knowledge and information.

Social networks Is basically a website that brings people to shared interest information and knowledge locally and globally.

Social Presence The feeling of community that individuals experience in Social Network Sites.

Social surveillance Social media users are more likely to spend time surveying and comparing themselves to other people's content versus maintaining their own content.

Student activities Any activity developed by a person in an educational environment.

Survey Asking a set of questions to a group of people to find their view point about some issue.

Sustainability It refers to people obligation to utilize the raw materials in an efficient way in line to keep it for the seventh generation.

Sustainability Maintaining harmony between biological systems conditions and humans to fulfill present and future generations' needs.

Teaching-learning Process This term is used to identify the educational activities that occur to teach something, and which result is that one or more individuals learn something new.

Technology adoption A frequent use of several devices and systems to support daily activities.

Time management The effective and productive use of one's time, often aided by strategies such as planning and self-monitoring.

University students in this paper, when we talk about university students, we refer to anyone enrolled in any university program, including bachelors, Masters, PhDs, teacher qualification programs, etc.

Usage The presence of an active social network account and making it a part of the daily life.

Virtual Communities individuals with mutual goals communicating, collaborating, and cooperating through a social network.

Web 1.0 The first phase of the world wide web whereby users were passive consumers of information posted by IT professionals without the ability to contribute and interact.

Web 1.0 allow users to read and share information via the Internet.

Web 2.0 allow users to connect and share information and knowledge via social networking with more interaction and less external control.

Web 2.0 Describes the evolution of the Internet from static websites controlled by the few to dynamic and user generated websites that support multi-user interaction and social networking.

Web 2.0 It is the collective name used to define various applications and websites which enable the user to build online information that could also be shared with other users. Blogs, wikis, folksonomies, social networking, content hosting services and podcasting are common examples of web 2.0 applications. A lot of commonly used websites are web 2.0 sites such as Facebook, MySpace, Flickr, YouTube, and Wikipedia.

Web 2.0 Refers to the second version of the Web, which is built on the precepts of user empowerment, collaboration, information malleability, user generated content and the technology that results from them. Web 2.0 is both a philosophy of internet use and a technology.

Web 2.0 Second version of the Web that allows users to work on interactive platforms, make collaborations and create effective web contents over the Internet.

Web 2.0 The second phase of the development of the Internet typified by user generation and sharing of content.

Web 2.0 the term refers to the developments of the world wide web (dating back to the beginning of this millennium) that have determined the shift whereby users of a website ceased to be just passive viewers to become content generators and members of users communities. Examples of Web 2.0 sites are social networking sites, blogs, wikis, video sharing sites, and mashups.

Web 3.0 refers to connecting intelligence and is known as the semantic web. In other words, it is used to identify web-based data so that searches can be more effective, and the information is part of the network.

Web 4.0 refers to the innovative intelligent agents; as it tells users about themselves; and neighboring; on other hand; is called the web of integration and incorporation in real time.

Web 5.0 refers to interaction between humans and computers. This web will allow users to feel, sense, and react. This web is called emotional web.

Web Types are based on disparities of web technology, namely, Web 1.0; Web 2.0; Web 3.0; Web 4.0 and Web 5.0.

Web Virtual environment - platform that enable users to view and use Web sites or applications developed via appropriate programming approaches in order to give visual forms to the digital information along the Internet technology.

World Wide Web (WWW) is derived from the term Web; it plays an essential role in obtaining the necessary information for the users with the help of the technology.

Index

T. Issa et al. (eds.), *Social Networking and Education*,
Lecture Notes in Social Networks, DOI 10.1007/978-3-319-17716-8

MIX
Papier aus verantwortungsvollen Quellen
Paper from responsible sources
FSC® C105338

If you have any concerns about our products,
you can contact us on
ProductSafety@springernature.com

In case Publisher is established outside the EU,
the EU authorized representative is:
Springer Nature Customer Service Center GmbH
Europaplatz 3, 69115 Heidelberg, Germany

Printed by Libri Plureos GmbH
in Hamburg, Germany